THE CAMERA ONLY POINTS FORWARD

A novel of television news, and stuff.

by

WILSON GAMBLE

Copyright 2013 Wilson E. Gamble

Published by Gamlewszqvskyicz Press, Filterboro, NC

ISBN 978-0-9894360-1-4

Fore word.

No, none of these people in this story are based on a single, specific Real Person. Well, most aren't. So, most of you who work in a newsroom right now can breathe freely. O, Vanity, thy name is television news. Having said that...yes, some characters are *composites* of real people I have worked with or known over many years in several newsrooms. Most, though, have sprung fully from my imagination.

Having said that, this is intended to be a work of fiction, not friction. There is no malicious intent here, only to relate the circumstances of which so many have asked about: "So, what is it really like back there, in a newsroom, you know--before you go on television?" When you consider that it takes dozens of people a good eight hours each to produce 60 or perhaps 90 or 120 minutes of television news every evening, one might appreciate that a few shortcuts are sometimes taken. In some places, however, as in the fictional Newschannel 99 newsroom, "taking shortcuts" becomes standard operating procedure, leading to a steady and inevitable decline in quality (and eventually, ratings).

Most of the events in this book—both in front of and behind the camera--are also fictional, but based very closely on real-world incidents. Some of the episodes, I will confess, did in fact occur, and I was witness to them. They are most likely the events many readers will shake their heads at in disbelief.

I owe a debt to many people, most of whom had no idea of the existence of this labor of love. Suffice to say, however, that there is a certain law enforcement Lieutenant, two television news journalists, and a Fudah Smith to whom I owe the largest debts. They may recognize themselves in this Forward but most certainly not in this story.

Finally, I owe a certain amount of artistic inspiration to a musician named Johnny Cash, who, like many reporters, has been everywhere, man.

1

We are parked at the kind of place that no traffic light will ever sprout. Or stop sign, for that matter. Or gas station to stop and ask directions. In fact, the only people we are likely to find--if they let us--are probably operating meth labs; it's so remote, no neighbor is close enough to smell the noxious fumes from cooking the methamphetamine. 30 years ago these folk operated moonshine stills, ran whiskey. Men got drunk on Saturday nights sipping out of fruit jars. Now the same operators make meth, and men and women grow into frail, sunken shadows of themselves within five years.

At this, the tiniest of all crossroads, two sets of dirt tracks converge at a break in the woods, lost in wild hills far from any city or cartographer. We have been following one of the tracks through this enormous state Wildlife Area. Lots of hollies and vines, but this intersection is no Hollywood and Vine. The dirt trails seemingly radiate to nowhere, unless you know them. Like the meth makers. In that case, they lead everywhere.

We don't know them.

Sergeant Mark stops our Jeep at the crossroads. He is a videographer at the television station, and a retired Marine, to boot. We don't call him "Sergeant Mark" to his face, but he sometimes calls me "Boot." A beefy man, he barely fits behind his seatbelt. He brushes away the late summer sweat, which beads freely in his crew-cut despite the Jeep's air conditioning, set at "Frostbite." Outside, the sun is obscured by no cloud. The only noise comes from a cacophony of crickets complaining about the heat.

"Okay, my man," Sergeant Mark addresses me, sliding the gearshift to "park" with some finality. "Which way do we go."

It's not a question, but a warning that we had better figure out where we're headed. Soon. Even after nearly two years as a news reporter at this television station, I haven't passed his inspection yet. His body language says he's had enough driving around, bumping along the uninhabited terrain like a Lunar Rover. For almost an hour we intrepid journalists have been searching for a small airplane that apparently crash-landed in the high, forested hills. It took a half hour just to reach the Wildlife Area. Now Sergeant Mark wants a true view holloa. Here in this hollow.

I'm studying the best map of the county that we have. But most of these oxcart paths aren't marked here. For all we can tell, the Donner Party may have been the last group to pass this way. Trees range all around the opening. High grass fills in the field itself. The Jeep's radio softly plays "Dueling Banjos." It feels like we are as far away from civilization as possible.

We got word of the crash in the late morning. One of the three emergency services scanners in our newsroom played out a brief drama: "Code One Thousand, in the vicinity of Wingo Ranch, three souls onboard." Decoded: a plane with three people is believed to have just crashed, the last known location near a remote place called Wingo Ranch. The announcement sent emergency services personnel scrambling, as well as reporters for all three television stations, a radio station, and the newspaper.

Every reporter loves this kind of "breaking news." It is much more exciting and interesting than the routine stuff of city budget cuts or school curriculum debates. Those daily affairs do help fill a lot of time in the newscast. One way or another, we have to "feed the beast" that is 22 minutes of news, sports, and weather in every newscast.

No matter what we have accomplished during that day or any other, our News Director, "Little Napoleon," patronizingly reminds us reporters of our unending duty as we leave work: "I expect you to have a lead story idea for tomorrow, Wilson. Preferably two. Don't come in without at least one."

Wilson. Gamble. My name. Truncated and morphed from my grandfather's Gamlewszqvskyicz, or something like that.

Today's Wilson Gamble Story Idea That Can Lead A Newscast is about how one or two local stores have failed to remove from their shelves dog food that has been recalled by the manufacturer. Bacteria in it has killed two dogs in California. See? Routine. So when the scanner call comes in the Assignment Manager hooks me up with a map and with Sergeant Mark, the videographer just coming on duty.

"Good luck finding it." The Manager smiles thinly, pointing vaguely at the map. "You're gonna need it."

We haven't had much of that. Luck. Phone service is spotty at best out here, so we can't count on often calling or texting anyone for guidance. First the state, and then the county roads run out. Our GPS unit is helpless, the display placing us in the middle of a field. Some ATV trails run on after the official roads end. As navigator, I advise Sergeant Mark which way to turn, based on the goal of reaching Wingo Ranch. Even that won't guarantee that we will find the wreckage. And I can't tell how far away Wingo Ranch is, even now--it appears as a tiny red square far from any road on the map.

We idle at the intersection of the two dirt tracks.

Before I can decide which way to go, to our surprise, a car pulls up next to us on Sergeant Mark's side of the Jeep. It is a battered, exhaust-spewing, black hatchback--a National Motors "Goshawk" that growing up we derisively called a "Chickenhawk." Two people are in it. Despite the secluded location, I guess it's not exactly shocking to find someone else out here. Disasters tend to draw spectators, even those whose appearance suggests they might normally prefer the privacy required to run one of those meth labs.

Their passenger side window rolls down. Mark responds by opening our driver's side window.

"Air yew lookin' fahr that plane wreck? Yep?" asks a skinny man with stringy black hair growing down around his ears from under an oversized John Deere hat. He has watery blue eyes that really do water. I wonder if he has an allergy or medical problem or addiction or what. He's leaning over an enormously pregnant young woman in the passenger seat to talk with us. He patiently awaits a reply.

"Ah, yes. Can you help us find a place called 'Wingo Ranch?'" I call over to him.

"Ah been lissening to the talk on th' amuhrgency frequencies, yep." He gestures toward a police scanner inside the Chickenhawk, easily the most valuable object there. Unless he has some meth in the glove box.

"I heard 'em say 'Wingo Ranch.' Yep, I'll take ye thar. Fala me!" Suddenly, he accelerates down one of the rocky, pitted trails that leads farther up into the hills. Sitting at this isolated crossroads, momentarily I believe this is the break we've been looking for. But just as Sergeant Mark gets us in gear, the worst kind of contradiction approaches. As we roll forward, a small caravan of fire trucks, ambulances, police squad cars, and Sport Utility Vehicles coated with the logos of the other media bear down on us and pass, slowly but confidently proceeding--the other way. Evidently, even the first responders don't have a fix on the location, either. But do they now have their bearings? A huge cloud of dust from the caravan settles over our Jeep.

"Do you think they know where they're going," Sergeant Mark again states, rather than asks. He brakes to a full stop once again. Videographers are also known as "Shooters," for shooting video. But he's not willing to pull the trigger on this decision. It's my call, it's on me. Gotta think quick. The Chickenhawk is pulling away without us. Do we fala, er, follow, this rather sketchy couple into possible oblivion...or follow everyone else? Then, the guy in the Chickenhawk notices my hesitation, grinds his chariot into reverse, and hangs out his driver's side window.

"Air ye comin'?" He asks back at us, almost shyly. "Yep?" He hopes he won't be stood up. I study his face a moment, watery eyes and everything, and decide that I believe him. He looks like he belongs here. It's not likely this guy would lead us to his meth lab, hidden up there in the hills.

And it's the only way we would have a chance to cleanly beat the other reporters, who have attached their hopes to the fire-rescue wagon train. Of course, it may mean we miss the story completely while everyone else gets it.

"Yep. Yes. We're comin'. Coming, I mean." I tell him, trying to sound decisive while clinging to my elocution skills. The man shows us his few front teeth, turns, and mashes the accelerator.

Off we go, trying to keep up with the little car. It's not made for off-road driving, or any driving, for that matter. So, after plowing through two shallow creeks and scraping over dozens of large rocks, I wonder how long the Chickenhawk will remain our escort.

After the emergency vehicles have disappeared, there's no other traffic. The voice traffic on our portable police and fire scanner sounds confused. No one seems to know where they are going. I check the map again and still can't tell how far away it is. No identifiable road approaches it.

"Have you ever heard of Wingo Ranch?" I ask Sergeant Mark. He drives like a man fending off a swarm of bees: big arms up high on the steering wheel, turning frantically to avoid endless sharp gouges and random rocks in the oxcart path.

He considers. Then makes a sharp, small turn around another gaping hole. "Yeah. It was a place for troubled teens, you know, kids in trouble with the law or abandoned by their families. But about 20 years ago the place was shut down when some of the boys claimed they were beaten by a coupla staff members." More evasive action behind the steering wheel. "Or, did they win a big award from the governor and move to a brand new ranch in Cheeseport?" he asks himself. "I forget which it was."

"Thanks. That's helpful," I tell him.

"Well, you're the reporter," he fires back. "You should know these things, man." No matter how talented, shooters are a defensive lot.

Similarly, I should know where the plane crashed. The odds are actually pretty good that the plane won't be found for many days, considering the dense forest and high hills. Amelia Earhart got lost in better-charted territory. It's true, we are only about 20 miles from the city, as the crow flies. But it's about 400 miles, as we drive, bumping crazily along. I check my phone. Absolutely zero signal strength. The hills are not alive with the sound of cell service. Check my watch. Again. Its 1:30 in the afternoon. Optimally, this is almost the time of day I like to start heading back to the television station to begin putting together my story. Today, things will be much different.

At 1:31 the Chickenhawk comes to a stop somewhere in the woods. We brake, too, but the stringy-hair driver motions out his window for us to pull up alongside. Its conference time.

"It ain't too fahr, yep. Just away over thar." He points where there isn't any road at all, only trees.

"Where is Wingo Ranch?" asks Sergeant Mark.

"Ah'd speculate about a half mile. Ah just wanted to give y'all an update. Yep." Another toothless smile.

"Can we keep driving towards it?" I ask. "Or do we have to walk?"

"Yep, we kin drahv. But only if ye don't mind drahvin' on a train trestle over the gorge."

A gorge? A train trestle? Quick. Calculate my worth to the television station. Also imagine the headlines: "News Crew Dies In Fiery Plunge Into Gorge." Otherwise, I worry what the other reporters will say if I decide this is a bridge too far, and give up.

Speaking of which, where are the other reporters, anyways? And the fire trucks? Then, another thought crosses my mind. "How often do trains come through here?" I verbalize. It seems a pertinent question.

"Ah never kep' track." He chuckles, shyly again. Kept track. Train track. Ho, ho, ho.

I glance at Sergeant Mark, he at me.

"I'll try it," he advises, shifting his bulk forward, lining up like a defensive tackle. I did mention he was defensive, right? Even shooters get their blood up for a news story.

His attitude is enough to push me over the edge. Metaphorically, of course.

"Let's go," I tell our friend in the Chickenhawk.

"Ah've done this afore, yep. Come along straight behind me and we'll be just fahn."

No smile from our tour guide this time. Just a cautious start forward. Then I see why he's driving with such circumspection. First the trees then the rocky terrain give way to--nothing. Okay, not completely nothing. Our path converges with the only sign of civilization we've seen in the past 20 minutes: train tracks. Heading out over a flat wooden bridge. I'm not going to look down but it appears the rocks simply drop away straight down some indeterminate distance.

"I'm guessing that it's probably, oh, about two tenths of a mile across," Sergeant Mark surmises with the air of a military strategist. To me it looks like 318 football fields. I strain to look for enormous, death-dealing freight locomotives bearing down the line. Nothing appears. Yet. The Chickenhawk starts across, rolling over one rail and taking each tie one slow bump at a time. We stay on his tail. One slow bump at a time.

Bump. Bump. Bump. I notice a swallow flitting about. Or is it a goshawk? Hey, there's an airplane, way up there. Wonder where they are bound? Cincinnati maybe? Bump. Wait. Something's bothering me. Oh, yes. We're on a DEATHTRAP TRAIN TRESTLE ABOVE SOME RIVER 16 MILES BELOW. Or so.

My blood pressure rises, my breathing gets heavy. I wistfully consider that untouched six pack of Coors in my fridge; hate the thought of never getting to taste it... . Wait. Bump bump. Cool it, bro. We're making progress. Bump bump.

Hey. Why is the Chickenhawk starting to pull away from us? There's a puff of exhaust from the tailpipe. Eyebrows drawn in consternation, Sergeant Mark is also focused on the growing distance between us and the lead car. Oh geez. We are proceeding quite prudently, I think. About halfway across. But they are gaining on us.

Bumpbumpbump. What do they know that we don't know? Is a train a-coming? Are the tracks a-humming? Bumpbumpbumpbumpbump. I frantically check behind us and before us--nothing there. Nothing we can see, anyways. But we can imagine anything.

Bump. Bump. Bumpbumpbumpbumpbumpbumpbumpbump.

The Chickenhawk is across, making a special effort to get over the rail and on to a dirt path on the other side. Then they stop. Because of the sudden gap between us, we make a panicky lurch forward. Sergeant Mark is focused like a laser beam.

Bumpbumpbumpbumpbumpbumpbump. My vision is shaken and

stirred; I can't focus on anything. Only hohohoping for self-prepreprepreservation. Can I jujujump from this J-j-j-jeep if I have to? How fafafar down? Uh, don't look. It doesn't seseseem good.

Suddenly, we're across. No train has come. Awesome. Knew it all along. I do a fist pump out the window. But now Sergeant Mark is furious, almost crushing the button to open his window.

"HEY!" he shouts at the Chickenhawk in his best drill sergeant voice. "HEY!"

The John Deere hat pokes out of the Chickenhawk window.

"Whutsamatter?"

"Why did you do that? You scared the profanity out of us!" Sergeant Mark hollers.

The guy almost blushes. "Ah had a hunch somethin' was comin'. Guess I wuz wrong, a-yup." Then, by way of apology: "It ain't but two minits to th' Ranch and that plane's got to be right close by."

Sergeant Mark cools. "No problem." Had it all the way, man.

We thump along behind the Chickenhawk, now over more oxcart potholes. But my spirit feels lighter now. In fact, I sense a light at the end of a very long tunnel. Thank goodness it isn't a train headlight.

Shortly, we pass an old brown wooden sign. Bingo, its Wingo. The sign, faded and covered by grasping vines, is engraved with the words "Wingo Ranch." A few log buildings sit, untenanted, on the top of a hill. Random weeds grow wild around it. My journalist's Spidey Sense tells me we are close.

Three minutes later, the Chickenhawk stops. We brake behind it.

The trees are heavy here. Even the trail peters out to a thin dirt path; we can't possibly push any farther, even with an ATV. No crickets. A reverent silence, except for mildly buzzing mosquitos. Patchy sunlight filters through the porous veil of trees. A breeze blows through the leaves. On the right, behind a line of trees, is a creek bed. Very little water in it. But something foreign to it is there. In a near trance, I exit the Jeep and walk forward past the Chickenhawk. The man and woman inside the car seem to understand that we are in the presence of death, so they sit, silent. I'm the reporter, the collector and conveyor of facts. By default, I am in charge.

Sergeant Mark shoulders up his black video camera and we walk about 20 paces up the path. We find a relatively easy spot to push through the trees and underbrush that guard the waterway.

It is an open area, filled with sunlight. And a rock-strewn creek. With a thin trickle of water...and a thousand pieces of a light plane that had burst apart when it slammed into the earth. The primary chunk of plane left intact--the fuselage--is smack in the middle of the shallow water. Did the pilot believe this would be his best shot at an emergency landing area?

Glance around: where are the passengers? Absolutely no way anyone could have walked away from this disaster. We take a few steps forward through the weeds but do not approach the wreck: everyone from sheriff's deputies to the NTSB investigator will want a clean incident scene. Finally, I spot a hand and arm, clothed in a white dress shirt, splayed out from under the fuselage. A tangled head of brown hair flutters in the light breeze. There is no other movement.

I feel moved to offer a brief, silent prayer for the man. Wonder who he was, and what his frenzied, fearful last few moments must have been like. How horrible it will be when his family gets the news. The news I will report on television tonight.

We spot two other motionless, battered, lifeless bodies nearby.

That's when I start to think about my story.

Next to me, Sergeant Mark expertly "sprays" the scene with his camera, recording a variety of shots.

"Do you see the tail numbers?" I ask him. That's essentially the license plate for the plane. We have to get it to research its registration and ownership. He points his camera at a spot at the opposite bank of the stream, where a piece of tail wreckage displays the letter-number combination.

Continuing to work, Sergeant Mark carefully avoids capturing a clear image of the bodies. A definite no-no. But he does motion for me to look in his viewfinder when he stops rolling. The camera's zoom function acts as a telescope, so we can see objects far away. I look at one of the victims. His eyes are wide open.

"He's dead," says Sergeant Mark, unnecessarily. "They're all dead."

I look back. The man and woman from the Chickenhawk are standing at the tree line, solemnly taking in the scene as well.

"You guys were great. Thank you for helping us," I tell them, quietly. "It isn't often that we are on the scene before the first responders." I wonder where the wagon train of emergency vehicles--and other media--is now.

"Its mah pleasure. Ah allus loved watchin' yer TV news, yep, so this is a great day for me." The woman, as allus, er, always, is silent.

"There's one more really important thing you can do. Find the emergency people and bring them here."

"But not before showing us a different way to get out," adds Sergeant Mark.

The next few hours are a blur. When the authorities finally arrive, they make us withdraw so they can secure the scene. That's okay with me because the other TV stations, still tagging along behind, aren't allowed in close enough to shoot video. They howl but it's no good.

To wait out the delay, we gather up at the Wingo Ranch. Broadcast reporters in one gaggle, shooters in another. The newspaper reporter and his photographer stand aloof. The other TV reporters question me like a subject of the story, rather than the recorder of facts.

"How did you get here ahead of us?" wonders "Channel 2 News On Your Side." It's his first job out of college, where he won an NCAA championship in gymnastics. His youth, athleticism, and looks are so striking that his career will never suffer for being beaten on something as irrelevant as news content. I give him the unabridged version of the tale, complete with the bridge.

"Newscenter 5" shakes her head, then brushes a string of raven black hair out of her eyes. "Why did you trust the redneck in the first place?" I don't have a good answer and she's not satisfied. "That's taking a pretty high risk," she asserts. What she lacks in height she makes up for in aggression. Now she is professionally ticked off. "All that for a television station? What were you thinking? Our boss would throw a fit if he thought we were endangering one of our station vehicles like that."

Ha. An unspoken television management truism: the equipment is much more valuable than the people. Despite her competitive frustration, "Newscenter 5" smiles at the irony a moment after speaking the words.

I smile, too, relaxed in the knowledge of a guy who can cry all the way to the bank. I have just beaten my competition, in spectacular fashion, on a major story in this market. In our newsroom, there will be high fives at five, six, and eleven.

From here on out, the process of putting together a news story for air is routine. We will all get the same interview with the lead law enforcement official, and maybe with my friend in the Chickenhawk, to tell us how difficult it is to find such a remote spot. The rest has to be done by the people manning our assignment desk. Out in the field, even the best reporters see only a small slice of a developing story such as this.

On a hill at the ranch I am fortunate to get a weak signal on my phone. With the tail numbers in hand, the desk will try to find out about the plane, the pilot, and the flight plan. Since many small plane pilots are well-to-do, this could be someone who had prominent connections. Our nightside reporter will go talk with the airport manager and other pilots. The desk will send us our satellite truck, so I can report live from the scene. To be precise, from Wingo Ranch, where there's a little clearing on the hill for the satellite transmitter to send its signal.

Despite their pleas to the lawmen, the reporters from the other stations aren't allowed in to the crash scene until it's too late.

For me, by 7:05, it's all over. Live reports at 5, 5:30, 6 and 7pm. I'm a star.

The couple in the Chickenhawk has disappeared, perhaps to make sure all the law enforcement officers roaming around don't stumble across their meth lab, or anything else they may be hiding.

On the way back to the station, I am jubilant. Even after nearly two years working at this station, many viewers don't really recognize me yet. But this is the kind of story that helps put me on the map. Especially since the lack of a map led to the "exclusive" elements I had in my story. Viewers don't get to know very many reporters, actually, unless they have a really special moment in the sun. It's what one of the other reporters at the station calls a "news high." Now, on the way back home, even Sergeant Mark becomes talkative, comparing this story with other wild TV news adventures he's had. I may have just passed his inspection.

My excitement increases as we pull into the station parking lot. I want to high-five a lot of people, pass around compliments and cigars to the people who helped us from the newsroom, and enjoy the sweet smell of success.

Unfortunately, the only smell prevalent in the newsroom is burnt coffee. No one is around to turn off the coffee machine. It's the "dinner void," between the end of the 7 pm newscast and beginning of preparations for the 11. The industrial fluorescent lights turn everything a shade more pale than the Great Outdoors we've been roaming through all afternoon. The only person in the room is a young assistant at the assignment desk, lost in an episode of "Entertainment This Night" and a newscast producer scanning state wire reports on a computer. Sergeant Mark is busy off-loading the equipment from the

Jeep into the videographer locker room. When he joins me, I am still staring at the coffee pot. It's been an intense day. He flips off the switch with one of his beefy fingers.

"Did you think someone would throw you a party?" he asks. Straightforward, like a non-commissioned officer. But not too unkindly.

"I guess not," I lie.

"Just remember. Three people had to die today to give us that great story."

Yeah. That. Perspective.

"Well, good job today. See you tomorrow," he says, turning around and leaving. That is all, soldier.

I feel wrung out and hung out to dry like an old chamois cloth. Yes, three people have died; those "three souls onboard" have met their eternal fate. I invested myself in this emotionally, though. Not in the death of two men and a teenage girl, but in the challenge of collecting the facts of their death and presenting it as a news story. The actual tragedy is something with which someone else will have to cope. Sadly, I realize that I'm looking for applause, not condolences. I kick myself, a little, being reminded of this. Still, I wonder: by what professional standard am I allowed to measure my work?

There is some small movement at one edge of the newsroom. A petulant, high-pitched voice rises out of the News Director's office. At least the boss is here. My spirits rise again, like an infusion of helium. Little Napoleon will want to congratulate me on my work--and congratulate himself on hiring me. Right? But I'll be cool about it, remind *him* of the dead people.

"Wilson! Come here a minute!" He commands in a screechy voice. Who? Shucks. Little ol' me?

I head on over, tripping lightly past the untenanted desks and echoing sounds of the emergency scanners in the nearly-empty, pale room. It's not too early to talk about my next contract, is it? My glow starts to return.

The Emperor's office is a continuous flow of stacks of paper and stacks of DVDs. A poster of Xena The Warrior Princess is about the only personal touch. That and an ancient Coleco handheld electronic football game, strangely out of place on his desk. Nearly hidden behind a pile of DVDs, the News Director sags far back in a leatherish and chromish office chair. Untied white athletic shoes rest on a tiny clearing on his desk. I wonder how his stubby legs can stretch that far. His face is a perpetual, puffy pout.

"Wil. Wilson."

Yes sir? You rang? His chubby fingers stab at the buttons on a remote control, pointed at a television/DVD unit on a nearby credenza.

"Can you believe this babe who wants to come here to report?" Little Napoleon asks.

What? A "Babe?"

He starts the disc in the DVD machine. First, a woman's name and address pop up on a blue screen, then a montage of shots of the reporter on camera. She seems a little unsure of what she's doing, but is strikingly pretty in a cold, formal way.

Little Napoleon regards her as Roger Thornhill did Eve Kendall: She's a big girl, and in all the right places.

"Look at her! Can you believe it? Wow! She was once 'Miss Bozeman'!" The News Director is envisioning this blonde vision working under him. *For* him, I mean. Whatever.

Ugh. I reply, "Yeah, wow. Hey, I gotta go write my story for the 11 o'clock newscast, and make sure the website is updated."

As I retreat, I hear the News Director call after me, his voice fading with the growing distance. "I expect you to have a lead story idea--or two-- for tomorrow, Wilson. Don't come in without at least one."

Don't worry, boss. After a day like this, it's about time to locate that six pack of Coors...and a new job.

2

Looking for work is a full time job in its own right. For television news reporters, it's an especially-painful level of purgatory. The routine goes like this: you begin by surreptitiously visiting your current TV station after work, several nights in a row (when the boss ain't there) to edit together a 10 minute audition "reel" of what you believe is your best on-air work. Its either burned to a DVD or uploaded to your personal website. Later, using your home computer (in case the boss is monitoring your online activities at work), you search for openings on industry websites like televisionjobs.com. Most people use a little (or a lot of) creative license in writing their cover letter and resume. Many submit their material to an agency for professional representation, but that's a different story with a different migraine involved. In this case, you eschew the agent, cross your fingers, and say a little prayer before mailing your carefully-prepared package to the News Director.

And then he loses your package, or your DVD doesn't play properly on their machine, and you never hear back from him.

Every once in a while a News Director gets exceptionally desperate and does reply with an email message. Mine comes about nine months after the airplane crash story, which figures prominently on my DVD. Shortly thereafter, I find myself starting over in another new town.

The sound of dresser drawers banging shut in the next room dissolves my slumber like dandelion spores in a puff of wind. But, ugh, I'm not yet fully awake. What time is it? A full hour before the alarm? Nerves, I guess. Think, buddy, think: What am I doing here? Oh, yeah: my first day on a new job.

I've started over before. And expect to do it again. Especially doing what I do for a living: "This Pen For Hire:" a mercenary television news reporter.

Still in a fog, I prop myself into a sitting position on the bed. Uncertain, darkened shapes start to come into focus. Industrial-strength curtains are pulled tight across--what? on the other side of the window. Light burns through the edges of the curtains, but I'm still hazy. What's outside? A foreign land, I'm sure. The geography of these fruited plains is defined only by the Nielsen ratings people, who ignore municipal and even state boundaries. This could be Greenville-Spartanburg-Asheville, or Champaign-Springfield-Decatur, or possibly Santa Barbara-Santa Maria-San Luis Obispo or any of more than 200 Designated Market Areas (DMA's), all according to Nielsen. Well, I'm no longer in the Appalachians, I manage to recall.

Outside the door I hear people moving around, yet I am alone: this is a hotel room. Few objects belong to me here. Some luggage, some baggage. An achingly empty bottle provides a vertical counterpoint to an otherwise featureless round and flat Formica table across the room. Ugh. I look around--slowly--head swimming from the effects of that bottle. What belongs to me in this place? The only personal touch is a Johnny Bench baseball card I stuck in the mirror frame. The Baseball Hall of Fame catcher from my hometown of Cincinnati will have to pass as my family here. No permanent place to live here, yet, either. Just another new job in a new town.

I hate trying new things. Hate it. I much prefer the known, the routine, the tried and true. But this is another gig, another steady paycheck, and I'm not working for Little Napoleon any more. Two years, says the new contract. The humorless joke about contracts?" Two years--unless the station exercises the morals clause." Okay, okay, two years. Time will tell whether everything I own actually gets unpacked this time.

Where's the clicker? Find a light, then the remote control on the standard hotel laminate nightstand next to me. There's time for some last-minute research. Snapping on the television, I look for the morning news. Want to see the top story on as many of the local stations as I can find. Concentrating on focusing my eyes, I turn to Channel 7 first: "Action News." The news reader describes a shooting and desperate manhunt for the triggerman. Quick, click to Channel 11: "Eyewitness News." Shooting and manhunt. Waving the magic wand again, I land on "Newschannel 99," where the news is just starting. Two minutes late? The news anchor is looking at the wrong camera. Now she's looking down. Someone else is talking. She glances up. Now over to the correct camera. She looks worried--for good reason, I suspect. She then recites details of a midnight foosball tournament for inmates at the state pen. The video, however, shows flatulent camels in Egypt. What about the shooting and manhunt? I turn off the TV in fear and loathing: this is my new employer.

Yikes.

Deep breath. My hangover just doubled. But it's time to get going. Newschannel 99 can't be that bad all the time, can it?

I won't find out if I don't find my socks. Hold on. *Matching* socks. I remind myself to not start sweating...yet.

It doesn't take long to clean up. Shower and a shave, and I'm starting to feel easy like Sunday morning. On Monday. Open collar, I head down to the hotel breakfast buffet for some solid nutrition. But I have to take a deep breath before diving in. The elevator doors peel away to reveal screaming kids and what appears to be a jostling crowd of NHL defensemen wearing business suits. I nearly decide to stay in the elevator and go back up. But, I neeeeed coffee.

Next to the coffee machine, there is a vicious scrum for a handful of supermarket Danishes. In a corner, waxy red apples look lonely in a wicker basket. A fearful hotel employee drops a new tray of bagels on the counter and withdraws fast: hungry patrons have sharp claws and teeth. I snatch an apple and two hospital-white Styrofoam cups of coffee.

Copies of "US Today" wait on a nearby counter, but I need the local newspaper to find out what's happening around here. There are boxes out front. I head out through the glass doors. Its suddenly sunny, a vibrant green of new spring and sparkly parking lot asphalt. I balance the coffee in one hand--gripping an apple with my teeth--and deposit 50 cents. I feel ridiculous, with the coffee perilously close to emptying. Victory. Whew. Arms laden, I head back to my room, the first foray into this new world a success.

Scanning the local headlines, I don't see anything about a midnight foosball tournament for inmates. But I do read a late leader about the shooting. And "Get Fotchy" in the comics section nearly makes me snort coffee out of my nose.

Okay, time to get going. Fasten the necktie, apply the suit coat. Everything I need for work is in the manbag. One last look: the mirror says 'go'. Check the tie and the fly--it's time for me to fly. The hour is still young, which is good. There is time to get a feel for this town's morning rush hour without rushing myself, and to listen to local talkers on the radio. The rental car feels foreign. Foreign made, and foreign to me, that is. On the floor in front of the passenger seat I spy a guilty empty bottle. Quick, stash it under the seat. Next crisis: how do I turn off the wipers that I had to use last night?

Now is the time to learn how fast the rats race in this town. Its competitive, but polite and slow. I crawl along with freeway traffic, past a miniature downtown skyline. "Filterboro," read the freeway exit signs. Tobacco billboards abound. I exit uptown. The roads are broader and newer than downtown. No traffic jams here, thanks to the wider roads. The traffic flows heavy but steady. Unhurried, I take it all in.

Unfamiliar buildings glide by my car. Few pedestrians walk the sidewalks, and there are many unfamiliar license plates. A lineup at the fast food drive-through window gets me thinking that this is a town well into its routine. Not me, though. I'm as foreign as the car I'm driving.

The radio guys are all following the manhunt story. It's getting repetitive, so I shove in a Johnny Cash CD to relax before the first day on the job.

We got married in a fever

Hotter than a pepper sprout

We been talking 'bout Jackson

Ever since the fire went out

I haven't worked work in Jackson. Yet. But its Market #90 this year, according to Nielsen. It may or may not be a big enough market to pay a mercenary like me. At least until a fresh News Director is hired to "cut costs." They usually begin by bringing in younger, less-expensive reporters. Who cares if it takes even the smart ones two years (the length of their contract) to really learn about the town they are supposed to cover?

This isn't Jackson, although it is The New-ish South, where some decent jobs are still actually available. Newer office buildings show off a fresh coat of money. Trees abound. The palms are sweaty. Not the trees, my hands. I drive on, worrying I may be lost. Where's this TV station? Finally, I turn in to a busy industrial park drive. It's a complex looking kind of, uh, complex. Multiple office buildings are arrayed like massive chess pieces around a checkerboard road pattern. Yet, a sign with a TV station logo finally directs me to the end of the last drive. Back there somewhere, I spot a soaring antenna tower pointing to the sky. But I'm lost; how do I get there from here? There are no further signs, and I prefer clarity in these things, dude. I double back, and drive around various industrial park boulevards. A little while ago I had a lot of extra time, but it is evaporating quickly. The clock is moving. No luck, no luck.

Wait. Behind a yellow road sign that reads "Dead End," a thin dirt road seems to wander on through a scraggly woods at the back of the park. Why not? I try it. Gotta drive slow over the washboard ridges in the road. But perseverance is rewarded this time: the trees part and a building with a parking lot appears. There's a fleet of Crossover SUV's with a TV station logo repetitively plastered on them. This must be the place. In a hurry, I stable my pony with the SUV's. I'll leave it here just for now, to get in the door on time. Whew. Okay, be cool, buddy. I adjust my interior mirror, and my hair. Take a deep breath, and go.

Stop. I realize the building in front of me looks pretty odd. Flat, two-story--that's pretty typical, early '80's utilitarian architecture. It looks like whitewashed stucco. Hold on, though. Its fronted by a four-story, rounded tower. Huh? Topped by a turret. Is this really the place? I double-check for a station sign. There it is, over an entrance, the same logo on the SUV's. Blue and gold lettering surrounded by a knock-off Nike-type "swoosh" graphic: WDMZ. Smaller print underneath proclaims "Newschannel 99." Even smaller letters on the third tier: "Where We're Right 99 Times Out of 100!"

Looking more closely, I spy inside a man cleaning the plate glass window that admits a view into the lobby. I look twice. He seems to be wearing a uniform: a long, gold-buttoned burgundy coat with epaulets. He energetically spritzes the window and carefully wipes it clear and clean. Wax on, wax off.

I hadn't visited this building the day I was hired. The News Director had what you'd call "outside interests." Allen Pratfall met me at a dog track, about a month ago. I actually enjoy the racetrack atmosphere: the kind of hollow, desperate enthusiasm generated by the prospect of winning and losing money. Hey, where else do you find so many "indoor" people with their pasty faces and soft, bookish postures actually spending time "out of doors?"

Pratfall is a bit of an "indoor" guy while attempting the look of a slick Player. You know, the guy lounging along the rail at Aqueduct, grasping a rolled-up racing program and gasping on a cigar. He introduces me to a couple of "business associates." One of them is a small, trim man in a brown porkpie hat who goes by "Alibi Wallace." Using a low whisper that implies everything he says is an important secret, for some reason Wallace thinks it necessary to convince me to join Newschannel 99. But I'm already won over.

Over a couple of beers during the Sixth Race, Pratfall offers me a general assignment reporter's job. This is a larger DMA than the one in the mountains, with better pay. Better hours and warmer temperatures make the deal attractive. The fact that my relationship with Little Napoleon quickly slid downhill after the plane crash report makes it imperative. Okay, I'm here.

Now, as I approach the entrance of the television station, inside the lobby I notice the man in uniform quickly donning a peaked hat and rushing to open the glass entry door. What's this? A doorman? I almost expect to find Phillip Marlowe sitting in the lobby, waiting for Colonel Sternwood.

"Good morning, sir," he offers, robustly. "Welcome to Newschannel 99, Where We're Right 99 Times Out Of 100!" The man, tall, round, perhaps in his 50's, touches the small plastic bill of his official-looking hotel doorman hat.

"Thanks. Reception?"

He points straight indoors, past a waiting room dominated by an ancient wooden Zenith cabinet-model television, picture all pink and green ("In Living Color!"). They must have one of those government-funded High Definition converter boxes attached to it. Behind a glass enclosure, complete with push-button speaker, a woman sits. Its Shelly Winters from "A Patch of Blue": floozy, round, beehive hair. She's really busy writing something with a pencil. I wait.

Finally, she turns on me with a nasal twang: "Well, good morning, sir. Welcome to Newschannel 99, Where 'We're Right 99 Times Out Of 100'. How can I help you?"

"Allen Pratfall, please."

Sweetly, musically, nasally: "Allen Pratfall no longer works here." Her meticulously-plucked eyebrows narrow. She sets down her pencil: "Dijyew have an appointment with him?"

"New employee. Reporter. My name is Wilson Gamble."

She sizes me up. Doesn't smile. "I see. I'll try to get Walter Wilson for you. Just have a seat if yew don't mind."

Pratfall gone? Do I have a job? Who is Walter Wilson? What was it that Shelly Winters didn't like about my appearance? Do I--offend?

Alright, I'm resigned to hanging out in the lobby, for now. A bank of orange leatherette chairs apparently stolen from a retired dentist's office waiting room look like my best bet. Circa "Atomic Age." Chrome legs splay out in four directions under every seat. 1959 may have been a creative year for interior design, but the chairs that remain are worn out. Sinking into the plastic upholstery, I scooch up to the edge of the seat--creating an awful squealing vinyl rubbing noise. Not comfortable; I relax again--and sink back in. Unfortunately, my knees are as high as my face. Ultimately, I give up and simply stand.

The Zenith shows a 30 second "newsbreak," featuring The Worried News Reader from this morning. She headlines the shooting, forgets the manhunt. She also mentions the foosball tournament, but there's no camel video, thank goodness. Then she takes a deep breath.

"Newschannel 99 exclusive! ... local newsman arrested! 39 year old Allen Pratfall of Filterboro Heights surrendered to authorities Sunday night. Police say an investigation found Pratfall ran a numbers operation at a local business. We're told it's a television station." Cheerful, now--got that out of the way. Probably a "scoop" on the competition, too, since he worked here. She continues. "And a bright, sunny day in Filterboro! Your complete weather forecast coming up at Noon. You're watching Newschannel 99, where 'We're Right 99 Times Out Of 100!'" Done. Whew.

The manbag slips from my grip with a surprised thud. What in the world have I fallen in to?

Surveying the room, I note the usual studio photos of on-air personalities smiling on the walls. They are known as "talent." Nice teeth, pretty girls. This, at least, seems normal.

Time passes, and I grow bored. I note several potted palms and red shag carpet dominate the interior decorating. Bordello remnants, perhaps? There's a network logo on the wall. Its familiar, of course, yet distant here: corporate. With time to kill I open the manbag and withdraw my phone. Send some unnecessary text messages, surf the web. The idea is to communicate that hey, I'm important, too. Lots of communications demanding my urgent attention. They just don't know that I'm busy texting my mother.

Random people come and go through the lobby. Otherwise its quiet except for the sound of the TV and the doorman hurrying through on errands.

I've been a reporter for years. On radio at first, which is nostalgic but pays nothing. Now I'm in television, which at first promised a career. I bounced around, sometimes two or three years at a time, sometimes not so long. Now, stations demand years of experience from applicants but only pay enough to attract college sophomores. No wonder everyone wants to be an anchor, they get paid. Which leaves me a growing rarity: a reporter with straight facts as well as straight teeth. I take this as leverage in looking for a new gig.

Time passes. I visit Shelly Winters.

"Any luck finding someone in the news department?"

You-still-here? expression. Take another drink out of that brown bag behind the counter, lady.

"Keep yer shirt on, let me check," she finally condescends.

Whispers into phone something about "won't go away." Sorry, I can't go away. No other job, Shelly. Check my manbag. Where's that new contract?

"Puhlease have a seat. Mr. Wilson will be right with you."

I have a seat, my body conforming and adhering to the space age chair. The only sound is that of the sucking leather noise of my body sinking, sinking.

"Mr. Wilson" rushes in. I struggle to rise as his words rush out.

"Sorry its taking so long we had our morning meeting and nobody wanted to do a package on the midnight foosball tournament at the state prison can you believe that and our News Director's in trouble and my breakfast burrito had green peppers in it when everyone knows I'm allergic to green peppers but I guess you probably are wondering what's going on with your job, right?"

I'm stunned into silence. He glances at a clipboard he clutches.

"You are Wilson Gamble aren't you because Allen told me he hired someone named Wilson and I remembered that because my last name is Wilson you know my name is Walter Wilson and your first name is, uh, Wilson if indeed--you are Wilson Gamble, right?" A sudden question mark at the end of the monologue. His eyes narrow. My cue to answer.

"I am Wilson Gamble," I affirm. It had been a unique name. I had liked it. Until now.

Somehow my brief reply befuddles Walter Wilson. He stands, overweight and sweaty. Swaying. Peering through big, thick, smeared glasses. Cheap tie askew. Breakfast burrito residue on a haphazard white shirt. He smells like a green pepper, even if he is allergic to it.

I move in, business-like, to offer a handshake and am greeted with a dead fish "grip." Yuck. Walter Wilson limply withdraws his hand, stops peering at me, and rolls into motion.

"Follow me back this way is the newsroom but first here's some offices, down that hallway is where the sales people work, they really seem to get a bad name but I like them especially when they get free tickets to all the baseball games and they let me go once in a while." He actually takes a breath. "Over here is one of the men's rooms. It has a machine that costs a quarter that sprays different imitation colognes so you might want to remember that the next time you need a little refreshing fragrance before heading out to represent Newschannel 99, you know what I mean." I don't, but still involuntarily feel my pocket for a quarter.

Keep walking. Red shag gives way to orange tight weave. No pad underneath, it is truly glorified concrete. "Back there is a break room and they usually have Pop Tarts in the vending machine but the vendor raised the price so it's a dollar for a package of two but my favorite is frosted strawberry. Do you like baseball?"

Yes. But...I happen to notice a hallway branching off. To the north, or somewhere. The orange floor and sterile walls are replaced there by flagstone floor and walls. Stone? Like an Irish castle I once visited. Dim lights. We walk past it. Suddenly, there's no commentary from Walter Wilson.

"What's back there?" I ask.

"Back there? Back there? You mean Miss Eriss' wing?" The overhead lights flicker.

"You tell me."

"Yes, that's where Miss Eriss lives and works."

Thanks. "Who's Miss Eriss?"

Funny thing: I'd swear the lights flickered again. Walter Wilson blinks through his glasses. How can he see through them? The lenses look like a car windshield coated with bugs. "Miss Eriss is your employer."

Walter Wilson's only declarative statement. But at least its evidence that I have a job.

"She lives there?"

"Yes, yes, yes. Upstairs. I was allowed to walk by the staircase once but I never actually went up there and you know she is very committed to the success of our company. She lives and breathes WDMZ and everyone loves her and you'll get to see her, soon enough. Let's keep going to the newsroom."

Walter Wilson resumes the bizarre tour.

"On your right is a water fountain and out through that door is the employee parking lot and there's an old desk in an old office that hasn't been used in a long time, at least since, uh, Aaron Altman used to work here but that was in the early 1980's and over there is a storage closet that someone locked me in one night I couldn't get out until the janitor came by the next morning boy that was a long night but I did get to read all of the old news scripts that are stored in filing cabinets in there... ."

We inch into the newsroom. Ah, home. It all looks high-tech, but is simply a made-for-TV set. Coffee slowly burns in a pot on a corner cabinet. Long banks of white-blue fluorescents glow overhead. Maps, wipe boards, and awards cover the walls. Digital clocks and High Definition television monitors cover the other walls. The room is divided by the low partition walls of cubicle clusters. Emergency scanner radios blare, the phones ring. Sections of the local newspaper are scattered everywhere. People chat on phones, peer into computer monitors, and generally act like they belong. Walter Wilson does not. He tries to shout into the noise, while pointing. It's like screaming into a windstorm.

"There's what we like to call the 'hub of the newsroom,' the assignment desk over there. Hey Gretchen, here's our new reporter!" His index finger is aimed at a cubicle island that rises in in the center of the newsroom. Phones, scanners, computers, empty breakfast food wrappers, and phones on chargers are all scattered about. Behind those ramparts, I spy: hair. Lots of brown, frizzy hair. Followed by a series of impressions: eyeglasses, distraction, granola, argument. Walter Wilson basically does not exist in the world of this woman.

"That's Gretchen Calzone, our Assignment Manager," Wilson says as an aside to me. Then, aiming himself towards her, he tries, "Gretchen? Gretchen? Gretchen?" Patiently. "Gretchen? Gretchen? Gretchen? Gretchen? Gretchen?" Back to me: "I guess Gretchen is busy"--she then looks up--"so over here is the News Director's office but Allen isn't here naturally since he's under indictment now and probably won't be coming back for five-to-ten years. But he had three of the best chairs in the newsroom in his office so I guess there will be a big fight to see who steals them first oh look they are already gone."

Nearby, at least three seated employees suddenly appear very busy trying to ignore this last observation.

"Over there those five rooms are our edit bays and then here's where the reporters all sit together in this cluster of cubes. We call it a 'cube cluster.' That's Jack Phillips, don't buy real estate from him, trust me; Sherman Follicle's there, he can get you free tickets to the dog track; and she's Tyler Hubbell... pretty girl, huh?"

Classic Platinum blonde. "Ugh," all over her face. Walter forlornly acknowledges her hate-stare. He sighs.

"Are you going out to cover the shooting, Tyler?"

Caught in mid hate-stare at Wilson, she's trapped. Must answer. "I'm waiting for the Public Information Officer to call back. Then we'll go get video of wherever the police are searching for the shooter." Turn to Phillips, "I hope it's near that new sushi bar over in Metronome Plaza, because I'm dying for tempura!" Smiles. No more Walter Wilson in her happy world! She returns to her email.

A different young woman approaches, unafraid of getting cornered by Wilson, or anyone else. She's, er, a little on the plain side compared to some of the Barbie dolls who work in television. But by her dress, appearance, and carriage, she's a professional. Aggressive. For the first time, Wilson has nothing to say.

"Jeanette Nettles," she offers, briskly. Gravelly voice sounds like Peppermint Patty. "General assignment reporter." Looking at Wilson, pushing practical, shoulder length brown hair behind an ear, she confides, "Don't call me 'Jen', okay?" It will take me a little while to figure out why. Wilson fidgets.

"Okay, uh, not-Jen. Jeanette. I'm Wilson Gamble. You *can* call me 'Wil.'"

Nettles smiles, pushes her practical hair behind her other ear, and quickly moves on. But it's nice to experience an interlude of normal human contact in a place that in some ways already resembles the Mad Hatter's tea party.

Wilson watches her leave; It's time to ramble on. "In the back is where the videographers hang out. With all the security fencing someone thought it looks like a cage so we call it, 'The Cage.' All their equipment is there, too. And up against the wall is where the producers sit that's known as 'Producer's Row' and you'll meet them as we go along but for now come over to my office and we'll see whether or not Miss Eriss wants to meet you right away."

No coincidence; the fluorescents momentarily dim once again at the mention of her name.

Walter Wilson's office sits on the edge of the newsroom. The blinds are closed, and the furniture here speaks of High School Classroom Fire Sale. Metal desk, metal filing cabinet, mostly-metal chairs. A drop ceiling encases recessed lights. A metal bookcase holds no books, but rather is filled haphazardly with DVD discs and gem cases.

Yellow splotches cover much of the metal. As I focus on them, they turn out to be sticky notes. "Feed manhunt vid. on sat. @ 3:30," "complain to restaurant re: brkfst brrto," "change litter box," etc. Photos everywhere of cats, or a cat. I can't tell. A framed photo of June Cleaver, or-- his mom? Stuffy cat smell. Yuck. I have a sudden, desperate urge to leave. Or hack up a hairball.

"Have a seat, have a seat, have a seat, just wait there because I gotta check something out online."

Behind his desk now, its Walter versus his computer. Typing. Mousing.

"Where do I click on this thing?" he wonders out loud to himself. Waves mouse frantically over pad. Further conversation with monitor.

"Where's that bookmark... okay... yes... there... well... okay... when? ... right, right... okay... ."

I wait.

"Buy... 65 shares... of... Washington Mutual... wow... sounds too good to be true... let's do it!" Decisions, decisions.

Back to me. "Buy low, sell high, that's my motto!" Walter smiles, frowns. Pause. Oh. I'm still here. Back to business. This business, anyways. "Oh, um, can I see your contract, Mr. Gamble? I don't have access yet to the personnel files in Allen's office, which they should let me see anyways but they don't so I have to ask someone permission and I don't know exactly who just yet." He waits, expectantly.

Ah, yes. My contract. I withdraw it from the manbag and hand it over with the same weighty solemnity of a head of state offering a weapons treaty to a powerful rival. Wilson reaches for it, notices something on his fingers, sets down my contract, wipes off his hand on a paper napkin. I grimace. He doesn't notice as he glances through the paperwork.

"Looks like Miss Eriss signed it and so did you and there's a notary seal so I guess you are cleared to go see Miss Eriss so lemme just call over to the front office and see if she is available because sometimes she's not."

He punches buttons on a standard black plastic office phone.

"Yeah Rose, its Walter. Isn't it a nice day outside but Arnold says it could rain if we wait long enough, what do you think, huh?" No apparent response. "I'm really doin' well on this day trader thing I have going..." Awkward moment. "Oh. Of course I'm not using the company computer for that." Quick, change gears. "I need to start a new employee file so can you get that for me? And, is Miss Eriss available to meet a guest because our new reporter needs to go on up."

Up? I wonder.

"You remember him, don't you? The guy you said had a funny, old-fashioned haircut." Burst of noise on other end. He hangs up without saying anything else. Absently, I pat my hair.

"Okay, do you remember where you first came in go back there and ask Rose to show you up to Miss Eriss and remember to be nice because she is the Station Manager and the last time I saw her she didn't seem very happy because of Allen so maybe you should consider... ."

Not knowing how he will finish, I'm out the door. Through the newsroom, I sense all eyes staring at the new guy, with some smiles meant possibly to be sympathetic because of Walter Wilson's rambling--which follows me through the room. Quick, help--where do I go?

Gretchen Calzone jabs one of her pencils behind her towards a hallway that I think I recognize that leads to the front office. "Good luck," she quotes.

Walk, don't run, I tell myself, venturing back to Rose. This time I approach her hideaway from within. The bulletproof cocoon dominates the lobby, telling visitors 'We are important enough to require special security protection.' No security, however, from behind. Surprise! Hastily, she drops a bottle into a desk drawer and slams it shut.

Smiling, I don't say a word.

A moment to compose. Rose punches a single digit on her phone. "Yes ma'am. New reporter. Walter Wilson sent him. Are you ready to see him? Yes, ma'am." Pause. Rose cups a hand over the receiver. "She's feeding her fish."

To whom?

"This could take a few minutes," Rose concludes.

23, to be exact. Ivory Eriss must have filleted them. Rose drifts off, humming snatches of broadcast commercial jingles. "It takes a husky mensch/to drink a lot of 'Quench'!" I stand around, uncomfortable.

Finally, the phone rings. Rose saunters over to it.

"Yes ma'am. I'll have Warden escort him. Oh. Uh, yes, ma'am. Of course. Yes. I will. Really, I will. Okay. Oh." Giggles. "You're welcome."

Hanging up, Rose presses the intercom button. "Warden, will you show our visitor up to Miss Eriss?" Now, the lights even flicker in the lobby.

Apparently yearning to serve, the doorman named Warden comes a-runnin'. His jacket tails practically flap behind him. Plastic smile plastered across his face as he approaches me. "Right this way, sir."

Back into building bowels we go. This time, though, we branch off down the flagstone hallway. It's cool here, dark. Musty. Quiet. We follow a winding path. Heavy wooden doors along the hall are adorned only with brass plates that identify the numerous inmates. Most are appended with an "Esq." after the name. Others end with "MBA" and related letter combinations. In any case, I have to trot to keep up with Warden The Doorman. Finally, we arrive at a gray stone spiral staircase. I notice that farther down in the gloom, another hallway branches off. I'm at such an angle that I can see down it. Distinctively, all the way at the end, a neon sign flashes on and off, like a garish beer sign at the bar: "Sales Dept.," I make out. Ugh. At least it's a long ways away from the newsroom.

"You will find Miss Eriss' apartment at the top of that staircase," advises Warden, leaving me staring upward at the cold stone steps.

I have to go up there? The thought gives me the creeps. "Her apartment?" I verbalize.

"Miss Eriss' office hours are from one until four," declares Warden. My watch shows 9:54 in the morning. "Therefore, at this hour, she will receive you in her private apartment."

Goodbye, Warden. Trudging up the tight circular staircase, I have to alternate between uncomfortably long and short strides over the tiny steps. Six, seven, eight. 23, 24, 25. Geez, Louise: 55, 56, 57. 'Round and 'round we go, where we stop, nobody knows. Huffing. Puffing. Sweating. Then I realize: I must be inside the turret I saw out front. I pass by numerous slit-like windows that are too small to admit much light or air.

Finally, I reach a landing, guarded by a heavy, rounded wooden door. 16th century Gothic, complete with metal strapping and odd engravings. Gotta catch my breath, wipe my brow. Okay, do I knock? Or just go in? In answer, on its own, somehow the door swings wide. Unexpected light makes me realize the relative darkness of the staircase. Blink. A large, open space confronts me. Blink again. I am confronted by oak floors, paneling, rafters, and candles. But, it is a living space. Little in the way of actual furniture. Long windows abound, but the sunlight is judiciously regulated by heavy curtains. A voluminous aquarium props up a far wall.

What else is here? A womannnnn confronts me as well. Very attractive, in a cold sort of way. Hmm, 27? 35? 51? Timeless, really. She's draped over a daybed in the absolute center of a Great Room that dominates the apartment. Silky gowns splayed all about her. Bony head thrown back, wrapped in a tight turban. Sunshine falls lightly on her pale and powdered form from a skylight. Lady Brett Ashley or Jordan Baker?

I pause, take in the scene from a Roaring 20's novel. Then, I move forward.

"Miss Eriss? Glad to meet you. I'm Wilson Gamble."

Pause.

"Mr. Pratfall let us down. Are you one of...his?"

This is not some fictional Jazz Age character. Instead, I am confronted by Lauren Bacall, or maybe Kathleen Turner. That husky, cultured, mocking voice is familiar from film. Meanwhile, Ivory Eriss retains her posture. And waits.

"One of his...what, Miss Eriss?"

She shifts, slightly. Almost condescends to look in my direction.

"His *hires*, my good man."

Yuck. I'm a servant. "Yes I am. One of his hires. But I wasn't aware of his, er, troubles, until today."

A cigarette burns and occasionally sparks like a bomb fuse in a long silver holder. "Do you have a signed contract?" she simmers.

"Of course. I have a copy here, if you'd like to see it." In the good ol' manbag. "In fact, you signed it."

She knows this. Taking it from me, Eriss holds the manuscript as if it was a germ. She takes a few moments to consider it. Sort of look it over. Apparently Eriss wants to determine if they really have to pay me. Too late, sister. She appears to relent. "You came all this way for...this much money?" she accuses me, mockingly.

"It's a job. And it is a raise in pay from my last job." But I'm not making her kind of cash: Sales Department money.

Having failed so far, she tries to puncture me again. "Why did you meet Mr. Pratfall at the...dog track?" Contempt.

"Not much choice; he wanted to meet me there. I'm a hired gun. Reporter by trade, I go wherever the work is."

"You're not an independent thinker?" Eriss twists on her daybed. "Insatiably analyzing life? Questioning those in power? Cynical? Critical of people and their motives? A crusader? Come now, Mr. Gamble, what kind of journalist are you?"

"Didn't claim to be one, Miss Eriss." I'm cool. But, um, what am I? Ah, yes. "I'm a reporter. TV news. I observe what happens and tell a story. Good at visuals, presentation, writing to video. I fill time in your newscast and, um, can read scripts with feeling."

Snap.

"Get a read on me, Mr. Gamble. If you have any allegiance to Allen Pratfall because he hired you, you had better lose it. He is not coming back. It appears you have a contract, so we will pay you for your services, evidently, for two years."

Suddenly, her voice slows. Deep husky again. Eyes far off, hazy. "But I may call on you...for *other* services."

Public appearances at Kiwanis meetings and school functions? I gulp. Then I think about that morals clause in my contract.

Momentarily, there is another movement off to the side of the room. Astonished, I spy the doorman guy, Warden, outside on a scaffold with his towel and bottle, clearing the streaks from a window. How in the world did he get up here?

Eriss notices my gaze, and condescends to explain. "Warden likes to keep the windows spic and span. A valuable service to me. He keeps them clean and I...keep a clear view on things."

I'm not sure if that's a warning. Eriss remains in repose. But then, there is another unexpected change of direction.

"Do you enjoy...art?"

What now? Quick, shift gears. Fortunately, I can feign some interest. "Like many people, I guess, I have my preferences." Better to hold out on this as long as I can. Number One, because I don't, other than occasional Norman Rockwell magazine cover art. And Number B, philosophically it's better to not express an opinion that is sure to be challenged by The Boss. I'm not looking for an argument. But my reticence won't last long.

"Such as?" she demands, shortly, expectantly.

Okay, okay. Think. I did a story for Little Napoleon on a traveling art exhibit. Right. "Realist school. Hopper, Homer...Bellows," I lie. Better than the Surrealist school that is indeed this weird place.

"How very...pedestrian," she breathes. Another cloud of cigarette smoke billows forth. "Some other day I may show you my collection. I have a taste for what some call...Late Gothic." She breathes, carefully. "I call it International Gothic. Altichieri, Bellini. Superficially one-dimensional, but the themes are suggestive. Persecution, for example. It is not quite so modern as you seem to prefer. But," a small smile forms, "I find it equally expressive."

"Umm, that would be, educational, I'm sure."

"Good bye, Mr. Gamble," she concludes. Smoke cloud billows in my direction. "I hope you won't come to my attention again before I...require you."

Its backtrack time, quickly. Thank goodness the stone stairs are much easier on the way down, although the tiny steps remain tricky. Still puffing, I happen to meet Shelley Winters at the bottom. She looks a little confused.

"Why didn't you take the elevator?" she asks.

I shuffle back to the newsroom. Avoiding Wilson, I step purposefully towards the assignment desk. Somehow, I sense an ally there. For the moment, though, Gretchen Calzone is distracted, ready to do battle somewhere else. Her impromptu frizzled ponytail is held together with a pair of battling Faber-Castell #2's. She's gnawing on a third pencil, working two phones at once. I am warned to Please Stand By.

"Whaddya mean you can't get Judge Barnswallow here to the studio by 11:45? No wait. Wait, Norman. Just wait. Maybe I can get Billy Fotch to go pick him up." She turns away from the phone, towards the far reaches of the newsroom. "Fotch! FOTTTTTCH! ! !" A primal, throaty yell directed at The Cage. The Cage doesn't respond.

More phone Calzone. She holds the first phone to her shoulder, while speaking into a second one.

"Judge Barnswallow, we are sending over someone to pick you up. I'm working it out. Please hold one moment." Switch phones. "Listen Norman. I don't give a rat's tail if they aren't done changing the oil. You get that Jeep back from the shop and you get over there and bring Barnswallow back here and I MEAN RIGHT NOW. AND CLEAN OUT THE FAST FOOD GARBAGE OUT OF THE PASSENGER SEAT!" Slam. Screaming at the entire phone, rather than just the handset.

Sweetly now, lyrically, second phone.

"Hello, Judge Barnswallow. Our representative, Mr. Norman Wallflower, will pick you up at the Courthouse in our limo in about 20 minutes. Oh. Uh huh. You heard? Well, uh, no. It's a Jeep. Yes, he's a videographer. Sort of. Yes, sir. No, thank you, sir. Good bye."

Billy Fotch wanders up. No hurry. Skinny, t-shirted, tattooed, black hair spiked with glue, he looks like a castoff member of the Sex Pistols.

"Meredith!" hollers Calzone.

Her line of sight is hampered by Fotch's hair. He zigs and zags with her; Harpo-Lucy mirror mime.

"Fotch, get out of the way, you idiot. Meredith! Barnswallow will be here for an on-set interview for the noon. Wallflower will pick him up. They'll be here by 11:45."

Distantly, quietly somehow across the newsroom noise, the noon newscast producer replies, almost dismissively, "Thanks Gretch."

Gretch isn't waiting for thanks. A call comes across one of the scanners, followed by static. Listening intently, she aims her eyes intently on the scanner, as if it would help hear it more clearly. Having learned what she can from it, she looks up with features contorted by sudden disgust. He's there.

"Fotch, what do you want?"

"You called me, babe. And here I am! What's your pleasure?" Slow, singsong. He would sound mocking if he wasn't so completely guileless.

"There's an accident on the interstate up near Oak Ledge. Sounds bad. Get out there."

"Um, okay." No pretense at professionalism. "Which way is Oak Ledge?"

Heavy, heavy sigh. "Moron. You've lived here your whole life and you still couldn't find City Hall. Oak Ledge is that town 15 minutes away from us on the freeway. You need to hop on the freeway and go--"

Another scanner burst. Urgent.

"Fotch GO. Now it sounds like there's a fire at the accident!! Entrapment! Go go go go go go go!!"

The motivation is suddenly sufficient. More indistinct but urgent-sounding scanner traffic immediately follows. Calzone phones the 911 call center to make sure of the location--wherever that is. I'm clearly not on her radar any more, Fotch finally gets the message, and he heads back to The Cage, equips himself, and is gone.

I'm still there.

"Who're you?" Calzone wonders, living in the moment. Not confrontational but momentarily lost. Blaring and flashing, the scanner streams out more emergency information. Then, a light flashes over her head when she recalls my status here. "Oh yeah, you. You can sit over, ah, uh, um, there until I figure something out."

Her pencil points to a cube cluster. Where some other reporters are deeply entrenched.

I wander over. Is there an open desk here?

"You can probably have, uh, Howard Beale's old desk. He's not coming back." Holding his phone handset away from his ear, Sherman Follicle snickers. Knowing looks abound. He motions with the handset. "It's over there."

Great. I'm glad for own my own space, such as it is. A chair and empty cube. Nothing but Potential here. I sit and explore the drawers: nothing but somebody else's history. Some old files, lint, pencils, hot sauce packets, and obscure business cards. About 200 pennies in a small box. Another voice interrupts my brief desk audit, coming from somewhere over one of the partitions.

"Hey, George. You may want to spray Lysol all over that cubicle before you touch anything."

'George? 'Is this comment directed towards me? The voice continues. "Beale wasn't very clean, George. He seemed to like extra ketchup on his burgers. Some got left behind."

Slowly, I rise up to look over the partition. There's a guy playing a video game on his computer. Very intent, focused on the monitor, but still talking--to me, evidently. "Whatcha do is wait until you can move into that other cube, two spots back," he suggests, not looking up. "It's against the wall so you can hang up more of your stuff. These partition walls are pretty short."

"I'll check it out," I replied. "I'm not 'George. 'My name is Wilson. Wilson Gamble."

"Jack Phillips." Momentarily, he turns from his computer. And, he's not so young, about 40. Hair thinning. Careful use of hair product. Expensive necktie. Fine shirt. Salesman smile. Trim moustache. Wait. How does he get away with having a moustache on TV? Many, if not most, stations require a clean-shaven look.

"You look like my old friend George Pierrot, who used to host a travel show here in the good old days when we did such things."

Whenever that was. I'm not sure that I should be flattered. And my thigh muscles are starting to complain from bearing the weight of my semi-standing position. As Phillips returns to his video game, I sink back into my seat to return to my cube reconnaissance. Okay. There is a computer, phone, and a blotter calendar with "February" still displayed--from last year. Dust.

"Hey, you can have one of these day planners, if you want." Follicle is now off the phone, handing me a black naugahyde bound folder. The cover is messily embossed with "Turk's Bail Bonds" in gold letters, with a logo of a jail door swinging open and a bird flying free.

"I got a whole box of these after I did a story on the Filterboro 'Bailympics' a couple of months ago. I know Turk Marion from high school."

Follicle's jowls are pulled up in a self-pleased smile. It's tough to gauge how old he is, thanks to too many pounds and too few, er, follicles. I'm guessing he's about 50.

"Bailympics?" I ask, taking the bait.

"Yeah, some people thought of ways to keep ex-cons off the street, and their big idea was a track and field competition. Sort of like Midnight Basketball."

"How'd it turn out?" I've never heard of anything of its sort.

"It was kind of a mixed bag. Five or six dozen cons, er, athletes, showed up for the competition, which was pretty good. But three were arrested right then and there on outstanding warrants, so not everybody was happy. But it made for a pretty good story."

Follicle settles back into his cube with a look of satisfaction that's probably only matched when he carves the Thanksgiving turkey.

The newsroom settles into a mid-morning lull as reporters finish their research and head out the door. Follicle is one of them. Phillips is not. He's polishing the dress shoes he has removed with the socks on his feet.

"What story are you working on today?" I ask him.

"Story?" Phillips blinks. "Oh, they assigned me something about garbage collectors skipping some peoples' houses. But I'm not going to do that."

"Oh? Why not?"

"Well, that's a pretty crappy story, so I'm waiting for breaking news," he answers, self-assured. Breaking news will be my story tonight, George."

"GAMBLE!" It's a shock to hear my name--my correct name--in this foreign place. It reverberates from the assignment desk: Gretchen Calzone.

Huh?

"Gamble do you have a crappy hillbilly rental car parked in the SUV Stable, blocking Billy Fotch so he can't get out? We have an accident to cover! Move it to a legal spot RIGHT NOW!"

Oh yeah, that. The keys are in my pocket--at least I don't have to stop to look for them. Hurrying, I follow Fotch's path to the back of the newsroom, through a pair of thick metal doors. Sudden sunshine stops me for a moment. Okay, there's my car--uh--rental car. Strangely, I feel glad to have a duty to perform, even a sheepish one. Inside, the car feels claustrophobic. Move, buddy, move.

I back out, and Fotch zooms away. He's wearing headphones plugged in to something. It looks like he's singing.

Let's try this parking thing once more, shall we? Scanning the parking lot I finally locate an open spot. Whew, I'm "legal." Relief: mission accomplished.

This simple success puts an extra spring in my step as I jump out of the rental car and head back to the sturdy double doors. I pull the handle...but it won't budge. Pulling again, I shake the handle. Locked, of course. Oh, no. Where do I go, now? The front entrance of the building seems a long ways away, on the other side of some wildly-overgrown vegetation. No walkway. I wonder if Shelley Winters will admit me this time.

I'm still standing there, wondering what to do, when the door opens. A neat salt-and-pepper head pokes out.

"You need an electronic passkey to get back in."

He's older than most of those on the front lines of this newsroom. Maybe 50-55, not as tall as me. Nevertheless, he has put himself together with great care. Precise. Nice tie. Tailored, pressed, manicured; could pass for a banker. Pleasant face, trimmed with character lines. A small smile brightens a pair of wise eyes. Is this the evening anchor? One of The Suits who run the place? Sales?

"C'mon back in. I'm Carl Collingwood," he says mildly. "Managing Editor." Baritone straight out of old newsreels. Yet, pleasant. "I've been editing copy for our noon newscast so I haven't had a chance to meet you. There's a doorbell buzzer right there," pointing to a button almost hidden by the masonry pattern on the exterior wall. "You can use that next time."

"Wilson Gamble. Call me Wil." Shake hands. I note cufflinks and a firm grip. But not grasping, insecure, over-reaching. I have to think for a few moments to find the right description. Then I have it: what we have here is a Gentleman.

"Let's talk in my office, Wil. Over this way."

Collingwood sets a steady but deliberate pace. He's solidly familiar with every inch of the newsroom. He carefully skirts the assignment desk chaos and heads into the office next to Wilson. The fluorescents are off and the blinds are half opened, admitting some sunlight. But the office is more evenly and warmly lit by a matching pair of desk lamps and a torchiere in the corner. In here, the newsroom noise is muffled. It feels...warm, fuzzy. Wait--it's also clean and professional. It's as carefully manicured as the man who works here. Framed and matted photos of Collingwood with...People...line the walls. Capital P, People:

Westmoreland, Polanski, Pele, O'Neill. Sitting slowly, I'm distracted in an effort to identify them. Why is this man in Filterboro, of all places?

"When I worked my first newsroom, it didn't smell like burnt coffee," Collingwood jabs a thumb at the newsroom. "It smelled like burnt coffee--and cigarette smoke. Tobacco haze everywhere." He moves behind his desk. Neat. Everything in place, even a cherry wood humidor. "Gotta go outside for that, now. But I have this air filter machine here my daughter gave me for Christmas, so I can offer you a cigar."

Tobacco? Not sure. A cigar takes too much time to smoke.

"I will later. I'm still trying to get settled in."

Diamond cufflink sparkles, hand waves, baritone blares happily, "Well then take one with you, take one. Put it in your pocket. Save it for later. I get these from an online cigar company out of Tampa. They smoke pretty good."

I notice another photo: Collingwood...with an older Collingwood. Having grown up on a strict diet of CBS News, I knew of him and his colleagues. Sevareid, Safer, Hottelet, Wallace. Charles Collingwood.

"I always admired Murrow's Boys," I observe, and it's true.

"My uncle," he responds. "He inspired me--and introduced me to a lot of people. But when I had the opportunity to join the network, I found I was committed more to my family than my family's connections."

"When did you make that decision?"

"Age 25. I'd already served at the end of Viet Nam. Wife and a little girl at home. Had a decent job reporting in Flint. My home state. I liked television, unlike Uncle Charlie. Now I find myself guiding young reporters who all hope to move into sports, "Entertainment Tonight," or anchoring. Which one are you?"

"I am a reporter."

"Really? A reporter? That's rare."

I'm not a rookie. This is my chosen profession. "Everyone here questions this. Why is that? I'm a reporter," I repeat, a little irritated.

"No offense, Wil. It's just that there aren't that many career news reporters any more. I had to get out, move into management, for my family's sake. Usually there's no future in it, no money. Most guys realize this and don't pursue it. So, it's almost all young gals getting into reporting, to fulfill a career desire. Eventually, they try to become anchors or meet a guy on the outside who can afford them. And then they are gone."

"But quite a few go to the cable networks, though."

"Yeah, and become like Jessica Savitch. Strung out and then dead. It's a fun business, kid."

Depressing. Collingwood stops, lost in thought. Did he know Savitch before she broke down? Getting tired, I break in. "What will happen in this newsroom now that Allen Pratfall is gone?"

"Oh, Gretchen and I will run the morning meeting. I'll worry about content. Walter is supposed to control the producers and the look of the shows. The big decisions, the paperwork, and the complaints will come to me. We can run on auto-pilot for a while. Bring us some story ideas to the morning meeting, Wil, ones you can turn each day, and you'll be alright."

I've heard that before, but manage to refrain from rolling my eyes.

"I need to know the players. A little history around here to get me up to speed. Can you help me?"

"Sure. We'll have lunch, or maybe better yet, dinner. Later this week. I'll fill you in. I want to talk to you about our news philosophy here, too, so you know where we're coming from, what's expected of you."

"Wouldn't the News Director do this? Will you be the next News Director?"

"No thanks." Collingwood emphasizes "thanks" with a definitive downbeat. "I prefer guiding the content of the newscasts--not figuring out budgets, personnel problems, viewer complaints, and resolving conflicts between the reporters. And normally, the N.D. would set content policy. But around here, they last about as long as an online message on "Tweeter." Collingwood's voice drops to lower, fake conspiracy tone. "So, we'll quietly discuss a deep, hidden, agenda in television news: Journalism."

Liking the Big J, I smile. But a noise burst from the newsroom startles me. It's the scanner. Fire. Structure fire, probably a house. Probable entrapment--meaning, people are inside the burning home. We tune in to the newsroom, er, discussion.

"JACK! Jack, that's you," ordered Calzone. Drop that stupid garbage collection story. Get Fakir and go! It's on Incendiary Street...you know, uh, um, behind the Spendthrift Supermarket Center."

The cube cluster reporter jackets himself. "Call me with directions to get there!" He hurries to the cage, quickly out of sight. Calzone turns to a computer and starts looking through a map program to find the specific location.

Collingwood turns to me.

"That's you, too, Wil," he pronounces. "We'll fill out your paperwork later. Go see how we do these things around here."

Suddenly, I'm in a hurry, playing catch-up. Stepping out of Collingwood's office, I blink at the overly-bright newsroom. Involuntary stop. Which way do I go? I try the Cage. Phillips isn't there but videographer Fakir Johnson is, fiddling with some piece of electronics. Evidently a member of The Geek Patrol. In his 20's, I guess. Near permanent bitter little smile, an attempt to demonstrate worldliness. He's thin but not all that healthy-looking. If someone with brown skin could look pale, I suppose its him. He blinks at me.

"Hi, I offer. "I'm supposed to tag along with you and Jack Phillips."

"Oh." He doesn't seem enthused. "Guess I'll have to clear some of the stuff out of the back seat."

Phillips rushes in. Impatient. "Let's go, Fakir, we don't need your GPS stuff to find a major fire downtown. The smoke ought to be good enough to lead us there, and the loud, red fire engines should give us another clue. This'll be a liveshot for the Noon, also."

"Liveshot? For Noon?" groans Johnson. "I'll need time to set up the truck, get you a working monitor, find that little battery-operated fan to stay cool with..."

"Let's just go and deal with one thing at a time, okay?" Phillips pushes. "We gotta get some pictures, first. Then we'll deal with the liveshot. I guess you're coming, George, right?"

"LIVE EIGHT," Gretchen calls. Like a peanut vendor at a ballgame, she expertly tosses the vehicle keys. Inexpertly, Fakir ducks, missing them. Now he has to search for them--under a desk, near a rack of electronic equipment. Desperation mounts... but, there. Phillips finds them and *hands* them to Johnson. Its almost 11 am. Time to go!

"I've gotta grab my mobile emergency scanner," Johnson announces. Phillips rolls his eyes. "I'll meet you in the live truck."

They split up.

I follow Phillips, talking to himself. "Phone, IFB, cigarettes, notepad, powder. Guess I've got everything." Powder. Even the guys have to think about their makeup. Don't ever let them see you sweat, even at a house fire in the mid-day heat.

11:02 A.M. We burst out of the double doors. Transitioning from fluorescent light to sun light, I stop again to blink. It feels fresh and clean, clearing my mind and stripping away a layer of artifice. Hmm, where's my car parked now? Since it is irrelevant this time, the car somehow seems far away. Where is the SUV Stable? I glance around, spotting the line of logo'd vehicles, reminding Filterboro viewers that we represent the station "Where We're Right 99 Times Out of 100." It's a motor pool of company Crossover SUV 's and full-size vans converted into mobile studios that can send reports from the field to the studio. A license plate on one of the vans reads "WDMZ 8." That's us.

Climbing aboard "WDMZ 8," Phillips is talking at his phone. Not "on" his phone. "At" his phone.

"Marv, we're gonna go live and you are going to put us where we need to be." Pause. He sits on the passenger side, straps in. There's no back seat bolted down in here, just a work chair bungeed to a counter that holds editing equipment. So I squat behind Phillips and find something to hold on to. Johnson carefully places his equipment around me and closes the door. So at least there's padding around me. Then: ignition. We back out and are gone.

11:07. "Marv. Marv. Marv. We're coming anyways and wouldn't you rather that we had a good view of the fire to show your brave firefighters hard at work? I don't care about Hazmat," argues Phillips. Hazardous materials. That gets Fakir Johnson's attention.

"What's burning?" he worries out loud. To himself. "Is it dangerous? I'm not sure I brought enough oxygen masks for everyone."

Ignoring Johnson, Phillips continues on the phone. "That kind of activity is visual, my friend. But we have to be close enough to see some flames as well as the smoke." He listens again, puts his hand over the mouthpiece, looks at me, winks. "City P.I.O.--Stooge."

Back to his phone, he talks down to the P.I.O.: Public Information Officer. "Marv, don't be stupid. You have to get us access to the incident commander." Pause. "Marv. Marv. Marvelous Marv. Marvie. Oh, Marv, you remember that little video clip..." sudden silence. More Jack Phillips. "Now you wouldn't want the Fire Chief to hear the things you said on that videotape, would you?" Noise on other end. Smile. "No, you just owe me. Pay up."

The conversation ends quickly. A satisfied smile for Jack. "We are gonna have great visuals," announces Phillips. He lights a victory cigarette, in a belligerent violation of the policy of every television station in America.

"Hope we can still breathe afterward," Johnson counters, glancing at

Phillips' smoke. "Do I need an oxygen mask? Its stowed in the back somewhere."

"He was just exaggerating. Didn't want us at this one, for some reason."

Johnson consults a GPS map display on the dashboard. He turns right.

11:11. Phillips' phone rings again.

"Newschannel Whatever, Jack Phillips. Hey Gretchen. Uh huh, yeah. What's the best way to this address? Okay. Yeah. It's close to where I thought it was. Shouldn't be a problem for the Noon if we can get a clear microwave signal back to you. Yeah, I know. Anything new on this? No? Okay. See ya."

We lumber along in our big truck. The shock absorbers evidently have been removed and I'm on an uncomfortable perch. Can't wait to stretch my legs. Out the front window, the smoke plume grows bigger as we approach. We hit one way streets again, sending us in directions that sometimes take us at right angles to where we want to go. It seems to take forever to get to this place. Check my watch: 11:13. Just how far away is this house fire?

Phillips pokes the buttons on his phone again. "Hey, it's me. Uh huh. I might be late tonight. No. No! Of course I know it's not mid-day yet. But they'll want me to go live at 6. And I'll have some stuff to wrap up afterwards." Wait. "That's not always true, Trudy. I try to get home as soon as I can. Tonight I may be a few minutes late. It's no big deal." Harsh sounds squawk out from phone. "Okay, to you it's a big deal. No. Yes. It's a big deal. How 'bout we talk this over later?" Glance at Johnson. "Trudy? Trudy?"

Silence. Phillips glances around. Nope, we aren't paying any attention at all, not us. Stopped at a traffic light, I intently study a panhandler trying to wipe a greasy cloth across someone's windshield.

"Uh, okay Trudy, sorry baby, I'll miss you tonight," concludes Phillips. End signal.

Silence. What can one say? Johnson adjusts his GPS dashboard device.

Change the subject, Wil.

Randomly, I ask, "Do you worry about dead spots for the microwave signal around here?" In other words, are the live trucks usually able to send a signal to the station from most locations in this market?

Fiddling with his glasses, Johnson jumps on the chance to educate. "There's not that many. Of course you always have to look out for big clumps of trees or tall buildings downtown. But there are a couple of funny spots where the signal just doesn't seem to get back to the station. It's all in the folder in that tray behind you. I wrote the book on it," he says with pride.

I glance over. There's a plastic binder, stuffed with a ream of paper. Sorry I asked. Phillips stares out the window.

"First, you can't tune in a signal anywhere in West Hamlin, but that's really far from here," Johnson recites. "Second, you can't tune in a signal in front of Sawbones Memorial Hospital, but you can for some reason in the back, by the emergency entrance. Third you can't tune in a signal at the north end of the dog track parking lot. Fourth, you can't tune in a signal... ."

I tune out.

11:15. Mature, leafy trees line bumpy-looking sidewalks, hiding mostly-older homes. It's a neighborhood slowly decaying close to downtown.

11:16. Suddenly, confusion. Smoke. Traffic diverted. The heck with "one way" streets, we go where we need to go. Police everywhere. The sense of a Big Event in the air. People gather on sidewalks, standing and pointing. It's okay to play hooky from work when there's a house fire to watch.

Johnson eases down the street until he can't go any farther. Multiple emergency vehicles block our path. There's just enough space for our van on the side of the street. He parks, making sure to leave room for emergency vehicles to get by. Stubbing his cigarette on the floor of the van, Phillips jumps out. I follow, straightening out the cramp in my leg.

"Okay, where's the incident commander?" Phillips asks the first firefighter to walk by. No verbal response but we follow his pointed finger. Stepping over swollen hoses, we inch by the fire trucks, emphatically rumbling with life. Strong engine exhaust fumes fill our noses; I cut short my breath, for the moment. We keep our eyes on the smoke source as best as possible. Trees get in the way, then other houses as we get close. There's no police tape, so we go where we want. But we remember to stay out of the way. Suddenly, we're there.

Phillips looks for a yellow fire helmet: Lieutenant.

I take in the scene. The stricken home is clapboard, standard two story. Yellow paint, green shutters. Everything seems normal on the property: bicycle in driveway, bird in birdbath, yard hose curled next to a spigot. But the place is suffused with smoke. Tiny bits of singed paper blow around.

Yet, looking up, orange flames crackle at upstairs windows. There is an unnatural heat of a building burning that comes at you with startling suddenness. Heavy smoke flows out from holes axed into the roof by firefighters. Water flows in from several streams.

Teams of firefighters and paramedics everywhere. And, blackened by the smoke, one man--a civilian--sits on the lawn next door to the burning house. Head in his hands, he gets oxygen from two paramedics. More smoke follows firefighters as they exit the front door.

Johnson gets close, where the sidewalk meets the driveway. Setting up his tripod, he "sprays" the scene with his digital camera, recording a quick succession of scene-setting shots. He tilts his head inquisitively, like a puppy dog, while studying the viewfinder. Sighs. Nice light, pretty picture. Slight adjustment. Sighs. "Got actual flames in the window there," he says to himself.

Four boys hang around, juiced by the excitement. The appearance of a TV crew is a part of the show. "Hey! Camera guy!" one of them shouts. Egged on by friends. "Put us on! Put us on!"

Johnson keeps sighing and shooting.

"C'mon camera guy! We want to be on TV!" They start to get in the way.

"Hey fellas, why don't you..." I start. Johnson cuts in.

"Okay, guys. Stay right there." He points camera at them. Observes viewfinder. Wait a heartbeat. "Okay, got it!"

"Hey thanks, man! What time will we be on?"

"Can't say. But tell your parents to watch Newschannel 99 all day to find out. Okay?"

"Wow! Cool! We will." They go pester someone else. Johnson smiles. He hadn't touched the red "record" button on his camera.

11:24. Phillips is back. "See those two women over there?" he asks, quietly. They are watching the fire from across the street, seated on a neighbor's low brick wall. "Get them."

"Can't really miss 'em, can I?" remarks Johnson, swinging the camera around. "They must weigh about 300 pounds each." Phillips tells him to shut up. Head tilt, sigh. Johnson does press the record button this time.

"They live in the house that's burning down," explains Phillips. "Nobody is sure where their father is. He's kind of old. They were sleeping in late, and rushed out at the first warning of 'fire.' The Dad might be inside, or he could be out at the mall. Or at the track. Or at the welfare office. Whatever. The only person who really may know is that guy over there."

He points, I turn and take in a strung-out, extra-skinny guy. Young: 20 yet? Stringy hair, soul patch. Sleeveless t-shirt and black jeans. Barefoot, on the sidewalk near us. Agitated. Suddenly, he makes a move for the garage, attached to the home. Firefighters restrain him, soon joined by a police officer.

"I need to get in there!" he shouts. "My stuff! My stuff!"

Talking quietly to him, the officer shepherds him away. A passing firefighter remarks to Phillips, "That guy ran inside once already. We found his stash in the garage." He snickers. "I almost wish we didn't have our Air-Paks on. He can't go back. Now, neither can we."

"Who is he?"

"Oh, he lives there. Ask around. You might know his dad." The firefighter raises an eyebrow, knowingly.

Phillips ignites. "Whaddya mean? Isn't his dad the guy who's missing?"

"Gotta go, Jack." The firefighter trots back towards the house.

The fire burns on.

We move across the street towards the two women. 30-somethings. Their eyes are now on us. This is a critical moment in getting The Interview: aye or nay? Their faces should soon reveal their willingness to talk to the press.

Moving deliberately so as not to startle his prey, Phillips approaches the two women with a bittersweet smile. Johnson stops short, and that's okay with him. Shooters are people who observe others for a living.

"We're running out of time before the Noon liveshot. But he'll get them to talk to us," Johnson confidently advises me. "Everyone calls him 'Jackpot' Phillips. Some think he's the luckiest reporter you've ever seen. Pretty much everything falls into his lap. But to be fair, he works pretty hard. He's smart. And he's very convincing."

Shock of the moment helps. As their lives go up in smoke, many people talk before they think.

Phillips chats up the women. Then they go quiet, staring at the house. More chat. Sympathetic looks abound. Gotcha.

"Hey Fakir, would you mind coming over here?" called Phillips sweetly. We obey.

"Fakir, This is Mildred and Marigold." They smile, politely. Johnson ignores them, quickly setting up the camera.

"Can you believe they have lived in this house for more than 10 years, Fakir?" Phillips continues. Ignoring him, Johnson pulls out the cable for a lavaliere microphone. Lavs are those little mics that pin to your lapel or collar. He stops. There's one mic, but two people. Johnson defers instinctively to Phillips. "Who do you want to 'mic up'?"

"Where's your handheld wireless microphone?" Phillips demands in reply.

"In the shop," Johnson answers. Distressed. Clearly, he likes having a very complete range of equipment.

"Marigold," Phillips orders. Johnson clips the lav on the collar of her blouse, and expertly disguises the cable by running it under her collar and over her back.

"Static two shot," Phillips instructs Johnson. Meaning, both women on camera at once, it's not necessary to zoom in with the lens.

"Just look at me, ladies. Pretend the camera isn't even here," he soothes. "We'll just have a conversation, okay? Just like we were having a minute ago." They nod, bovine-like. Lead us to the slaughter, sir.

"Got speed," announces Johnson, indicating that the camera is recording.

"First, tell me your names again, so we have them on tape, just so I'm sure."

Slow look at one another.

"Mildred Ratskywatsky," offers the woman on the left. Instinctively raises palm of hand to base of skull, pats hair in place.

"Marigold Ratzkywatsky," follows the other sister.

"Uh, you'll need to spell that for me, so I get it right," tries Phillips, a little stunned.

The first complies. "M-i-l-d-r..."

"No, Mildred. Your last name."

She does.

"So, Mildred," started Phillips. "Are you worried your father is dead?"

Shock.

But the camera is rolling.

"Uh, no. Yes," tries Mildred. She sweats a lot. Slowly. "Well, we don't know. The firefighters have been saying the longer we go the less likely he's in there. Or was it the more likely?"

Marigold just nods.

"We just don't know if he's in there or not. He's our father and I don't know what I'd do without him," Mildred announces. Sob.

Phillips glances at Johnson: soundbite. Use it for the noon liveshot. Johnson checks the time code display to make a mental note of the place on the video to which he will cue up.

They need more material, though.

"Who is the young man who was trying so desperately to get inside the house?"

The women look at each other.

Mildred speaks. "That's Robby." Good enough for you, mister?

It isn't. "Who's Robby?"

"He's our step-brother. He lives in the garage. Daddy fixed it up for him. He locks the door so we don't see him much."

"Step-brother? Who is his real father?"

The pair stops again. How did he know to ask?

Finally, Marigold: "Mr. Rooker." Margaret adds, "Mr. Rodwell Rooker. I don't like him much."

Phillips face lights up like Christmas morning. "Roddy Rooker? The city councilman?"

No answer.

"Why did Robby want to get back in the garage?"

Marigold frankly states, "Must have been all that marijuana he's growing in the garage. I told him he'd get caught sooner or later."

Jackpot.

Phillips asks two or three more questions. Answered by Mildred.

11:35. Done with the women, who remain seated, faithfully waiting for their father. Fakir Johnson hustles over to the live truck, fires up the generator. He scrambles to lay out cables and hook up the camera for Phillips' report at noon.

Phillips dives into the back of the truck. Pulls out the chair and flips on a laptop editing computer. Inserting the SD card from Johnson's digital camera, Phillips swiftly pieces together the video: the stricken house, firefighters, the strung-out guy trying to get in. Then he edits Mildred's soundbite. Done.

Now to the front seat. I'm in the way, so I move back.

"George," he calls to me. There's no time for a ridiculous conversation so I acknowledge.

"Call in to the station and let Meredith know we are almost ready to feed, and that I have an anchor script for her."

"What's the number?"

"Uh, try 555-9369. That's the newsroom hotline."

As I call in, Phillips scribbles a shorthand outline for his script. Stops. Looking out at scene, he notes the firefighters getting it done, maybe too quickly for his purposes. Phillips grimaces. "Hope we still have smoke for the live hit."

Something else catches his attention. And instantly, he hammers the door lock with his fist.

A thin, intense face presses up to the passenger window. Sucking-a-lemon look. "Jack!" it shouts. He has to look up at Phillips, sitting on one of those big captain's chairs. Inside the air conditioned truck the voice sounds a long ways off. "Jaaaaack!"

"Hi Marv," Phillips answers serenely, looking down through the glass.

Marv is short. He stands on tiptoe just to look up. "Jack open the door. I need to talk to you."

Phillips opens the window one millimeter. "No time, Marv. Gotta liveshot to prepare for."

"Jack. Help me out, here."

Phillips fixes him with a stare. Then pulls on the handle and heads out the door. I follow. Fakir Johnson scrambles inside. Must feed the video Phillips edited back to the station before the liveshot, and time is running out.

Outside: "Marvin Finkbeiner, this is our new reporter. I've been calling him 'George' but that's not his real name. Doesn't he look like George Pierrot? What's your name again?"

"Wilson Gamble. Nice to meet you, Marv."

"Marv is the city's Public Information Officer," continues Phillips. "He will gladly get in the way when you try to get some work done. Like right now."

Finkbeiner begins. Breathy. Less than commanding, but still demanding. "Jack, I got you a good parking spot. I got the incident commander for you. I got you as close as possible for your liveshot. Show the firefighters keeping it contained. And you need to move this truck as soon as you're done."

"It'll still be awhile, Marv. Fakir will have to break down the equipment from the liveshot and I still have some very interesting things to follow up on with this fire."

Marv's pale face gets whiter. "What do you mean?" Low voice.

"Nothing bad about the fire department," soothes Phillips. "Don't sweat it. Just some extra details that could make this fire story more newsworthy."

"Anything I can help you with?" A weak attempt to learn what Phillips knows.

"Sure. Where's the kid the police had to pull away from the home?"

"Don't know who you mean. Um, look at the time. Gotta go!" Finkbeiner quickly departs.

"Oh yes, look. At. The. Time," answers Phillips in staccato, under his breath. To me, "At least we got rid of him."

11:57. Camera ready. Phillips loops his IFB (Interrupted FeedBack) earpiece into place. Johnson attaches the lav to his necktie—he's not wearing a jacket out here. "Wish I had the handheld wireless," mutters Phillips, perhaps just to rile Johnson.

No answer. Johnson moves behind camera. Sighs. "Wish the sun wasn't so bright." Glare creates shadows on parts of Phillips' face. "I can get you the reflector to even put that light on you," he suggests.

"Don't worry. I'll get a cloud to come in and cover the sun when we go on."

"If that happens I'll have to white balance again," warns Johnson. White balance corrects the colors the camera sees.

Phillips reviews his script, rehearses once. Stops. Someone is talking to him from the control room over his IFB.

"What's that? Mildred Ratzkywatsky?" he repeats. "Hold on, let me check that." Phillips checks his notes for the spelling. Got it. "M-i-l-d-r... . Oh. Sure. R-a-t-z-k-y-w-a-t-s-k-y. You're welcome, Meredith. Ready for an audio check? Okay, testing, testing, audio check, 1-2-3. Can you hear me."

Affirmative. More IFB chatter.

Phillips glances back at the house. The insides are probably gutted pretty bad, but the outside retains the form that has graced this street with for the last 50 years.

"Still looks good. A lot of smoke. We've got a great visual here." To Johnson: "Which shoulder?"

"The fire is over your right shoulder," Johnson replies. He connects a cable from the truck to a television monitor, which now shows a feed of the Newschannel 99 programming. It sits at the foot of the tripod so Phillips can see what's happening.

"Good. You might need to zoom in on it after the soundbite."

Clock ticks. Phillips focuses. House fire, smoke, firefighters, onlookers suddenly feel a mile away. Eerie quiet. Then, a massive and sustained cloud drifts in to block the sun. The diffused light is now perfectly even, so there will be no odd shadows on Jackpot Phillips.

"Told you," Phillips says, holding up his notepad in front of his face so Johnson can "white balance" the camera a final time.

Johnson turns on the toplight and resets the camera. There's a nice glow on Phillips. "Ah, much better. Stand by!"

I'm observing from the sidelines. Phillips and the monitor are both silent now as they await their 15 seconds of fame. On the monitor I can just see the anchor reading silently, smiling. Phillips looks up from notes, nods head. On screen, he appears in one graphic "box," the smiling anchor is in the other. Phillips listens, listens...and then he's On.

"Amy, just a short time ago intense heat drove out firefighters from this home on Incendiary Street." Phillips turns to the fire, and points, perhaps unnecessarily. "Smoke is still billowing out of the top story windows, making it difficult to see the home at times. Firefighters continue to pour water on the house, but it appears to be a losing battle. Now they are working to save the neighboring houses. As you can see in this video shot just minutes ago, the vinyl siding on one of those houses has melted in several places." Phillips consults his notes while Johnson's edited video rolls from the control room.

"A family of five lived in the burning house. We know that four made it out safely, but we are still not certain of the fate of 54 year old Ignatz Ratzkywatsky. His daughters tell us they aren't sure if he is still trapped in the house because they were awakened by the smoke alarm and rushed out right away."

Phillips pauses for the soundbite to play. His mic is off, for the moment.

"Fakir!" He whispers harshly while the tape rolls. He points. "Push in on that police car that's parked over there."

Johnson must wonder why he's not going to get a closeup of the fire instead. But there's no time to question Phillips, so he swiftly obeys. Swiveling on the tripod, he catches the squad car.

We are back on the air.

"You can't see him very clearly, but the man in the back of that police car is Robby Rooker, son of Filterboro City Councilman Roddy Rooker. Robby is the stepson of the missing man, Ignatz Ratzkywatsky, and lived in the garage that is attached to the home that's on fire." Johnson pulls out, pans over to Phillips. "Sources tell me he may be in a lot of trouble over a stash of marijuana that was discovered in his garage apartment while firefighters were attempting to put out the blaze." Smile. "But he hasn't been charged yet. More on this tonight at Six. Reporting live from the east side, Jack Phillips, Newschannel 99, where 'We're Right 99 Times Out of 100.'"

Phillips remains stock-still, smugly smiling, until he gets an "all clear" from the producer through his IFB. 90 seconds after he has started, he is done.

The cloud departs. Its suddenly sunny again.

"It's a lead story," observes Johnson, looking up from his viewfinder. Meaning, for 6. The Important Newscast.

"Yup," is Phillips only reply.

His phone rings. No more smiling; we are back to work.

Things start to happen fast at the conclusion of Phillips' report. Marvin Finkbeiner calls: Councilman Rooker has no comment. No one knows when Robby Rooker will be booked by the authorities. Quietly, Phillips calls a contact with the clerk of the court's office. Robby Rooker will see the judge at 2 pm.

Soon after the newscast ends, firefighters finish off the blaze. It turns out that there are no casualties: While getting a $6 haircut at a neighborhood barber shop, Ignatz Ratzkywatsky saw his home burning on TV. He has no comment about his step-son.

Some neighbors do have a comment, though. One calls Robby a "dopehead" who lights up while sitting in a lawn chair in the driveway. "The kid offered some of his pot to my daughter. I went over and told Iggy it better not happen again. A few minutes later, I see him chasing Robby around the backyard with a tire iron, screaming at him to get straight. Everyone knows Robby uses drugs. That councilman's son is a maroon," he finishes dismissively.

"Maroon?" Isn't that a Bugs Bunny quote, as in 'What a maroon!'? Utterly certain to make air.

Phillips moves on to interview the incident commander. Without calling it an illegal narcotic, he describes the stash firefighters saw inside the garage.

Next, we race to the Reproach County Courthouse. Rooker has to make a First Appearance as a legal formality. Thanks to our noon report, everybody knows this. In fact, Channel 11 and Channel 7 are already there. So is the *Daily Repellent* and the NPR radio affiliate, WTDS. We park, grab the camera ("I wish we had that wireless mic," Phillips complains again), and rush into the building. It feels dark here, cool. Marble everywhere. Our hurrying comes to a halt for a security check at the entrance. Then, we wade through a crowd of misdemeanor crooks waiting for judgment, on into an elevator. Up we go. Its awkwardly quiet inside. Johnson shifts the weight of his camera. Phillips clears his throat. I stare at the escalating numbers on the panel over the elevator doors: 5, 6, 7.

Finally, the doors open and we hurry to magistrate's court. Specifically, Magistrate T.T. Book. It's a sterile white room, divided by a tall, judicious counter that blocks us from an inner hallway that leads to chambers in back. Reporters, videographers, microphones, and notepads are everywhere. The floor is elevated behind the counter so the magistrate can look down. No Robby Rooker yet. A clerk looks busy behind the counter, but is enjoying the change in her routine. No phones allowed here, what's Jack to do? He motions to the other TV reporters. "Hey, Sam. Katie. This is our new reporter. I've been calling him 'George' but he doesn't seem to like that because it's not his name."

"Wilson Gamble," I introduce myself. Shake hands.

"You do kind of look like George Pierrot," Channel 7's Sam observes.

Otherwise, the TV reporters show little interest in me. The newspaper and NPR types have already paired off in a corner, observing us mournfully.

Now that the gang's all here, the room fills with an awkward, expectant quiet. You can sense it sometimes if you listen very carefully: news is about to happen.

But it doesn't.

We wait. And wait. Channel 7/Sam, asks, "Are they gonna arraign him soon, Margie?"

The clerk answers in a monotone, "Anytime within the hour."

"And it'll be Magistrate Book, right?"

"Yes, it will."

More waiting.

Phillips grows quiet now. Thoughtful. Why isn't this happening? Well, Rooker is a City Councilman's son, that's why. We need a little help.

"I'm gonna go make a call and have a smoke," Phillips says. He goes.

Bored now, Channel 7 and Channel 11 inspect the new kid.

"Where'd you come from?" inquires Katie absently, holding her handheld wireless microphone with a modern-font "11" emblazoned in red on the mic flag.

"The mountains. DMA 57. And yes, it's cold in the winter."

"You like it here?" asks 7/Sam.

"Can't say. I'm still figuring things out."

"What about Allen Pratfall?" tries 11/Katie, her eyes glowing just a little. Let's cut to the chase: TV reporters are by nature, insatiable gossips. Inquiring minds want to know.

"Wish I knew. He hired me last month, and today I finally show up and find out he's been arrested. Guess I'm lucky to still have a job."

11/Katie smirks. "Ivory Eriss must like the look of you."

"What does that mean?"

Now 7/Sam smirks. "Oh, you'll find out." He turns back to the counter.

"When's this gonna happen, Margie?" he asks tiredly.

"I can't say, Sammy. Sometime this hour." She goes diligently back to her paperwork. Whatever that may be.

Phillips strides in. Big rush. He looks annoyed. "We gotta go," he tells Johnson.

"What? Go?" Johnson wonders. Everyone else looks, hard.

"They need our live truck back right now and we still have it. Stupid jerks. We have no choice. Let's go." He's halfway out the door. I can see the reporters calculating: What's going on? Doesn't Phillips want video of the arraignment? But they are suspicious. This doesn't seem right.

"Waitaminute, Jack," tries Johnson, who is not naturally suspicious. "You drive the live truck back, then come get me. Or have Wil here drive it back."

"My license is suspended and Gamble isn't cleared yet. Let's go, Fakir, and we'll get back in time for the arraignment."

He's out the door. Expecting us to follow.

"Unbelievable," mutters Johnson. Other videographers shake their heads. Another stupid management decision is gonna hurt the news content again.

Cursing and spitting, Johnson grabs his gear. I follow. Phillips is already at the bank of elevators.

Johnson starts. "This is just about the stupidest thing..."

"Shut up," Phillips answers, quietly but firmly. "I needed a good excuse to get you out of there. Shh, wait," he pauses, conspiratorially. 7/Sam wanders around the corner, just to look at us. Busted, almost.

"And its asinine decisions like that which are just killing us!" Phillips rants to no one. Loud enough for 7/Sam. "I pull off this huge exclusive and they're worried about repairing the live truck! What a bunch of..." muffled expletives! as he enters the elevator. Johnson and I dash in behind him, heading down.

"Okay, here's what's going on," explains Phillips, quietly. "I talked with Collingwood. He's tight with someone in Magistrate Book's office. Rooker has been already booked in, uh, Book's private office in the back, so we couldn't see it. But the police still have to walk him from the Courthouse to the police garage. They didn't want anyone to know. Too bad, it'll look just like a perp walk."

Perp walk. Perpetrator. Images of people with coats pulled over their heads. Handcuffs. Police escort. They always look guilty, which is why police often tip off reporters about them. Not this time, though. But it's a public street between the courthouse and garage... .

"Which door will they come out?" asks Johnson.

Phillips thinks for a moment. "Not sure. Let's cross the street and wait on the side of the police garage. They have to walk over there. We can see almost all the doors from there, and then go get 'em no matter where they come out."

We exit the building, burdened by our equipment as well as the hope that the other reporters won't figure things out. Sudden sunshine blinds me again as we walk out the doors.

Jaywalking across a busy five lane city street, Phillips points to a tree shading the opposite sidewalk.

"Set up there," he advises. "They won't see us quite as quickly when they come out. And maybe the tree will screen us if any of the other reporters look out one of those upstairs windows."

Johnson complies. Tripod extended, camera mounted, he lines up the courthouse in his viewfinder. "I'll get a nice steady shot from here, and then go on the shoulder when they get close," he explains.

The Gothic era Courthouse is a dark hulk, but is enlivened by activity. People come and go. And come and go. Time passes and the deadline pressure grows.

"I hope Collingwood was right," Johnson says. If Rooker is actually booked like everyone else, we will be the only station with no video.

Feeling the pressure, Phillips fidgets, then looks into a seventh-floor window. A man looks back. The tree screen didn't work.

"Uh oh. Sam from Channel 7 sees us. He'll know something's up."

I do some calculations. "He needs a couple of minutes to make some calls and a couple more to get his videographer together, and two or three more minutes to actually get down here."

"We gotta hope these guys come out soon, or it'll be a real scrum," wishes Johnson.

Nervous waiting. Maybe we are wrong. Should we be here or in the magistrate's court? At least if we are inside, we will rise or fall with all the other reporters.

Looking through his viewfinder, Johnson breaks the tension.

"I see four bogies in formation at twelve o'clock." Three abreast, one with a hand on another's arm. The fourth man follows close behind. Everyone is dressed in plain clothes. But two are plainclothesmen. Another wears a suit that is most definitely not off the rack--and a ponytail pulled back tight: lawyer.

"Get 'em," Phillips orders, unnecessarily. Johnson is already recording.

The group of men waits for a break in the traffic. Halfway across, they spot us. In response, Johnson immediately dismounts the camera from the tripod and shoulders it up. He and Phillips move forward to meet Robby Rooker.

It's the strung-out guy from the fire, swaggering now. Not the police detectives. Their physical bulk towering over Rooker, they maintain an attitude of professional grimness. They hadn't expected any cameras and they don't plan to stop for a press conference. But they won't get in the way, either. Not with this little weasel. They march on. The attorney, acting important on his phone, catches on just a little too late.

Phillips falls in step with Rooker. Walking backwards, Johnson records the little group. Tied together by a mic cable, it's a crude waltz. Walking a step ahead, I guide Johnson with a hand on his back.

"Robby, why did you have such a large stash of pot in your garage?" Standard. Always presume guilt on perp walks.

"Pot?" he sneers. "The firemen was just mad because they said I was gettin' in the way. I just wanted to find my step-daddy."

Naturally, Phillips isn't buying. "So that's why you're handcuffed?"

The attorney, with the air of the Master regarding Oliver Twist's request for more gruel, tries to run interference. But he's not physically substantial, and Phillips brushes past him. Rooker, with an attitude of a smug insider, has the gall to answer the question.

"Listen, man. I haven't done nothin'. I'm just here for protection from those firemen. They manhandled me!"

Out of the corner of my eye I see figures rushing out of the Courthouse, trying to catch up. Too late.

"Did you offer marijuana to all the neighbor kids, or just a few of them?" Phillips persists.

"Bite me," answers Rooker. No more polite answers from him. And the attorney finally manages to interpose himself between the camera and his client.

Just for sport, Phillips keeps going. Trying to bait Rooker. Johnson looks for ways to get a clear shot of Phillips' victim, the perp.

"Are you worried about going to jail and meeting all those people there who don't like your father very much?" No response. "Did one of your sunlamps fall over on some dried hemp and start the fire?" Keep walking. "What did your Dad say to you? Why did you get preferential treatment when you were booked?" Silence.

The detectives turn Rooker into the parking garage. It's off limits to us, so we're done. Nevertheless, it's another Jackpot.

"I love this story," says Phillips.

Panting, 11/Katie catches up first. But her photog, on the run, records no useable video. They are simply out of luck. 7/Sam had stopped across the street and ordered his shooter to tape a brief wideshot of the perp walk. But we were in it. The newspaper and radio people don't need the visuals but would have loved to be over here where the "news" is. Or was. All the other reporters get nothing more out of this small skirmish. They have been beaten on this one, for the second time in one day.

"Sorry boys," smiles Jackpot Phillips. "Guess we'll get that broken down ol' live truck back to the station now."

Happy Jack hums and smokes while strolling back to Live 8. On the drive to the station, he pulls out the trusty phone again. Pressing the numbers, he applies the phone to his ear and waits. And waits. It must be ringing. No answer. No voicemail? I wonder, silently. Phillips shrugs at nobody, gives up. "Trudy has Caller I.D," he explains out loud to nobody. Ah, the woman who hung up on Jack earlier. A small rift in his otherwise endlessly-happy day. He burns another cigarette.

The sun is falling but the light feels sharper on our return to the station. Johnson and Phillips drop me off before heading back out to fire scene for a another liveshot, this time at 6pm. I plan to finish the day at the station.

On the drive back, I wonder about Ivory Eriss. Phillips isn't the guy to ask--not the guy who keeps calling me "George" for sport. I admire his reporting savvy. But we're not going to be friends.

Back at the station, I'm locked out of the building again. This time, however, I know where the buzzer is, and press it. Wearing a wondering look, a very young production assistant or intern or somebody's visiting daughter opens the door. High school age?

"It's okay. I'm Wil, a new reporter," I explain.

"Hi, I'm Aimee." The girl vacantly flutters her eyes as I pass through.

The daily chaos is growing in the newsroom. Deadline equals pressure. The 6pm newscast is all-important, but first they have to plan the 5 and 5:30 as well as the 6. Game faces everywhere. Laughter takes on a tense tone. Gretchen Calzone hollers. The scanners scan. Cursing increases. Small arguments flare. Unnoticed, some leftover coffee burns down thick in the pot.

"FOTCH!" Calzone yells. Into a telephone this time. "Where are you?"

Pause.

She physically collapses in disbelief. Stops yelling. Small voice.

"Yes. No. Yes. It was nice of you to stop to try to change a tire for the helpless lady broken down along the freeway." Her voice picks up energy. "But no, you probably should not have driven her all the way home and then accepted a plate of fudge brownies! Not if you DIDN'T GET THE STORY WE WERE COUNTING ON, YOU NUMNUT!"

The entire newsroom stops flat for a moment. Then, in a moment, bedlam. Eyes roll knowingly. General bitter hilarity.

"You got 'Fotched,' Gretchen!" exclaims Sherman Follicle in a sing-song voice on his way to an edit bay.

I go back to Howard Beale's old cube and sit. I don't know Fotch, or the dynamics here, but it isn't tough terrain to figure out. Faced with nothing to do, I turn on the computer, realizing its a futile activity. I have no login ID, so I don't exist.

Of all people, Walter Wilson lurches by to save me. "C'mon over to Carl's office because we're having our afternoon editorial meeting and you can sit in on it and have some coffee and maybe a Danish and get a feel for what's gonna happen during our evening newscasts and then plan for tonight at 11 even if nobody watches it but I watched last Tuesday night and that'll help you understand how we do things editorial-wise and what we look for in our stories here... ."

I follow the sound of Wilson's relentless monologue. We pass a row of edit bays, where the video recorded by each shooter is edited into coherency. The bays are starting to fill with activity. Inside each one, shooters swear as their intentions fail to be understood by the computer editing equipment. Reporters sometimes stop by to see how things are turning out. Often, they quickly leave under the pretense of having to do something else for the newscast.

Quietly, I slide into Collingwood's office. All the chairs are filled, everyone studying a packet of papers stapled at the top left corner. With no pace left to sit, I lean against a door jam.

"Here's a copy of our afternoon 'News Outlook'," Collingwood advises, handing me one of the packets. Okay. The Outlook is a summary of various items that could make the newscast, prepared by the Assignment Desk. It has different names at different stations, but I'll accept the presiding terminology here.

My last station ran newscasts at 5:30 pm, 6, and 7--after the network newscast. The Newschannel 99 programs are one hour-long newscast at 5 and then the half hour "flagship" newscast at 6.

"Guys, this is Wilson Gamble, our newest dayside reporter," offers Collingwood to the group. "Wil, you know Gretchen and Walter, and this is the Evening Producer, Tracy Scott. That's the nightside producer, Marshall Hurd. Jefferson Adams and Lavinia Fern are the main anchors." He identifies three or four other people as well.

"Hi's" all around.

My observations start with the producers. Tracy Scott seems, um, focused. Professional suit, hair marcelled. Could pass for on air talent. Hurd looks quite the opposite. T-shirt, sandals, opinions. Then to the anchors. Adams lives in a Savile Row suit, pointy shoulders. He started out a big man and added lots of extra poundage along the way. Now he sits and walks leaning back, like he's perpetually sucking in his gut. That gut is fashionably adorned with a tailored and monogramed dress shirt, silk tie. Smells of cheap cologne and expensive cognac. An affected attitude of disinterested omniscience. On the other hand, Fern feels intense. All of her: suit, expression, hair. Intense. Her sharp facial features seem locked into a permanently unsmiling attitude. I bet she grinds her teeth at night.

"On the speakerphone is Brian Fantana from our Soyfield bureau," Collingwood explains, pointing to his telephone. "Soyfield picks up a nice mix of agriculture stories and drug crimes in the eastern part of our market."

"Werk rol, ellyod firl," greets the static-distorted voice.

"Uh, thanks, great, I guess," I answer, hopefully.

Collingwood is ready to start. "We'll have to get someone in engineering to look at that speakerphone." He consults the Outlook. "Okay, first in both newscasts we've got Phillips live at the fire, or what's left of it. You've already heard that he nailed Rooker's son. We also have the manhunt for that shooter, and video of the Tree Sloths' baseball stadium construction. Soyfield, what do you have on the school bully story?"

Phone speaker crackles. "Huzz gudd fjrl..."

Collingwood curses, hangs up and dials again. During the short interval, some small movement outside the building catches my attention. I glance through the cracks in the venetian blinds and catch bits and pieces of Warden The Doorman wiping down the window. But by his persistence I wonder: is he watching us?

In Soyfield, Fontana picks up.

"Try again, Brian," Collingwood speaks at the speakerphone.

"The bully story is good," Fontana tries. Magic. Much clearer this time. "Some parents in Washerville have called a PTO meeting for tonight to try to force the principal to do something about the kid who's going around threatening all his 5th grade classmates."

"Washerville?" I mouth to Calzone, next to me.

"A little east of Soyfield," she whispers. "On the Washer River." It sounds like a long ways away.

Fantana's voice certainly sounds a long ways away. "Bully's parents say they'll be at the PTO meeting, starts at 7:30. Some of the other parents will be there, too. It could get ugly tonight, so we should send somebody to cover it. For the 5, though, we've got a couple of ticked off and worried parents on video. The principal isn't making any statements yet."

Back here, in Collingwood's office, Scott breaks in. "This should be pretty high in the 6. The stadium construction is taking months and months, and there's nothing really new there."

Adams answers. "But I heard that Wallflower got some footage of an I-beam that got loose from a crane and knocked over a port-a-john. Its great video!"

The trump card: great video. Everyone nods sagely.

"Okay," sighs Collingwood. "The bully, then the stadium construction thing, and then the feature on the new lottery jackpot, and a v-o on the water main break in Khalishes." He proceeds through succeeding "blocks" of news divided by commercial breaks. A few questions from Lavinia Fern, some gutter humor from Jefferson Adams. We shape the 5 and 6 pm newscasts, and plan for the late one, over the course of 20 minutes or so.

Collingwood prefers a team approach in preparing a newscast. Likes a lot of input from a lot of people. One person, however, does not gain admittance to this meeting.

"We gonna cover the Cloverbell Farms ice cream eating contest?" asks an Italian suit standing in the doorway. Perma-smile installed on a red-cheeked, clean-shaven face. VO5 hair. Thin leather briefcase. "Free ice cream!" he offers, teasingly. Seems like a happy-go-lucky guy. Except, I recognize Satan. In fact, I think I can almost see a long, pointed tail swishing happily behind the tailored suit.

"Get out of the newsroom, Hornswoggle," growls Collingwood.

Retreat. Swishing tail between his legs.

"Sales department," Collingwood explains to me. No need. They'd love to squeeze their clients into newscasts everywhere. Like Cloverbell Farms.

Finally, Marshall Hurd asks, "Will the fire still be going tonight for our 11pm newscast? 'Cause I'd like a liveshot there, too and you guys always leave out the 11."

"That's true!" Walter Wilson adds. "Troo-oo" in two singsong syllables. Note of parental patronizing.

Collingwood just blinks. Adams laughs. Calzone leaves.

"Marshall, the fire is already out."

"But you said Jack Phillips was going live from the fire for the 5 and 6!" Hurd insists. Childlike hurt.

Fern leaves. Adams leaves. Fantana hangs up.

"From the fire location. Location. Its shorthand conversation. Jack is fronting the lead story he developed with breaking news information that he gathered and from the place where it started." Collingwood responds patiently. "Phillips won't be reporting at 11 tonight."

Hurd gets it, sort of. "What will we have for tonight, then?"

"Let's see." Collingwood thumbs through the packet. "Liz?" He turns to a nearly-middle aged woman in a blouse and pants who has remained behind. "You can follow the Rooker story. Get city leaders' reaction. I'm sure the Mayor and maybe some voters would have something to say."

"Alright, Carl. I have a couple of ideas," she responds.

Collingwood turns to me. "Wil, say hello to Liz Pendens, nightside. Then, say goodbye to Liz Pendens, nightside. She's headed to P.R."

Out of the business, straight to the dark side: public relations. The flip side of journalism, but The Land of Silk and Money.

"Oh? Where at?" I ask. Who knows if I will be calling on her sometime.

She smiles. "National Tobacco."

Okay, I'm immediately certain I will be calling on her sometime. In a place called Filterboro, I don't have to imagine that tobacco manufacturing is pretty big.

Hurd interrupts the conversation. "Carl, can I still get a liveshot out of that?"

"We'll see." Collingwood's tone suggests he drop the issue.

Following everyone else, Hurd and Wilson leave. Undertone of arm-in-arm whiny sympathy.

Collingwood sits quietly behind his desk. Taking a moment for himself, he lightly pats his chest, as if something is missing. Oh, yeah. His pocket was once full of cigarettes. "Sometimes I really wish I hadn't stopped smoking. Maybe Liz can send over a quiet supply," he jokes drily.

"You always have your cigars," I suggest. An image of the two beers left in my motel mini-fridge suddenly pops in my head. Collingwood breaks up the image.

"Yeah. It's not the same."

He picks out a cigar. Observes it, then the sliver of bright newsroom that can be seen out his door from my vantage point. "At least today we didn't have any epic battles over the kicker." The "kicker" is the brief, light-hearted feature at the end of most newscasts. "You wouldn't believe the arguments that rage, and the grudges kept, over the dumbest little things." I would believe. Collingwood has an example handy. "Just last week Lavinia and Gretchen were screaming obscenities at each other over the video of a candle-dipping contest. The fight was infinitely more interesting than the story itself, which was just like watching paint dry."

"Or watching candle wax dry," I offer...drily.

Rolling the cigar with his fingers, Collingwood lights up. He searches for his Christmas present--the air filter ashtray--and punches the on button. Soft buzzing noise. Puff, puff. The smoke is coaxed into the machine. "Okay. I guess we need to have you fill out the usual paperwork. You will have to choose which health insurance plan you want. We have a guy in Personnel who could answer your questions. His office is over in Administration, you know, the place that looks like a wing in a medieval castle. But you probably want to stay away from there as much as possible. He lost most of his staff recently in cutbacks, so he probably won't return your phone calls. I'll do my best with your questions but don't take anything I say as Gospel."

"That's okay," I reply, wondering how long I will really be here." But I need an extra day off to get back to the Mountains to finish making my move here. I flew in and rented a car over the weekend, so I have to get back there to bring my stuff down here."

"When do you want to go?"

"First I'd prefer to find a place to live. But either way, by this weekend."

"Where are you staying now?" Collingwood wonders.

"The Placid Place Motel, near the downtown freeway."

Collingwood lets slip the smallest head-nod and smirk. What kind of memory or association does he have with that place? I will never know.

He stamps out the reverie with a flick of his cigar ash. "If nothing else works out, I'll try to help you find something. Walter is always talking about a friend of his who runs a kind of old-school boarding house, if you don't mind that kind of thing."

I do mind. Much prefer an apartment. My own place. By myself.

"We'll get Rose to put together your paperwork for when you come in tomorrow," he continues. "For now, you might as well get a feel for the newsroom heading into the 5. Now get outta here. I've gotta copy-edit Hubbell's story so I don't think it'll be safe to be around me for the next ten minutes."

Time to head back to the cube cluster and my new desk. I find a station I.T. guy there, making things work.

Standing aside, I sense a growing wall of noise all around the newsroom. Videographers, production assistants, engineers, assistant producers all come and go. Videotapes are played. Phones ring. Scanners squawk. Tyler Hubbell serenely stares into mirror the size of a note board, arranging her hair. Sherman Follicle hammers on his keyboard. His round face is red and sweating. He's nearly panting. Gretchen Calzone furiously bangs on her computer, searching for something. "There's got to be another convenience store near that exit!" she hollers at no one.

Fern and Adams sit quietly on one end of the room in more spacious cubicles with higher partitions. Hey, they're anchors. Both appear to be checking scripts on their computers. But a second look shows they are both quietly lost in what appears to be separate telephone conversations. Jeneatte Nettles reviews a videotape in an edit bay. Along Producer's Row, Scott displays the attention span of a fruitfly. First, she types on a keyboard. Next, flips through the photocopied pages of a court ruling while crushing her ear with a phone. Then, she has ten seconds for each of three people waiting to see her. Suddenly switching gears, she stares at a postcard of a tropical beach before glancing at a cable news channel on one of the wall monitors. All the while ignoring Walter Wilson blathering at her about milkshakes. Glad I'm not her.

The computer is now functional. Its mine. First, I have to create a password. For some reason, perhaps still thinking of my encounter with Ivory Eriss, I'm thinking of art. Time to retrieve the little I know once more. Edvard Munch? Uh, no, too cute. How about George Bellows? That's real enough for me. I try "cliffdweller." Nope. The login ID must have at least one digit. Okay, "cliffdweller#1." Nope. Can't have a symbol. Well, okay then. Frustrated, I drop the symbolism, try, "wilson1." Too easy; I'm in. The computer shows me the standard generic blue wallpaper, a handful of PC icons. Checking out my "Facespace" social networking webpage will have to wait. Aside from the web browser, there are two other programs worth opening: the email program and "ENPS," a news software program designed by the Associated Press. Along with "iNews" and one or two other newsroom programs out there, ENPS is familiar territory to me. It displays wire copy, newscast rundowns, scripts, and News Outlooks for the next few days. Since its always the flagship newscast--the one that matters most to advertisers and Nielsen--I check out the 6pm newscast rundown first. A spreadsheet of story titles appears in chronological order, top to bottom. Clicking on one story, I can see the script for it. Back in the rundown, most of the titles are in red. That means their authors are not yet finished writing, or the scripts are not yet approved by a copy-editor. A few appear in green, meaning they are approved, ready for shooters to edit the video. Some stories are in "yellow" limbo: someone had better start typing.

Speaking of "limbo," Fotch wanders back in to the newsroom, oblivious. He missed the car wreck/fire by two hours. His timing doesn't improve: Collingwood instantly spies him. The Managing Editor stands in the door of his office, arms folded, practically tapping his foot. "Billy, I just finished approving Tyler's story. You go edit it, and don't miss deadline...or I'll stab you."

No answer. What can he say? Spiky hair a little crestfallen, Fotch takes the paper copy of the script and heads over to Hubbell. She doesn't appear all that willing to be associated with an also-ran, but together they find an edit bay.

The clock ticks. With just 30 minutes to air an unusual silence prevails. Call it: The Last Big Push. Affecting an "I've done everything I could do" attitude, Calzone changes the pencils in her hair, wraps up a leftover Pop Tart and replaces it in a box in her desk. She may need it tomorrow. Wilson hovers around the edit bays, checking video, muttering endless stream-of-consciousness observations to no one but himself. Collingwood quietly chats with Marshall Hurd about the 11pm newscast. Reporters disappear, off to liveshots or edit bays or the green room to comb their hair. Anchors observe scripts, ask questions of Scott, make small changes. The loudest sounds come from an ancient industrial-sized printer that simultaneously produces scripts in several different colors: pink and blue for the anchors, and other colors for the producer and director. Production folk shuffle the scripts together like poker aces.

With ten minutes to air, it's time to mobilize like Europe after Sarajevo. Powdered and hair-sprayed, Fern and Adams move stately towards the studio. Camera and audio technicians, technical operators, and the show director head into the Control Room. Sweating, Follicle rushes into the studio for an "on set" report.

Nobody seems interested in watching the early newscast. Its "just" the "5." It's a money-maker, added on to the existing newscasts and using much of the same staff and other resources as the "6." Hosted by a second-string anchor, it offers light features, live interviews, more weather reports. Butting heads with syndicated shows on other channels, this show holds its own, but no more. But since it literally costs nothing extra to produce, it is a Bottom Line winner.

Collingwood stops by my cube. Thinking about Robby Rooker, I ask. "How did you know the kid wouldn't be arraigned in Magistrate Court?"

"Well, since he has such a prominent father, you start to get suspicious right away. Then I called a clerk in Book's office. He wouldn't answer, but saw my phone number on his telephone caller ID display. He took a lunch break, and called me back on his cellphone." The smallest of smirks. Tiny. "He gets a quiet bottle of good wine shipped to his house every so often."

"You've gotta be careful using information from a guy like that."

"Yeah, don't want him to get fired. But today Phillips caught up with Rooker out in the street, not directly outside Book's office, which would have been a red flag to someone up there. So I'm not worried about burning him."

"You send out very many bottles of wine?" I ask.

"Let's just say I have an account down at the liquor store," he answers. "And, I have the word out that I'll slip $10 into the pocket of anyone with a good news tip." Smooth operator. Then, Collingwood changes direction. "Have you been able to log on to your computer yet?"

"Uh Huh. But can you show me a couple of things about how you use ENPS here? The way you use it appears to be different than my last shop."

We adjourn to my cube. Collingwood goes over some details. "Glad you know this program. Most places have ENPS or iNews now, so I guess I shouldn't be surprised." He shows me what I need to know about the program, as it is used at Newschannel 99.

Eventually, when he moves back to his office, I realize the newsroom has turned into a Waiting Room. Calzone loads fresh paper into a fax machine. An engineer tweaks the lighting for the newsroom camera. I open my Facespace page to post a new photo and status on my profile ("Shotgun start to Filterboro gig") and type a quick email to a pal at my old station, to make sure my new account works.

People begin to migrate to Producer's Row. One at a time, they gather at the television monitors. Its almost 6. Wilson rolls in, like a nor'easter. A "Slim Jim" hangs off his lip but naturally, his mouth isn't too full to talk. "Everyone watches the 6 together even if you're not doing a story 'cause we gotta see what we're doing and what 7 is doing and what 11 is doing and compare and then afterwards its dinner time and, you know what? tonight is meatloaf night at my house. My wife Margie who isn't really that old makes a great gravy with the meatloaf which is a lot better than ketchup on it unless we screwed up and got beat on a story then we try to figure out how to catch up and do the story at 11. C'mon." He gestures to me. No need to ask twice. I don't want to hear how his wife might put A-1 sauce on baked turkey.

The volume controls are manipulated by Collingwood. First, we focus on Channel 7. "They start one minute earlier than everyone else. They think it gives them an edge," Collingwood states.

"All it does is loses them 60 seconds in commercials at the top of the hour!" snickers Calzone.

Wilson does play-by-play. "It looks like Sam is going to handle the Rooker story for them and all he's doing is playing catch-up to Phillips except Jack has him beat BUT OH LOOK AT THAT they misspelled Rooker's name in the super! 'R-o-k-e-r! 'Overall not too bad but not as good as that time Sam beat us on that story when Polanco Hotels announced it was moving its headquarters out of town." Collingwood cringes. "Looks like 11 is leading with the Luther Post shooting instead of Rooker, I guess they didn't get any video of the perp walk so to them it's not a lead story and look, they are doing a liveshot from the crime scene where that taxi driver was shot but that's like 20 hours old now."

But it feels so immediate since they are appearing live there. Wilson takes a shallow breath and continues. "Uh oh, now 7 is doing that traffic wreck and fire that Fotch missed. Maybe we should have GPS installed in all the station vehicles, that way maybe he could have got his bearings faster and still got out there and back in time... ."

Collingwood mutters an oath.

Next, Volume Up on Newschannel 99, seemingly always the last to start. Theme music urgent, "newsy." We see the video of the fire neighbor, exclaiming, "Everyone knows Robby uses drugs. That councilman's son is a maroon." Studio announcer then proudly proclaims, "The Six O'clock News on Newschannel 99, Where We're Right 99 Times Out of 100!" Dramatic music surge, graphics dissolve to reveal Fern and Adams. If nothing else, they are slick. She's brisk, he's loose. She's sharp lines, he's big hair--even though its thinning. She's all business, he's all pleasure. And opinions. Not always overt opinions. Quite often they are conveyed with smirks, voice tone, body language, and raised eyebrows.

The anchors introduce Phillips out in the field. He walks and talks, taking us through the story. We go down the sidewalk with him as he reveals the house and then the garage.

"That's okay," mutters Collingwood, critically, to himself. "Maybe we should've focused more on the garage."

"I would've focused more on how worried everyone was about the missing Dad," comments Wilson, gamely. "Its human interest." He must feel that he's not a player here if he doesn't share an opinion about everything.

"He hasn't been missing for six hours," states Collingwood dismissively. Wilson's commentary stops, but only for the moment.

More opinions follow from Adams. A sympathetic reading of the closing "tag" after the Rooker story ends with, "...Robby Rooker was released on bond and tonight is safely back home with his family." Safely? He was in danger? Adams turns to a different camera and a "two shot" of he and Fern. "And it's always 'innocent until proven guilty,' right Lavinia?" She stares at Adams a moment. This isn't scripted. "That's the Constitution, Jeff." Back to the news, please.

Back in the newsroom: "Adams is a poker partner of Councilman Rooker's," Collingwood advises. "Their families go camping, they invested together in one or two enterprises." No kidding.

"Is Adams that secure here that he can say anything he wants?" I wonder out loud.

Collingwood isn't the one to make that call. He's not the News Director, or the Station Manager. "You never can tell, can you?" he replies.

Playing his remote control, Collingwood ratchets up the volume on Channel 11. Reporter Katie tries to catch up on the Rooker story. One nugget Phillips doesn't have: "Robby Rooker was arraigned in the private office of Magistrate T.T. Book, which was unusual. Magistrate Book explained to us that it was simply more convenient for his schedule."

"A soundbite with Book!" exclaims Follicle, back from his on-set appearance. "How'd she get that?"

Of course, Collingwood knows: "Book is friends with Calvin Jarvey."

"Calvin Jarvey?"

"Station Manager of Channel 11."

Oh. Sometimes you're a lucky reporter. Sometimes you're good. Sometimes your boss works for you.

Since we know what's in the Newschannel 99 rundown, we focus on the other stations' newscasts (except to offer gossipy critiques of every reporters' performances). 11 proceeds with the fiery car wreck and some new unemployment figures.

"What do you think, maybe we should have had unemployment in the A-block, Carl," whines Wilson.

"It's in the business segment at 5:30. No spectacular news there," replies Collingwood.

"Not real visual," adds Hurd, thinking ahead to his newscast at 11.

The next few moments are like watching a three-cornered tennis match. We volley between channels 99, 11, and 7. Then, we turn up the volume on Lavinia Fern in time for the manhunt story.

"...elusive triggerman accused of shooting a taxi driver this morning." Fern turns to a second camera. She's in one graphic "box," Tyler Hubbell is in another. Uh oh. Hubbell is not ready. Her hand absently pats her blonde tresses. She's lost in thought. Evidently, her IFB isn't working, meaning she can't hear. But in the heat of the moment Fern can't really tell, and couldn't stop if she wanted to.

"Newschannel 99's Tyler Hubbell is live in Ashton Heights tonight to tell us what progress deputies are making in this search. Tyler?"

Switch to full screen view of Hubbell. In front of a brick building. Is it a school? I wonder why she's at that particular location. Never mind. She's practicing her lines. Mouthing them, really, not saying them. Off camera, we hear a panicky "Go!" Must be the videographer.

"At least Wallflower is paying attention," remarks Calzone.

Hubbell's engine roars to life. "Well, Jeff..." Calzone rolls her eyes at the error. "This is the Command Center for the manhunt for Luther Post. Several witnesses told deputies that Post pulled the trigger on cab driver Reddy Chowdhury. He is considered armed and dangerous, and the shooting launched an urgent manhunt." The camera pans off Hubbell to see the wooded hillside. Two deputies are seen laughing over a joke nearby. Not urgently.

Hubbell ignores them. "Post is 52 years old and had been living in Otis Mills. But tonight, the wild hills of eastern Frippin County are Post's new home as he runs from the law." The director cuts to the "packaged" story on tape. We see worried residents, kids playing 'cops and robbers,' Sheriff sure he has Post cornered.

The package ends and we go back to Hubbell. She's ready this time. "Deputies describe Post as a black male, six foot three, 250 pounds, and bald. Even though he's on the run...deputies say he walks with a limp." She allows a small smirk, which says, 'I'm clever'. Groans in the newsroom. "If he doesn't turn up tonight," Hubbell continues, "K-9 trackers will be brought in tomorrow morning from the State Police to find this dangerous fugitive from justice. Reporting live in eastern Frippin County, Tyler Hubbell, Newschannel 99, Where We're Right 99 Times Out of 100."

"Convicting him so soon?" asks Calzone airily, wandering away.

"Sounds like it," decides Collingwood. He turns down the volume. All three stations finish their "A" blocks. Other staffers drift off. Channel 11 ends its block with the Cloverbell Farms ice cream eating contest.

"I guess those guys will be eating free ice cream tonight," comments Follicle, sadly. Everybody likes "free," even reporters who make a decent living.

Moments later, 11 airs a commercial for Cloverbell Farms. I envision dark countenances in our sales office tomorrow.

Back at my cube, Calzone drops off supplies: station-issued cellphone, two reporter's notepads, ink pens, paper clips. "You got an IFB?" she asks, popping her chewing gum.

"Don't leave home without one," I reply.

"Okay. We'll get you some business cards in a week or so. Send me an email so I get your name spelled right," she concludes. Then, she's gone.

I'm not alone, yet. Jacket on, impossibly thin leather-bound briefcase in hand, Collingwood comes by one final time. "Looks like you are ready to report tomorrow," he observes my office supply treasure trove. "Or at least take dictation."

I almost salute. "Got everything except a story."

"That'll change tomorrow morning at 9." He checks out.

Other station employees drift away. It's quiet again, as the newscast fades into the lighter fare of weather and sports. Everyone has either disappeared or is in the studio keeping the show afloat. Time for me to fly. Gather my stuff, orient myself--which way out, again? Start walking.

I spy Hurd, tapping at his computer. It's time to think of dinner.

"Marshall...are there any decent...uh, Latin places to eat around here?" Guess I have a craving.

He stops. Thinks. "There's a Taco Belt over on Spatterdash Street... ."

I'm outta here.

Back at the Placid Place Motel--my "home away from home." It's not the usual bland representation of modern overnight lodging, with neutral tans and pale blues. Although its hard by the interstate, it more closely resembles the "motor inns" of the 1950's: two wings of rooms anchored by an office in the center. Faux cupola built over the office. Pool out front, "family-run" restaurant to the side. It caters to the traveler just passing through. They check in at 9 pm or so, leave by 7. But it was designed to have folk come on down an' set a spell. They checked in at 4 pm or so, plenty of daylight left. Each room is fronted by a pair of metal garden chairs with looping pipe-like arms arranged on a small cement slab just outside the door. At one time folks actually sat in those chairs, swapping road stories with one another. That may have been before air conditioning was invented. Out of nostalgia, I occupy my chair, but wait in vain.

I sip on the first of the two brews left in the fridge. Night-time deepens slowly when there's little to do. Giving in to the boredom, I slip on a "Dewey Webber Surf Board" t-shirt and workout shorts and find the alleged "fitness center" that had been perfunctorily added on to the motel behind the office and next to the ice machine. Inside sits a dusty universal machine and a stair stepper. No one is here. Looking up, I see: mirrors on the ceiling? Hmm. Maybe I won't go there. The pool's closed for "repairs." Aside from the restaurant attached to the motel there's nothing worth visiting within walking distance--unless I want to hazard crossing the freeway interchange on foot. No thanks. So I amble back to my room, grab the last drink, and smoke Collingwood's cigar.

Oh, those ugly idle hours. I don't enjoy reading books or pondering over Sudoku puzzles or surfing the internet. The term "veg out" is foreign to me. Drinking, on the other hand, has been a recreational activity in my family for generations: A long line of beer drinkers. I, however, am an equal opportunity imbiber. And those last raucous semesters of college instilled in me a taste for the liquid bite that has never abated. Now, out here in The Real World, the pervasive culture of drinking in television news does nothing to inhibit me. So, I return to the empty lounge chair out front and take another deep sip--and vow to never again leave myself with two measly bottles of beer on hand.

The motel starts to fill up. Phones pressed to their ears, overnight visitors hurry from their cars straight into their rooms, to watch Sportscenter or a pay-per-view movie. No one slows down to sit in a metal garden chair and swap those road stories.

Eventually, the cigar burns down and my drink evaporates, so I head back inside my room. It smells of stale disinfectant spray and a stubborn, vague mold. "Folsom Prison Blues" plays on the computer tablet. Out the window, I watch the cars go by on the interstate. Time to meditate with another drink, this one water. And wonder: are their destinations any more meaningful than mine? Newschannel 99? Who knows. I iron tomorrow's dress shirt, sloppily; pick a suit. Okay, I'm ready for tomorrow. No more beer in the fridge, unfortunately. By the way, are there matching socks in the suitcase? Okay: Good to go this time.

My unfocused eye catches the Johnny Bench baseball card tucked into the side of the mirror. Where did I pick that up, anyways? I grew up a Reds fan, sort of, but didn't really collect baseball cards as a kid. Something about this one appealed to me. It's what they call Bench's "Rookie Card"--his first. I guess I admired the bass-ackward cap and his nonchalant confidence. It helps to possess the hindsight of knowing he turned into the greatest catcher to play the game.

This reminds me: a baseball game is on TV. Reclining on the hotel bed, I click over to it and watch Astros-Dodgers, disinterested, for a while. But at 11 its time to watch the news on WDMZ. Anything new tonight?

The graphics and voiceover promise lots of updates. "New, Tonight! ..." Fern and Adams again. They lead with the Robbie Rooker story, same information. A reporter does a weak "follow-up" report. Turns out the kid has a couple of drug-related arrests but no convictions. The pony-tailed lawyer is evidently pretty good at what he does. At least Hurd got the liveshot he'd been whining about, this one outside City Hall.

As to the Luther Post manhunt, Pendens "follows-up" by interviewing the victim's family.

Then Adams starts to read the School Bullying story. There was a meeting tonight, right? We had someone covering it, right?

"Angry parents on the warpath in Washerville," Adams intones. "They say its time a school bully got reigned in. They say school officials aren't doing enough to protect their kids from a man-child who has flunked the fourth grade three times." A soundbite from an angry parent follows. But, then, waitaminute. Didn't we have this same stuff at 6 pm? Uh oh.

Back to Adams. Video shows daytime footage of the exterior of a school building. At 11 pm, though, "daytime" = "outdated." More Adams: "At a special PTO meeting tonight, parents expressed their frustration and anger to school district administrators. No word yet if the alleged bully has been suspended." We weren't there to find out? If not, didn't anyone call to find out what happened? Ewww. That's just not good journalism.

Fern pops up. Tells of the traffic wreck and fire we missed earlier. No video. A graphic map shows the approximate location of a 12 hour old accident. Any video Fotch may have shot has apparently died.

"So that's the big update," I tell myself. The "new" news at 11 was old news we failed to report at 6. Not a sign of a healthy newsroom.

Eventually, the newscast ends with the kicker, hoping to close on a positive note. The video is contributed by Cloverbell Farms while Adams reads a story about an ice cream eating contest.

3

Up 'n' at 'em. 8:30 am, I am in the newsroom. On tap is the Morning Meeting. Most every newsroom in America has a Morning Meeting at the beginning of the day. Reporters, producers, managers, some videographers, are present. Everybody is supposed to pitch story ideas, brainstorm, critique, receive their assignments, and sort out other ideas. We also offer suggestions regarding each story, while mapping out the day's plans. It's an expanded version of the afternoon meeting I observed yesterday. More like a battlefield, since fewer "management types" are around. The gloves are usually off.

People drain from points around the newsroom into seats around a conference table in front of the assignment desk. Coffee steams everywhere. Mine is in a borrowed mug, hastily washed. Eventually, other reporters range around the table. Collingwood presides, looking fresh in another new suit. His manicured hands coddle a new Outlook filled with story ideas. Calzone, Scott, Meredith Angle--the Noon newscast producer--and some of the videographers also join us. Wilson sucks a sloppy breakfast burrito ("The restaurant, which is El Indio which means The Indian I think, by the way is over on Polyglot Street, got it right this time," he confides to me, mouth full). Fantana is on the speakerphone.

"Okay Brian," begins Collingwood. Already, there is a note of stress in his voice. "What happened last night?"

Another garbled connection. But we hear something about the PTO meeting didn't take place. In fact, the bully was arrested for carjacking a Humvee in the mid-afternoon, trying to leave Washerville.

"A fifth-grader?" asks Wilson.

"Yerp," affirms the speakerphone.

"We reported that the meeting had happened. It's a major fact error. I thought Marshall was going to follow up on the phone with one of the parents or a school board member--to see what happened at the meeting?" asks Collingwood, already patting his empty pocket. Where's that cigarette?

No reply. "Anyone know what happened?" Collingwood tries again.

"Well, uh, there's nothing in the nightly 'After Action Report' that says anything about that story," starts Wilson. "Just that Marshall wrote there was a mis-spelled graphic and Jeff forgot to put on his microphone at the beginning of the newscast and a backlight on the set needs replacing and..."

"Okay, okay," Collingwood interrupts. "I'll have to ask Marshall when he gets in. Brian, unless you've got anything else, you need to follow that up today and straighten out our coverage on this."

"Nuh probrm, bosh," answers the speakerphone.

Muttering about the audio quality of the device, Collingwood turns to the Filterboro reporters. "Alright. What are you guys pitching today?"

Wearing a pair of reading glasses that look more like a prop than a prescription, Hubbell is quick to pitch an easy one. "I should follow up the Luther Post manhunt again today."

Before she can go much further, though, Jack Phillips cuts in.

"Actually, last night I had a conversation with the District Attorney, who owes me one. Says deputies are gonna get a search warrant for Post's brother-in-law's house. That's over in a neighborhood in Khalishes. I'll know when the warrant is granted and can be over there when the place is searched."

Around the table, nobody speaks for a moment. People look at one another. It's a challenge and there's a sudden tension.

See, this has been Hubbell's story so far--and it's obviously a big one. In many newsrooms its sacrosanct that a reporter gets to keep working a story until it's over. Unless they give it up for reasons beyond their control. It's also largely an unspoken rule, which can be threatened by new information developed by another reporter. So, etiquette may have called for Phillips to make no attempt to claim the story...but practically-speaking, all journalists desperately want to tell the most important stories. So this morning, Hubbell can't claim the story outright. She has to convince Collingwood that she still owns it.

"The Sheriff told me they'll catch Post today, for sure," she tries, and glancing at Phillips adds, "And they're looking for him in the Frippin Hills, not over in Khalishes!"

Phillips rolls his eyes, loudly. "I've got a surefire visual. It sounds like you'll have more of what you had yesterday."

Hubbell ignores him. "Carl," she tries, "We'll go up in the woods on an ATV with a couple of deputies to get the latest on the search. And we will still have time to show up to see the pointless search warrant executed."

Picking up on Phillips' criticism, however, Collingwood asks, "What will you do different in your story if the deputies don't find anything, Tyler? You had 'worried neighbors' in your package yesterday. Can't rely on that angle again."

"You could find out who does Post's hair," Phillips gibes.

Hubbell shoots him a death-ray look, but refuses to be drawn in to a personal battle. "I'll talk with the cab driver's family," she replies to the moderator, Collingwood.

"We did that last night at 11," he answers. "Has anyone gotten through to Post's family? What do they have to say?" asks Collingwood.

"I called, left a couple of messages," replies Calzone. "No reply. Last night the reporter knocked on their door. No answer."

"None of the other stations had them last night at 11, either," comments Angle. "And by the way, there's no update on Chowdhury's condition."

Glancing at Phillips, Scott tries, "Well, we could do something on the manpower drain on the Sheriff's Department, considering they have so many people looking for Post--how much of it is for show-for the TV cameras? What are they not able to do now that they're all working on this case? One of the visual elements to that could be the deputies serving the search warrant."

Phillips grimaces at Scott. It's a pretty good approach.

"That's a possibility," agrees Collingwood. "Tyler, start with the Post family. Go to their home, see the neighbors. Dig into Post's background. Since you'll have to talk with deputies anyways, ask them about the manpower situation. And if you are real nice to Jack, he might just help you with the warrant information." Now it's Hubbell who rolls her eyes. But her voice remains sweet long enough for one more request. "One more thing, Carl. I could front it live out at the command post, like yesterday."

"We won't go live unless there's something new," he answers. "It didn't seem real urgent there last night."

Hubbell has to answer that. "It wasn't my fault. None of us knew we were on the air."

"Don't forget to plug in your IFB next time," Collingwood answers, pointedly, then quickly moves on. "Jack, what kind of follow up do you have on Robbie Rooker?"

Phillips is ready. He probably didn't truly expect to cherry-pick Hubbell's story but thought it was worth taking a shot. "I've been trying to reach Rodwell Rooker. He's got a city council meeting tonight but I hear that he doesn't plan to attend. With the primary election coming up, nobody had even thought about challenging him. That could change though because I hear a couple of heavy hitters may think he's vulnerable. They could actually mobilize their campaigns as early as today."

"Rooker is dead meat," announces Nettles. "His own county party chairman is ready to run. That would suck for him."

"Martin Contestable? Try to develop that, Jack," directs Collingwood. "What else? Sherman?"

Follicle suggests a feature on a cow chip flinging contest. It's in Blue Hill, at the northern end of our market. "These guys are good at it, and it's real visual," he assures us.

"How in the world do they practice?" wonders Scott.

"It's a long ways away," warns Collingwood. "Can you find some vosot up there to bring back as well?" Vosot: voice over/sound on tape report. A report that the anchors read that includes a soundbite from someone.

"I'll be back by 2:30. No sweat," Follicle answers. He looks sweaty. But then again, he usually does.

One by one, Collingwood checks with the reporters. Each ends up with an assignment. Then, to me. An easy out is to suggest a local angle to a current national story--such as finding how many flights have been delayed at the local airport when the national on-time flight statistics are released for each airline. Other than that, I don't have much to offer. No contacts here, yet. Collingwood, however, has an offer I can't refuse, in the form of a ready-made story.

"The Reproach County Health Department is starting a new flu vaccination program today. They are starting early this year because it takes a regimen of two shots instead of just one. People can get them for free at the clinic. How bad is the flu season going to be later this year? We actually had a couple of older people die last year. The Health Department isn't far away from the station, and Gretchen can hook you up with the right people over there. 'One stop shopping,' when it comes to shooting video, you won't have to go anywhere else. Should be an easy enough assignment to get your feet wet." "Feet wet?" What foreshadowing. Okay by me, not having anything else to do. This should be simple. No worries.

Collingwood goes to a wipe board on the wall. Fills it in with reporter assignments. Then assigns videographers. He gives me Billy Fotch. Now I'm worried.

Everyone disperses from the meeting. Some head to their desks to begin research, others are able to hit the road immediately. Before they go, Calzone calls out additional work. "Jack! I need you to stop by Ten Smedleys Elementary School at 1:30 to get video of the groundbreaking for their new wing. Tyler! Pick up an interview with that union guy about possible layoffs at the transistor radio factory. Jeanette! Get a quick update on the workers setting up for the Prune Festival this weekend." Moans and groans. "Wil!" A crooked smile as she inserts the first pencil of the day into her hair. "You've got Fotch so I'm not giving you anything extra to do." Small favors.

Grab Fotch, reading a *Mad* magazine back in the Cage. "How long do you need to get the SUV loaded and ready to go?"

Not a hard question. But the answer takes a while. "15 minutes?"

He's questioning me? Okay. I'll hold him to it. "15 minutes is fine. I'll get my stuff together."

First, I call the Health Department. They're expecting some media coverage today. Full access, everybody will be willing to talk. Going to be a little touch-and-go, however, with patients. Laws protect their identities so we can't record video of them without asking. There are often ways around that, such as to simply avoid shooting their faces.

Check with Collingwood.

"Any history around here? You mentioned a couple of people died last year. Any flu epidemics? Problems with inoculations?"

Thinking for a moment, Collingwood smooths down his pomaded hair with a hand. "Nothing of great significance. Every year people seem more concerned than ever to get a flu shot. Like many places, there was a temporary shortage in the vaccine recently. And what they got was virtually useless. So the Health Department is trying to stay ahead of things this year, evidently. There's no strong historical angle. The Health Director there is brand new, trying some new things. Do what you can with it."

Time to go. On the way out I grab my manbag. It's not a gym bag or a computer bag; also not a briefcase. Its zippered everywhere. Has the saving grace of being faux black leather, the color of cool. My professional life resides in there. Notepad, IFB, phone, makeup, aspirin bottle. Lots of aspirin.

Time to return to the Cage, to find a Fotch. Floor-to-ceiling lockers dominate the utility room, most filled with equipment. In one corner sits an easel covered with black velvet. That's used for shooting closeups of photographs, court documents, newspaper articles.

There is one person here. Not Billy Fotch, though. He sits at a table, working on a camera before him. Extremely thin, raven black hair askew, uneven moustache. Tired lines about the eyes betray his age as he looks up to me. He pauses, as if it will take an effort simply to ask what I want: "Can I help you?"

"I'm looking for Billy Fotch. We're supposed to head out on a shoot."

"Somebody's always looking for Billy Fotch," he sighs. "He went out to grab some breakfast sandwiches from the place around the corner."

I glance at my watch. "Do you think he packed his gear first?"

The Person checks over his shoulder. "Looks like his locker's full, so I'd say, 'no.'"

Not a good start. I go back to the desk, sit. Have another cup of coffee. Look around. Most other reporters are gone. Collingwood is on the phone. Wilson wipes something off his tie with a post it note. Calzone is in a fury at the assignment desk, yelling at someone on the phone--and it may not even be Fotch.

I turn on my computer. Wait for it to get the electronic synapses to fire before typing in my shiny new password. Wait some more. Ah, finally. Click on an icon to open an internet browser; wait again. Search for "flu shots" and "inoculation" and "vaccine." Wait. Inoculation is spelled with one "n." The results show nothing remarkable. CDC says they had been 70 to 90% effective until last year, when they didn't predict the right strains to inoculate against. Hmm. I didn't know scientists de-activated the virus in the vaccine. There's no chance it can give someone the flu.

Alright. It's been ten minutes. Let's go check on Fotch again.

The Cage still holds one inmate.

"Sorry. Fotch isn't here." The Person bites into a breakfast sandwich.

"Looks like he came back with your breakfast."

"Yup. But he had to go get gas for his SUV. Guess it was low."

I take a deep breath. Calm blue ocean. Okay, is this some sort of initiation rite?" Is he screwing around on purpose? We're going to be late." I forget Cardinal Rule Number One: never push videographers. You can only pull them.

The Person smirks. "He's just doin' his job. The SUV needs gas. If you run out of gas, you'll be even later."

Walk away. I strongly dislike Reasoning For Seven Year Olds.

Go see Collingwood. I wouldn't normally go over a guy's head like this, but I'm not sure I'm missing some point of protocol--and its clear Billy Fotch is in regular need of authoritative babysitting.

"Get Gretchen to call him. She'll set him straight. And wait for him in the Cage. Don't expect him to wait for you."

"Who is the guy working on his camera in there?"

"Oh, that's Norman Wallflower, the Chief Photog. He's been around here as long as me. He's been planning to do something else as long as he's been here, but nothing has ever worked out."

"Like what?"

"Shoot documentaries, films, pro sports, porn, whatever. Anything else and anywhere else but here."

"Don't all videographers have that plan?"

"Most, I suppose. Norman's just been dreaming longer than most, and doing less about it."

No word from Fotch, so I stop by the Assignment Desk. Calzone is more than happy to screech at Fotch. He asked for it.

Manbag in hand, I roll back to La Cage Aux Fous one more time. Wallflower is still fiddling with his camera. I take up a post by the door. Drop the manbag, fold my arms, and wait. Over my shoulder, I hear Calzone barking at Fotch. Better him than me.

"So you got him in trouble," observes Wallflower, listening but not looking up.

"He got himself in trouble," I answer.

"Not a good start," he warns.

"I'm used to being tested by people when I start a new job. That doesn't mean it's any less juvenile."

Smirk. No reply. I wait. He fiddles. A clock ticks. Well, it ticks somewhere, not here. Meaningfully, there are no clocks in The Cage. Photogs keep their own time.

Finally, Fotch ambles in.

"Whoa, all I needed was to get some gas," he explains pre-emptively to my foot-tapping.

"On the other side of the county?" Best to establish a little incredulity. Face-value doesn't work with me, buddy. At least, uh, on the face of it. "We need to go," I conclude.

Suddenly a man on a mission, Fotch busies himself. Grabbing gear, checking bags. I watch. Finally, he appears ready. But, no.

"Lemme just hit the head and I'll be ready to go," he announces.

A flu epidemic could have come and gone and we would have missed it by the time he finishes. I'm burning mad and sure I show it.

"Must have been a big breakfast," he explains. Off we go. Really, this time. It feels like it must be noon by now.

We head out the door. It's a warm, moist day. Spongy clouds. I start thinking about my bladder. Oh no. Fotch went. Now, I sense the need to go. Must have been the extra cup of Joe while waiting for Billy. No way in the world am I going to say anything until we get there. One step at a time. Climb into the SUV, focus on the story assignment. Unfortunately, it smells like coffee inside. I tightly cross my legs.

The ten minute drive feels like three hours. Liquid references emerge everywhere. A Frank Ocean song plays on the radio. I try to think of other things: Wondering which brand of beer I should buy tonight does not help. We drive by a swimming pool. "Looks like rain," observes Fotch, while I squirm.

Finally, we park in an alley behind a tall building downtown. Looks to me like a tow-away zone. "Media parking pass," explains Fotch. That trumps all. He inserts a red card on to the SUV dashboard. "We pay money for this to the city, so Norm says we should use it as much as possible."

We circle to the back of the SUV and open the hatch. I grab the tripod, Fotch gets the rest. We haven't really talked, but now he starts a conversation.

"Wow, thanks for carrying the tripod. Not many of the reporters will do that. Hey, are you thirsty? I'm thirsty. It's hot. When we're done maybe we can stop and get a 32 ounce Thirst Squasher at the store. It's only a $1.50. Wow, I can almost taste... ."

"Billy, how do we get to the Health Department?"

He points to a seven- or- eight story concrete block building. Standard impersonal municipal issue. I walk quite rapidly down the alley toward it. Fotch tries to keep up.

"Think it'll rain?" he asks. I grunt. Or gasp.

We head around the front of the building. A fountain plashes. I spot a soda pop billboard. Uh oh. Hurry... . I feel like I'm moving awkwardly, straight out of the Ministry Of Silly Walks. For a moment a memory flashes by: my childhood neighborhood in Cincinnati, a little friend of my sister who had a propensity to wait just "a little too long." She suddenly has to go home. To get there, she swivels her right leg tightly in front of the left, then does the same with the left in front of the right, to keep herself as tightly bound up as possible. Swiveling-slow locomotion, I'm not sure she always made it in time.

Now I'm not sure about myself, either. Fotch and I head through double glass doors. Heavy air conditioning coats the lobby. Hallways branch off somewhere. Elevators must be nearby, right? The place is crowded with people, mostly patients, I guess. All seem to be drinking something. Coffee, water, sodas from a machine. A toddler slurps on her thumb. Hnnnnnnnnn.

A desk sits heavily in the center of the lobby. Information, please. The people there point us to the sixth floor. Yow, I've really gotta go. Briskly, briskly to the elevator. Some other people are waiting also. I shift my weight. Ugh. Nearby, out of sight, I hear someone getting a drink at the water fountain. What's taking so long for the elevator?

Ding! A crowd of people shoves onboard. The door shuts, I press "6." Notice every button from "2" to "5" is also lit up. Naturally. Sweating now, I bounce on my feet. Hum the National Anthem or "Electric Blue" or something. Everyone (except the oblivious Fotch) seems to be staring. I dimly begin to catch a conversation in back.

"...and then we floated down the river right to the bottom of the Falls."

"Did you get wet?"

"Oh yeah! They gave us these big raincoats, but we still got soaked... ."

I'm going cross-eyed.

Ding! Sixth floor. I'm out like a shot, not waiting for Fotch. Desperate as a late groom. Where's a bathroom? Go left, no--over there! Running with the heavy tripod, I cut people off. Who cares about people staring! Never so glad to see a restroom in my life.

Four minutes later, me and my tripod emerge. Light as a feather, cool as ice, ready to cover flu shots.

The county Health Director, Dr. Juniper Wetlands, is cordial. She wears a white lab coat over a healthy physique. All carrots and fitness centers. Reading glasses hang from a lanyard around her neck. I wonder if they are there to embellish her academic persona more than anything else. Nail polish, but no lipstick. Mid-30's? I wonder. Her office shelves are empty, but her chairs are full. We can't sit down because several large white cardboard moving boxes are in the way.

Wetlands shoves a box aside for me to sit down.

"Sorry about the mess. I'm still moving in, and something always pops up to distract my attention from getting unpacked."

"I'm new in town, too," I try, competing with a stack of papers for space on a chair.

"In any case, I'm glad you're here to do a story on the flu shots. It looks like the other stations aren't coming out today. Before you came, I tried to do a little research on the history of influenza and vaccines in Reproach County, but I'm afraid I can't tell you how or why this particular vaccine was chosen for our county this year."

"What can you tell me about the local history from what others have told you, over the past year or so? Did many people get serious cases of the flu around here?"

Wetlands shrugs her shoulders. "I understand some people got sick last year, as they do every year, but the mortality rate was low. At the moment I'm better able to talk about national trends. And I can explain the two-shot regimen that is new this year."

"Can any of your subordinates help out with some other local specifics?"

"Well, one or two, I suppose." Dr. Wetlands stops and lowers her voice. "But completely off the record--do not report this--part of my job here is to re-organize this office. My predecessor was a bit lax when it came to paperwork, staff discipline, the like. That's one reason things may appear disorganized."

The journalist inside me strains at the leash. Can't sound too eager or interested, though. "In what ways were they lax?"

No way. "I'm not going to tell any more than that to a reporter." She smiles, nail-polished fingers combing her straight brown, shoulder-length hair behind her right ear. "But it wasn't exactly anything to threaten the health of the residents of the county, so it really isn't newsworthy anyways."

Wish I had a dollar every time someone told me that, hoping I'd go away. This time, though, there's nothing more concrete to go on. Maybe it really isn't serious--especially since Wetlands is willing to share this off-the-record insight with a reporter she has just met.

"Okay," I reply. "Going back to the flu shots, can we start with another doctor here?"

Off we go. Reading glasses, white jacket flapping, Wetlands gives us a quick tour. We weave our way down hallways, through patients, nurses, records staff. Eventually, we interview a staff doctor and a couple of patients. Get pictures of people wincing while they get their shots.

Along the way, I notice that the Director's office isn't the only corner of the Health Department loaded with boxes. 11 or 12 brown ones are piled up in one place, oddly blocking a closet door. The whole place seems a little disorganized, not just Wetlands' office. I guess that's because there's a lot to do. Kids cry, patients wait impatiently, nurses work around the boxes and other obstacles with a practiced skill. I try to find interesting story angles and get Fotch to shoot video with a little creativity. Or, at least so it's not completely fouled up.

Soon it's time to record a "standup," where I get a little face time to end the story. A nurse stands by. Fotch gets a closeup on my arm, and then-- the nurse jabs me with the needle. Fotch widens camera shot to reveal me in patient's chair. With my sleeve rolled up as the nurse finishes, I start.

"A lot people have to overcome their childhood fear of needles to prepare for flu season," I recite. "But the doctors here say this pinprick can save the average person three missed days at work and hundreds of dollars in medical expenses if they would otherwise get the flu this year. Reporting downtown, Wilson Gamble, Newschannel 99, Where We're Right 99 Times Out of 100."

Nothing to see here, folks, please move along. Just routine stuff being recorded for the Six O'clock News.

We're done and say goodbye to Dr. Wetlands, busy unpacking yet another box in her office. Fotch and I head back downstairs, through the busy lobby towards the double doors. A small crowd blocks the way, staring at an empty sidewalk. Empty that is, unless you count a thick rain falling on it. Looks long term. Fotch immediately stops. "Hey man, I forgot a microphone upstairs. Meet you in the SUV."

He gives me the keys and hurries off. I've still got the tripod. Wait here or in the SUV? I don't like crowds, and there isn't one in the SUV. I look up. The rain isn't going away any time soon. Get wet now or get wet later. Okay, there's no time like the present. I'll just dry out sooner rather than later.

Out the door, I race along the pavement, trying to avoid puddles. My head down--hurry, hurry. Quickly, it gets wet on my neck, my back, even on my shins. I 'round the corner to the alley. Slip in the key, lift open the back. Here I can take a breather, standing under the hatch. I sling the tripod into the back and hang out here for the moment. I don't want to subject my dress clothes to any more of this downpour. An idea strikes me. Can I crawl through the back of SUV into my seat? Yup.

Here I go, over portable lights, extra batteries, a microphone boom pole, and other stuff. I point my leg over the back seat, step into front seat, done. Oh no. I forgot to close the hatch. Geez. Trying the gymnastic routine again, I head back, close the hatch, and return to the front. Finally.

I turn the ignition from the passenger seat and turn on windshield blower right away, for the fog on the inside of the glass. Still no Fotch. Turn on the radio, no sign of Frank Ocean now; only an old song about A Horse With No Name. I'm getting bored.

A door opens in the rear of the Health Department, half a block up. Hmm. It catches my eye because nothing else is moving outdoors in the deluge. And, who knows where Fotch will reappear. Anyways, a figure emerges--a man, I guess, hunched inside a dark rain poncho. Hood pulled over head. It's not Fotch. He struggles with a brown box. More bulky than heavy. He staggers into the rain away from me. Where to? Still watching, the wipers squeak over my field of vision. Visual good, visual bad, good, bad, good, bad. It's like watching every third frame of a movie.

The man dashes along the alley. It's difficult to make out, but 500 feet farther down, I make out a garbage dumpster lid opening and closing. That's it. He's throwing something away. My idle curiosity satisfied, I turn the channel on the radio.

Now, waitaminute. Who would choose to perform this chore during a monsoon? And, was that one of all those boxes cluttering the Health Department? I wonder what is inside it.

But, why bother to check it out? The rain isn't letting up. My story is done. When Fotch remembers where the SUV is, we will return to the station and dry off. Take time to get accustomed to my new work-setting to write and edit my story. Turn in something easy and predictable--but most importantly, done on time.

But I just can't do things that way. I have to find out if there's something interesting here. Professional inquisitiveness, you could call it. Curiosity may have killed the cat, but it launched a thousand careers in journalism. There may be nothing worth finding, but I have to look. "No stone left unturned," I guess. Or, the definition of a journalist: "Once nosy, always nosy." Whatever, let's go.

No Fotch still. Clambering over the back seat again, I find a station umbrella. Armed with this, I head out the door, into the cruel elements again. As I trudge along, the puddles seem to grow, the soak spreading on my legs. Dumpster, right ahead.

I throw open the rubberized lid but it's tough to see anything inside, it's too high. So I slide the small steel access door in front open and peer inside. Dozens of trash bags, one or two burst open. Mostly wet shredded paper. A pile of flattened boxes in back. On top of the trash, like a cherry on a sundae, sits one square, wet brown box. I look for a packing label but I'm at a bad angle and the rain doesn't help. But I can make out "RCHD" printed on it. Reproach County Health Department, right? Now I've gotta get a look inside. How? No choice but to dumpster dive...in the driving rain.

The umbrella is no good now. I have to position my right foot in one of the slots into which the garbage truck inserts its lift arm. Keep a grip in the wet, son. The cast iron feels cold and a little slimy. Hoisting my left foot over the top, I teeter for a frightening moment. Why am I doing this, anyways? Okay, stable again. Sitting on the edge of the dumpster, I test the interior mash of trash. Will the garbage support me? Okay, it seems packed down. I'm in.

The rain keeps coming. I take long, slow steps over the slick refuse, like an astronaut on the moon. There's the box sealed with packing tape. How to open it? No knife--and I left the SUV keys in the ignition. My personal keys are safe and dry in the manbag. Looking around, there's nothing handy. Okay, fine. I start scraping at the packing tape with my fingernails. I get a little panicky in the relentless rain. Anyone watching me, by the way? Never mind. Fragments of tape pull away, stick to my fingers. The cardboard grows soggier by the second. Finally, though, I gain traction. One long tug, and it's an open box.

Pandora would be proud.

The box is filled with used needles and syringes. Wow. Can you say "lead story?"

Hurriedly, I close the box, shove it toward the front of the dumpster. I scramble over the side. Gotta haul it back to the SUV. Get Fotch and the all-important camera.

Oh no--the SUV is gone! How? I'm flabbergasted. So, the box will have to stay here for now.

Grabbing the now-impotent umbrella, I race back to where the SUV had been idling. No SUV of any kind there, idling or not. Next, I race to the front of the Health Department. Inside its dry and cold but, of course, to those huddled by the door inside, I appear to be a soggy lunatic. Where's Fotch? Glancing around the lobby, I decide that I don't want to inquire on the sixth floor--not with my Lead Story melting in the rain as we speak. Looking out the front glass doors proves fruitless; Fotch isn't circling the block looking for me. Then the glass starts to seriously fog up so I have to go to Plan B.

I need a phone. Mine is safe and sound in my man bag--in the SUV. Time to find one, away from here. Heading back out into the rain, I desperately look around an unfamiliar downtown street. That water fountain is mighty superfluous in this downpour. Behind it, across the street, is a tobacco shop. "Pillar and Post Tobacco" reads the sign. At the moment it is the only sign of life in the middle of the city block. I'll try there. Splashing across the road, I run breathlessly into the shop. A large, middle-aged woman sits behind a counter; no one else is there. Mousy gray hair--evidently styled with a kitchen implement-- disparages her face. So does a frown. Creases line her face, hands, arms. She's reading a magazine, not smoking. The walls are lined with glass cases. Tobacco. Cigars everywhere. Ad posters everywhere else.

I'd really like a cigar, but not right now. "Can I please use your phone?"

Okay, "dubious" was invented for the woman's reaction. She did not move, except to lift her eyes. They simply settle on me. I'm out of breath, thoroughly soaked, hair matted down. And I'm carrying an umbrella that presumably should have warded off at least some of the elements.

"There's a payphone around the corner at Goldini's. They're probably still open after the lunch rush." She still does not move.

"Thank you. But I don't have any change. Look, I'm a new reporter for Newschannel 99... ." That transforms things, but not for the better. The lady finally moves. Lurching along, down the back of the counter towards me: "Get out of here right now. I don't want any TV news people in this place." I hesitate before the downpour, and the onslaught. "Go on, buddy, before I call the cops!"

Alright, already, I'm outta here. I plunge back into the rain, like diving into a swimming pool. Goldini's, huh? Will they treat me any better? Who knows, just go. But where? Didn't see any restaurant the way I approached the tobacco shop, so I just keep going, away from the Health Department. No one at all is on the sidewalk. In my hurry I pass storefronts too quickly to tell what they are. I turn a corner, and there it is, the red and green striped awning providing a welcome, uh, welcome. Under the awning I slow down a minute, catch my breath, smooth my hair in the reflection of the window as best as possible. Okay, somewhat presentable. Entering through a glass door, I encounter an unguarded host's podium. Is there a phone anywhere? Bar's empty. I look past a partition into the dining area. There is one patron: Billy Fotch.

I march straight to him.

"Billy, why on God's green earth did you leave me in the rain back there?"

He's seated at a square table with white linen. Looks to be at peace with the world. Hands folded. Just waiting for his cannelloni, thank you. Out loud, he replies wondrously, "Oh, there you are! I had no idea where you went. Want some lunch?"

Speechless, fists growing, I stand above him, dripping on his menu.

"But remember I said I was thirsty? so I came here. Its close by. Then I remembered I didn't have lunch yet so I decided to eat in. Here's a menu."

I am mad. Extreme, firestorm mad. I mean rockets-red-glare, broiling-molten-lava-on-the-surface-of-the-sun-angry.

The slow, deep words I growl work magic. "If...you...don't...leave...with...me...now...you...will...have...to...pick...cannelloni...out...of...every...hole...in...your...body."

Fotch hurriedly leads the way to the SUV. It's neatly placed in a parking lot across the street, out of sight from the direction I came. Finally, off we go. I explain as much as I can to him without expletives. It's a short drive. We travel around two corners, and stop on a street before the alley.

"Why here?" Fotch whines.

"I don't want them to see a big white SUV with 'Newschannel 99' on the side, Einstein."

"I can't shoot in the rain. There's no rain jacket for the camera. And I'm still thirsty," he finishes, mumblingly.

"Then you will just have to stand underneath my umbrella. First, we stake out this place here for a little while. See if the guy comes back out with another cardboard box."

We stand and stake. Fotch, the camera and tripod under the umbrella. There's no room for me, so I get wetter. My anger subsides, though; we can still get this story.

Time ticks on as we possess our souls in patience. My arm begins to hurt, holding the umbrella. Fotch practically envelopes the camera, leaning over it, while trying to stay dry under the umbrella.

Payoff. The dark rain poncho suddenly appears once more out of the building, heading down the alley. Carrying another brown cardboard box.

"Roll tape!" I whisper viciously.

To his credit, Fotch does his best. He quickly zooms in, finds focus, records. "Hope the lens isn't real fogged up," he mutters unhelpfully.

Poncho man lifts the box, rests it on top edge of the dumpster to get balance. A moment later, over it goes. He races back inside the shelter of the Health Department building.

Key moment. "Did you get it?"

"Well, it was raining."

"No. I hadn't noticed. Check tape, uh, Fotch-stein." Ha ha, "Fotch" and "Einstein." I may have found my own critical nickname for Fotch, just by accident.

"Quit calling me that," Fotch tries, sounding bullied. "And it's not 'tape,' Grandpa, its digital," he adds, trying to fight back. I shrug my shoulders; some trade phrases involving "tape" and "reel" will simply persist.

Anyways, Fotch cues the video time code in the camera viewfinder and hits "play." Only one eye fits into the viewfinder: his. Fotch assesses his work.

"Looks pretty good. I can see the dude. Maybe I should have 'gained up' because the clouds make it kinda dark outside, or used a different filter, and I'm not real sure about my white balance and..."

"Shut up. Take the camera off the tripod and come down here with me."

I need video proof of what's in those boxes. Jumping back into the SUV, we speed down the alley to the county's newest Hazardous Waste Dump. I grab my phone, safe and dry in my manbag. I have to call in this fabulous late change to my story.

There's very little signal, however, only one bar on the display. Maybe the close-in buildings around the alley create a dead spot for the cell signal. I try to send a quick text message to the station. Anyways, seconds later, we reach the dumpster.

"Fotch, you record me while I climb into the dumpster and get the box."

"But the camera will get wet!"

Another reminder of what's more valuable. I'm thoroughly soaked, could get sick. I think for a moment.

"Okay, turn around and park the SUV so the back end faces the dumpster. Open the hatch and stand under it."

That's logic clear enough even for Fotchstein. He sets up. I wait, impatiently. What if the poncho guy comes back outside with another cardboard box before we get our evidence recorded? I grab a handheld wireless mic and try to think about what I'm doing here.

"Okay, go," Fotch advises.

I clamber over. Fotch focuses through the open sliding iron door in the dumpster. Now there are two brown cardboard boxes inside. I grasp the first one, open it for the camera. Don't want to touch the contents, so I shift them around so Fotch can see.

"Be sure to get a closeup of the Health Department label," I advise. "But now we need to open this second box on camera, to see what's inside." I pause. This is TV, remember.

This may be the golden moment of the story. As the reporter I want to be a part of it. "Fotch, start on me. I'm going to do a standup."

I've already decide this will be a "bridge" standup, connecting two halves of my story. So, what will be the content of those two halves? I must think fast.

Fotch adjusts the camera, then declares, "Rolling." Even though it's not video.

"Dumpster diving may never have been so hazardous." The camera pushes in on the box. I take my keys, rip a line in the tape. "This box was discarded here this afternoon." I pull open the lid. *Voila ici.* "Another box filled with needles and syringes. All heading for the local landfill instead of a sanitary disposal site."

Pause.

"Not bad," starts Fotch. "Maybe you want to..." But I cut him off.

"Billy, there he is! Quick, get a shot of him!"

A man in a dark rain poncho is standing in the frame of the Health Department door. Frozen for a moment by the sight of us. Carrying another brown cardboard box. For a moment he's unsure what to do.

I try scrambling out of the dumpster. Slipping, sliding.

"Sir! Sir! Why did you dump these boxes in this dumpster? Can you explain why there are needles in these boxes?"

He's gone, door banging. I slip again on the trash, losing my grip in the rain. Fotch doesn't get a clear shot of the man, but moves quickly to the back door. It isn't locked. A wooden wedge keeps it open, probably for poncho-man to quickly get back inside to escape from the rain.

I catch up to Fotch, and we simply go inside. Cool in here, no humidity. Flashes of yellow cinderblock walls, cast iron steps, and fluorescent lights way up high somewhere. Claustrophobia. It's a stairwell. The stairs are slippery wet heading up. We hear echoing steps, and someone breathing heavily moving somewhere above.

Fotch pauses. "What are we doing?" He's asking for a command from the ranking officer in this outfit, me. Deja vu: Sgt. Mark.

"We're heading upstairs," I reply. "We have to follow these wet tracks."

Up we go. We hear a metal door clanging shut, up there somewhere. The wet marks keep going all the way up to the Sixth Floor, stopping at the door to the interior.

Okay, it's time to pause to catch our breath. The door's closed, is it locked? I depress the thumb latch. It won't budge. We can't get in. I peer through a small square window in the door. The nerve center of the Health Department should be secure, I reason with myself. Fotch just stares at me: we labor up all these steps and we have to go back?

Nope. Somebody is heading out.

Collect yourself Wil, look nonchalant. Pretend you come this way every day. A bearded man in a suit, a stranger forever, pushes open the door, engrossed in reading a handful of papers.

"Thank you," I coolly offer to the distracted Good Samaritan, grabbing the door.

"You're welcome," he replies, not noticing Fotch and his camera. Waving his umbrella, reading his papers, he moves along, down towards the rain.

"Billy," I hiss. "Go back down a couple of stairs and get some video of me going through this door. In the story we can say we followed the man in the poncho here to the Health Department headquarters." It doesn't occur to me until later that we could be recording me committing a felony.

Nevertheless, Fotch retreats and rolls tape, even if there's no actual tape. I walk through the door, and Fotch follows soon after. Now what? It's a long office hallway. Gray tight weave carpet, mauve walls. Fluorescents every few feet. People move between closed cherry wood doors with brushed aluminum handles. Very antiseptic looking. But hiding at least one dirty secret.

A white coat, presumably borne by a doctor, hurries up to us. He scratches hair fragments on the side of his head.

"I thought you guys had finished," he says, trying to lead an answer out of me. Like I said before, inquiring minds want to know.

"Um, we got a little turned around when we were leaving," I try to explain. But the sprinkler system has not gone off and we're both soaked pretty thoroughly.

"But you shouldn't be filming anything back here."

"We're not." At the moment. "If you are worried, take us to Dr. Wetlands, and I'm sure she will give us all the clearance we need."

The doctor's bedside manner cools. "I'll let security take you, if they choose to. Wait here."

We wait until a small patch of rainwater soaks the carpet under my feet.

A uniformed city police officer approaches with the balding doctor. The officer is bummed out to be taken away from the daytime "reality show" he's been watching in the security office.

"What are you guys doing?" he demands. "Which station are you with?" He doesn't recognize the new TV guy.

"Newschannel 99. We are attempting to track down a person here who is breaking the law," I reply. A simple gimmick, in the hope of converting the law enforcement officer to my side.

"What do you mean?" he wants to know, nearly putting his hand on his gun holster. So I tell him.

"Alright," he decides. "Let's go see Dr. Wetlands."

He leads. We tramp down the corridor, through a heavy security door and into the sixth floor lobby. Another door opens up to the public reception area for the Health Department. People there are still waiting for flu shots. The receptionist recognizes us, despite my now-soggy appearance, and calls Dr. Wetlands on an interoffice phone. We stand at the counter.

Moments go by. I feel my story momentum draining away. Consider: the clock is ticking, and I have recorded no interviews for this new story. The righteous indignation of the crusading journalist--yes, it is a rare but real phenomenon--can be tempered by such logistics. Okay. But there is still an important story here. You don't just discard hazardous waste in the dumpster. Somebody could get hurt. It's a lead story, for Pete's sake, on my first day on the job.

A further delay. I shift on my feet and realize that my clothes are actually starting to dry in the air conditioned environment. Fotch seems to enjoy watching a small blonde haired girl picking her nose. That somehow reminds me that I really must call in my whereabouts to the newsroom, but the sound of the cop's fingers drumming on the receptionist's countertop gets her attention, and this time her call produces a nurse.

"Dr. Wetlands will see you now," she announces in the superior manner of the medical professional. I put away my phone.

Hurry. We follow the nurse through a door to Wetlands' disheveled office. She's waiting behind her desk. Wearing her glasses this time. Her tone is measured. "I understand there's a problem, Mr. Gamble. But I didn't imagine you had already enlisted the aid of law enforcement."

"Actually, he's here to watch me."

"Okay. Thank you, officer. I'll call if I need you again."

But he doesn't leave. "Actually, I think I may need to hear what this reporter has to say, and what is going on."

Wetlands looks surprised. "Okay, I guess." She turns to me, with a tone of curiosity rather than anger. "So, why were you in the garbage dumpster?"

I calculate that she might actually bend our way on this. She's new, this wasn't her mistake. "I witnessed someone throwing away boxes of used syringes and needles. We recorded it on video. I'm now trying to find out who did this, who approved it, and why. Can I ask you some questions while Billy here videotapes us?"

"I'm not ready to answer these questions on tape," Wetlands fidgets. She doesn't know. But she's responsible. Sigh. "Most places have a contractor that handles this. But I'm not sure of the routine on this here."

"Who was supposed to take care of this?"

"I'm not going to say anything more until I investigate this matter further."

The clock is ticking and I have a story to produce. "I will wait here until you find out. Otherwise, I will tell Billy here to start recording with his camera, which could make this look even worse than what it might be."

Wetlands shows anger now. "You don't have to threaten me, Mr. Gamble. I'm well aware of the ramifications. My instinct is to throw you out of here," she glances at the officer, "but I want to show you we are ready to clean house, right here, right now. So please be patient while I do what I can to explore this situation."

Um, okay. That's reasonable. In a difficult moment she has given me more than most would. I sit tight while she and the officer leave to confront someone. Or, I should say, we "stand tight." The guest chairs are still covered in...boxes. Cardboard boxes. Memory flash. There's a pile of boxes somewhere else here. They are brown, though, not white. I ease out of Wetlands' office. Think. Look for some cue to jog the memory. Boxes. Yes, piles of boxes. In front of me is yet another medical office hallway. People, doors, carpet, drop ceiling, fluorescents. Doors. A closet door. That's it. The brown boxes were in front of a closet door, right?

I have to talk to someone at the station. I pull out my phone and start to punch the numbers, but my attention is quickly drawn away. At the end of the hallway Wetlands re-appears, accompanied by three others. One has a white coat, the other wears a suit. The third wears a blue work shirt and jeans. The officer is not there. They confer. Flustered talk, rising and falling in volume. They disperse. Wetlands breaks away, comes towards me, eyeglasses flapping purposefully at the end of a lanyard. She looks angry. This is not my fault, I remind myself.

"The Board isn't going to like this. At all," she tells me, adding to herself, "And in my second week, too."

I offer a sympathetic look but stay silent. Let her talk. "Where's your cameraman? Let's do this."

As we return to her office, Fotch jumps, caught fiddling with some knickknack on her bookshelf. "I wasn't doing anything!" he protests, unnecessarily.

We ignore him.

Wetlands sits down behind her desk, and looks out the window. Still raining. "If I'm going to straighten up things here, I guess it might as well start with this." My heart flutters with the joy of a lead story. And I feel bad for Wetlands. In that order.

"Billy, set up the camera," I order, quietly. Don't want to startle the quarry.

"All set, boss. Just pin the lav mic on her and we're good to go."

So he has been doing more than just fiddling around with the knickknacks. Good boy. Roll tape.

"Doctor Wetlands, how long have boxes of used needles been piling up in a closet or hallway here in the Health Department?"

She's thrown off by my immediate frontal assault, but recovers quickly. "I guess you noticed the boxes when you were here earlier. It looks like needles have been improperly disposed of for about six months."

Feeling merciful, I keep the interview short. Wetlands tells me there's apparently no current contract for disposing needles. Somehow it expired half a year ago. They were simply collected and stored in a closet. Eventually, a janitor took it upon himself to dump the boxes. He didn't know it was illegal but did realize it was a shortcut; that's why he did it quietly. My appearance in the dumpster freaked him out. No kidding. This never happened before, to her best knowledge. I can put it down to poor past management, but Wetlands wouldn't pass the buck.

"Who was responsible for letting the contract expire and allowing the needles to collect in a closet?" I ask.

"I'm the third Health Director in a year, so it may have simply slipped through the cracks," Wetlands tells me. She's not claiming a mea culpa. The Board of Health has been here all along.

"When do you think it would have come to your attention, had we not seen what happened?" A tough one to ask someone who is clearly trying to fix things. You never know, however, what a sharp edged question will provoke.

Under the circumstances, Wetlands can't become angry. But the question is audacious. So she allows herself to be glib. "I'm certain that I or one of the other managers here would have questioned the janitor as to what he was doing." She tries for self-assurance. "It would have been only a matter of minutes." So there.

Our welcome is officially worn out. I don't plan to bother any patients to get their reaction. With time growing short, I've got to get back to the station to do some research. Among other things, I have to find out which agency may be responsible for oversight on something like this. Federal? State? Local? The officer has departed without a word, but I assume he will be pretty busy the next few hours.

Oh yeah, I have to write and edit the story. I glance at my wristwatch-- its due in an hour and a half. Yow.

We head out the front door this time. The rain is subsiding, I'm a mess, but I still reflexively open my umbrella. Time to try the phone again, to call the station. Got a signal this time. Calzone answers.

"Gretchen, this is Wil Gamble."

She's perpetually distracted, even while directing a forceful question. "Gamble where in the world are you? Did Fotch get you lost?"

"Long story, Gretchen. But you'll--"

"I don't want to hear it. Talk to Tracy Scott about your story." Sudden telephone muzak. I'm on hold. Moments later, Scott's rich voice fills the phone. She sounds like she needs to be assured this new guy can manage his simple assignment.

"So do you have the flu shot story or not? I'm planning it for the B-block in the Five o'clock show."

"Tracy, I haven't been able to call before now, but the story has changed pretty seriously." I explain in a hurry. Instead of sounding excited or thankful, Scott's voice is angry. I hear cursing.

"You mean at this hour of the day I've got to rip apart my newscasts and change everything around? Why in the world didn't you let anyone know what was going on over there?"

Again, I try to explain. But producers rarely comprehend the challenges reporters face in the field. To be fair, Scott is telling herself that reporters don't comprehend the challenges producers face of blowing up a newscast at the last minute.

Ultimately, I end up with the lead story at 6. To me, that means a few extra minutes to prepare. As a result, another reporter's deadline just got bumped up, so that person won't be too happy with the new reporter, either. I'm making friends everywhere.

We pull into the SUV stable and park. Fotch grabs the camera, me the tripod and my manbag. Finally, the rain has stopped, leaving behind a steel gray sky. Many parking lot lights are on despite the hour, ignited by trigger-happy light-sensors. I am still somewhat heavy with humidity, until we hit the door. Sudden, evaporating air conditioning sucks us in. In five minutes my hair is dry.

In the meantime, Fotch removes the SD card from the camera, heads to an edit bay. It's a standard videographer quality assurance check, even for substandard videographers. They want to be the first to see their triumphs and mistakes. Especially, so they can explain away their mistakes.

I toss down the manbag in my new cube; gotta comb my hair, straighten my tie. In the cool indoors, my clothes suddenly feel quite clammy.

"You aren't going to front this live, looking like that," observes Collingwood, coming over. "I don't suppose you have a backup wardrobe here yet."

"Nope. Tracy Scott says she'll just take a straight package." That's a pre-recorded report, without me appearing live on camera to introduce it.

At least we shot that standup inside the trash dumpster.

In any case, Collingwood wants to know what I've got. And he's not just curious. What proofs do we have? Is anyone being left out who has a stake in it? What information do we still need? Will it be interesting visually?

Walter Wilson comes puffing up. A post-it note dangles haphazardly from his sleeve. How did he learn about this report?

"What about the Board of Health?" he inquires, distractedly. "What about the Board members? Aren't they going to look bad here because you know the Director is new and I hear that she's pretty hot but they, I mean the Board members aren't. I mean, they might be hot but they aren't necessarily new."

"Doesn't the Director speak for the Board?" Collingwood asserts.

"She didn't even consult with them!" he answers.

"Okay, Walter, which one of them called you?" asks Collingwood, quietly. It's pretty obvious.

Wilson is instantly flustered, his moral right to intervene nipped in the bud. So he simply doesn't answer the question. "Shouldn't we consider running this story later, like tomorrow, after we've had more time to check things out?"

What's left to check out?

"We've got everything on video, Walter," I answer. "There aren't any questions left to answer, other than: 'Who's going to jail?' If a Board Member wants to give me a quote, I'd be glad to include it."

"You're new here." Wilson starts with me but immediately turns to Collingwood. "This guy doesn't know anything about the way things work in this town because you know people will blame the Board Members and they really didn't have anything to do with it so let's get one of them on camera for an interview to include in this package."

"No, Walter. The story is airtight. At this point a quote will do. And then we can keep it alive better with an on camera interview tonight or tomorrow, if they still want to do it. Anyways, if we're really missing something, it's a resident who is outraged about this hazardous neglect of public safety."

Beaten, Wilson retreats, sniveling. "Well, if the station gets sued, I did what I could to stop it."

Collingwood watches him go, then turns to me. "Walter isn't much good around here when it comes to news content. But he is well-connected in this community. A lot of people would like to control our content by controlling him. You can't forget that. Fortunately, without meaning to, he helps clarify the 'right and wrong' in journalism by just opening his mouth. You just have to do the opposite."

Sherman Follicle has been following along from his cubicle. "That's pretty easy, Carl, coming from you. Walter's contacts bring us some good stories."

Collingwood considers. His conscience is pricked, for gossiping like this with a newbie. "Yes, Sherman, they do. They just shouldn't expect to control the content of those stories." Back to me. "Wil, go to it. Should be a good story."

I head into the edit bay just as Fotch ejects the SD card from the machine. "Looks good," he assesses, handing it to me. He doesn't look me in the eye, though, as he heads out, a little too quickly.

Alone now, I sit. The edit bay is the size of a closet. There's two linked monitors, computer tower, digital upload device, and keyboard ranged across a work counter. A tape machine sits lonely for those times when we need to use footage from the station's old tape archive. The overhead lights are set low, about 40 watts, to make it easier to view the editing monitors. A second computer, for script-writing, waits on the side. I insert the SD card into the upload machine and watch it work. Despite the obvious rain, I see fairly-clear video of a man tossing a brown box into the dumpster. Cool. Each time Fotch stops recording ends a video clip. Next one: Dr. Juniper Wetlands appears in close-up. It's the interview after our discovery. Except...she's in a fog. It's a gray haze clouding her appearance. Oh, no. The video is bad: I've been Fotched!

Must find The Fotcher.

Blindly, I stagger into the bright lights of the newsroom. No fog here. "Fotch!" I holler into the vacuum of growing deadline-induced noise. Naturally, there's no response. Everyone there has heard this desperate call before. I run towards the Cage. Some people watch me, knowingly.

"Fotch!"

A couple of photogs are in the Cage. Fotch isn't one of them. Norman Wallflower is. Does he ever leave?

"You looking for Billy Fotch? He went to get a sandwich."

"His video looks screwed up. It's important."

Wallflower looks as if my priorities are what's screwed up.

"You didn't give him a lunch break. You took him away from his lunch." He pauses as if to begin a college lecture, or to lodge a union grievance. "Okay, you're new. Here's your lesson for the day: you need to give your shooters a lunch break."

"I couldn't plan on breaking news, buddy," I responded, bitterly. "And he left me standing in the rain."

"He says you left him. He couldn't figure out where you went, so he thought he was clear to take a federally-mandated break from work."

"My video is fogged up. Are you saying this is the price I'm paying because Fotch didn't get lunch?" At my age, I should know better. It's not cause and effect. But in the eyes of the videographers, I had better learn The Facts Of Life.

Wallflower pauses. "Let me come look at it." He moves slowly; I'm wound up. I could race to the front office, up all the steps to Eriss' apartment, jump out the window, and circle the outside of the building two times holding hands with Warden The Doorman before Wallflower languidly makes his way to my edit bay.

But I already know nothing can be done. Anyone who wears eyeglasses knows what it's like to move from humid and hot to dry and cool. Outdoors to indoors, your glasses fog up. So can a video camera, even a professional-grade one. Our camera began recording in a climate-controlled setting, then moved out into, well, thoroughly "humid" conditions outside. Then we moved back to the dry air conditioning inside. Fotch simply couldn't tell in his viewfinder, or chose to not to.

Wallflower can't do anything about it. He doesn't say a word--doesn't have to--before he departs. He shrugs, wordlessly, after viewing a few seconds of the Wetlands interview. Can't "fix this in post"--the post-production facility--the way you can with some other video recording errors. Soon after Wallflower departs, Nettles hears my ranting, alone in the edit bay. Assessing the situation, glancing in at me, she shrugs her shoulders and advises: "You've been Fotched."

Yes, I noticed. Still, it's remarkable. His misadventures have acquired the status of a verb? Breathtaking. Despite this, he's still employed.

Needing Collingwood, I rush into the newsroom and make a right turn towards his office. Not there. Gretchen is too busy to say where he is. Walter Wilson? My God. Okay, I try him.

"Carl?" he responds. "Why do you wanna know where Carl is? Do you want me to tell him something for you? It's true that he owes me a breakfast burrito on account of this bet we had when that big hurricane hit North Carolina last year. I said it would be a Category 3 when it made landfall and Carl didn't think it would be that strong so I bet him and I was right but he never paid up, 'cause he said he never agreed to bet on something that might destroy and kill..."

"Walter!" I nearly howl. "Where is Carl right now?"

"In the men's room," he replies, meekly and succinctly.

Don't remember where The Head is located, but I'm not going to risk more conversation by asking the original Talking Head. I rush by Gretchen; she recognizes my panic. "Men's room is down that hall," she points, guessing the wrong need but the right answer.

Adrenaline flowing, my vision is jarred by my pounding feet. I have no peripheral vision. People, sounds, objects become non-entities. My focus is solely on getting down the hall. Where is the restroom, where is it? Now I hear something quiet and remote: a toilet flush. Whoosh. I'm drawn to it. Hurrying down the hall, I slam through a wood door and spy Collingwood washing his hands.

He doesn't look up. "What's the matter?" he asks, quietly.

I explain. Collingwood methodically works the problem.

"How does the audio sound?"

"It's fine."

"Normally I'd say to go back and interview the Health Director again. We have standards here, such as not using video that is so flawed that it distracts the viewer. In this case, I'm guessing there's little chance the Health Director will want to do that interview a second time. And... her comments are essential to the credibility of the story."

I try, "We could run a soundbite from her and explain what happened to the picture."

Uh uh. "That has to get by Walter Wilson, the Executive Producer--who is in charge of the look of the show. No good. That would give him his excuse to keep the story from running, or at least, limiting it." Collingwood briskly leads me out of the restroom and back towards the newsroom.

"It seems like the only option," he continues, "is to run the best soundbite from her and cover most of it with b-roll--extra video of the dumpster and the health department. You will just have to report the story live on the set in the studio. No taped package this time."

Seems reasonable. That also takes much of the deadline pressure off. I won't have to edit an entire "package," just one soundbite and various b-roll shots. We reach the edit bay. Observing my clothes, Collingwood gives me something else to worry about.

"I think you will want to borrow an extra jacket and tie I have in my office. Come and look."

Uh, yeah. I don't want to be introduced to this town looking like I slept in my clothes all night. In a pool.

Heading back into the edit bay, I'm calmer now. Funny, I nearly forgot that it is my first day on the air here. I edit the video, go to my desk and write a script. Selecting a soundbite from Wetlands is something I want to handle carefully. She took a chance in speaking with us, hoping to seem upfront with this sudden scandal. It's easy to manipulate small segments of an interview to twist the meaning of what the speaker said. And it's complicated even further by the foggy video, which could subliminally communicate that she is somehow shady. I don't want Wetlands to take the fall for this.

Return to the restroom to clean up. Collingwood's silk tie knots nicely but his jacket feels a little snug. And, uh, I do indeed spend a quarter on a spritz of imitation cologne from the dispensing machine that Wilson told me about. Back at my desk I find my IFB earpiece and review the script a final time. And then take a moment to resolve a unique identity crisis. For reporters new to a newsroom, the easiest thing to mess up is the "sig out." "Signature out" is the self-identification that closes the story. It becomes second nature to refer to yourself as "Wilson Gamble, KRAM Channel 8 Action News" after the 500th time. I have a new identity here. "Wilson Gamble, Newschannel 99, Where We're Right 99 Times Out of 100." Would hate to get that wrong.

Okay, it appears that I'm good to go. Story is ready, I feel confident. A few nerves. Ready for my close-up, Mr. DeMille. Everything is quiet in newsroom. I'd better find my way to the news set. The news set? Uh, where is the studio? I didn't get to that part of the station tour. Don't panic. Where'd everybody go? Of course--over at the panel of televisions to watch the newscasts.

Gretchen Calzone is willing to lead me there. She weaves down a meandering hallway. "You cleaned up pretty well," she remarks. Instinctively, I glance at my tie, my sleeves, my fly. Knotted? Buttoned? Zipped? Good. Ignoring a red flashing "On Air" light hanging from the ceiling, Calzone pushes through a pair of big iron double doors. Instantly, we are behind the news set. Waiting in the "wings." The only lights in the room are directed at the news set, around the corner. Calzone and I face crude 2x4 wood framing. On the other side is the plywood background that viewers see every night: a bank of fake monitors. It's a Potemkin Village scene. Beyond this partition I spot cameras, a floor director, and the darkness shrouding everything behind them. I hear but can't see Lavinia Fern reading. Her voice echoes in the cool, warehouse-sized studio.

"That's our Five O'clock News, thanks for joining us." She almost smiles.

Jefferson Adams offers a goofy grin of his own, concluding, "I'll be back, with more news and Lavinia too, coming up next, here on Newschannel 99, Where We're Right 99 Times Out of 100."

By the way, who in the world came up with that tagline?

The red microphone light inside the studio goes out: Commercial break. That's my cue, so I wander out to the set.

Ignoring me, Fern leafs through some updated 6pm scripts just delivered by Tracy Scott, marking little changes. Adams holds up a brown compact with a rather, uh, compact mirror inside. It is way too small for his large features, so he revolves it in front of his face, taking in one section of his wonderful features at a time. There is a third chair behind the granite and wood news desk. The position is marked "sports" underneath. A floor director seats me, points out a circle marked on the edge of the desk. "Belly-up there so we can set up your camera," he says, attaching a microphone to my lapel. I insert my IFB. My hand shakes slightly while plugging in to the IFB receptacle box hidden under the table. New job. Jitters, even after all these years.

Fern notices me, formally. "Looks like you got a good story today."

I nod. Adams adds, lightly but not sympathetically, "I heard your video got Fotched." Before I can answer, the station theme music flares up. The clock waits for no man.

Over our IFBs, Scott announces, "Stand by. We open under video, it's a cold open. Lavinia and Jeff start on Camera 2. Both turn to Camera 3 for a 'three shot' to introduce, uh, Wilson. Wil... your close-up is on Camera 1." I look around. Which camera is which? Numbers are printed on each one but the location of each is still not yet familiar.

The newscast is underway. Newschannel 99 graphics fly in, pictures of the "news team" appear while an announcer tells everyone which station they are watching and what city we are in. Next appears video of the poncho man and the dumpster.

Fern projects a steady, cool, professional voice. "It's hazardous to your health--and it comes straight from the Health Department. Good evening, I'm Lavinia Fern."

Now the picture dissolves to the two anchors live on the news set.

"And I'm Jeff Adams. Caught, red-handed by a Newschannel 99 camera. A Reproach County Health Department employee improperly disposing of hundreds of used needles and syringes. And the health department 'fesses up, on camera, only to us."

Both anchors twist slightly in their seats at this pre-determined juncture, while Adams addresses me.

"Newschannel 99's Walter Gamble joins us with the exclusive on this needle nuisance."

What--"Walter?" Okay. Mistake with my name? Intentional? Slip up? Name confusion: Walter Wilson, Wilson Gamble? Whatever. No time to lose. I begin by addressing the anchors, then turn to a single camera. At least I'm thinking about this possible slight rather than worrying about nerves.

"It's playing with fire, and the flame is disease, Lavinia and Jeff." At this point I turn away from the anchors and to my own camera. "Needles and syringes come into intimate contact with disease every day. And today, boxes of used and potentially-infected needles and syringes were simply tossed into an open dumpster behind the Reproach County Health Department. And we've got the proof."

The video rolls.

"This afternoon, we discovered this man--later identified as an employee of the Health Department--throwing away brown cardboard boxes in this garbage dumpster behind the Health Department. When we checked the contents of the boxes, it was clear that a major mistake was being made. That's because this is a highly-regulated activity. There are strict federal and state laws that require medical professionals to properly dispose of their needles and syringes. But those laws were clearly disregarded this afternoon.

"Health Department Director Doctor Juniper Wetlands has been on the job less than two weeks, but still took responsibility for what she called 'a failure in the chain of command.'"

I wait for the soundbite to play. Take a deep breath, try to remain focused. All has gone well up until now. The video is foggy, of course, but only on screen for three seconds. It looked worse in the edit bay, perhaps because I expected it to be perfect then. That expectation is now gone.

More b-roll pops up while Wetlands speculates on how this error could have happened. She finishes, and my face returns.

"The Health Department is in the middle of a Flu Shot program, so it appears that most of the needles and syringes were used for that purpose. Wetlands insists this is the only time this has happened. She refused to name the employee we caught at the dumpster, but says he has been already suspended with pay while the Health Department conducts an internal investigation. There will be other investigations, however. We learned late today that the state Division of Public Health and federal Department of Health are both considering their own investigations, and whether any charges should be brought."

I turn back to the two anchors on a "three shot."

"After examining the dumpster, investigators say it appears all the needles and syringes have been accounted for. But it remains to be seen who will be held accountable for this blunder."

Fern asks a scripted question.

"How are needles and syringes supposed to be disposed, Wilson?"

"Well, first, there are medical 'sharps' boxes that take needles, and other hazardous materials disposal containers for syringes. They are carefully marked--and don't look like brown cardboard boxes. Professional disposal companies are often contracted to remove these boxes and recycle the materials." I expect a "Thank you, Wilson" from the anchors, a medal from the station, and at least a beer from Collingwood. But Adams throws me a curve.

"What are members of the Board of Health saying about all this?"

Oomph. Television equivalent of a sucker punch. Ask a question someone isn't expecting and for which he may not be prepared. A clever one, too, in this case, perhaps straight from Walter Wilson. The Health Director should be able to speak for the Board. But this Health Director was not in place when events led up to what happened today. So it's possible she does not speak for the Board. If I have to, I can reply with the trusty but rusty "I'm looking into it" and will report the answer in a later newscast. And in this day and age, some newsrooms counsel their reporters to answer, "That's internet content, visit our website to find out!" But this is my first day on air--my introduction to Filterboro. A good reporter knows his story and should be able to cover everything. Quickly. My mind competes against my body, however. I have to consciously restrain my hands from becoming fists. No time to think of places I'd rather be. Can't think up creative insults. I must think of something of substance.

"Well, Jeff," I start, sharp emphasis on "Jeff." "I think, uh, that they may not be happy about this." No kidding. Fern twitches. Adams smirks. Must do better. "All this developed late in the day." That sounds like an excuse. I think of Wilson once more. "Newschannel 99 has been in touch with at least one Board Member who was not happy with our investigation." Well, they were in touch with *us*, but I'm not splitting hairs. "They have to meet together before taking any action. And with an internal investigation getting set to start, few Board members may be willing to speak their minds." Better, I hope.

Finished with games, Adams turns back to a different camera and moves on.

"The manhunt for an accused murderer moves into its second day. Still no success for investigators searching the wilds of Frippin County for Luther Post... ."

Quietly, I unplug the IFB and detach my microphone. Insults, curses, threats reel through my mind. Adams finishes introducing Tyler Hubbell's package. The microphone light goes out while her pre-recorded report plays. I'm off-balance due to the rush of nerves and anger. Must cool out. But I have to say something or the pompous anchor may typecast me as helpless or weak.

"So this is the way you want it?" I ask.

Adams coolly leafs through some scripts. "Gotta be ready for anything on live TV, buddy." Fern glances at him disdainfully.

"If that's all you can think of, man, this is gonna be a breeze." Peace out. Stride through the wings, out the double doors.

Engrossed in the competition's newscasts, nobody pays attention to me as I re-enter the newsroom. Wilson is on the phone, Calzone is gone for the day. Collingwood lightly pats my back, offers a "Good story," and turns to the monitor displaying Channel 11's broadcast. Nevertheless, this is more thanks than Little Napoleon ever gave me.

No medals, no free beer. But real satisfaction. On my first day on the job, I turn lemons into premium limoncillo. High stress, obstacles, conflict, overactive bladder, diplomacy, sacrifice, bad fortune, and good fortune. A good friend once called it a "news high." But to station management, the final accounting is that I filled one minute and 38 seconds of our newscast in a way that probably was not detrimental to the station's interests. The content had better not turn out to be wrong. In any case, my day will not be over until I fill some space on the station's website. A drink beckons tonight. Another 1:38 or so to fill again beckons tomorrow.

4

On anybody's first week of work, each day seems finely detailed and self-contained. The small discoveries of meeting new people, arranging the workspace, and learning the office dynamics are all a part of establishing one's routine. "Oh, let's see. Tuesday was when I learned where the break room is!" The individual days don't start to run together until later, when patterns become old-hat. For me, right now, even the routine things aren't routine yet. There's still a little buzz each day when I pull into the tree-shrouded drive and turn into the WDMZ lot. Unfortunately, I don't notice the more telling details of that little drive through the property until later.

Wednesday comes. Despite a mild hangover, I follow-up on the loose needles story (after an extraordinarily-rapid investigation, the poncho man takes the fall; he's fired. Prosecution may follow). Viewers aren't outraged, however, and only one other media outlet picks up the story (on Saturday the NPR station, WTDS, does an 18 minute report after the story is effectually finished). Collingwood advises that the Great Silence is a matter of professional pride; even reports on matters of public safety are occasionally ignored by some media outlets when a competitor breaks an exclusive story. If they don't run the report, then they didn't get beat on it--right?

So, the story seems to lose steam quickly. No congressional inquiry, no cable network picks up the story, no one in the hierarchy is losing their job, so the story has no "legs." There could be federal and state investigations but that could take a while, so the story is suddenly...not a story. This happens sometimes.

Thursday comes. Since Newschannel 99 is tired of the needles story, I end up reporting on rumors of a textile mill closing.

Friday comes. I am assigned a report on the aftermath of an overnight fire at a lumberyard.

To begin the day, I finally submit my employment paperwork. I appreciate attention to detail, so everything is neatly and fully in place when I walk it up front and hand it in to Shelley Winters, er, Rose. Five minutes later--just before the Morning Meeting--my desk phone rings. It's Rose.

"Mr. Gamble, the records indicate that your paperwork is incomplete.

You will want to come here now and finish it. Until everything is complete, you will not be added to our payroll."

"What's wrong? What did I forget?"

Machine-like response. "Your driver's license was issued by a different state. You need an in-state driver's license to prove your identification with us and to be able to drive a company vehicle."

"I don't have a new license yet because I don't have a permanent residence here yet."

"Looks like you'd better find one," the machine in the beehive hair replies.

Later in the day, Collingwood says he will try to talk to Ivory Eriss to break the logjam. I really need to get paid. My meager savings account is rapidly becoming depleted and I hate to put anything on my credit card.

Then I consider the looming weekend, my first in a strange town. I've got too much time on my hands that could t-t-tick away with my sanity.

"What are you doing this weekend?" I ask Collingwood.

"Gonna have a few people over on Saturday," he replies, mildly. "Why don't you come by, about supper time. I can show you my boat."

"Your boat?"

"Sure. I've been working on it for years, never put it in the water. Getting close, though. And it gets me out of the house for a while, even if it's only out to the driveway. You'll understand that better when you have your own family."

"Okay, Carl." No, I don't understand. But I plan to, one day.

Another night in a motel. So transitory, depressing. Just me and the Johnnys: Bench on the mirror, Cash on the computer tablet, Walker Red in a plastic hotel cup. Rinse down and repeat. The only baseball game on cable is a laugher between the Yankees and Indians. Channel surfing quickly becomes tiresome.

I open a small window at the back of the room. It's about eye level. The sounds of the freeway roll in like ocean waves: roaring engines, rolling tires, rumbling semis, the occasional jittering of airbrakes as a truck slows to exit. The trance-like lullaby of the road.

It is a strange land along the interstate. Motels belong to the freeway, not the community where they happen to sit. They are a permanent fixture on the sideline of the flow of life. Nobody is planning for a future here. Inside my room there is no settled place to for me to drop my keys when I walk in. Certainly no empty wall for my Rockwell "Life" magazine poster. At least I can link my tablet to a Wi-Fi internet connection. And, a small fridge keeps my drinks cool.

No luck finding a permanent domicile so far. Saturday will be my first full day to look. Soon I will have to get back to the mountains to bring down the rest of my belongings. I miss my stuff, the familiarity of it. The motel is unfamiliar. The vague antiseptic smell. The way the drawers slide open too easily and the way the cheap comforter brushes roughly against my face. For now, I'm locked in lonely limbo. Back in the room, fast food arrayed on the bed, non-fast food drink in hand, I dig out a phone number and begin to dial. Long distance.

Voicemail. "Hi this is Megan. I'm out with Meathead right now. Or I forgot to recharge the battery on the phone. Or I'm looking for a lost bowling shoe. But you know what? I don't think I have ever been bowling. In any case, leave a message and I'll call you back, if I can remember the security code to check my messages."

I nearly hang up but change my mind.

"Megan, its Wil. I'm in Filterboro for my new job. Say 'hi' to Mamie for me. And don't forget to feed Meathead."

Megan: Pillow fights. Springtime meadows. The freshness of feathered blonde hair against my cheek. Happy, unassuming welcome. Bright, waiting smile. Pouty lower lip. For her, each new day is fresh and full of promise. She is untroubled by the past, largely because most of it slips daily from her recollection. Somehow, she recollects me, though. Mostly, anyways. We met in college in Pennsylvania, living on the same floor of the dormitory during our freshman year. Weeknights drinking iced coffee, munching biscotti, studying. Weekend nights drinking "shooters" and carousing. Long walks, cookouts, college football games, exploring by the river. She loved spicy Buffalo wings. There was school, then there was Megan. Not much else was important to me. The summer after our freshman year we found jobs near campus, stayed in the summer dorm. No classes, deep friendship. She was the substance, the light--not the heat--of that single summer. Each day had a morning, noon, and night. But romance never really occurred to us. We were friends. That's all. In fact, she dated several other guys. It didn't occur to me to wonder, "why not me?" I dated several other girls. Even as we double-dated, we seemed quietly linked. After the date we would check in with each other, chat about everything. For some reason, I simply believed her romantic happiness must be linked to another guy. Just figured we'd grow old together as friends.

Then, in the late fall of our sophomore year, her father died. Heart attack. So unnecessary. So unexpected.

Megan couldn't stay in school. She returned home to be with mom-- Mamie--in Youngstown, righting the family ship. My, how quickly the nuclear family can blow apart.

As it tends to do, life moved on at this crucial age. Megan fell behind by two college years, so she didn't come back to school. Eventually, though, she returned to Life As She Knew It. With a vengeance, apparently, I learned later. Informally interviewing several people who knew her at that time, I was able to piece most of it together. Community College in Youngstown led to drinking parties. A sketchy boyfriend. Drugs, eventually. At a party one night, she overdosed on something. Unconscious. Nobody called an ambulance; that would have ruined the party, dude. So she laid there, in a basement, the drugs eating away at her mind. Two days later she somehow staggered home. Been there ever since. Mother and daughter against the world. Believe me, living young in Youngstown, Ohio is Payment In Full for people on a payment plan.

We had been out of touch for a couple of years. College can keep you busy and Youngstown just seems so far away, no matter where you live. Then one night Mamie called, explained some things. But there was no way to prepare me for meeting Megan. Her feathered hair had become bottle-blonde and wildly teased. So was her smile and pouty lip. Heavy makeup--all of it a little off center, like a smudged watercolor. Her eyes were as vacant and gray as an old steel mill. She started calling me "Willie," as if that had always been her pet name for me. And the careful but stylish outfits of the past were replaced by leopard-print, spandex pants and a waist-length fur coat. Oh my. Who is this? Freak show? Freak out. I left ASAP.

Several Megan voicemails followed. Imploring. "You can call me if you want."

I didn't want, but eventually I did. Tough call, to make that first call. Megan had lost most of our shared memories, our secret language, our dreams. Yet she had hung on to some vague recollections and somehow held on to the belief that I was a friend to be trusted. And yes, I confess that I missed her presence. Megan isn't all there. Yet I love what is left just as much as what left.

To me, Megan represents the poignancy of innocence lost, the pain of life used up, yet meandering on. Almost like the parts of the space shuttle Challenger when it blew up, propelled pointlessly for a while by the force of the explosion.

So, my thoughts often return to college, recalling that long, hot summer. Thanks to my memory-editing, it gets better all the time. It's a difficult paradox for the journalist in me to accept, but in this case, "when the legend becomes fact...print the legend." So, today's Megan remains happy, as long as she is kept at arm's-length.

My previous job working for Little Napoleon was situated only three or four hours away from Youngstown. I rarely made it back there, though. It's much farther away now, here tonight in The Placid Place Motel. Yes, it's a strange land along the interstate. In a cellphone age, the motel landline has become an ornament; this phone does not ring. Lost in my unhappy thoughts, I take another sip. Eventually, even the sipping stops. The empty room recedes, and finally, I sleep into the weekend.

For once, a Saturday lives up to its expectations. Sunshine. Late-spring cool. One good thing about the phone's silence: I sleep 'til noon. That's too late for the motel breakfast scrum. I opt for a much more pleasant meal at a nearby family restaurant. While sitting there, I hear a good story idea.

Reporters publish or perish with their story ideas. Whether or not better news reports are ready to be assigned to them, news ideas are pitched during every morning meeting. We must present at least one that can be "turned" into a package that day. Its irresistible daily pressure, which changes your perspective. You are forced to look at all of life as a potential news story. This is where the resume cliché about "motivated self starters" becomes very real. You stay tuned in to as much as possible, always considering: how can I make a news story out of this? Your barber faces a new, somewhat onerous state training requirement. The convenience store always seems to be sold out of lighters. You overhear high school kids debating the hardest bike lock to pick. Wastewater utility workers seem to spend a lot of time near a creek that you pass on the way to work. There are many ways to develop story ideas. Keeping your eyes open is one of the best.

So. The restaurant. Old school family-style, straight down to the chrome-edged tables and mini-jukeboxes installed in each booth. This morning, a strange sign hangs from the host's podium. Rough, hand drawn letters on computer paper state: "No guacamole today." During my eggs, ham, biscuits and coffee I keep up a running conversation with the waitress. She's kind of pretty, so I don't mind that she lingers a moment after giving her my order. "Guacamole?" I ask. "This doesn't look like a Mexican restaurant." And, "How are you really supposed to pronounce 'guacamole,' anyways?" This disguises my real interest. You can't tell when some people will decide its none of your business. She lightly skips around my real question so later, when it's time for the check, I come to the point. "So, why no guacamole?"

The waitress thinks about the tip--her tip--at this point. She quietly explains the last two shipments of avocado have been bad, the boss wouldn't even offload them from the truck because they were frozen. Yes, other restaurants are in the same bind. Over the past two days, many customers have complained. And, no, they don't expect any more shipments for a couple of days.

There. A ready-made, home-grown news story to pitch. Not exactly a lead story, but something a lot of people will be interested to learn. What you call a "talker" or "water cooler" story because it's what co-workers will superficially chat about when they are tired of talking about the weather. It's a relief to have something to pitch Monday morning. It may be better than some other story they might propose for me to do, say on something like a shortage of leader dogs for the blind. The difference is: this is my story, I own it.

I begin my search for something else of my own or, at least, to rent. First, stop in at the Pump 'N' Run gas station next door. Prices along the interstate are a little high, but the rental car is running only on the memory of fumes. A minor but curious incident happens while I'm there. The payment device on the gas pump does not accept my debit card because it's from out of state. So I must head inside the convenience store to pay at the register.

The jangle of the bell over the door echoes inside the lonely aisles, filled with maps, muscle car magazines and enough junk food to keep Larry Groce happy for months. But there is a brief burst of activity behind the clerk's counter. I do a double take. One moment the clerk is aiming a camera at me. The next its nowhere in sight and he offers a welcoming smile. Creepy balding guy, jowly, with unhealthy-looking blotchy skin. My Spidey Sense tingles...or, in my case, my news story radar fires up. But I'm not even sure what I just saw, so there's nothing to do but pay my bill, pump the gas, and run.

The search for an apartment is just as mystifying. Co-workers have warned me that the market is tight and expensive. I start with the newspaper classifieds, check the free real estate magazines I find in the supermarket, and look around online. My phone calls weed out most places; they are full. Visits to two others shows why they are not. At one apartment complex I step around bullet casings, piles of trash, and at least one drug deal--just to get up to the office. Once there, the iron gated door is locked. I speak with someone inside for about 20 seconds on an intercom before realizing they aren't coming out. And I am not going in. So I move on.

Finally I find an apartment complex that happens to be a short drive from work." Shoddy Acres." Incredibly, an apparently-decent--and affordable--apartment is suddenly available. The agent, a tall, itchy woman named Lucy Clearinghouse, scratches her wild brunette head a lot. But she shows me an apartment that fits the bill. Clearinghouse explains someone pulled out of a lease agreement today, two days after signing. Wow, good timing, I guess. I make mental plans for the place: laying out my effects, finding the nearest supermarkets, liquor stores and restaurants. Don't forget the dry cleaners. I trace a new route to work. A fanfare of triumph follows.

After this success, even the Placid Place Motel doesn't depress me now. Back inside, there's even more excitement, such as it is. The light is actually blinking on the phone in my room, perhaps for the first time in a decade: Message for you, sir. Anticipation, as I punch in the antiquated security code. Who is it? Parents? Collingwood? Megan? Turns out, it's Everyone. The Trifecta.

First, laconic Collingwood. "Wil. I tried calling your cell, no answer. Want to let you know to come around five. We'll catch a few innings of the "Game of the Week" before the multitudes come tumbling in." He finishes by leaving road directions to his home. Quick, look at my cellphone. It has been off.

Beep. Followed by an admonition from my father to call my mother.

Beep. Then: "Hi Willie!" Bright, fresh sound. Lots of ambient noise in the background. Muzak? Children?" I'm in a mall, sitting and watching kids running around a play area. Wow, there are a lot of little kids here! I don't really know why we're here today but Mamie will be back soon to get me, I guess. I got a new blouse and a pair of... Oops! Waitaminute." Muffled sounds of Megan helping a child get up. I wait impatiently for several seconds. "There you go!" she launches the child back into the fray. Back to me--well, my voice mail. "Thanks for your call yesterday," she says, shyly. "I hate playing phone 'hide and seek' with you. But you can call me again if you want. It was raining here when we walked into the mall. Right now, though, I think Mamie and I have to... ." The message times out. It just ends. And I know I will never learn what Megan was going to say, because she will forget it and her mother probably will not know what she meant. Heavy sigh. But I save the message so I can listen to it over and over for the next seven days, lessening my loneliness.

I close the back window to the motel room and turn on the clunky old air conditioner, inserted below the front window of the room. Time for a nap to refresh. Unsurprisingly, I dream of a car ride with Megan on a river road. We are both silent until I turn into a school parking lot. Then, she unpacks something from the back of the pickup truck. It's a photo album, but I can't see it because of the glare of the sun. Megan drifts away as my dreams flit away to other trivialities.

The glare of the sun is starting to falter as I shower and dress. Fingering the directions written on the back of an abandoned news script, I drive out to Collingwood's house. On the interstate, it's the opposite direction of the television station. After I exit the freeway, my route takes me up long, straight hills. It's a freshly suburban area outside of Filterboro proper. The Land of Blooming Subdivisions, Sporadic Trees, Corner Gas Stations, Strip Malls, and Fast Food Restaurants.

I'm early, of course. Bouncing to another Cash CD, I force myself to drive around the neighborhood several times to be at least a few minutes late. The homes are spacious Spanish Colonials. Lots of arches and stucco. An SUV in every driveway, a chicken in every pot. Or, on every grill. As I park, the air is pungent with burning charcoal, lit propane, and smoking wood chips. My stomach actually growls. Telling it to shut up, I pass along a neatly trimmed walkway. Professional landscaping everywhere. My short-sleeved casual shirt flaps slightly in a breeze. Through a short courtyard entryway I find a double front door.

Collingwood answers with a smile and a beer. Good man. He's in dress slacks, golf shirt, and stainless steel magnetic sports bracelet. As at work, he looks at home, here at home.

"You came at a critical time. The grill is getting hot and the Tigers have a man on. Game's tied."

I offer him a six pack at the altar of the curious American tradition of trading beer for the promise of: other beer. Collingwood delivers, handing me a Newcastle Brown Ale. It might be a domestic tradition but I don't mind drinking an import.

We head into the house. It's wide and open: vaulted ceilings, wood floors. Chunky new furniture arrayed throughout the great room. Clean, white walls, dotted with artwork. One pretty piece of human sculpture waits for us.

"Welcome to our home," offers a handsome woman. Cultured, buttery voice. Hint of an accent. She's thin and cool, black hair pulled back severely. Pearls and upscale casual clothes. Although she's past 50, her sleeveless brown top reveals taut and smooth arms, topped with a tan. Neither is her back heavily swayed; a disciplined person. Definitely not now or ever before a fulltime mom.

"Wilson Gamble, this is my wife, Marie."

She moves a highball from right hand to left, so I may take her hand. My left hand holds the Newcastle. We exchange a couple of pleasantries, but she doesn't know who I am, and really couldn't care less, even though her courtesy won't allow me to escape without a few formalized questions. She moves in a completely different world. Distracted, Collingwood is drawn back into the baseball game so I soon follow him. We sit, he on an overstuffed recliner, me on a leather couch. Marie heads out to points unknown. A flat screen HDTV occupies a choice spot on the wall, where a Warhol might have rested.

As a kid, I was more of a fan of the game of baseball than a fan of a single team. One of the players I loved was Johnny Bench. But I preferred to try to copy the swing of Bench's teammate, Joe Morgan; the way he flapped his arm while waiting for the pitcher to throw the ball. Unfortunately, I could flap my arm but couldn't hit a curveball. Anyways, a Tigers-Blue Jays game doesn't particularly mean much to me. Yet I stay engaged, out of respect for Collingwood.

"I remember my first game at Tiger Stadium," he recalls during a half-inning commercial. "Rain threatened. But Al Kaline and Norm Cash hit home runs and Hank Aguirre beat the Yankees. My Dad and I sat in these green wooden box seats, with a warm, thick chain separating our box from the one next to us."

"Sounds like a happy memory."

"It was. But as a kid, other things stay with you. I remember counting the number of times the hot dog vendor came by. Must have been eight or nine times before my attention wandered. Even during the game we listened to Ernie Harwell announce the play-by-play on a transistor radio. Afterwards we ate dinner at a Daly's Drive-In." Collingwood stops. "And then I remember there was a solitary Yankee fan who wasn't intimidated by being completely outnumbered. He hollered like crazy early in the game, booing the Tigers, cheering his own team. He was obnoxious and unpopular, and he made me mad. But he hung in there even when we took the lead, didn't give up or back down. That really impressed me."

The present-day Tigers score a run, drawing Collingwood's attention back to the present. "C'mon, boys," he mutters.

Soon, however, the doorbell rings, echoing in the oversized room. Unwillingly, Collingwood breaks away to get it. Voices...ah, yes. This is only the start of the evening's festivities. I stand in greeting as two men in their 40's enter the chamber.

"Wil, I'd like you to meet the Mayor of Filterboro, Fulsome Parody. And this is Marvel Thyme, the Boss of Reproach County." His eyes twinkle at me. "Gentlemen, this is Wilson Gamble, our newest reporter."

They shake hands but regard me warily. As a "Reporter," I'm nature's predator of any politician. Thyme wears all white--like a cricket player--a cheap hairpiece, and a vacant expression. But Parody isn't vacant, he knows stuff. I can sense it. He can sense that I sense it. Et cetera.

"Didn't you do the story on the needles being thrown away at the Health Department?" he asks, cautiously. I nod, warily.

"Don't worry about it," interjects Collingwood. "Wilson's alright." Turns to me, with a jest. "You're not looking for any stories here to pitch at Monday's morning meeting, are you?"

Looking straight at Parody, I reply, "In fact, I've already got something." I pause, just to have fun with him.

Sure enough, everyone stiffens, ever so slightly. I guess I made an impression in my first week. They smile, though, when I tell them about the guacamole.

"No scandal there," observes Thyme, who speaks whinily. Parody shoots him a quick, keen glance. Why use the word, "scandal?" I ignore it.

Everybody now has a beer and we adjourn to the ballgame. Let's be buds, with some Newcastles, at least on this Saturday.

A grill sits in heat out on a back patio. I can see it through side-by-side sliding glass doors that open to an oversized screened-in pool area. Marie moves quietly in and out of the room on unknown errands. She might throw a salad together but is clearly not the grilling type. Finally Collingwood pays it some attention and we ultimately get some beer-soaked bratwursts to go with the game.

No one, it turns out, is a Tigers fan except Collingwood. So, as the game starts to disintegrate, everyone's attention moves elsewhere. Music plays. The sun fades to black, the liquor cabinet opens, more people arrive. Many from the station. I find myself pleased to see Gretchen Calzone enter. She seems smaller in civilian life: less substantial, more vulnerable. Her brown hair now looks teased--intentionally--not frizzed. Her blue eyes are clear, focused. With a hint of innocent pink lipstick touching a smile, I realize she really looks attractive. Best part is, she walks straight over to me. Thank goodness, for once she isn't yelling at the top of her voice.

"Hey, buddy. Didn't know that you'd be here." She smiles. "Not much going on over at the Placid Place Motel this evening?"

I have a reply all dressed up and waiting. "Well, the Fraternal Order of Moose convention was getting a little out of hand. You know, older guys wearing nothing but huge furry hats chasing the maids down the hall. Polkas 'til dawn. The Pabst Blue Ribbon was flowing. I almost stayed for it."

"Sounds tempting. Have you found a permanent place to live yet?"

"Actually, just today. An apartment at Shoddy Acres."

"Oh. Pretty close to work, right?"

"Yeah. Even closer to the Laundromat. I'll be hitting you up for quarters."

"I spend them all in the soda machine. Once you find enough of them it'll be the highlight of your week."

She doesn't know it, but it just might be. I start to ask where she does her laundry, but Gretchen is suddenly distracted. She half turns toward the door. "Artie! Over here." Turns back to me. Suddenly, she seems a little embarrassed. "Um, I want you to meet Artie, the, uh, guy I'm seeing. He was parking the car."

Oh. Okay. Guy in black leather jacket saunters over. Big. Overdose of suntan. Maybe steroids. Bored. Removes reflective teardrop sunglasses with a swoop of his paw, er, hand. Stops to slick back his black hair. Way cool. No way we're going to have a conversation involving more than two syllable words.

"Artie," begins Gretchen. "This is Wilson Gamble, our new reporter. Wil, this is Artie Torpid."

He grabs the tips of my fingers to crush them in a "handshake."

"So, you're one of those," I observe, looking him straight into his chin.

"One of those...what?" he replies, squaring up, assuming a challenge. He's ready to rumble on a moment's notice, baby.

I call him out. "One of those people who doesn't feel he's quite on the same level as everyone else until he attempts to make someone feel weak."

"You don't have much of a grip, man."

"Boys..." Gretchen attempts to insert.

"That's okay. I'd rather shake hands with Jim Beam. You keep practicing with your squeeze ball toy...Artie. Nice to see you, Gretchen."

"See ya, Wil," her voice trails off as I leave. I know she's watching me as I move away. Also, I know Artie Torpid is pretending to focus on something else, to buy time to decide if he's just lost a testosterone battle that just a minute ago he appeared to have won.

Heading to the liquor bar, things soon get whiskey hazy. Next thing I know, there's a hundred people in the room. I'm occasionally one of them.

This is not a party that will echo down the corridors of time. No crazy hijinks, drunken fights, or unusual hook-ups...yet. No police, except Sheriff Don Dank, who as a guest is "arresting" a pretty brunette with some stories about high speed pursuit techniques. Maria Collingwood is everywhere, quick-chatting the lonely, filling glasses, introducing people. Everyone seems very intent on drinking. Old school drinks like Tom Collins, Brandy Alexanders, and Panamas. Anything with liquor.

I'm not very involved in this. My major in college might have been Observation. A People Watcher. Studying human nature. Now, I observe an endless number of fairly-interesting people flow by. To anyone who will listen, a woman in red and in her late 40's introduces herself as President of Reproach County College. She stands just a little too close to every guy she with whom she talks, including me. Breathily, she tries to engage me in a discussion about continuing education. It's not registering with me. Then there's a slickly-groomed young guy who is a salesman for National Tobacco. I'm not buying. Walter Wilson spills a drink on Marvin Finkbeiner but doesn't stop talking. For a moment I catch a glimpse of Gretchen and Artie arguing near the front door. But at that point I am distracted by a guy with a huge smile, who tries to convince me to do a story on a printing company that is performing a crucial community service by taking donations for the area Boys Club. They aren't giving anything themselves, just setting out the cardboard box. He wants me to get the word out so others will donate. Eventually, his grin starts to blur and I lose track of what he's saying. That isn't taken as being rude; stirring his drink, the salesman loses track, as well.

Breaking away from the Human Smile, I return to the bar to refill my glass yet again. I prop myself up against the furniture. Someone mentions the time and I check my watch. It takes five or 30 slow seconds to focus on the numbers: 2:30. Don't see Collingwood any more. Nor Calzone. I assume she and The Leatherman have left the building. Perhaps, I tell myself, fresh air would mix better with a fresh drink.

Unsteady, I kind of slowly bull my way through the room and slide through a glass door to the patio. Warm, moist air intoxicates me almost as much as my drink. Must stop to catch my breath. It's easy to take air conditioning for granted after being in it for a few hours.

Making my way across the patio, from a distance I turn back to observe the party. The lights seem harsher from out here in the gentle night, but the sounds are muffled. That's more my style: from the outside, looking in. Like sitting along press row. Inside, familiar faces mix with the others. Tyler Hubbell, surrounded by about 15 men of varying ages and prospects. Sherman Follicle, showing off sing-along skills on the piano. Lavinia Fern, earnestly plotting with two other stylish, pearl-laden women.

Another sip from my glass. Warmish. Think I forgot ice this time. Or, maybe it melted, who knows? Wobbly, I look around. My eyes are still adjusting to the night. Low lights glow everywhere: from inside the pool, along the landscaping. A few dim bulbs burn along a lengthy patio that runs along a wing of the house. It's covered by an awning. Everything outside of it, I learn, is wet; there has been a light rain. Evidently, that's why no one else is out here. So I stay away from the pool and wobble along the patio. Mostly padded chaise lounges and little cast iron cafe tables under the awning.

There, reclining, is Ivory Eriss.

She wears what looks like a collection of flowing silk scarves. Her silver cigarette holder smolders. Hair let loose this time, creating an entirely different effect than in her apartment. More of a wuh-man, you might say. Appearing a little younger, also. Her head lazed back on a pillow, she hums something complicated. A little off key. Or, perhaps I'm just hearing it off-key. In my moment of recognition, her head lolls my way. Too late. I'm frozen like a bunny on a freeway.

"Bill?" she asks, unfocused. Mistaken identity. Still time to get out of this. Before I can move, however, she looks closer. "Oh, it's...you." Voice drops an octave on "you." The temperature of her voice plummets also, from warm butter to polar icecap. Clear disappointment. Fine by me.

"Miss Erish,"I greet her open-endedly, or perhaps simply to acknowledge her. In my condition, I'm not sure. Also because of my condition, I carefully over-enunciate. "It is so nice to see you tonight." She does not move.

"Mr. Gamble," she returns, shortly.

"I didn't notice that you had arrived..." I start.

"Really. And you said you were a journalist."

"Nope. No ma'am. I said I was a reporter."

"Ah. A journalist would have noticed."

"Tonight I am not even a reporter, Miss Erish." Gesture towards the house lights. "I am just a new guy relaxing and meeting new people in a new town."

"Just relaxing? Exactly who are you meeting? Community leaders, contacts essential to your job? Weak politicians, failed businessmen, 'community college' Presidents--oh yes, I noticed *you*." Funny. She seems a little jealous. "Connecting with them is as much a function of your profession as the recorded interview."

She draws on her cigarette. We've each scored a point, of sorts, so I let it go. Anyway, my vision, coherence, and inhibitions are starting to go south. Which means, she's looking better by the moment.

The party is a distant swirl of laughter, clinking glasses, and sporadic tinkling notes from Follicle's piano. That's inside, far away, where it's cool. I'm outside, where it's humid. And for some, hot. Under the collar.

"Well, maybe I'll go on back inside to connect with somebody like... ." Uh, I carefully consider. "...the construction foreman for the new baseball stadium."

Eriss is silent, for the moment. She will let me go. But as I turn away, I hear, "Why not connect with a television executive?" The butter is warm once more.

Connect? Err, does she mean, "hook up?" Stopped in my tracks, my back turned to her. Eriss has not moved from the chaise lounge. But I can sense her yearning. That's her weakness, which she is loath to reveal. The problem is that our worlds or so completely different. She seems to live in 1925. Maybe I don't live in the now, but at least in the 21st Century.

"What are we going to do with you, Mr. Gamble?" I hear her wonder. And I wonder. "You don't look like you're in any shape to discuss Bellows."

"Ah, but I am in fine shape to discuss bourbons!" I try, flailingly. Small smile from Eriss. Bad show, old boy.

"Miss Erish..." I try again.

She replies, sulkily, "Tonight, it's 'Ivory'."

I don't really know where I'm going with this. But suddenly my boy Johnny Cash sings something about it in my head.

I fell in to a burning ring of fire

I went down down down

But the flames went higher

Face burning, I look at Eriss more intently. Got to bring her into focus. It's difficult, though. Misty, even a little foggy. The light is dim, but it throws distinct shadows. She remains in repose but is focused like a laser beam on me now. She sets down her glass, stubs out the cigarette. She will make a move in the next few seconds, I just know it. How many drinks tonight? Not sure if I've had too much or not enough. Suddenly, an image of Megan comes to mind. Or is it Gretchen? I smile at my own confusion, which is immediately misunderstood.

"Come hither, Mr. Gamble. The light is dim and I want to see you better." Her voice is low, beckoning.

Eriss finally shifts, swinging her legs off the chaise lounge, planting her feet on the patio. She lifts herself up in a rather graceful motion, almost as if she is the master of gravity. I'm drawn in by her tractor beam, and kind of flop down next to her, side by side. Resistance is futile. Suddenly, it occurs to me I never got to see Collingwood's boat. What a strange digression! But, oh, Eriss beckons, and this ship is about to set sail. Her breath is warm, sweet, a little smoky. And the sounds of the party recede to nothing.

5

Well, I woke up Sunday morning

With no way to hold my head that didn't hurt

The beer I had for breakfast

Wasn't bad so I had one more for dessert.

Except that I don't feel like a meal, especially that kind of dessert. Where am I? Everything looks sideways. A swimming pool is tilted upright over there. Gray morning. Its light, but even the sky seems hung over. Why am I out of doors? It's drizzly. Everything feels damp. My clothes, blanket, hair, and this... what is this I'm lying on? A chaise lounge. Face down. Hold still; breathe. I can tell there is no way I'm going back to sleep, as much as I'd like to postpone this Morning After.

Summon all my strength. C'mon, dude. I throw my legs off the edge of the lounge chair, push myself up into a sitting position. Dizzy...okay, stabilize. Pulling the blanket around me and over my head, I'm hoping to ward off a small chill and the evil spirits brought on from last night's intake of Spirits. Sunday morning, coming down, hard. Focus. Okay, this is Carl Collingwood's house. There was a party here last night. No one else out here on the patio, however. Hold on: yuck. My mouth tastes like a septic tank. Burp. I'm not feeling very pretty right now.

I'm tired but my eyes refuse to stay closed. Especially after they spot a long, silver cigarette holder, placed like an offering or a sacrifice on a nearby patio table. What is that thing doing there?

I have no desire to move for, say, the next three weeks. Except that the damp is collecting in the creases of my clothes. Still huddled in the blanket, I rise slowly to my feet. Ta-da! For my next trick...never mind. I shuffle towards the sliding glass doors. Takes me, oh, about an hour to get there. The doors are locked, of course. I peer inside. It's darkish inside, no movement. But I spy a human form on the couch. Do I wake him? I debate for about ten seconds. My body is beginning to make some demands. I must pee. Then inhale coffee, Coronation instant breakfast drink, bagel, granola bar, something. I tap on the glass window. Ouch. Even the reverberations make my head hurt.

No movement inside. I tap again, louder. The couch form moves, rises, glances about. Looks frightened, like a child. Then focuses on me.

Huddled under a blanket, the very definition of disheveled, I don't look reputable. Neither does he. Hairpiece missing; a few natural long, loose strands float everywhere. Pasty pale. Slept in his cricket uniform. Marvell Thyme tries to get up, stumbles, and finally makes the door.

"Uh, hello?" he bleary-eyes me.

"Hi. I've been on the patio all night. I need to clean up a bit."

"Oh." Thyme falls back on the couch. "Who are you?"

"The new reporter at WDMZ."

He thinks, remembers, lays his head back down. "Oh yeah, right. The smart guy."

I am hardly listening while I lumber over to the bathroom. Soon, returning to the kitchen, I feel like a stalking animal. I must eat something to settle my stomach and my nerves. Where's the fridge? The Great Room opens into a kitchen unfettered by walls on two sides. A kitchen island provides a low barrier to the dining room. I find a loaf of whole grain bread; toast a slice, smear peanut butter on top, and bite. Chew. Bite. Umf. Need water. Where's a glass? After a slow five minutes of chewing and slurping, I begin to notice details in the room. Empty bottles, ashtrays, bowls of mixed nuts, trays of hors d'oerves. Mm, hm, just like a party had been here. I fill the glass with more tap water to finish washing down the peanut butter. Better let that sit for a minute. I park on a kitchen bar stool at the island. Looks like the toast will stay down okay. I'll probably survive.

Evidently Thyme can't find sleep, either.

"What were you doing out on the patio all night?" he asks, using a tired yet plaintive little boy voice. There's that whine again.

"Oh, I just crashed there. Couldn't drive, and had to sleep somewhere," I offer, sounding careless.

"Last thing I remember was talking with Tyler... ." He trails off, in thought. "Now there's a smart reporter for you."

"In what way?" I ask. This is gonna be fun.

Thyme stretches on the couch, then contracts again. Looks out in space, as if contemplating the meaning of life. Of course, right now it feels like our thinking caps have been sent to the dry cleaners. "She knows what's important. She listens to reason. She understands the value of getting to know people. And work with them. Important people."

"Like you," I offer, agreeably. Nastily.

He bites, naturally. "Yeah, like me, smart guy. And Mayor Parody. And a lot of the people who were here last night. We're all connected, in a way, running this town and this county. It's..." he stretches, "organic."

"A living thing," I offer helpfully. Nastily. What a goober. But this is good fun.

"Yes!" Thyme's juices are starting to flow. "It used to be that Wall Street investors thought they were 'Masters of the Universe.' I thought about becoming one of them. Instead, I decided politics was where the real decisions are made." In his excitement he sits up. "With our taxes, we take peoples' money. With our schools, we indoctrinate the kiddies. With our police force, we have an army. With our utilities, we control how people live in their own homes. Think about it! Some wise guy in a Swiss suit wearing an Italian watch thinks he's important because he makes a business deal? *We* are the Masters of the Universe, not them!"

"But doesn't he pay the bill for your political campaigns that keep your people elected?" I ask.

Phhhhht. Thyme deflates faster than the Atlanta Braves in the playoffs.

"Not always," he replies, defensively.

"You mean that, when the politicians sit down with the money men, the politicians call the shots? And the money just says, 'Yes, sir? '"

Thyme is silenced. Except to mutter, "*Tyler* is a smart reporter." He goes off into another room. Far from me, I guess. I really am starting to feel better.

In the quiet, I notice the diffused, damp outdoor light lends a coat of gray to everything indoors. Fuzzy, dark shadows remain. But I hear something stirring in a far corner of the house. Soon, Collingwood brightly steps in. Showered, shaved, cologned. In a fresh golf shirt, warm-up pants, and tennis shoes.

"Wilson!" he greets, brightly. Then he takes a closer look. I'm a mess. "You don't look so good, son."

I stand in my own defense. Somehow I feel compelled to go shake his hand. Don't know why. But that's too formal for this setting. Instead, I simply stand, awkwardly. Maybe I should explain why I'm in his kitchen, with a smudge of peanut butter on the corner of my mouth.

"Spent the night on the patio." Oh, that explains everything.

"You aren't the first," Collingwood waves dismissively, flipping on an overhead light in the kitchen. "Though maybe it's not such a good idea with that Luther Post running around--and the police chasing him, guns drawn. We're kind of on the fringe of civilization out here in this neighborhood."

I hadn't thought of Luther Post. Gawd. Glad I hadn't thought of Luther Post.

"Anyways, let's get you warmed up. I'll get some hot coffee percolating and see if we can't wake up the rest of the house."

"Who else is here?"

"I have no idea. We have a couple of spare rooms, and I went to bed way before the party ended." He grins. "We may stumble across stragglers the rest of the day."

The coffee truly does "perk" here. Collingwood actually pulls out an old school, tin, stove-top percolator. A glass bubble projecting from the lid shows the coffee's progress. The smell alone is a balm to my senses. Then, however, I recall something about last night. The way it ended. Now, I'm almost sick. Knees shaky, I sit.

"Carl..." I start, not knowing where to go with it. He turns to me. Try to be conversational, Wil. "I saw quite a few Newschannel 99 people here last night." A statement. Allows for an open rejoinder.

"Yeah," he smooths the back of his slick hair with his hand. "I wouldn't say anyone at the station is really a close friend. But there are a few folks I like, so I'm glad to have them over. It makes for a nice mix with everyone else."

"By 'everyone else' you mean, like community leaders, that sort of thing?" I ask.

"I guess you could call them that. 'Movers and Shakers' would also work, I suppose. 'People Who Get Things Done' is the way I like to think about them." He chuckles. "Call them 'Players' if you want."

"Boss Thyme thinks they are the Masters of the Universe. At least for this corner of the universe."

He chuckles. "I don't know about that. Mostly, though--and don't laugh--I just consider them to be my friends."

"I wouldn't laugh at that," I respond.

"Some would in this town. Some who were here last night." But it doesn't seem to bother Collingwood.

"Why was Walter Wilson here? You don't consider him a friend, do you?" I ask.

Collingwood considers, slicks back his hair with his hand once more.

His tic, I am learning. "Well, no. But like I say, he's close to a lot of people, so you can't keep him out. And, when it gets late enough, he can be quite funny."

"I guess I could see that."

"These parties also sometimes just take a life of their own. And the Walter Wilsons magically appear." He considers further, and mutters, "Like the mushrooms in my backyard."

'Boss' Thyme wanders back in. His hair is back on but he looks pretty bad, and flops heavily back down on the couch. "Where's the clicker?" he nearly demands. "I wanna watch 'Meet The Nation' on Channel 11."

A lengthy search commences. At a party like the one here last night, a missing remote control unit is like a lost child at the bus station. Finally, Collingwood shows Thyme how to manually ignite the television; the show is half over.

Collingwood furrows through cabinets for breakfast fixings. I look down at the crumbs from my peanut butter toast on the plate. What I swallowed now feels like an entire melon growing in my stomach.

"I thought I saw Ivory Eriss here last night," I trying to extend the conversation we've been having.

Collingwood looks at me closely. "She comes and goes places on her own schedule. I don't go out of my way to invite her, but she is friends with Marie, so she's always welcome here. I'd be real careful what you say in her company after having a couple of drinks. She remembers everything...just like me."

"I'm not sure I said much of anything to her last night." Well, that much is true.

"Good idea." Collingwood piles a growing mound of food on a plate on the kitchen island. A quick sparkle lights in his eye. "Hey Marvell!" Moaning on the couch. "Marvell...want some scrambled eggs with salsa? I won't make them so runny this time."

Without a word, Marvell Thyme rises quickly and lumbers out to the bathroom. Urp. The thought almost churns my stomach as well.

Eventually, I wash down some hash browns with coffee. That, and a shower renews in me a semblance of respectability and consciousness. Thyme and two or three other party left-overs make their exit, stage left. Collingwood invites me to hang out.

He does indeed finally show me his boat, parked behind the garage. I note the grass has grown up a little higher over the chocked wheels than elsewhere. Having worked one summer on a charter fishing boat at a tourist spot in the Outer Banks of North Carolina, I can talk a little boat language with Collingwood. So we spend two or three hours putzing around on his dry-docked yacht, *The Dutch Tilt*.

"So, what about Marvell Thyme and Fulsome Parody?" I ask, watching him tinker in the engine compartment. We're both sipping sodas this afternoon. "Is Thyme some sort of 'Boss Hogg,' the power behind the throne? He doesn't seem capable."

Collingwood nearly snorts cola through his nose. Right on. "That's a good story. A long time ago, in college, Fulsome ran for student body President. That was downstate at Inimitable State University. A lot of people around here went to college at ISU since its in-state. Well, this big, goofy kid with enormous hair starts showing up at Fulsome's organizational meetings and rallies."

"Enormous hair?" I interject.

"Oh yeah. Like you wouldn't believe. A bird's nest perched straight on top of his head. I've seen pictures, it was a phenomenon. Most everyone else's hair grows out or down; Marvell's hair grew up, snarled in about five cowlicks. It was memorable.

"Anyways, he worked hard on Fulsome's campaign, putting up banners, handing out fliers, making phone calls. He wasn't a visionary, just a very committed foot soldier. Well, all the hard work paid off and Fulsome was elected. But shortly before the actual election, his opponent accused Fulsome's campaign manager of not being an ISU student. Of course, he meant Marvell, who wasn't the campaign manager by a long shot, but was that closely associated with it by that time. It turned out that Marvell was attending a little community college in the next county but wanted to hang out at the Big University."

"That doesn't seem like it should have disqualified him from helping with a Student Body President campaign," I observe.

"You're right. But it sounds like there was a lot of controversy, name-calling, nearly a fistfight or two. Fulsome was confirmed the winner, and kind of became, well, accustomed to Marvell. Since then, Marvell lost his hair but worked on several election campaigns for Fulsome, including the last four for mayor. So, I call him the Boss of Reproach County."

"Mayor Parody doesn't seem like anybody's fool."

Collingwood contemplates for a moment. "Nope. It's funny. I mean, it's interesting. Even though he has a prominent public position, he's really the power behind a lot of other thrones in this area. If you watch long enough and carefully enough, you'll see his hand involved in a lot of things. He's quietly invested in some business ventures, also."

"Are you close with him?"

"That's hard to characterize. We take in ballgames, go out to dinner...but most of all, we find each other useful. We can work with each other."

"Isn't that...a little dangerous? Couldn't that turn into giving aid and comfort to the 'enemy'-- you know, the people we are supposed to cover as reporters?"

Collingwood sips his soda. Considers. "In a vacuum, yes. In the midst of competition, no. There are too many other watchdogs like us out there for me to conspire against the public good. But... ." He looks away from me. "I guess it's a bit of a compromise. Not that anyone has ever kept me from running a story. We have, however, covered stories they pitched to us. We'd check everything out, get the other side. But they help set the agenda by giving it to us in the first place. That does happen."

That's the way of the world, I think. I have no problem with that. Making contacts is an utterly essential part of the job. Players want to be on the inside, know stuff before it happens--or before it airs on TV. Good journalists cultivate those contacts, trade them a little information. Occasionally do a positive story for them when it is warranted. Sometimes sit on a story until everyone agrees on the best time to release it. And then we let everyone else--the viewers--in on the little secret.

"How well do the Players know Roddy Rooker?" I ask.

"Very well. Good friends, if not always allies."

"Do *you* know Roddy Rooker well?" That's more to the point. I find myself testing this man.

"Yes. He's a friend. And he would have been here last night except he's embarrassed by his son and doesn't want to face anyone right now. You won't see him at next week's city council meeting, either. He may have to answer questions as to why his son seems to have received preferential treatment in the courts."

"Did he?"

"Of course he did. Rod behaved like a Dad, trying to shield his son."

"But you helped Jack Phillips find out. And some people might have construed it as Roddy Rooker trying to protect his political career."

Collingwood pauses again. "Yeah." Another pause. Another soda sip.

I bore in. "Why did you give that information to Phillips?"

"Can't help myself, I guess." Collingwood looks away again. "I have to get the truth out there, or at least what I believe is the truth. Or, if I were to feel a bit more cynical, I'd say I just wanted my station to have a better story. In any case, if I have any kind of reputation in Filterboro, it's because of that. Someone smart who knew what they were talking about--it might have been my uncle--told me a long time ago that 'Integrity is your best calling card.' That might sound old fashioned, but I am deeply committed to it without even thinking about it."

Now it's my turn to pause. Deep down, I relate to this reflexive behavior. I find myself admiring this guy. Even as he sweats over a recalcitrant engine in a boat that never sails. Few may know he has real power in this city. But abusing it does not seem to enter his mind.

6

Homeward bound. At the end of the following week I get a three day pass. I arrange my air ticket and say goodbye to the Placid Place Motel on Friday morning. The sooner the better. I need to move into that new apartment, get a driver's license, finish my WDMZ paperwork, get a real paycheck, and become an upstanding member of this here community. Collingwood has arranged a stipend out of the News Department budget to get me by. But that arrangement can't last long.

The flight north is fine. Mountain weather greets me, a reminder to not stay long. Finding my pickup truck in the endless long term airport parking lot isn't easy--where did I park? There it is. Ah, Big Blue. The familiarity of my truck is comforting. But the familiarity of a town I don't belong to any more is unsettling. I'd rather cut ties and move on, making connections in my new town. So I decide not to call my few friends or stop by the old TV station. Driving west, I decide against visiting a favorite barbeque joint in favor of a more generic experience: a fast food restaurant. Afterwards, I head to my storage unit. A guy in the office helps me load up the truck with my stuff, for a small fee. And then I'm gone.

South by southwest on the interstate, down out of the mountains and into the countryside. The open road holds a fascination for me. Not just the freedom to roam. Actually, as a Professional Wanderer, I am instead grateful for fixed points. Towns, villages, even freeway exits. Each are an oasis, proof that we are not traveling solely for the sake of movement. They are evidence that one can *arrive*, eventually. Each exit represents some unclaimed opportunity, some unknown friend. They also are reminders of civilization in the midst of the interstate desert. Oases named "Dry Ridge," "Sadieville," and "Renfro Valley." Older travelers drove through these towns on two lane roads, experienced their diners, filling stations, Five-and-Dimes, and hotel lobbies. Now we drive past the green freeway exit signs that bear these names and wonder what the towns look like.

Behind the wheel of Big Blue, me and the speed limit are tight. Yes, I drive like a tourist. There are plenty of other drivers on the road, but most of them pass by, unblinking, at a higher rate of speed. This remains a lonely place. The independence of automobile travel reduces inhibitions, elevates selfishness. The buffer of speed and metal between each driver creates more autonomy. And more separation. A gray Toyonda "Preclude" passes, followed by a green Fort "Ecarte" and a conversion van. Each ship piloted by captains who believe they are in control of their own passage. We are *not* all in this together, they think. They are wrong. We may exit at different places, but all of us will indeed, exit.

The day peters out, cracks in the light slowly filled in by the dark. The radio is off; I've had my Johnny Cash fix. My driver's side window is cracked open, creating a loud, steady streaming white noise. Elbow resting on the open driver's side window, I flow along with the wind rushing by. Strange sensation, really, the body so sedate while hurtling forward more than a mile a minute. The thin gray ribbon rolls on over sloping hills and through crowded thickets of darkening green trees. Little to see except sudden clusters of lights that herald each new intersection. I think of Megan, and even Gretchen. I like something about her spunk, her verve. Gretchen, I mean. I'm trying not to think of Ivory Eriss.

Exit eastbound and down into a valley, I head towards a different mountain range. Its full night now, I'm getting tired. Soon I come across a cheap motel, truckers, and HBO. A Placid Place Motel in a different place. Nothing worth watching on TV, of course. So, I drink. And then, I sleep.

Normally, I prefer a lazy start to any day off of work. Especially after a couple-ish of cheap beers the night before. But I start to consider the 5pm deadline to pick up the keys for my new apartment--and the distance to get there. Driven by this, I get driving. Thankfully, another clear day. Egg biscuits and coffee, to go. More interesting scenery, through and over the mountains. But the steep grades are a more difficult drive in a loaded-down pickup. Once I'm through the hills, the road suddenly becomes a straightaway. It joins another interstate, and I'm on my way...home? Such as it is, I guess.

As the mile markers diminish, the wheels roll faster. Even on the straightaways it feels like I'm driving downhill. I'm not interested in a speeding ticket, but I'm excited about having a few hours to set up my new place. Can't wait to begin the next phase of my life. The radio is on, and I'm searching for Filterboro stations even before I'm close enough to tune them in.

Finally, it's my turn to exit the interstate. This will be *my* oasis. I try not to notice the Placid Place Motel. Five minutes later, I'm pulling in to a different parking lot, out front of the rental office for the Shoddy Acres apartment complex.

Rest a moment. It is both exciting and settling to have my belongings and my place. For two years, at least, "unless the station exercises the morals clause... ."

It appears quiet around here for a Saturday afternoon. I plop my feet out of the truck and onto the asphalt, and head to the office.

Inside its cool and dry. Clinical. A single majesty palm is browning over in a corner. Everything else is white Formica. A Woman With Big Hair works a Sudoku puzzle (apparently to look hip) and looks, well, puzzled. She's chewing gum, quite actively. Then she sees me and frowns.

"Can I help yew?" Voice straight out of a Lily Tomlin character.

"Hi. I'm here to sign a rental agreement and pick up my keys."

Confused look. She pops her gum. "What's yer name?"

"Wilson Gamble. Should be..." I consult my memory, "Let's see, apartment 202-B, I think."

She searches a computer screen. It's taking too long. "Which apartment?" she asks, note of disbelief.

"202-B."

"And your name isn't George Townsend?"

"No, Wilson Gamble."

"Do you have any paperwork for this apartment?"

I pull out a lease agreement from my manbag. "Here."

She studies it. "No one signed it from Shoddy Acres."

Uh oh. I'm confused for a moment. Wait. It comes to me. "The apartment agent said someone would sign it when I came in today, as long as it was before five o'clock."

"Who was the agent?"

Look again, this time for a business card. "Lucy Clearinghouse."

"Hmm. But she didn't sign the lease, and she's not an employee of Shoddy Acres." Tiny, ugly smile. "And my computer says apartment 202-B was rented by a George Townsend, um, yesterday."

Flabbergasted. "My apartment is gone?"

Lily Tomlin hardens. Chewing stops. "It's not your apartment."

I guess not. "But I had an agreement!" I yell.

She's cool as I heat up. "Did you? No one signed the so-called paperwork you are showing me." Gum chewing resumes.

"But we had an agreement!" I repeat.

"A verbal one? Can you prove that?" she smirks. Now she's moving away from Customer Service to Customer Annoyance.

Catch your breath, buddy. "Okay. I had an agreement for an apartment here. Do you have any other suitable units available? I really can only afford a one-bedroom apartment."

She softens again. "Let me see." Checks computer. Bites her pen. Scratches her head. Drums her fingers. I want to scream.

"Okay," she says to herself. "Here's something. Yes." Looks at me. "When were you hoping to move in?"

Not a good question. "Today! I drove here from out of state and I had an agreement and I'm here to move in right now!"

Lily Tomlin shifts into automation-mode. "I'm sorry," she replies in a bright, rehearsed, sing-song voice. "There's nothing available for another two weeks. I'd be glad to show you a model apartment and put you on the waiting list."

Think for a minute. "I'm going to call the agent. Uh, Lucy Clearinghouse," I tell her as I pull out the trusty phone from my magic manbag. We are going to straighten this out, right now. Fumbling with her business card, I dial the numbers. It rings. And rings. And then an automated voice to match Lily Tomlin here: "The wireless customer you are trying to reach is out of the service area. Please try your call again later."

I curse. Stomp. Throw my stuff into my manbag. All to the amusement of Lily Tomlin.

"Alright." I say to her, hot as a frying pan. "I want to speak to someone in charge. Someone is going to be held accountable for this. Who is your supervisor?"

She doesn't cower. "I'm the only one here right now. It's the weekend," she adds, unnecessarily.

"This is ridiculous. Thanks to you, I have no place to live now. Tell me who I should take this up with. Who is the manager of this complex?"

"The manager of the premises? Or the company's General Manager?"

"Well, the General Manager." I'm really mad. Boy, am I going to give them a piece of my mind. Grr.

"The General Manager of Shoddy Properties, LLC, owner of The Shoddy

Acres Apartment Complex, is named Ivory Eriss. I'd be glad to give you her office number."

Huh? I pick up my jaw and shuffle out to my truck, utterly defeated. Didn't think I'd ever go back to the Placid Place Motel, but off I go. The shadows are lengthening as I pull in. A young, tattooed clerk checks me in.

"How long are you staying?" he asks. Boredom reigns in his world.

"Wish I knew," I respond wearily. I explain why. "I had better say 'a week.' My apartment rental fell through and I have to find a new place to live."

"Ah," he responds, busy slowly checking me in. Then he stops, checks me out. "You were here the last couple of weeks, right? You need a new place to live?"

What? I must gauge what he's about to say. He looks a little unkempt in a Skinhead kind of way. One of his tattoos creeps up his neck out the side of his collar. He's wearing several earrings, some of them in his nose. His eyes seem earnest, but I'm wary.

"Uh, I have a few leads on some places, but it's getting late in the day today so I probably won't be able to check them out until Monday."

The clerk isn't deterred. "If you need a place, there's this boarding house here in town where you can rent a room month-to-month. It's a pretty good deal if you don't want to stay at a motel." He looks around disdainfully at the lobby. "Especially *this* motel."

"A boarding house?" Didn't I hear something about a boarding house somewhere before?" I didn't know they still existed." But it sounds better than staying here.

"Well, she doesn't serve meals, but you can use her kitchen. And there's a fridge. You have to share the bathroom, but there's a couple of them to choose from. It's in the historic district downtown."

"How do you know about this place? Do you live there?"

He scratches a tattoo on his arm and smiles. Missing a tooth. "I used to. Until I got this job, found a permanent place to live over at a pretty nice apartment complex not too far from here. Called 'Shoddy Acres'. But they are usually full-up."

Gripping the counter, I resist a manic urge to strangle this clerk.

"You want the phone number?" he asks.

Stop seeing red, Wil. "For the boarding house? I guess so. Sure." But I'm not. Sure, that is.

Flinging an old phone book on to the counter, he flips it open. "Okay," he says. "I'll write it on your receipt here."

"Thanks."

"Ask for Mercy Haversack. Just call her 'Miss Mercy.'"

In a different room at the Placid Place this time, I pull the heavy curtains slightly apart. Have to keep an eye on my stuff that remains in the bed of the truck while I'm in the bed of my room. Of course, this also invites preening eyes by those who would optically invade my room.

Ignore this. What to do about lodging? I felt pretty fortunate just finding Shoddy Acres. And it turns out the place is run by Ivory Eriss? You have gotta be kidding me. Did she know I had a deal ready to sign there? I have no answers.

Fitful sleep in another motel room. Sunday comes and I'm still tired. The long drive, loss of my apartment, and the looming workweek force a yawn. I have to push myself out the door to follow housing clues from the classifieds. But on a Sunday, nothing works. Everything is rented, as before. Middle of the month, it's a tight market.

Still no working signal for Lucy Clearinghouse's phone. But I have given up the idea of trying to fight for the apartment at Shoddy Acres. Not sure I want Ivory Eriss to have access to a key to my apartment.

Finally, a different agent tells me that in a month-and-a-half a couple of second floor rooms over a record store in the old downtown section of Filterboro will be available. If I want it, there's a short waiting list: none. Leaving my number with the agent, I jump on it.

What to do until then? I'm still driving around with furniture in the back of the truck. Not helping the gas mileage. Don't think I can stomach any more of the flaccid place I'm staying. I start thinking about the boarding house. I'd enjoy something homey right about now. Historic district, huh? Long rows of homes intimately cared for by people who value their neighborhood? I wonder about Haversack House--Victorian, Federal, maybe Gothic Revival? A cozy room of my own? Walking distance to downtown? Matronly landlady to welcome me there? Milk and cookies? We've got a winner. Back at the motel I dig out the phone number on my receipt and call Mercy Haversack.

Seven rings. Eight. I'm about to hang up and give up when the receiver is picked up. "Good afternoon. Haversack House." Sounds like "Heh-vah-seck." Wavering, elderly, rich-sounding voice. Measured, genteel, belle of the Old South. I already feel a warmth about her.

"Hello. My name is Wilson Gamble and I'm calling about renting a room."

"Wilson. Such a nice name. I had a guinea pig named Willie once."

"Yes ma'am. But I prefer Wil, not Willie. Do you have a room available?"

"Oh yes. But first I need to know more about you, Willie. Who are your mother and father?"

I'm baffled at this. "They don't live anywhere near here... ."

"I would still like to know." She is steady, unexcitable, insistent.

"Okay, if you'd like. My father is Morgan Gamble of Upper Sandusky, Ohio. Mom is Ida Gamble. She doesn't live in Upper Sandusky, Ohio."

"A Yankee, ah see. And youah famalee is not tah-geh-tha." She clears her throat. For once I'm momentarily uncomfortable admitting my birthplace. Miss Mercy continues her slow stream-of-consciousness monologue. "Well, that's okay. I ("Ah") once ("wunhss") visited the state of Ohio and was treated quite respectfully. And we are at peace now, aren't we?" Phone smile.

A hearty, "Yes ma'am" to that.

"And, what is your profession? Where do you work? I only take in professionals."

"Uh, Newschannel 99."

Silence. There's no reply at all. Is anybody listening?" Ma'am? Mrs. Haversack?"

"Miss Mercy, thank you." Miss Muh-see. "You work at a...television station?" Ugh. How low can you go?" What do you do there?"

"I'm a reporter."

Again, silence. What's the problem here?

"Well, now, Mr. Gamble, I'm a quiet person who takes in quiet lodgers. I'm not used to having someone here who pokes around into other peoples' business for a living."

"I have a private life also, Miss Mercy. I respect the privacy of private people. Unless, ha ha, they are breaking the law!" Ha ha.

A coughing spasm is all I hear. I hope she's alright—Miss Mercy sounds so frail...like someone you would want to protect. "Also..." My voice rises; I'm a little desperate. "I really need to find a place to stay for a few weeks."

She bends, slightly, clearing her throat. "Do you have any references? How did you hear of my home?"

"Around here, so far I only really know people at work. Carl Collingwood, for one. And the guy at the front desk of The Placid Place motel mentioned your place and gave me your phone number." Swiftly, regrettably, I recall his teeth and tattoo: he may not be the best reference. I swiftly discover how wrong I am.

"Little Jerry? Bless his heart. Well, in that case, I suppose it's okay. Come look at my place and we'll sit down and talk in person."

Uh, ok. "Little Jerry" is my best reference?

We agree to a time and I get some complicated directions. In my current situation, no time is like the present. Let's go.

Settling back into the cab of my truck, I head away from the interstate culture of fast food and all-night gas stations. Zig-zag my way through acres of neighborhoods, punctuated with corner strip malls and convenience stores. Past an auto mall of some half-dozen dealerships. No one shopping there on a Sunday. Now through an older business area, some boarded up shops, some pawn shops. Only the weeds truly thrive here.

Along the way I think how my attitude shifted so quickly on the phone. At first I wasn't sold on the boarding house. But as I felt rejected, I began to want it. Human nature, I guess. This realization dawns on me as I pass out of the dying business district and slowly make my way down a residential street filled with older homes. Front porches and sidewalks still exist here. Indeed, there is an abundance of Victorians, Federals and Gothic Revivals. Many look freshly painted and recently landscaped. Not many weeds here.

I pull into a driveway and observe the Haversack House. It glows in the warm sun. But it is definitely not a Victorian, Federal or Gothic Revival home to be featured in "Southern Existence" magazine. So far as I can tell, it's late Plain Jane Revival. A sagging farmhouse on what used to be a busy thoroughfare--a hundred years ago. White clapboard, two gabled windows oversee a boulevard known as Mulberry Street.

The home is shoehorned between beautiful homes of varying shape and heritage. Haversack House is clean, yes, and whitewashed. As I disembark from the truck, an elderly woman slowly materializes at the screen door. She waits, wide and round, coated with a floral print dress. Her head looks heavy. Spectacles. Round face, hanging lower lip. Large features, framed by tightly curled white locks.

"Hello, Mr. Gamble," she offers in singsong 3:2 time, with the tone of a grandmother. After all I've been through, I want to shout, "I'm home!"

But...it's not my home. I'm here to transact a business deal. I saunter up four pine steps to what once was a standard-issue front porch. A wood swing rocks unsteadily in the breeze a few feet down.

"Welcome to Haversack House. It's one of the oldest continuously-inhabited homes in Filterboro," offers Mercy Haversack. Her syllables are methodical: Fil-teh-buh-rah. "Step inside and I'll show you the parlor."

She is slow. Glacier slow. As slow as the check in the mail. Sundials move faster. Every single motion is carefully considered, debated, then executed. No movement is wasted. She shuffles past the heavy front door, swung open to reveal the hallway.

We are immediately confronted by a mammoth but creaky-looking staircase on the right. Plain white walls, aging wood floors. The hallway zig-zags to the left around the staircase. The place smells like a clothes trunk after years in the attic: warm, muggy, mothballs. We proceed over numerous throw rugs haphazardly tossed over the worn hardwood. Then, Miss Mercy opens a plain wood interior door and ushers me in...to the 1890's.

A beautifully-appointed parlor. Walls lined with bookshelves filled with hardcover books and framed prints of classical paintings. Antique furnishings seated on intricately-woven rugs. A baby grand piano anchors one end. A fireplace, the other. Little tables and knick knacks abound. "Old fashioned" comes home to sleep here at night. The single, quiet capitulation to modernity is that the parlor, unlike the hallway, is freshly air conditioned. Oh, then I spot another nod to the 21st Century. In a large ante-room, a place whose walls seem to be covered with more books, I notice a television quietly buzzing. My fleeting glimpse identifies a horse race underway somewhere. Anyhow, back here in the parlor, I shear off my shoes and apply a pair of slippers offered to me. We sit.

"My weakness, Mr. Gamble. I do enjoy the television. It puts me in touch with an outside world that advancing age increasingly compels me to withdraw from."

"Well, if you are a fan of television, we ought to get along just fine!" I try.

A reaction of actual disdain? No, I decide she may just have gas. Miss Mercy continues.

"Mr. Gamble, welcome to my home. I try to run a quiet but

distinguished business here, and attempt to make my lodgers feel welcome. But you will find that a handful of my previous guests over the years did not behave themselves in a gentlemanly fashion. So, I was compelled to draw up this list of regulations."

In slow motion she presents me with a list of rules. Eleven pages' worth...single-spaced. The ones I take the time to read seem reasonable: no tobacco, no women, no loud noise after 10pm, lower the toilet lid, etc.

"I guess I can live with this," I say.

"The terms are $100 every week, due on Friday, in addition to a $300 deposit. By the way...do you follow the sporting world?"

"How's that?" I ask, caught off guard. "Not much, really." I start to ramble. "I'm a Cincinnati Reds fan, and in high school I lettered in racquetball, but that's about it. Why do you ask?"

"It is not important. So, I understand that you work at WDMZ?"

"Yes. ma'am."

"Do you have a reference or two from your employer I may contact?"

I give her the work numbers for Collingwood and Gretchen Calzone.

"This will be sufficient, probably. Allow me a few hours to check these, and see if your deposit check clears. After that happens you can move in tomorrow if you wish."

"Can I see the room first?"

She laughs. But it's a harsh, slow old laugh that surprises me, deep from some old, hidden, roustabout days. Days of raucous fun--or running conflict, I'm not quite sure which. Mercy collects herself.

"Oh yes, of course, my dear. I will allow you to take a look upstairs. Go ahead. My knees are not strong, so I hope you will not be offended if I don't provide you with a guided tour."

Actually, I'm grateful. A guided tour might take until the summer solstice.

Back out of the parlor and air conditioning, the humid musty smell returns. Down the hallway, up the staircase. The stairs are worn somewhat, and creak just a little. Up, up, and angle left to the second floor landing. A long hallway with a low ceiling confronts me. More throw rugs. One window behind me, at the front of the hall. Ahead, four closed pine doors. Mine is second on the left. The flooring is solid and the walls seem thick. No noise apparent at the moment. I like peace. A darkened brass doorknob twists to permit entry into my new room.

I peek inside. It's a new hotel room, alright...circa 1895. I wonder if O. Henry wrote about this place. Is it lit by gaslight? The ceiling is low, the trim a well-rubbed pine, there's room to move around. A queen-sized, four poster bed is covered with a macramé bedspread. Dark, wood dressers, tall and wide, surround me. Next to a window is an old-timey secretary desk and chair. The only item that looks 20th Century is a window air conditioning unit. That's *mid* 20th Century. Doesn't smell old, however, thank goodness. Faded wallpaper, more hardwood floors. But this floor seems to slope a little, from the entrance to a far corner, near the closet. It's spacious: plenty of room for sit-ups and pushups, should the mood strike me. In all, the room is unremarkable but still acceptable. Okay. Two long windows admit light. What's outside? I wander deeper into the room, looking to check the view. But when I pull aside the heavy curtains I find...skyscrapers?

Whaaat? Can't be. Open the set of curtains over the other window: same image. This is not real. The windows are lined with cityscape poster pictures, like those used in the deep background of furniture advertisements in the newspaper. Look closer. New York, 1930, I'd say. Is the actual view of Filterboro that bad from here? This is a little unreal.

Retreat. What is that all about, anyways? I back out the door, leave it open, and stare at the window from a more distant vantage point. Did I enter the right room? What's really out that window? Think. Based on my quick look at the exterior of the house and the neighboring buildings...I can't even guess. It's not frightening, really, it just does not compute.

Alrighty, then. Take a breath, close the door, head down the hallway. Check out the bathroom. Musty, like the hallway. Small pink tiles populate the floor and the walls. Very neat, no open tube of toothpaste lying out. Got all the amenities, even a modern toilet. I flush it just to make sure it works.

So...I trudge back up the hall, slowly, pondering. The train of throw rugs have no backing, and are lightweight, so they tend to slide around under my feet like an air hockey puck. Back to the landing, I clump down the stairs. The window treatment in the room leaves a weird impression on my mind. I stop midway down the staircase. Think for a moment. Okay. Ask what the window thing is all about. If there's a satisfactory response, go ahead and take the room. If not...well, plod back to The Placid Place Motel.

Eventually, I make the ground floor, round the staircase, and slowly trek back into the parlor. Sunlight glows on the piano. A grandfather clock ticks. Mercy Haversack is actually knitting something. Stolid reassurance. This feels like home, right?

Enter the parlor. I realize I'm still wearing the slippers. That's okay.

"Miss Mercy?"

In her ponderous fashion it takes five seconds to tilt up her head. Was it a brief look of derision? No, no, of course not. It just takes a few moments for her smile to warm up. What kind of question do I formulate about the windows? Buy some time.

"How many people share the bath?"

"Only two people use it now." A curious, shy smile appears momentarily. "I use the one downstairs."

"How often do the linens get changed?"

"Once a week, on Saturday. A hired woman comes in to do some tidying up."

I think of my computer tablet. "What about an internet connection. Is WiFi available? I notice my phone doesn't seem to have any signal in here."

Haversack shifts almost imperceptibly. "Well, no. It is so difficult to keep up with all those computers and smarty phones that are coming out these days."

That's okay. Guess I'll have to stay connected at work, I guess. Next, I get to the one thing that's really bothering me. "Miss Mercy, why are the windows covered with skyline posters? Was I in the correct room?"

"Oh my, yes. Don't you like the pictures? I had them carefully laminated on the windows by Slab."

This sidetracks me for a moment. "Slab? What's that?"

She answers as if I should have known. "My son, of course, Mr. Gamble."

Um, ok, of course his name would be "Slab." But the skyline photos?

"My dear Willie," she replies, slow speech decelerating further. "Up there the only view you have is of the rooftops next door. And it provides a measure of privacy."

Wouldn't the curtains do that? Well. They aren't bad pictures. And I don't have too many options here. If Mercy Haversack will have me, I will move in tomorrow.

Next day, she checks my "references." Calzone doesn't have time to listen and hangs up on Haversack. But ever the gentleman, Collingwood gives her 15 slow minutes. After that, I'm in. That night, I drive my truck up the gravel driveway and onto a cement parking pad at the back of the house. Three other cars are there, but one spot is open.

On foot, I crunch back down the gravel to the front of the home. I knock on the front door. This time, Haversack calls for me to come in and I enter the musty hallway. She is wearing another floral print, leaning heavily against the door to the parlor.

"Come in, Willie, come in," she invites. As I settle into a seat, an enormous farmhand enters the room and descends into another chair, at about the speed of a man being sucked into quicksand. He simply looks at me, emptily. He's not really a farmhand. He has the dimensions and the indifferent expression of a movie rental kiosk. A big boy, glowing pink with a fringe of fuzz on the peak of his pate. It occurs to me that perhaps he is a refugee from "Hee Haw." But he doesn't look like he does any pickin' or grinnin'.

"Willie," Mercy starts, slowly but obdurately, "this is Slab. He lives as well as works here." Farming the back 40? I wonder. She turns to him. "Slab, this is Willie Gamble, our new boarder. Willie, this is Slab Haversack."

"Uh, hi, uh, Slab," I try, knowing the attempt to communicate will fail. He moves as little as his mother. In fact, even less: he does not work his jaw in reply.

"Slab lives here in my home and takes care of the, er, maintenance of our operation. But you must come to me if you have any maintenance requests."

"Operation?" Interesting word. Whatever. Anyways, it's all okay with me. I don't foresee any long conversations with Slab about Edward Hopper, politics or Descartes. Or crayon colors, nose wiping or dead spiders, for that matter.

As I sign the tenant agreement, Miss Mercy looks firm. Slab shifts slightly forward. "You can leave your truck in the parking lot to unload your things, but afterwards you will have to move it to the street."

"Why? Do other tenants pay more for parking?"

"No. I just know them better and they've been here longer. Unregulated parking spots are marked on the streets. But you can't park in front of my home. Mulberry Street is a "No Parking" zone during the overnight hours. Instead, you just park around the corner on Chainlink Street."

That doesn't sound like fun. "Any chance I could earn one of those spots in your parking lot?"

Sloooooow smile. "Not unless you plan to live here a very long time."

Night-time in a strange room. New room, old hat. Quiet, except a radio that plays on the other side of the wall. It's not loud, just there. Three empty bottles lounge around on the floor. Hey, it's time to celebrate a small victory, right?

I occupy myself by moving my boxes around, plugging in a few appliances, ironing a shirt. Tuck Johnny Bench into the mirror frame. Where's my manbag? Ah, I left it in the truck, now parked around the corner. Don't feel like chasing after it tonight. Tired from the work and the drink, I hit the hay in my new digs.

Next morning. Up and at 'em, an Atom Ant cartoon plays on a TV somewhere in the Haversack House. Undistinguishable noises identify other human activity. I'm not much for a big breakfast, but I must ingest caffeine. My personal coffee maker has an honored place in the room, on top of the desk. Add bottled water and grounds, and life can ignite.

Okay, it feels a little weird making my way down a semi-public hallway to the bathroom. Carrying my bath stuff, suit, and towel. I tell myself that I will get used to it. Everything in the bathroom works, even the old-fashioned dual-faucet sink. Attached to the mirror, however, is my first run-in with what I later deem the "Mercy Rules." It is a white, lined, 4x6 card with shaky but very proper pen scrawl across it. Taped neatly to the corner of the mirror.

"Plumber has advised us, shaving cream clogs the drain. Please wipe used cream on tissue and flush down toilet."

Oh. I have never heard that one before. Cleaning a razor with tissue is a sloppy proposition. But I decide I will do my bit to get along, for now.

Eventually, I descend the staircase. No one else is in sight. On the way down I notice another 4x6 card, taped to the wall halfway down the stairs.

"Please do not touch the walls. Use handrail for balance, if necessary."

Um, okay.

The ground floor seems empty, so I head out the door, thinking about work. A fresh, new day. Leaving the Haversack property, I round the corner and head to my truck. There, I discover another card, this time on my windshield. This one is different, 3x5, and written in a hurry.

"We have lived here for years and worked out everyone's parking spaces along this road. So please park somewhere else tomorrow night. Jerk."

Welcome to Filterboro.

7

Midway through the morning meeting, Walter Wilson enters. Talking nonstop, naturally. His voice intrudes itself on my consciousness quite slowly while I consider today's Outlook--but it intrudes, just as sure. Someone follows him in to the room. Wilson waddles, his guest lumbers. A prodigiously immense but stubby man. Wide as he is tall. Not muscled, not flabby. Just immense. Like a walking street corner mailbox. I think of the Master Cylinder, nemesis of Felix the Cat. The only tiny feature are his eyes. Two dark, unblinking points, coated with luxuriant eyebrows. Untroubled expression. Massive balding head runs down into enormous shoulders, chest, and everything else. Dark, double-breasted suit. How did they find enough material to make it? The meeting crashes to a halt. All stare in awe and wonder at this apparent freak of nature.

"...and the carpeting was replaced one year later, in 1993. Or was it 1994?" It's Wilson, on tour. The man-mountain follows, ignoring Wilson but responding to everything with a low, dry chuckle: "Heh, heh, heh."

Wilson carries on. "But it's an open secret that the job was done by members of the Filterboro mafia, which means they were probably 'casing the joint,' as they like to say on those reruns of the Untouchables that I like to watch every afternoon on that cable station. In any case it's hard on the feet so I don't think there's any padding under the carpet... ."

Collingwood interrupts both Wilson and our meeting as the odd couple approaches the conference table. He's in the know, natch. "Everyone," he announces. "We want to introduce you to our new News Director, uh, Vlad Macula."

Silence.

"You guys did some fast interviewing to replace Allen Pratfall," finally remarks Follicle.

"Actually, Sherman," replies Wilson, self-importantly, "Vlad here was the other finalist for the job when Allen was hired. And," he adds, serenely, "he was really the first choice of Miss Eriss and I. We wanted him, couldn't wait for him to get here from Billings. But others overruled us."

"That's ridiculous, Walter," Collingwood responds, dismissively. "Vlad, you are just in time to witness our morning meeting."

The mound of humanity answers. "Thank you, Carl." Slow, careful syllables. Lugubrious, deep bass vocal tones. Barely perceptible Eastern Euro-accent. Its speech time. "Permit me to be clear. I understand it's always a little, shall we say, 'nerve-wracking' to acquire a new manager." Okay, so he's sensitive to us? Great!" That is as it should be." Nope. Not sensitive. Not Great. "I have already reviewed several weeks' worth of taped newscasts. I will call upon each of you for a one-on-one meeting in the next few days. I am not immediately planning any personnel changes, but..." another sinister chuckle follows: "Heh heh heh...I will be watching each one of you verrrrry closely. Heh heh heh."

That brightens up the morning meeting.

"You may proceed with your work," commands Macula. "I will retire to my office, and become acquainted with the computer system here. Good morning." His shoulders turn away, followed stiffly by the rest of him. He leaves us with another, "Heh heh heh."

Wilson leads Macula into the News Director's office. We sit in stunned silence. Gretchen Calzone conspiratorially catches my attention and rolls her eyes. Uh oh.

Brightly, Jen Nettles breaks the ice. "Well, that was fun!"

"Nice knowing you guys," says Jack Phillips.

"We have to find out which market he came from," Scott adds. "We might be able to find out a little about him. One of us has to know someone working at his last station."

"I'll run a Gargle search engine check on him," offers Angle.

"What for?" Follicle challenges. "What's the use? He's here. Ivory Eriss wouldn't admit a mistake and remove him."

"But I for one would like to know what to expect from him. See if Chuckles here has the reputation of being a slasher, a stalker, or if he's just full of hot air," replies Nettles.

Can't argue that. In fact, in a newsroom--where everyone has an innate need to know everything, and First--it will become a contest to find out this man's background.

No time for that now, though. Everyone moves into their work day. My news report is about how a majority of the security cameras used in smaller businesses don't operate properly. The people who run gas stations, pawn shops, and convenience stores often plant cameras around their business--but don't turn them on. Or, they mistakenly point the camera towards the wrong spot. If there is a robbery, all anyone can see of the perp is his feet, or the top of their hair, or simply nothing of value at all.

While interviewing Sheriff Dank about this, I throw in a question about Luther Post, who still hasn't been caught. His response it telling. Without telling. "Wehhhhhhhlllllll," Dank drawls, tobacco wad deep in mouth. "He isn't caught yet."

No kidding. I appraise Dank. He is what you might call "wiry." Lean, tough, gristle, topped with a cowboy hat. But sporting a kind of crude charisma that appeals to voters in Reproach County. It doesn't extend to reporters.

"We've got our eye on a couple of people he was known to *con-sort* with." He's practically reading a press release. Chew, spit. "And we are following up several *meaningful* leads in this case. I am certain we will apprehend this suspect in the very near future."

Thanks for the scoop. Clearly, Post is long gone or completely lost in the woods of Reproach County. "Should people who live around here be concerned for their safety? Should they take any special precautions at places such as public schools?"

"There is no need to be, er, alarmed."

"But he was considered armed and dangerous just a few days ago."

"Wehhhhhhhllllllllllll, he's back up in the woods somewhere, probably cold and hungry. I'd say he's runnin' out of *vim* and *vigor* about now. Not tah mention food and water."

"But what makes you think you're gonna catch him sometime soon when he's evaded you for so many days?" I have to ask. I brace myself for the answer.

Dank's dark eyes narrow. He draws himself up to all of his six feet two inches. "Because I said so," he asserts.

It's time to return to the station. I'm starting to hit my stride, learning how to get my work done in a timely fashion at WDMZ. I have a personal Timetable--and making it back by 3:30 means I have just enough time to write my story. No time to remove my jacket or grab a cup of coffee. Scanning my video, I quickly transcribe soundbites. Once I'm finished writing by 4:15, Collingwood or Tracy Scott or maybe Lavinia Fern can copy edit the script. It's obvious that I shouldn't go to Walter Wilson, who changes words he's never heard of("It's a 'boon' to the community, don't you mean 'boom' to the community because I just don't get it"). My photog and I have to start editing by 4:30 to make the 5pm newscast. Those deadlines are loosened slightly when my stories are placed in the 6pm show. For the organizationally-challenged like me, remembering the Timetable makes a pretty big difference in making sure we get done on time.

So I get to work. On her way back to The Cage to yell at Fotch for some reason, Calzone stops by. "Chuckles has been keeping himself busy."

"Chuckles?"

"Don't tell me you didn't notice his conspiratorial little laugh: Heh, heh, heh. I've been stuck in here listening to him in his office all day. I'm pretty sure that I'll have a nightmare about his voice tonight."

"Oh, you mean Macula. Yeah, I heard it. Anybody fired yet?"

"Nope. He hasn't come out of his office since he started exploring on his computer. Not even at lunchtime. Walter tried to get him to go to his taco joint, but Macula just grunted at him. Walter fled his office in a big hurry. I don't think he'll be going back in--voluntarily, anyways."

"Smart thinking," I reply.

"Not Walter's strong suit," Gretchen judges, and moves on.

Walter's true strong suit is providing a running critique of the competing newscasts at 6pm. Although our news programming begins at 5pm, this is considered the "flagship" newscast. We wear our Sunday Best for this show. Everyone gathers, by habit, except Macula. He's still working, I suppose, in his office.

Wilson is revved up. "Okay so Channel 7 is up first and look at Ken the anchor's hair, its sticking up in the back just like Opie or was it Alf-Alfa. But it looks like they are gonna lead with the Hairdresser who was attacked in her shop this morning. Its way down in our newscast BUT LOOK they got an interview with her in the hospital! Wow! Tyler didn't get that, I wonder why... ." (Tyler's about to do a liveshot at the salon) "...and now they are going to do that dirty election campaign between Roddy Rooker and Martin Contestable boy do those guys hate each other... ."

I try to tune out Wilson and focus on the newscasts. That must explain the very similar intense look of concentration on everyone else's face. Fern and Adams appear as our newscast starts. It's immediately evident that something is wrong with Adams. He's looking off set...okay, now he's focused. His body seems unsteady, like a cork riding a wave. Lavinia introduces herself. Pause. She turns to Adams, lost in his thoughts. Suddenly he arrives to the moment and starts.

"And hi, I'm Jeff Adams. Hmm. Looks like the Soyfield Fire Chief has got himself into some trouble! We always knew it would be just a matter of time!"

Shock in the newsroom. Is he drunk? He's not slurring, but he doesn't seem together. "Brian Fantana is in our Soyfield Bureau and Brian, what in the curses is going on out there?"

Uproar. Fern looks shocked, Fantana starts to stumble out his report. Now the newsroom goes crazy. I glance over at the other side of the room, where Macula remains in his office. A bulk shadow, unmoved. Is he watching? Does he notice the burst of excitement over here at the TV bank?

None of us can hear Fantana's report. Everyone is talking at once, to confirm what we just heard and speculate as to what is wrong with Adams. Someone wonders why he seemed together in the 5pm newscast but not now. Collingwood and Wilson march to Macula's office. Wilson stays in the doorway while Collingwood plunges in. From here I can only see their backs as they engage the News Director. Can't hear anything that far away, of course. Wilson gestures wildly. Collingwood folds his arms. Macula does not emerge from his office when the pair departs.

By this time, looking worried, Fern is reading the next story. But we all know who's on deck. And there he is, chin on balled fist, imitating Rodin's "The Thinker." A pretty big stretch, I think. Deep in contemplation, Adams slowly rises to his full seated height, and addresses the camera. "Nothing like a tax increase story to make your bowels move. Since mine are getting ready, let's take a break. We'll be right back after this."

I wonder if Adams will be right or back. Ever again. There is momentary control room confusion. The camera stays on him, unrelenting. He was supposed to throw to Nettles at City Hall. Serene in his little corner of outer space, Adams placidly waits. Finally, the picture fades to black.

Collingwood strides quickly across the room, grabs me by the arm and keeps moving. "Your package is supposed to be coming up," is his only explanation. Wilson tags along.

We're off and running, heading to the studio. Down the hall, through the big double doors. It's cold inside here; they have to protect the temperature-sensitive equipment. Something else is chilling: Adams leans back in his seat, still serene. Arnold the weather guy and Lavinia Fern simply stare at him. Adams lost in thought, or something. Oblivious.

"Alright Jeff, you're done. Get out of here. Wilson Gamble will sit in for you."

What? That blindsides me.

And Adams. For him, its instant lucidity. He doesn't like me. "This guy? He's only worked here a week!" Two weeks. And a day, buddy. Adams doesn't move. "I'm not leaving."

"You crossed the line, Jeff. You need a break."

"No, Carlie-boy. I'm in the game. I'm fine. Everything's cool. Just give me some space and it'll be fine. Break's ending. Hey, I've got the munchies. When you go out, do me a solid and get me a Snicker's bar from the candy machine, Will." Adams tosses a dollar at me, which I simply let flutter to the floor. His attention shifts. He looks behind Collingwood to the floor director. "Which camera am I going to be on?"

"15 seconds," announces the floor director, shooting a concerned look to Collingwood. But it's Wilson who responds the quickest.

"He'll be alright, Carl," Wilson implores. "He was taken by surprise because he thought that Lavinia was supposed to read those lines."

"He'd better start reading between the lines," starts Collingwood. But the fact he was distracted is enough to save Adams for now. His intransigence and the pressure of the ticking clock are enough to sway Collingwood. He catches Adams' eye, just for a moment, and holds it.

"This is the last time, Jeff. I am going to watch in the control room. You will only read what is in the teleprompter and say nothing else. Nothing. Or you are out of here."

Adams pretends to review copy in front of him, whispering something about "not a robot." Lavinia Fern remains silent, reviewing her own scripts. She is a separate Entity. The opinions not expressed on this program are necessarily those of this co-anchor.

I trail Collingwood and Wilson behind the news set, through a different heavy door. Inside is the Control Room. It's dark. Shadows work here, illuminated only by small electronic lights and multiple television monitors. No windows. At times they say it feels like there's no air.

One monitor shows the broadcast picture seen by viewers at home. Next to it is the "preview" monitor, to show the director which shot is lined up next. Others display the shot seen by each studio camera. There's four on the news set, one in the newsroom, one in the Soyfield Bureau, two from liveshots in the field somewhere, and two from network video feeds. A final monitor displays the script as portrayed by the teleprompter. The back story of the newscast is told right here. I find a small open spot along the wall, and watch. One of the studio cameras is labeled the, er, "Studio Camera." Mounted high above the news set, it's only used for a few moments at the end of some newscasts, to show the studio, perhaps as a parting gift to the viewers.

It gives me a bird's eye view of what's going on out there. Wilson leaves. Collingwood moves in behind Tracy Scott's camera. She gives him a look of disgust. But the break is ending and she has a job to do.

On the studio camera, I can see the floor director pointing at the middle of three floor cameras. The red tally light glows. Fern talks. Adams waits his turn.

"Welcome back." Hey, nothing weird here. The co-anchor was whacked out but we sobered him up. Everything's good. She starts.

"Numbers can be deceiving. But in some ways, the latest crime statistics seem to show that Reproach County is suddenly a much more dangerous place to live than a year ago." She stops. Adams seems to be catching up. There's a collective catching of breath in the control room. Finally, he reads. Very Carefully.

"County leaders say most of the increase is due to explosive population growth in the past twelve months. But Newschannel 99's Jeanette Nettles reports, some of the victims say they don't feel safe in their own neighborhoods anymore."

Cut mics. Cue liveshot. Big sigh. But there's no time to celebrate.

Scott is burning up the intercom microphones. Reminding Fern she reads the next story on Camera 3. Telling the technical director when to display "supers"--the titles on the bottom of the screen that identify the people talking. Reminding Nettles to "stand by" in the field after her taped report ends. Asking Arnold Paul if he can add 30 seconds to his weather segment, and the Master Control operator to add 30 seconds to the next commercial break--because she wants to kill stories that Adams is supposed to read. The director remains busy setting up camera shots and firing commands to his technical staff. The next five video segments, including mine, have to be in place. The audio operator needs to lower the volume on my package. The person running the character generator has to have the next "super" ready to go. The camera operator has to set the next shot. It's a ballet of bedlam.

Nettles finishes her report and Fern reads the next story. It's only a 20 second "v-o," or voice over. Meaning, the anchor reads copy while matching video appears on screen.

Then, Adams. Everyone stops and watches. This must have been what it was like for the helpless people on the ground to watch the Hindenburg burn and crash.

"Residents of northeastern Frippin County may soon flush their septic systems if a proposed urban sewer line is approved by county commissioners tonight." Adams pauses. What now? By chance I check the monitor that displays the teleprompter. The squeezed script does indeed look quite awkward:

"NERS TONIGHT.

FRIPPINRESIDENT

IAL CUSTOMERS..."

Surely remembering Collingwood's warning, Adams dutifully reads, "Frippin Resident Ial Cus.. uh, Ial? Uh." His confusion is quite evident. He checks his paper script, known as "crash copy." He's crashing; copy that.

"Ah, er, Frippin *residential* customers may have to pay a special utility tervices sex, er, services tex, tax, to have the lines run through their neighborhoods. Commissioners tonight, uh, will vote tonight on the issue."

Adams looks dismayed. Cut to Fern. She reads the intro to my story, and then eventually together they tease the upcoming weather report and this "block" of news finally ends.

Collingwood shakes his head. No longer serene, Adams looks for a hole to stuff himself in to. Fern stays busy, trying to distance herself from the faux pas. But...we can't dwell on mistakes. Scott isn't sure what happened.

"I was talking to Master Control about the break when that happened. Is Adams in trouble again?" she asks.

"No," Collingwood replies, quietly. Whoever wrote that story failed to put a space between 'Frippin' and 'Residential.' A simple press of the 'space bar' on the keyboard. So when it appears on the small prompter screen on the camera there wasn't enough room for that whole mashed-together 'word.' So, it wrapped around at a very bad spot."

Scott shakes her head. She's seen it before.

Commercial break. Arnold Paul, the meteorologist, is in his "Weather Center" about ten feet away from the main news set. The floor director rolls a studio camera over towards Paul. On a monitor in the control room I can see he is intensely focused on his computer. A late update from the National Weather Service? No. Reflecting in his mirror, Paul pulls out a brush and fixes some wayward strands of his wavy silver hair. Then, he fixes the knot on his silk tie and begins his forecast.

I'm ready to duck out. Collingwood's anger seems to be dissipating, but he needs to get to the bottom of the Adams Calamity.

"Any idea what happened, Tracy?"

Scott keeps her eyes on the clock--it's essential to provide time cues to the meteorologist, so he knows whether or not to pick up the pace. But she has a timely thought.

"During the break between newscasts he said he had to make an emergency visit to the restroom. He came back and all this weirdness started."

Without a word, Collingwood heads out. To the head. I'm behind. The closest men's room is just outside the heavy double doors from the studio to a hallway. Collingwood plows in. He sniffs--thankfully the washroom has been, er, out of use for a while. But there has been some smokin' in the boy's room. From the trashcan, Collingwood fishes out the end of a doobie. Its soaked wet, evidently to put out the flame.

"There's no way to prove anything," Collingwood confesses, half to himself, half to me. "But I'm pretty good at math."

The broadcast races on. Weather, done. Sports, over and out. The "kicker" closes out the newscast. All without incident, thank goodness. When it's all over, Collingwood instantly moves to intercept Adams. They go visit Macula, along with Walter Wilson, who carries in a small mountain of his "thoughts" scribbled on sticky notes.

I hurry out to the newsroom. What's the popular verdict on Adams? How many calls from viewers? Was that crazy stuff, or what? ! ? ! ?

Uh, no frenzy. In fact, few people are there. Marshall Hurd is engrossed in "The Garlic" news parody website. At the assignment desk, young and blonde Aimee Flotsam is eating a Lean Cuisine frozen dinner that smells like burnt cheesy noodles.

I hang in there awhile, finishing up my work while keeping an ear on Macula's office. Loud but indistinguishable voices erupt from behind the closed door. Eventually, Collingwood retires, alone, evidently vacating the field to the likes of Macula, Wilson, and Adams.

That's it--I'm vacating also, heading out the door. Hit the supermarket and the liquor store, then head to the Haversack House. Quietly, I park around the corner, in a different spot. But this one had better work. I'm not willing to play too many more rounds of "musical parking spots." Entering the front door, I find myself still impressed by the homi-ness of the porch, and wonder why builders don't make them anymore. I carry my two bags of groceries into the kitchen.

Mercy Haversack floes in. Wearing another floral print and a dour, business-like expression.

"Miss Mercy, where can I store my food?"

"Not in here," she advises--abruptly, for her. "Out on the back porch there's a refrigerator and some shelves." She hefts a finger, slowly pokes it behind me. "And by the way, that's the proper entrance for, er, boarders to use here. Your key will work in the lock on that door."

As a, er, *boarder*, I struggle on back, through a wood-framed screen door. The long, rusty spring that retracts the door screeches and bounces obnoxiously, of course. Going through the door leaves me in a ten-by-ten enclosure. A glorified summer porch, really. Screened in, but no air conditioning. Against a far wall--the house exterior--is a 40 year old Kelvinator refrigerator. A little thing, by today's standards. Rounded top corners. Tilts awkwardly to one side, due to age, or an uneven floorboard, I guess. It hard to believe the thing is actually operable, except that I can hear it wheeze, mechanically. Six cabinets are mounted on another wall nearby. Two have nothing in them, so my stuff piles in.

A 4x6 card commands guests to "Close cabinet doors when finished." Another informs, "Refrigerator temperature set on 'Low' at all times. Saves energy. Do not adjust."

Once my stores are stored away, I grab a can of something pasta-like and fixings for a sandwich. Back to the kitchen. It's cooler here. Mercy sits at an obscenely-cluttered table, nearly unmoving, ignoring me and reading a magazine. It's the "Saturday Evening Post." A closer look: March 10, 1956. She's chewing on a roll.

"Miss Mercy, what are the kitchen rules?" I try to ask politely, looking around for little white cards. There's not much counter space to set down my stuff.

Haversack deliberately places the magazine on the table, erasing some of the last open space in the room. Swallows the roll. Challenges me with a steady gaze.

"Try not to use the oven. Water is a precious natural resource, don't waste it. You can use the stovetop and microwave once in a while. Use only the dishes in the drain, not in my cabinets. And, of course, clean up after yourself."

"I always do," I tell her, setting to work. Hard to know how to balance friendliness with establishing the fact that I'm not that easily bullied.

Returning to her magazine, she grows quiet. I stir up a warming can of ravioli, assemble a Dagwood sandwich. Lots of meat and cheese, maybe a slice of tomato. Sensing what's coming, my stomach makes noise. I carry my plate and bowl to the table and set down to dig in. Mercy looks up once again.

"Don't use that plate," she admonishes.

What?

"Why not? I got it out of the drain next to the sink." I try to make sure my voice doesn't rise petulantly. "You know, where you told me to get dishes."

A smirk slowly unfurls across her heavy face." Yes. But, I use that particular one to feed the cat."

8

No notes are left on my truck the next morning. Yay. My new spot must be approved by the invisible Parking Nazis. Truck's wet, though. Mother Nature may not have approved.

On the way in to work, I wonder about this Vlad Macula. Looks like a bean counter. A giant bean counter. And when management turns to giant bean counters, it's a bad sign for programming. Cutbacks may be imminent. I've got a contract, of course, but those are one-sided, ever designed to benefit the station, not the employee. 'For Cause' or not, if Macula doesn't want me, he can find a way to get rid of me. Fine. Would be a perfect ending to an all-around weird experience at this place.

In case he keeps me, this is another day towards regimentalizing my new routine. Exit the freeway, battle the surface street traffic. I can almost hear the fast-paced, canned, 1961 movie short theme music playing: "American Industry at Work." I cruise down the office complex drive, passing all the block-like buildings, and head past some greenery into our parking lot.

The sunny day quickly dries the overnight rain. And the bright light strikes the tall, white turret of WDMZ. As I drive by to find a parking spot, I spy Warden the Doorman inside the lobby, busily abusing a cloth towel on the front windows. Why does that man spend so much energy cleaning the windows? He doesn't seem to notice me--or anything else-- on this side of the glass.

Carrying my manbag and suit coat, I use my new electronic key to get in through the back double doors, into the artificial atmosphere of the newsroom. Although the early crew has been churning out the morning newscasts, it's pretty quiet. One TV on the bank of monitors plays softly. Meredith, the Noon producer, is typing something on her computer. The scanners squawk steadily but not insistently. Coffee perks up the second pot of the day on its cabinet perch. It smells like morning. Sedate. Gretchen Calzone hasn't gotten truly fired up yet.

Sherman Follicle is already on his computer when I sit down nearby. We exchange a brief "hello." The two of us don't have much in common, except that he's from Michigan and I'm from Ohio. There's that major college football rivalry thing. But we really don't even have that to talk about. He attended Central Michigan ("you know, that's where Dick Enberg went," he reminds people) and I went to Case Western. He studied broadcasting and I studied sociology. He enjoys landscaping; is older, rounder, family-oriented. Irritates me with his nasal Michigan twang (He hails from a place called "Iyann Erber," home of the University of Michigan). Although he seems tired in person, Sherman is remarkably energized when the red tally light comes on over the camera. He is the master of happy, first-person features where he gets to try things himself, from riding along in an F-14 jet to dressing up as a clown in the circus. To him, every day is a national holiday. Today's holiday happens to be National Taxidermy Day. Therefore, Follicle has his story idea ready-made: a local taxidermist is offering to show him how to stuff a wild coyote.

My stories aren't that fun. I have to actually prepare for the morning meeting. I hadn't noticed anything noteworthy on the ride in to work that I might look in to. Notepad and pen handy, I make some phone calls. There's nothing new on the search for Luther Post. I'm responsible for Frippin and Ersatz counties, so I call the sheriff's departments, city hall clerks, school superintendents. Nine times out of ten, they have nothing of interest. But I chat them up anyways--the secretaries, usually. The courtship starts with the weather forecast. Who doesn't complain about the weather? I tell them harmless inside stuff about Arnold Paul, our Chief Meteorologist. They watch him, like him--but don't know much about his life. So, I make myself their conduit inside Newschannel 99. In a few weeks, we will move to more personal joking. By then I'll know about their issues and operations, and can chat about more stuff. Eventually, someone will put me to the Trust Test. Off the record, they may tell me something, say, about an investigation that I shouldn't know about. It might look like a good story. But it is really a harmless bit of information. If I report it, they will never trust me with anything truly valuable ever again. And word gets around about trust; trust me.

The pace of the newsroom picks up as others arrive. The coming morning meeting is on everyone's mind. Pressure. Some did their homework the night before or early in the morning, and have story ideas ready to pitch. Others worriedly check the newspaper for tidbits in the classifieds, obituaries, advertisements, or elsewhere. Some visit websites that provide nothing but feature story ideas, the Public Relations wire for media releases, or look for ways to localize a national news story. The problem with these sources is that six other people could pitch the same idea. Others simply throw out vague suggestions to follow-up ongoing storylines--such as Luther Post or Robby Rooker.

Today, one of my local calls scores. The town clerk in West Hannibal says she heard that an unidentified man entered the local elementary school an hour ago. Possibly carrying a gun (most do in West Hannibal), he slipped past the front office and was able to roam free until the principal came across him. He ejected the man from campus and then called police. By the time they arrived, the interloper was gone. Okay, it looks like I could be heading to West Hannibal today. But it's an hour drive--one way, so I keep digging, just in case.

The other calls don't yield much. The Ersatz County Sheriff's Office has scored a coup in luring civil rights leader Theophilus Walker to talk to students about how school resource officers can be trusted to keep them safe at school. Perfect. West Hannibal is in Ersatz County. I'll suggest we cover that at the morning meeting as a nice "bridge builder" story. Every now and then we are able to do a happy story...so we can make a friend. Next time we do a negative story there, they will be reminded of the "nice" story in case they complain.

Armed with my story ideas, I confidently march off to the Morning Meeting. Poised at a huge dry erase board, Collingwood presides like Professor Kingsfield from "The Paper Chase." Some days I feel like Timothy Bottoms. Butterflies flutter by. Don't call on me, don't call on me. Sooner or later, he will. Some days, the answer sounds like, "Uh, I, uh, saw a report on, uh, tooth decay, uh, on the network morning show that we could, uh, localize..." Eyes roll. Some snickers are heard. But what's worse is that Collingwood stops and stares at you. Wipe board marker stopped in mid-air. Then he simply ignores such poorly-conceived story ideas and moves on. Uh...ugh.

Not today. Nettles pitches a strong idea. Murmurs of "that's a good story" echo around the table. A "good story" is more than just a story with strong content. It consists of a combination of three elements: A) clear news import; B) potentially interesting video; C) obtainable interviews for "sound," that is, soundbites. Stories that do not potentially have these elements are not "good stories." For local television news, Watergate would not have been considered a "good story." Think about it. The Assignment Manager berates the investigative reporter: "What? Your only video is the outside of a hotel and your only interviews are with lawyers who said, 'No comment'? Are you out of your mind? It's a newspaper story!" That, by the way, is an epithet. In a visual medium, nobody wants to look at 90 seconds of a city council meeting. Who cares if they approved $900,000,000 to renovate the mayor's summer home?

My story idea is duly approved. I hear at least one, "That's a good story" grudgingly murmured somewhere around the table and am secretly satisfied. Can't wait to go. I notice that no one has mentioned Jefferson Adams' on air blurtings from last night. Wonder if he'll be around for tonight's newscast.

This is the first day that starts to feel routine. Fakir Johnson and I settle into a SUV and make the long drive out to West Hannibal. When we arrive, we find the story is as advertised. There's no suspect, no arrest, but the principal confirms the guy had a rifle and plenty of parents are upset. The kids don't seem worried, but what do they know? The school will tighten security. No reason to pitch a liveshot to the assignment desk for our 6pm newscast; the school will be quite empty by then. So we plan to shoot our video, eat lunch, make one more stop for a second story, and return to the office by 3:30 or so.

Planning the lunch break is a big deal, especially when we are far from the station. Videographers expect their hour-long break. It would be utterly mandatory if this was a union shop. Even though it's not, reporters usually try to keep them happy...because the boss insists that everyone gets their federally-mandated break. The day's schedule planning often starts with deciding where to have lunch; namely, identifying which restaurants are in the vicinity of the story. Everything else has to work around that. I know of some stories that actually changed because the news crew preferred to interview someone who lived closer to a favorite lunch spot. It turns out that Johnson knows a family restaurant outside of West Hannibal. It has red checkered tablecloths and a good hot turkey sandwich. I've learned to trust videographers and their stomachs--even Billy Fotch. They always know a good place to eat, including locations as remote as West Hannibal.

The patrons all watch us as we enter the restaurant. Our logo-covered SUV has their interest, but they don't recognize me, certainly don't recognize Fakir, the guy *behind* the camera. But we still sense a certain amount of respect that some people have--not for members of the working press, but for somebody they saw on television. We saunter in, self-conscious. Just here for the grub, ma'am. The waitress is solicitous, in a curious sort of way: are these not men?

After lunch we stop at the Ersatz Sheriff's Department. Classes have just ended at a different elementary school close to headquarters, so a dozen or so kids with their parents mill around, ready to hear from and meet Theophilus Walker. Chief Deputy Roscoe Flamm eagerly takes me around. Good P.R. for the department. Good P.R. for Flamm, who plans to run for Sheriff in a year or so. After interviewing a parent, I let Johnson loose to shoot whatever he wants. Flamm pulls me aside. He's a little shorter than me but clearly spends a lot of time in the gym. Uniform is fitted to show off his "Body By Roscoe." Big arms pop out of the uniform shirt, already tightened by body armor underneath. Close buzz cut. A fairly young guy making some plans. He speaks in 90 rpm bursts, like an M-16.

"This is great. I'm glad you could make it. Will this be on the 6 o'clock news?"

Stifling a yawn, I reply, "Probably. I wanted to show you I'm not only interested in the bad news. We like good news stories at Newschannel 99." No we don't. Viewers don't watch good news stories. They tell us that in every single ratings survey. But Flamm doesn't know that. I'm paving the way for a little future co-operation from him. It comes much sooner than I expect.

"You are the only reporter I could get out here for this. The Sheriff didn't think we'd get any coverage at all." Flamm hooks his thumbs into his service belt, and squares up on me. "I've got something else for you."

My Spidey Sense starts to tingle. But I must remain nonchalant. "Oh yeah? McGruff The Crime Dog coming for a visit?"

Flamm ignores that. "We're ready to bust some perverts. Computer guys, you know, who surf the internet all night. Meet young girls, proposition 'em, try to hook up with 'em. 'Cept they are about to hook up with us, instead."

"How are you going to do that?" Suddenly, this is cool. Whatever the process is, I'm in.

"Internet Crimes Squad. Deputies go online, pretend to be young teenage girls--or boys." He grimaces. "It doesn't take long before some perv starts chatting. Next thing you know, he's set up a date. But I'll be there instead. You can too, with a camera, if you want."

"Are you kidding?" A key question remains. "But my boss might not be all that interested if it's just a photo op that everyone's invited to."

When Flamm smiles, it's like his whole body flexes. "You're the only one here today. You'll be the only one there on that day."

I instantaneously become a big believer in Woody Allen's insistence that 80% of success is just showing up.

Fakir Johnson has no idea why I'm smiling all the way back to the station. "Your story isn't that good, man," he advises me.

"I have one that will be," is all I tell him. Can't tell anyone except Collingwood. Word must not get out on this. We drive on.

"What do you think of Macula?" Johnson asks, conversationally.

Tread carefully. "Hard to say. I haven't really seen enough of him. But a lot of stations are only hiring 'one man bands,' so we all could be seeing some changes."

"That's true. Bigger changes for reporters or shooters?"

"Well...I've never saw a change in News Directors that benefitted me," I reply flatly. Even if they aren't trying to make everyone a one man band--a single employee shooting and reporting--most prefer to bring in their own on air "team." Just for the sake of bringing in new people. That "freshens up" the look of the newscast, especially if it's in last place in the ratings. Forget the fact that most newbies are from out of state, entirely ignorant of the new community they are about to cover.

"Maybe he'll get us some new cameras. I'm tired of mine always being in the shop for repairs."

"That and your wireless mic," I remind him from the liveshot with Jack Phillips.

Showing me a sour face, Johnson doesn't say another word all the way back to the station.

As we pull in to the SUV stable, I find myself about 20 minutes behind my Timetable. Gotta hurry. Johnson can grab the gear. But before I make it into the building, I can hear a muffled shouting match. It explodes in volume when I pry open the double doors.

"You didn't even try!" It's Tyler Hubbell. "Did-ent ee-ven try! I thought you were shooting! And you missed it--you missed it! How could you miss a boat sinking in the river? Were you picking your nose or straightening your comb over or studying the science behind how Velcro works?"

Norman Wallflower deflects the verbal assault with a pair of arms folded over his skinny chest. But he suddenly lets loose, hard. "Hey Prima Donna--Prima *Tyler*--if you want me to do something specific, get out of the SUV! Take a break from putting on your lipstick!"

Walter Wilson is the only person there with a job title high enough to officiate the conflict. But he's oblivious. He's trying to talk to Hubbell in mid-shouting match. "Tyler? Hey Tyler? Tyler? Tyler? Tyler?" All this while Hubbell is screaming at Wallflower: "There's no reason for me to put on lipstick when the standups you shoot of me have your stupid thumb in one corner of the lens!"

Wilson keeps trying. "Tyler? Tyler? Hello, Tyler? Tyler?" His voice is patient, steady, persistent. But she twirls away from Wallflower, splashing some of her iced caramel macchiato on Wilson. She stalks back to her desk. Wallflower follows. Wilson quietly leaves in search of a napkin, or perhaps a sticky note. Food stains seem to happen to him a lot.

"It's not my *thumb*, Prima Tyler," responds Wallflower, evidently enjoying his clever new nickname for her. "It's my middle finger!" He shows her what he means. That sets off another round of hollering.

No one else pays them any mind. It's getting too close to deadline. Same with me. I move right past as they snarl at one another. This dispute has the sound of someone who didn't get his lunch break. A different kind of trouble waits at my desk. A Walter Wilson sticky note. Cold fear unnaturally grips me. The gist is: I am summoned to see Vlad Macula as soon as I get in.

No time like the present: I am "in," despite the deadline pressure. Get it over with, whatever "it" is. I have to walk past the Hubbell vs. Wallflower firefight once more to get to the N.D.'s office. Their battle runs from her cube to an edit bay. I glance over at Calzone; she's not paying attention. Tracy Scott seems to act as if this is normal.

"Will they kill each other in the privacy of the edit bay?" I ask her.

Scott seems surprised at the question. "Tyler and Wallflower? Oh no, no, no. They do this once a month. Neither one of them has any discipline, so it naturally just kind of, um, gushes out at one another." She almost giggles at that.

"So I don't need to call Warden The Doorman," I guess.

"Don't bother; he's busy cleaning the windows. If any blood comes trickling out the edit bay door, we'll call in the cops. At least we'll be 'first on the scene' on this one," Scott smiles and turns back to her work. I march on to Macula.

In his office, Vlad Macula betrays no recognition of the ongoing blow-up. The door's open, but little light finds its way inside the office. Blinds drawn, overhead light out. An antique table lamp glows 15 weak yellow watts. Cloaked with another dark suit, Macula sits heavily behind his computer. The monitor flickers a bluish tint on his face. His massive body is planted, unmoving, like a boulder. One of his hands, seeming to act on its own from behind the desk, motions me to close the door. I sit on the edge of a chair in front of his desk, but it's difficult to see around the widescreen monitor. I wait. The tiny eyes come up to me from around the monitor.

"I wish to meet with all of you so that you may learn your fate." Each word spoken meticulously, like the care of a brand new car. Then, the mirthless laugh: "Heh, heh, heh." Unnerving. When I do not respond, his flowing eyebrows narrow into a single unit. He goes on, ponderously.

"Wilson Gamble, eh? Like to gamble a little, eh? Heh heh heh." He chuckles at his own joke. "You have not worked here for so very long." It sounds like he's charging me with something.

"Two and a half weeks," I reply. Gotta let him know I can speak.

"So you are not so set in your ways, correct? We have too many people working the dayside newscast. You are the newest." The tiny eyes do not blink. They wait.

"And what does that mean for me?" Steady, can't get worked up. It seems he is baiting me, waiting to see how I will respond. The 15 watt bulb seems to dim further.

"A change, I think. Although you are new here, your file shows you have many years' experience. We need someone with such qualifications for our morning newscast."

"You want to move me to early mornings? What about the reporter doing the job now?"

Slower than ever: "He does not fulfill my requirements. Heh heh heh."

Wonder if the guy was thrown in a dungeon or merely fired. I don't know him, but I don't really want to share his fate. "So you want me to take his place. Reporting for the morning show."

"Yes." Macula leans in on me, as best he can, across his desk. His bulk actually edges it forward an inch. "How does that...appeal to you?"

Our least-watched newscast doesn't appeal much. But this guy seems to relish making people miserable. Common trait among News Directors. So, I resolve to not allow him the satisfaction of rattling me. "Part of my deal for coming here was to work dayside." I have to tread carefully, while establishing a few things.

A long, slow, evil smile cracks his face. "Do you have that in writing? Is that in your contract?"

Of course not. Very little in any television contract actually favors the employee. They can get rid of you but you can't get rid of them. They build a cage with their legal limitations, and it's not bounded on the west by Tulip, Texas or on the east by Somaliland. So, I don't reply to the question.

Macula chugs slowly along. "Any agreement you may have verbalized with Alan Pratfall is hardly binding in a court of law, and certainly carries no weight with the current administration of this news department. Heh, heh, heh. And I prefer to work with what are often called 'team players' while I am in charge at Newschannel 99."

Heard that phrase before. "You don't know me well enough to know that I do my best no matter what the assignment is, "I reply. Then, the conversation with Chief Deputy Flamm comes to mind. "But I have a big sweeps story I've been developing and it would help me to do it if my schedule remained consistent with a standard 9-to-5 work day. It's a pretty good story."

Macula's momentum melts. "Sweeps story? I failed to understand that any had been assigned. We shall have to discuss this in greater detail at a later date." He glances momentarily at his computer. "In that case, we shall wait two weeks before making any definite changes. That should be sufficient time to finish your work on that report. We will talk then." He does not punctuate this with his trademark chuckle.

Having dismissed me, his attention drawn back to his computer.

Not so fast, my friend.

"There's one other thing," I interject. Macula seems surprised that I didn't simply disappear. Yes, I'm still here. "I'm in a bind with my paychecks," I inform him. "I haven't been paid. Evidently the payroll people need an I.D. with a permanent address. But I haven't been able to secure one yet."

"Well, you need to do this, then."

I explain my situation. A small smile quietly returns to Macula's face. In his mind I will end up owing him a favor. "Heh heh heh. I shall investigate the matter as soon as practical. You will successfully manage your financial affairs until then, hmm? Good day."

Thanks, Chuckles. I withdraw from the vacuum of the dark office, making a quick, blinking adjustment to the sudden light and noise of the newsroom. I feel some relief over postponing the change to the morning shift, but feel a detached concern for that colleague who may be out of a job soon. I check my watch and the stress jumps right back on my shoulders. Now I am 35 minutes behind schedule. Gotta run.

A reporter I worked with a couple of markets ago calls a finely-produced report "n'art"--the grammatical contraction for "news art." What a joke. The process of editing a news "package" is as creative as assembling a circuit board and technical as painting a landscape. Okay, maybe it's the other way around. In some ways, it is like paint-by-numbers. Getting a story on the air takes several essential but standard steps. Once we return from the field, I take my SD digital recording card straight into an edit bay. Reviewing the images, I look for compelling "soundbites" and write them on a notepad. Back at my desk, checking my facts, I start writing. The key is to make the creative juices flow under deadline pressure. Then I find someone, usually the Managing Editor, to copy-edit the story. While they look at the script I bite my fingernails. Even if the editor doesn't technically improve the script, a second pair of eyes covers your asparagus, in case any legal or ethical issues pop up later. Then, I head back to the edit bay to stitch together the sequence of video clips to match my narration and the soundbites. It's called a "package." You have to count on at least one or a dozen malfunctions to slow things down. Finally, I press the "send" button to electronically deliver the finished product to the control room.

And after a day's worth of blood, sweat, and fears...some bug in the system confuses which video to play--and something unexpected runs instead.

Well, not every day.

Only your best stories. During ratings periods.

The usual suspects are crowded around the bank of televisions at 6. Adams introduces my report (calling me "Wilson Gimble" this time), but instead of watching my exclusive on the crazy man with a gun in an elementary school, we are treated to video--with no narration--of civil rights activist Theophilus Walker. Before any shocked noises burst from the gaggle around the TV's, I launch like a North Korean missile out of the news room.

In the cool dark quiet of the Control Room, lights and monitors blinking serenely, you'd think nothing has happened. "What happened?" I cry.

Scott briefly looks my way; the show must go on. "The wrong video was sent to the Control Room."

"No it wasn't, I made sure of it!"

A tall, goofy 20-something busy viewing the latest video posts on f-baumsworld.com at a laptop computer at his work station flicks an eye up to me. "Dude, you sent your video to the wrong production channel here."

"Couldn't you check it before the 'cast, make sure it's the right video?" I ask harshly, glancing at the computer screen to which he insolently remains glued, pointedly ignoring my presence. "You just associated a man who was arrested for marching in Selma with a fool with a gun in an elementary school!"

"I'm working here, man," replies the Goof, dismissively. He clicks "start" on another entertaining online viral video.

"Why don't you pay closer attention to your work, then?" I spit out. "Try to earn your four dollars an hour!"

The Goof smiles for the first time. "You get what you pay for, man."

The newscast is over. I am sitting in my cubicle with my head in my hands when I hear a voice over my shoulder.

"Hey George. I heard you had a problem getting your paycheck. This'll help."

It's Jack Phillips. Can anything good come from that corner of the newsroom?

"Come and see," Phillips replies. He holds out a laminated plastic card.

I lift up my head. It's a driver's license--for this state. Insensically, I stare at it. My face stares back at me. It's the picture from my Station Identification card. My name is on it--my real name. It appears to be a state-issued driver's license.

"Are my eyes really brown?" I ask, with no intent.

"Only if you want the proper identification to get your paperwork in order," answers Phillips. "The address," Phillips winks, "is the house where Robby Rooker got busted."

"Why in the world did you go to all this trouble for me?" I wonder.

"That's easy. I owed old George Pierrot a very big favor. Long story. He's gone, you reminded me of him."

Wow. From the outhouse to the penthouse in five minutes. Looks like my Cash-22 dilemma between no address, no identification, and no paycheck is suddenly solved.

Back "home" at the Haversack House.

I'm still trying to be optimistic about this arrangement, so I park far away at the "closest" available street side spot. As directed, I enter the back door, heading through the enclosed back porch with the refrigerator-refugee from "Leave It To Beaver." Silently passing Miss Mercy, melted into her kitchen table, I grab a bag of "Fritos" and a bottle of Gatorade for dinner. There are other voices in the parlor. But I need some privacy so I head up the stairs and down the hall. Something white and unusual is crumpled on the floor in front of my door; my bath towel. A 4x6 Mercy Rule is neatly placed on top.

"Towels may not be left in bathroom. Please keep them in your room."

Arrrggghhh. I already served my time as a teenager. And these daily lectures by note card are starting to get on my nerves. Why not a brief tete-a-tete request rather than a stark, impersonal demand? Some people have no diplomacy, I tell myself. Wonder if this is just a breaking-in period, or permanent oppression. Signs are that Haversack has the corner on 4x6 cards in this town.

A noise behind a neighboring door slowly intrudes on these thoughts. Its TV noise, meaning another boarder is home at this time. Towel under one arm, Fritos and Gatorade in the other, I move down the hall. I offer a friendly knock at the door. The television goes silent. I tap again. Quiet footsteps inside the room. Finally, the door opens about three inches. Eyes look down on me. Way down. For a moment I wonder if it is standing on a chair. The eyes stare but the mouth does not move. Is it a troll? A vampire? A basketball forward?

"Uh, hi. I'm Wil, the new tenant. In the room next to you," I try. No response. The door sullenly remains at three inches. As if all the air will escape if it opens any farther. I try not to breathe too much and use it up.

"I was wondering about some of the rules here... ." Pause, looking up for reaction.

The mouth finally forms words. The voice cracks like puberty itself.

"I saw your towel in the bathroom. You are supposed to hang it on the rack in your room."

"Uh, yeah." Okay. Looks like I'm talking with a Disciple of Mercy. "Does Miss Mercy always communicate through, uh, notes like this?" I hold up the card.

"Oh yes. Quite efficient, I'd say. Boarders don't have to be confronted face to face." A life goal for this troll? No wonder I hadn't seen him until now.

The opening in the door slowly starts to recede. But I'm still trying to connect a little here.

"I put food in the cabinets on the porch... ."

The troll interrupts. Breathlessly. "You mean the 'pantry.' We call it the 'pantry.' Food is kept in a pantry so it's the 'pantry.'"

Who is this, Walter Wilson's younger brother?

"Uh, okay, the 'pantry.' Looks like a porch. I just wanted to make sure I hadn't put my food in the wrong place. Didn't want to get a 4x6 card from someone."

Still no blinking. But the door is definitely closing. "Yes, it's fine. Thank you for your interest." This last part is muffled behind the fully-closed door. Nice to meet you.

Head downstairs, towel in hand. Now I want to connect with Miss Mercy, in a mildly violent way. Down the steps, around the corner, into the parlor. Slab sits motionless in the ante-room at the far end of the parlor, and I sense the presence of a couple of other people there, too, but don't actually see them. I guess they are other boarders. They are apparently engrossed in something, perhaps the television, so I move on.

Down the hall, through the dining room, I glance into the kitchen. Mercy is settled in there, self-absorbed. Slowly destroying a complete box of cheap chocolate-covered cherries. Other than the repetitive hand-to-mouth reflex, she's solid and unmoving as Asia. She pretends not to notice me when I enter the room. Magazines, knitting, and old telephone directories are piled up like ramparts to hide behind.

"Miss Mercy," I start. She affects a slight startle.

"Oh. Mistah Willie. I didn't see yew come in theyah," she tries. I know better. She had already twitched involuntarily in recognition of my presence. Now she claims I didn't exist until I spoke to her. Why do people play games?

"I'm sorry about leaving my towel in the bathroom. I didn't know that rule but I wish my towel hadn't been left on the floor of the hallway."

She regards Exhibit A in my hand.

"But it wasn't left on the floor. I made sure it was on your doorknob."

Mebbe, mebbe not. But I proceed cautiously. "In any case, next time just mention it to me and I'll be glad to abide by your policies."

"Well, I feel my 4x6 cards are quite efficient and preclude the necessity of finding you boys each time you trespass upon my house rules. That way we avoid, shall we say, unpleasantries. Like this."

"Next time, mention it to me in person," I insist, a little more assertively. "Then I won't find the need to be...unpleasant." She stiffens, not expecting a challenge to her ways of doing business. But I've got her. "That way you won't have to worry about your minion carefully placing your card on top of my towel that was left crumpled up on the floor."

No answer to that. I drop the 4x6 card. Adios, amiga. But me, my towel, my Fritos, my Gatorade, and my dignity are heading back upstairs.

Before passing out--that Gatorade mixes well with Southern Comfort--I check out the 11pm newscasts. The Newschannel 99 lead story restores some of my sobriety. Police say that Luther Post robbed a convenience store near Ashton Heights...and shot the clerk.

9

It's a mad scramble at the morning meeting to determine just how much coverage to give the latest incident apparently involving Post. In addition, the Sheriff's Department is now offering a $5,000 reward to the person who provides information that leads to his arrest. The bigger question is who gets the reward of being the lead reporter. After another challenge from Phillips and even Fantana ("hzz shootrng vvvktm lvvvfd out hrrr" he tries, via speakerphone), Hubbell wins out, owing to her previous coverage of the story. I'm not in the running: I'm off to find some child sex predators.

The Internet Crime Squad does not have an impressive suite of offices. Wallflower and I ride up a herky-jerky, chain-driven elevator to the fifth floor of Ersatz County Sheriff's Department headquarters. We sign in at a desk hidden behind security Plexiglas, and wait for Chief Deputy Roscoe Flamm. Dim light accents the dark wood walls and floors. While waiting, we sit on old style wooden benches, heavy and dark. Many initials are carved into mine. I watch a spider weave a web on a filing cabinet behind the desk. I'm almost ready to sing a church hymn in these pew-like benches.

Collingwood gave the go-ahead to develop a report on internet predators for an upcoming "sweeps" piece. Television stations set their advertising rates by the number of people watching during four month-long ratings periods: February, May, July, and November. "Sweeps" refers to the way the Nielsen ratings company used to send out ratings diaries to viewers, "sweeping" from one coast to the other. Of the four sweeps months, May and November are the most important. The result is yellow journalism at its most jaundiced: sensational stories *you just can't miss!* Overweight pets! Killer fungus on hotel beds! Kids who smoke pencil shavings! Radio DJ's who don't play requests! News anchors with enlarged prostates--an inside look! ! ! Occasionally, there's an opportunity to really investigate something. I hope we have found one of them.

Flamm's compact form strides in to the room, carrying a protein drink. Probably spent his lunchtime muscling around the gym. He introduces us to Sgt. Terry Sherman, head of the geek squad. Petite, blonde, unsmiling. Veteran. Hates the media, because she's been told to. We are a distraction: we will get in the way, ask stupid questions, yada, yada, yada. Sometimes those stupid questions are ones she wishes she had thought of while investigating some crime.

Nevertheless.

This story could help her in a lot of ways. We can scare potential predators, keep them from stalking children in the future. Publicizing the value of her program, we might generate more funding for it. So, for today, Sherman is civil.

Wallflower and I follow her and Flamm behind the reception desk--past the cobweb on the filing cabinet--through a door, down a dark hall. Are there no windows in this place? Heavy, dark, wood trim around doors and windows, like that of an old schoolhouse, appears darkened by years of cigarette smoke and other atmospheric pollution. Such as swearing. Doing so, under her breath, Sherman marches on, over the cool, hard tiles into a big, open room. Here, tables are coated with piles of computers and wires. Two or three offices line the back wall, blinds pulled down on the windows looking into the room we occupy. More thick wood. No papers or files in sight; nothing for our prying eyes to see. One deputy is working quietly in an office. Otherwise, we are the only ones in the area--until we start chatting online with some very sick men.

"This is it," announces Flamm. He's staying where the camera is. "This is Sgt. Sherman's show. She's here to answer questions about procedure, I can speak about larger criminal issues." He'll get his air time, with pleasure. Hey, I owe him.

There are some windows here, but blinds cover them. The artificial light is kept low to more easily view the computer screens.

"Okay," Sherman starts, addressing my cameraman. "How do you want to do this?"

Wallflower considers: for any videographer it is a treat to shoot video with some planning and creativity, rather than simply "run and gun" style. He walks around the tables. Then starts talking to himself. "Put up a couple of lights here...and there, to throw a shadow. Use a colored gel one of the lights. Uhhhh...tripod behind the chair. Have to fix my shutter speed for computer screen shots. Maybe a wireless lav for the sergeant." Then, finally, out loud to Sherman. "Would you normally use any one of these computers, or just one in particular? '

"Doesn't matter. They all have the same software set up."

"Then go ahead and sit at this one."

She does, and somehow doesn't seem any shorter for having been seated.

In his sullen, plodding manner, Wallflower unpacks. Lights, audio, tripod, camera. It takes a while. Sherman describes to me techniques her team uses to catch the attention of online predators. In what is called a "pre interview" I ask a lot of basic questions, which will help me ask more focused and intelligent questions when the camera is rolling.

Finally, Wallflower pins a wireless lav microphone on Sherman's blue uniform collar. Away we go. First, I interview her. Initially her answers are stiff as starch but when we talk about young lives she is helping to save, Sherman warms up nicely, giving more emotional answers. Afterwards, Wallflower changes camera position. It's pointed at me now so I can ask a couple of the same questions again. These "cutaway" shots might come in handy when we edit the video. Then, he moves to an angle behind her as she faces the computer. Flamm and I lean in to see the screen, careful to stay out of Wallflower's shot. Now Sherman can get to work. She enters a chat room, fishes around for a while. In eight minutes, though, someone takes the bait. Screen name "W@nkr" pushes a conversation. Sherman responds in the guise of a 14 year old girl.

"HIG?"

"fine but i have so much hw, mostly algebra... i'm so tired i'm aak"

"LOL! What school? '

"guildenstern ms. hate it"

"ASLP? ?"

"14/f/Filterboro. U?"

"23/m/Filterboro"

Sherman keeps a digital photo of an anonymous young teenage girl handy. In response to the Age/Sex/Location/Picture request, she accesses the file and forwards it to the predator.

"U r cute! !"

"tu"

"What do u do 4 fun when u don't do hw?"

"uno, chill w/ friends, go to the mall"

"Really! Which mall, maybe I'll see u there"

"pestilence ridge mall, by the hwy"

"What else do u like to do?"

"what do u mean? ? ? ?"

"When ur parents aren't home"

"oh, watch tv i like Bachelor but my mom doesnt like me to watch it"

"Did u evr want to hook up with a bachelor?"

"why? !"

"To get with a guy, we could hang out"

Behind us, Flamm makes a disgusted noise. I second that emotion. The conversation rapidly progresses. Or, regresses.

"what do u like to do?"

"Don't laugh!"

"what do u mean dont laugh"

"Oh, I like to get sexy sometimes, get together with someone and have some fun, uno"

"what kind of fun?"

"Well I kind of like to do the wild thing, j4g, uno"

"that's cool"

"ATM I'm NIFOC, what about u"

"tmi! ! ! :-O"

"lmirl? ! ? !"

At this point Sherman has to translate for us. "He says he's naked in front of the computer. I tease him by saying that's too much information."

The guy is not deterred. He presses on, hoping to move to a webcam and then to hook up. Grimly, Sherman claims she has no webcam, but after initially resisting finally gives in to the request to meet. Her 14 year old character lets slip her mother is going away next weekend and she'll be watching the house by herself. W@nkr is so revved up that he immediately seizes on the opportunity. They set a time and Sherman gives driving directions.

"Shooting fish in a barrel," she observes.

We spend another hour. Sherman invites two others to her little party. "By a week from today, our unit will have lined up about 25 of these perverts. About half will show up and we will take them down."

Mentally, I'm rubbing my hands together. Literally, too. Muuaahaha. This is going to be great sweeps stuff. Saturday can't come too soon.

Back at the station. I'm reviewing video from the Task Force shoot. The frizz is gone from Gretchen Calzone's hair; its early Friday afternoon. Her Dollar Store reading glasses hang limply from a lanyard around her neck. Evidently she's thinking about her weekend plans. I try not to imagine her spending it with Artie. The scanners are peaceful. Most of the work is done that can be done in the office, leaving reporters and videographers to finish the job out in the field.

The quiet had been such a balm to her nerves that Calzone's smile lingers even when the phone rings. I can't help but hear the one-sided conversation, which starts out brightly enough.

"Newschannel 99, Where We're Right 99 Times Out of 100! Yes ma'am, I'm a 'boss.' The Assignment Manager. You can talk to me." Long pause. "Ma'am. Ma'am. Yes, ma'am, I've been taking notes. You're from Greenville and you say your charter bus broke down on the highway here at... six o'clock this morning. 60 or 70 people going to a family reunion in Texas. The bus company finally sent a replacement at 11... oh, sorry, 11:30... but it didn't have air conditioning so no one wanted to get on it. The little babies are crying. And now the bus company is hanging up on you when you call to complain. Yes ma'am. Calm down, please, we want to help."

Calzone attempts x-ray vision through a wall into The Cage.

"Excuse me, ma'am, don't go away." Phone receiver to chest. Deep breath. Best Alexander Graham Bell imitation. "WALLFLOWER COME HERE I WANT YOU!"

Nothing.

"Ma'am, where are you now? Everyone is in the parking lot of a Frendy's restaurant at the freeway exit? Can I get the phone number you are calling me from? Mm hm. It's a cell phone, right. Okay. I am looking for someone to send out to you right away. Yes ma'am, I understand about the little babies. Okay. Mm hm. Thank you. Okay. Thank... thank... thank you bye." Quick disconnect.

"NORMAN!" she somehow growls at "howl" volume.

Tracy Scott now informs Calzone that Wallflower left with Sherman Follicle. "Had a standup to shoot with someone, I think."

Checking her assignment wipe board, Calzone mutters. "Norman's gone, Fakir's with Tyler, everyone else is busy. Which leaves Billy, naturally." She looks around. No need for the office public address system. "FOTCH! WHERE ARE YOU?" The walls shake.

Sudden commotion in an edit bay, the sound of someone falling off a chair. Fotch emerges like a hibernating bear, rubbing his eyes. The spike seems lost from his hair. "What is it, Gretch?" he asks, wondrously.

She quickly recounts the story. "The second bus took them to a Frendy's restaurant parking lot off the freeway, but they refuse to go any further without a bus that has air conditioning. Certainly not all the way to Dallas. So they are all standing around, trying to keep an eye on their little babies, er, the kids, and wondering what to do."

Fotch seems to get it. "What town are they in?"

"Cheeseport. It's the Cheeseport exit, number 235. Easy. Go south on the freeway, get off at the Cheeseport exit, and I guess the fast food restaurant is right at the end of the exit ramp, although I've never been there. Should take you about 30 minutes to get there, so get going right away just to be safe."

"Why were they going to Texas?" asks Fotch, randomly. He scratches an ear ring.

"That doesn't matter JUST AS LONG AS YOU GET GOING TO THE FRENDY'S AT CHEESEPORT!"

"Yes ma'am!" Fotch salutes. He's out the door, man. Focused like a laser beam. Or not.

"FOTCH!!" Calzone screams.

He peaks back in.

"Don't forget your camera."

Smile. "Right." Back to The Cage. Equipped, gone.

I have time. I saunter up to the Assignment Desk. "Can Billy really do this alone? I'll go with him if you want." Not malicious, just willing to help.

"Sure he can do it." Calzone's busy working. "All photogs need to be able to go get stories on their own like this." Confidence is the company line. But then she tips her hat to reality.

"Its three hours before the show." Calculations. "It'll take an hour round-trip, maybe 20 minutes to shoot, 40 because its him. That leaves an hour and a half to edit 45 seconds of video and write a quick story. If necessary, you can write the story. No sweat." But she wipes her forehead with her fingertips. Her smile is gone now that the clock is ticking on a decision to (shudder) Trust In Fotch.

News crews start making their way in, like partners to an Allemande Left at a square dance. Hubbell and Johnson. Follicle and Wallflower. Nettles and Frank Sturm. Others. Noise and tension start to rise. The afternoon shift arrives, and the newsroom is now full of life. The afternoon meeting starts. Collingwood is busy and Macula is hiding behind his computer, so Calzone presides from the Assignment Desk, her knowledge of all things superior to reporters who know only their individual stories. Then, however, the hotline telephone rings.

"Newsroom. Yes, Fotch, where are you?" We all know a flurry of exasperation will follow. "Where? Exit 301? You went the wrong way!" Something on the other end. "I DON'T CARE IF THERE'S A FRENDY'S AT EXIT 301. That's 40 miles north of here! I told you to go south! Even people who flunk Driver's Ed can figure out when interstate mile markers count up or down! Turn around! Turn around right now, go south until you hit Exit 235! Now!" She slams the handset down, really hard. Doesn't that kind of cheap plastic ever break?

Collingwood has heard much of this. He moves to his office doorway. Hands on hips, he calls over to Calzone. "Now he's an hour away. Is he gonna get there on time?"

"There's still time," Calzone growls, definitively, defensively.

Tracy Scott is interested. This is supposed to be a story for her show.

"Should we send someone else and call back Billy?"

Calzone figures again.

"Everyone is still tied up with stuff for the show. Videographers have to edit or get ready for liveshots. It's really up to him."

"Alright," Scott looks wary. "But I'm not sure where I'm supposed to put this story in my show. I'm starting to doubt that he's going to make it back on time."

"He'll be back on time," Calzone responds with confidence. Stirred, not shaken. One concession, though. "Put it in your 6 o'clock newscast, not the 5, to buy a little more time."

"He'll probably drive all the way to Dallas," offers Follicle, head down in his cube.

I'm researching my story on the computer when Calzone takes another call.

"Whaddya want now, Fotch?" Pause. She takes a real deep breath. Slowly, now. As to a child. "Listen, Mr. Rand McNally. I know they aren't at the Frendy's at Exit 287. They are at the Frendy's at Exit 235. That's south of there. Keep going. AND GO NOW. Thank you, Billy." Calzone actually hangs up the hotline phone delicately. Her self-control is amazing.

Three minutes. Hotline again. The frizz is back in her hair.

"OF COURSE THEY AREN'T AT THE MCDONARDO'S AT EXIT 287! THEY ARE AT THE FRENDY'S AT EXIT 235! GET ON THE FREEWAY AND GO SOUTH OR I WILL STRANGLE YOU WITH THIS TELEPHONE CORD!" The slamming of the receiver breaks off a piece of the phone, which flies away sharply.

A deep murmur emerges from Macula's office, like a slowly-forming belch.

Calzone glances his way, doesn't reply. She's almost panting. Deep breath, now. Calm blue ocean. Its Friday, still, right? She finds another phone, dials.

"Yes ma'am, its Gretchen Calzone from Newschannel 99, Where We're Right... oh, never mind. There's been a delay but our videographer is on his way. Any word yet from the bus company? No? I'm sorry for that. We are calling them also to see what they have to say. Yes ma'am. How are the little babies?" Long, long pause. "At least you won't have to pay for the damage, right? I hope not. Well, Billy is on his way, should be there in a little bit. Thanks for your patience."

She hangs up. The hotline rings again. I notice Calzone staring at the back exit doors, wistfully. Several people jump up to answer it, but Calzone coolly lifts it to her ear.

"Yes Fotch." She's very quiet now. Eyes closed. Mechanical. "You go south on the freeway. South to Exit 235. Cheeseport. Get off the freeway. The Frendy's is right there. I can see it on the computer on "Goggle Road View." Got it? Please, go. Please." There's a pathetic note of pleading. She mouths the word "please" again after hanging up the phone.

Back in my world, I find my videographer, bring her up to speed on an interview I need to get for a quick story on a groundbreaking ceremony for a new library. We need to leave in about 15 minutes. I make a couple of phone calls, set everything up. There's an hour left before the newscast and I am making sure my manbag is prepped when the Newsroom Hotline phone rings yet again. Calzone just stares. It rings again. She can't bring herself to get it. I do, for her.

"Newsroom, Wilson Gamble."

"Hey, Wil! How are you?" asks Billy Fotch.

"Hi Billy, I'm fine. Where are you?"

"Cheeseport, of course! Exit 235. But I don't see a Frendy's. So I found an Orby's Roast Beef place."

Wordless, Calzone leans forward, staring daggers at the phone pressed to my ear.

Glancing at her I take one step back and say, "And did you find a group of70 stranded people with a large charter bus there?"

"No, but did you know that they have 39 cent roast beef 'n' cheddar sandwiches this day only? I ordered some for everybody at the drive-thru."

"Wow. Fabulous, Billy. But you had better order a bullet-proof vest if you don't find that Frendy's right away. It's got to be around that exit somewhere."

Pause on his end. "I'm trying to look around while I'm stopping to eat. Oh. Wait! Frendy's has the big sign that says 'Frendy's' and has a red-haired girl and a hamburger on it, right? with the word 'Frendy's', right?"

This boy needs a doctor. Or a bodyguard. Gretchen stares at me, uncomprehending. But understanding.

"Yes, Billy. I strongly recommend you go there immediately. Eat your lunch on the drive back."

At this, Calzone rips the receiver out of my hand, slams it on the desk. She keeps whacking the desk with it. She doesn't stop. More pieces break off. I stand back. She stops when she cuts her hand on the jagged plastic. The blood catches her attention. She can only muster up an, "Oh," as we all stare at the wreckage.

Walter Wilson springs from his office. He is so furious that he speaks in short declaratives. "That is going to cost you, Gretchen Calzone! That phone is not yours, its company property! You will pay for this out of your next paycheck!"

Staring down Wilson, Tracy Scott intervenes, soothing Calzone back to the break room where they can locate the First Aid kit. "It's okay, Gretch. Cool down, honey. He'll find them and he can still get back in time. Don't worry. I've got it late in the 6 o'clock. He can still get it back. Plenty of time."

"Yeah, yeah. Plenty of time. Right," Calzone breathes, heavily. They exit, stage left on this Friday.

The end of the story only came to me later. I leave to shoot an interview and missed the, er, excitement. Over beers during the weekend, Collingwood fills me in.

"First, the good news. Fotch actually found the place, and the people. He videotaped an interview with the woman who called us, shot video of the 'little babies' she had talked about, and the bus. There was just enough time to get back. I called the bus company. They were rude but told me another bus was on the way."

"Did it have air conditioning?" I ask. Smart aleck.

"Of course. It got there a couple of hours later."

"What about Gretchen?"

"She finally calmed down and came back to the Assignment Desk. She even was thinking about packing up a little early. But Follicle started joking that Billy was going to call to ask for directions back to the studio, or ask if he could pick up his dry cleaning on the way back."

I smirk. Collingwood takes a slug from his beer. "But it turned out worse than that."

I'm semi-stunned. "How is that possible?"

"Do you know that small lake along Traction Avenue when you get off the freeway? Fotch noticed a small group of people gathering around something. The journalist or whatever inside him came alive. Turned out, an alligator was strutting around the lake, scaring people. So dear old Billy thought it would be a bright idea to shoot some 'breaking news' video of the alligator."

"He stopped? Knowing how late he was with his bus video?"

"He stopped. Shot video of the gator. And was very proud of himself when he rolled in to Newschannel 99 at 6:25." Way too late to make the evening newscast.

"Was Gretchen there when he finally came in?"

"Yes." He drinks again, enjoying himself. "Jack Phillips and I had to pull her off of him. I mean, physically. He was scratched up a bit and there was a welt on his neck from the phone cord but I think he'll be okay by Monday."

"Too bad," I joke. "She should have punched him in his viewfinder eye."

Smiling, Collingwood concludes, "Either way, I don't think he'll press charges against her."

10

Another week rears its ugly head. To me, with an exciting sweeps shoot to look forward to on Saturday, the work-week seems to drag on. My stories are varied, as always, but fairly run-of-the-mill. City council is thinking about enacting a new tax to expand the airport. A drugstore closes its doors after 48 years in business. Several students get sick eating mystery meat at an elementary school cafeteria.

Work is, well...work. At "home," I try to keep a low profile at the Haversack House, quietly imbibing in my room while I'm there. I discover more Mercy Rules on the ubiquitous 4x6 cards. "Do not throw leftover food into the garbage can." I wonder what I'm supposed to do with it. "Do not set the air conditioner in the window below 76 degrees." Since there's no thermometer, I don't really know the temperature. "On odd-numbered days, please walk on edges of throw rugs to keep them from getting worn in the middle." I find myself wishing my odd days were indeed numbered here.

Increasingly, I find myself avoiding "home" as much as possible. Primarily so I don't have to interact with Mercy or Slab, who I have not once seen with an actual repair tool in his hand. Not that I can recall him in any kind of actual forward motion. Since I have so much free time on my own hands during the weekend--much if it necessarily spent at Haversack House--I don't much look forward to Saturdays and Sundays. This weekend is different, when the hands of the clock finally sweep around enough times.

Naturally, Wallflower doesn't contemplate working a weekend. He hands off our Very Important Sweeps Project to one of the weekend videographers, a 30-ish guy named Don Wash. He's wearing the videographer uniform: jeans and a novelty t-shirt that merely reads "Think First." And...he's vertically challenged. No more than 5'5". Which is not a helpful attribute for shooters. Often, they have to compete to take pictures of a news subject who is sometimes surrounded by an assorted scrum of other videographers, reporters, photographers, security people, and hangers-on. Sometimes you gotta go over the top when you can't go through them. But Wash also appears to be a veteran of the gym, his bulk protruding out from the t-shirt. This *is* a helpful attribute, especially when we may be challenged by angry internet sex predators.

We meet at the station, early. He packs up the gear while I go over the game plan. Wash is excited to be in on this story. "Buddy, I have got a

13 year old baby girl at home and if anyone ever tried to mess with her... ."

I glance at his t-shirt and smile. "Think First." Woe to that poor sucker.

Using my Big Blue pickup rather than a station SUV to remain anonymous, it takes 15 minutes to drive to the house. It's a two story vinyl-sidedlate-1970's job in the center of an aging subdivision. Not run down, really, but the neighborhood has seen somewhat better days. Lawns. Lots of trees. Empty-nesters practice yard maintenance on a Pleasant Valley, er, Saturday.

We meet Flamm at the door. He has briefed the other deputies detailed to the Internet Crime Squad. He says they don't mind our presence but we still run a gauntlet of stares. They regard us with a single expression: don't screw this up for us--or you will never feel comfortable in this town again.

Finally, we get in to see Sgt. Sherman. She seems more welcoming than our first encounter. Perhaps she's a little more used to us now. She explains the set-up. "A relative of mine is in the kitchen, through that door over there, who has a little girl voice like you wouldn't believe. When the doorbell rings she will call out for them to come in and wait here, in the living room. When they say something about the rendezvous, we all come in to make the arrest. There are eight other deputies in and around this home, so no one gets out un-arrested."

"Whose home is it?" I wonder.

"Yours," she answers. "And mine. The city owns it. Sometimes they hold retreats here, other times they host out of town, um, dignitaries. Visitors."

Not too-dignified dignitaries, I hope. Not in this faded Brady Bunch-ville home.

"Where can we put our camera?" asks Wash.

Sherman points up. An open stairway leads to an upstairs walkway. Despite the relentlessly white-painted walls, its dark up there. A low wall divides the hallway from the large, open living room underneath us. The low wall is topped with a variety of houseplants. We have the high ground; it's a perfect vantage point over the trap that is set below. "We'll disguise you there," indicates Sherman. "After we apprehend the suspects you can come on down right away and get up close and personal."

"Can we hide a wireless microphone somewhere downstairs, to make sure we pick up all the sounds down here?" asks Wash, carefully. Don't want to frighten the prey, now.

Sherman considers. "Is it the little microphone that you had on me during our interview?" I nod yes. "That should be no problem. We'll put it in this desk drawer here and just leave it open a little."

While Wash moves equipment upstairs, I ask to see Sherman's "appointment book" for the day. It's pretty simple. Every half hour a new perv is scheduled to show up. Each one is identified only by their computer screen name. Contacts made to their internet service provider give us some clues to their identity. I see "W@nkr" is scheduled to arrive at 10:30am. Sherman tells me her unit traced the IP address on the man's computer, cementing the evidence against him.

Soon, everything is in place. The 9 am "appointment" is due in a few minutes. I climb the stairs to the special perch next to Wash and Flamm and we wait, camouflaged. My heart beats fast as the house grows quiet. I listen to Wash make little grunts while he adjusts his camera and watches through his viewfinder. There are no second takes with something like this, so it had better be right the first time. Glancing down, I note that the living room is furnished plainly. It doesn't actually look lived in; there's no detritus of life laying around, like magazines, knickknacks, or even some dirty dishes. Not my problem, though. My position gives me a clear view of the front door. It'll be the portal to jail for some people today. The sun beams through large windows to provide a well-lit lair for the offenders stupid enough to come.

For some reason I expect the high-pitched, confident sound of the doorbell ringing. It doesn't happen. Instead, I hear a light tapping at the door. As if someone doesn't want to make too much noise. A teenage girl's voice downstairs calls out, "Come on in! Door's open!"

It does. Open, I mean. Despite the abundant light in the room, its brighter still outside. At first, the visitor's features are not distinct. As he slinks forward, they clarify. A small man wearing brown polyester pants, an old golf shirt, and a bad moustache slinks in. He looks around, carefully.

The girl speaks again from the back of the house. "I'm just getting out of the shower! Have a seat in the living room if you want."

The shower? An oily smile crosses the guy's face. Yeesh. He doesn't sit. He doesn't even move. Then a different female voice, this one much more commanding, hollers "Freeze!" Four deputies bear down quickly, force the man on to the floor--it isn't difficult--and read him his rights.

One checks his pockets, leafs through his wallet. "Uh huh. Jerry Pilager. 118 Sprawl Street, Filterboro. Hook up with kids much?" The trapped man's eyes are glazed over.

My photog, Wash, doesn't fritter around. He bounds away, down the steps in a heartbeat. It takes a moment for me to register that he doesn't have his camera. And he's shouting curses.

"You pervert!" He curses. "I'm gonna beat you senseless!"

Fists clenched, Wash rushes headlong at the man, still handcuffed on the floor. He scores a couple of slugs to the jaw, but there's too many deputies. Despite Wash's righteous fury, they manage to hold him back. Flamm pins his arms behind him. Sherman and I get in his face, which is blood red.

"What are you doing?" she screams. "You can't do this! It'll ruin everything!"

I try to intervene. "Don, what's going on?"

Wash is still livid. But in a moment, he realizes the need for clarity. "That's my daughter's soccer coach!" He sputters.

Ugh. Sherman and I look back at the guy in disgust. We would love to let Wash have a few minutes alone with him. Instead, we talk quietly with him, lowering the temperature. Eventually, Wash heads upstairs to call his family, chat with his daughter a little. See if there's anything to really worry about.

There's still a news story happening, so I grab the camera. It isn't foreign to me, being a "one man band." So I head back downstairs.

Deputies take their time moving Pilager The Perv out the door. I find my chance. "What are you doing here?" I ask, smarmily, while pointing the camera and holding out the stick microphone.

Still stunned, the man starts to answer, but thinks better of it. I get to the point. "Did you meet a 14 year old girl online and come here to have sex with her?"

Stumbles, mumbles, bumbles, fumbles. "I, ah, no, I, you know, she said she was 18, but I, uh... ." then he falls silent. Nothing good can come from talking to a video camera.

But I try some more. "Are you a youth soccer coach? Have you ever touched any of your players?" And, thinking of Wash, "What would you say to parents?"

A look of fear crosses the perv's face. He rubs his jaw. But still, no answer. Pilager is led out the back to a car in the garage and disappears to his fate in the court system, and a long, dark prison filled with grim and menacing shadows.

Sherman returns, looking grim. "You had better talk to your cameraman and see if he's going to flake out again. I don't care if the next perv to walk through that front door is his wife and she's buck naked and carrying a cucumber--he cannot lose his cool, not one more time." Looking at me, a thought occurs to her. "Say, you don't have any daughters, do you?"

"No, no, no," I reply, holding up my hands in half-surrender mode. "What I care about most is winning an award for this story."

I head back up to Wash. He's finished on the phone, but doesn't look at me. "Everything's fine at home," he says, quietly.

"I think we'll be okay here, if you don't flip out again," I say, a questioning tone in my voice. "Can you hang in there?"

"Yeah, yeah." Even quieter. "Yeah. no problem. I got it under control, it's okay." He tucks in his t-shirt, pulled out in the scuffle. "I'll go talk to the lady in charge down there."

I let him go alone. In a few minutes he comes back to our stake-out position. Sherman shoots a warning look up at me. Yes ma'am, we're cool.

The mini-drama finished, everyone resumes their places. Flamm takes a position more suited to potentially containing Don Wash than actually seeing anything downstairs. The doorbell is supposed to ring at 9:30. But it doesn't. So we wait. 9:45 comes, no new perv. My watch reads 10:19 when we hear it. Everyone tenses back up, stops breathing for a moment. I wonder if it is the 10am "appointment" or W@nkr, due at 10:30.

The girl's voice calls out as scripted, "Come on in! Door's open!"

Pause. The door does not open. I can almost sense the struggle going on inside the perv on the porch. Go ahead with this, or turn back?

Perhaps prompted by Sherman, the girl calls out the next line. "I'm just getting out of the shower! Wait in the living room if you want."

The shower? That ends the struggle. The door opens. A thick shadow fills the door. I crouch a tiny bit lower. But I can still see. And, why is Vlad Macula down there? Did he know about this set-up, this sweeps story? He sports a jogging suit rather than a double breasted suit. The breath catches in my throat.

Heh, heh, heh.

He didn't know about the sting.

Chuckles is a perv.

No wonder he spends all that time at his computer. Wash is still taping but throws me a look of OMG shock. What a morning. Our News Director is about to make news. On our newscast.

Everything happens very fast. Macula is skillfully flung to the floor, despite his great bulk. Quiet in the realization that he had not chosen wisely out on the porch. He is not chuckling.

Then we show up.

He is startled. "You!" he says, accusingly. Like I suckered him here or something.

"So this is what you do on your office computer all day long, huh?" I ask. The shot in the dark hits its mark; Macula winces.

The officers have him secured, but they look at me, wondering how this crazy news crew knows all these pervs. Sherman also sends a questioning look my way.

"It's our boss," I remark, and turn away. Heh heh heh. Guess I won't be moving to the morning shift any time soon, after all.

Sunday breakfast at Mercy's. Well, call it "Sunday brunch" after sleeping in. I wonder if anybody's in the kitchen. Maybe I can make some toast and see about frying an egg. Hope it's not too much to use the stove. I head on down in my sweatpants, t-shirt, and Cincinnati Reds ball cap.

Sure enough, the mountainous form of Mercy Haversack is planted at the kitchen table. Does the woman ever move from this spot? I try not to roll my eyes.

"Good morning, Miss Mercy," I offer, non-committally.

"Hmmm," she answers, engrossed in a magazine. "Ladies Home Journal" must be running another "What Men Really Want" investigation. Primal instincts exposed. Speaking of which, I'm a hunter-gatherer at the moment. That category's probably not in the article. I need to move from caveman to a more civilized mode.

"Mind if I use a burner and frying pan?" Ask to be polite. If she hadn't been there I would have just done it, as part of our agreement.

Heavy sigh. The magazine lowers at about the speed of Congress. Mercy stares into a corner of the ceiling, as if contemplating this non-essential sacrifice. Whatever her answer is today, the underlying message is that I had better think twice about asking in the future.

Ultimately, she breathes a small sound, like "Hyeh." It seems affirmative, so I move into the porch/pantry. Rustle up some bread, butter, eggs, peanut butter, juice. Oh, it's gonna be a feast.

While I work, I notice Haversack eyeing me over her magazine. She has nothing to say. But I try for small talk. "How's everything in the neighborhood?"

She works herself up into an answer, and when it finally comes, shockingly, it's at full blast. Slow-motion full blast, if you can imagine it. "The waste management collectors left a lot of garbage strewn on the road this week. Then young Warren, who is in the room next to you, paid his rent late. That meant I couldn't deposit his check with the others at the bank yesterday. And then Mrs. Trollopson who lives across the street and three doors down had the nerve to ignore my advice!"

Gosh! Can you believe that? I flip my eggs and think about my toast, but try to remain in this conversation just to fill the dead air. "Why's that, Miss Mercy?"

"I told her she needed to trim that hedge at the end of her driveway. I told her that for years it's been too high and she wouldn't see someone coming when she backed out into the street." Her words suddenly move faster. "And then finally she told me to stop nagging her about it!"

"Did she have an accident?" Where's a knife for my peanut butter?

Mercy's voice rises in defense. "No! But that's not the point! She's going to! And it's because of that hedge!"

I never associated Mercy Haversack with so many exclamation points. Try a calming tone, instead. "How long has the hedge been there?"

"Let's see. It was planted back in...oh, I'd say it was more than 15 years ago."

I wonder how many times that cars have successfully navigated the Trollopson driveway with no difficulty. Okay, my small meal is finally ready. Find a plate--not one belonging to the cat. Sit at the table with Mercy. There's nowhere else to go. Now it's her turn for a question.

"Why are you starting your day so late?"

None of your business. "I had to work yesterday."

"Late into the night? You came in very late last night. And I'd have to guess you had something to drink." She might be right, but there's no charity from Mercy. No delicacy, either, despite her genteel veneer.

I clear my throat. "I have lots to do today, so I better get moving," I respond, followed by the fastest kitchen cleanup you have ever seen.

Exit, stage right. My day is pretty empty, but I'll find a way to stay away from this place as long as possible.

The neighborhood is considered historic. In fact, parts of it are like a giant, open-air museum, showcasing beautifully-restored homes. It also features an element missing from newer neighborhoods: sidewalks. Sunday afternoon is a great time to look around, so I go for a stroll. After a few blocks something eventually enters my consciousness: there are no children here. I quickly realize that mostly older people populate the neighborhood. I guess they are more likely to have the time and resources to maintain these Victorian gems. Two or three have been transformed into Bed and Breakfast Inns, idealized monuments to a past that really didn't exist. They are perfect in adult-only settings because children are known to make a mess.

Eventually, I wander into a small neighborhood park wedged into the end of a block. Houses stand proudly, guarding the flanks of the park. It is nicely landscaped, with a smattering of benches and picnic tables. A cast iron slide and swing set--practically untouched--are a nod to folk here who receive the occasional visit from their grandchildren. For now, however, the place is barren.

11

Once my work pattern is established, time slips by quickly enough. By Monday morning, everyone has heard about Macula's arrest. Sure enough, Sherman's detectives are at Newschannel 99 bright and early, confiscating his work computer. Two of Ivory Eriss' lawyers emerge from their offices to watch, silently. The detectives tell Walter Wilson that they traced Macula through his home computer to his work computer. It's the only time I've seen police tape put up in a newsroom; I'm sure the police enjoyed "forgetting" to leave it up after they go.

Leaderless again, things actually seem to return to normal. For me, the only interesting story I cover this week is that a fortune teller is called in to look for Luther Post. She sends deputies on a hilarious search through a food bank while volunteers serve meals to the homeless. With news crews from all three stations--at the invitation of the Sheriff--in hot pursuit. Despite speculation and worries to the contrary, Post has not "struck again." It turns out, the latest shooting was committed by someone else, who has been apprehended. The countryside is not terrorized. And, it seems, Post must have slipped out of the region.

My personal life has not found a pattern. In this town I haven't connected with anyone my age. Living in the boarding house is driving me crazy; it's not my own place. I keep missing Megan on the phone, leaving messages.

And I'm ducking any further encounters with two other women: Mercy Haversack and Ivory Eriss.

It's been a couple of weeks since Eriss and I last, er, talked. I'm hoping she just forgets--intentionally or otherwise--and moves on. Around the office, I haven't seen her and I don't think she's seen me. Unless she has an observation post in that turret up front. Or security cameras hidden in the ceiling of the newsroom. If they are there, they catch my mixed reaction on Friday when I find two gifts waiting when I come back from the field. One: my first real paycheck. The other: a huge bouquet of flowers.

I fell in to a burning ring of fire

I went down, down, down

And the flames went higher

And it burns, burns, burns

The ring of fire.

Another hint of Eriss' attentions awaits me the next Monday morning. A second bouquet of mixed flowers sits on my desk. To me it's like a funeral arrangement. Mine. It's so big I can't see anything on my desk. The bouquet drops an occasional loose petal and a strong hint or two. Oh, no.

With that arrangement plopped down on my desk, everyone stares at me as I enter the newsroom. The fluorescents feel brighter and, um, bluer, today. There's the familiar smell of coffee but the unfamiliar sensation of being the center of attention. Gretchen Calzone looks at me for a moment but says nothing. On Friday, I had managed to quietly dispose of the flowers before too many people came back from shooting their stories. No such luck today.

"Oooh, what's this?" Nettles glides by. She teases. "'Say it with flowers,' huh, Gamble?"

"Well, we're all dying to know," says Sherman Follicle, kindly. "This has me thinking of doing a story on secret admirers. Did a viewer send the flowers to you?"

There's no "admirer's" name. No card, in fact. At least there's no summons upstairs attached. There's only one person who would have sent them. And it's not Megan, who never even thinks about flowers, except the wild ones that bloom haphazardly in Mamie's garden or along the side of the road. This display didn't have that far to travel. But I'm not exactly going to share that with everyone. And I fear that anyone who has been around here for a while may have already guessed.

"It's a mystery. I really have no idea who sent them. Probably a viewer. I don't even know anybody here in Filterboro yet. Anyone know when these came?" I ask, looking around, checking the clocks on the wall, to deflect the one question of real interest. "These must not really be for me," I conclude.

Tyler Hubbell answers. Just arrived, still standing at her desk, rummaging through a huge Coach bag. "Rudie the weekend producer told me they came late last night. Sunday. Kind of a funny day to send flowers to the workplace, dontcha think?"

"Yeah..." I can't figure out that one. Also, I don't like this being the topic of conversation among people such as "Rudie" and other I don't know.

Tyler tries to be nice. "They're, uh, real pretty, Wil. You had better check to see if there's enough water in the vase."

I check. Very little, actually. Gives me an excuse to retreat for a while, get some H2O for the flowers, some O for myself. When I come back from filling the vase, the attention of the newsroom--forever populated with overly-curious types with short attention spans--is focused on a new object. At least the intense attention is drawn away from me. This new object is about five-and-a-half feet tall, wearing a form-fitting, carefully-tailored, double-breasted and very shiny charcoal gray suit. Black dress shirt, Windsor-knotted light gray tie. Thinning hair and moustache wiped by restless hands.

This refugee from The Sopranos is standing under, er, next to Walter Wilson at the door of Wilson's office. He pretends to pay attention to Wilson's drivel while discreetly scanning the newsroom. He's checking us out. Well, we're checking him out. New News Director?

"New News Director *Candidate*," corrects Follicle, comprehending my significant glance his way. Follicle pretends to not pay attention while shuffling through a sheaf of papers on his desk. "Don't know his name but he's someone Wilson worked with in the Reno market, back in the day."

Must be a last roll of the dice for this guy to need to come here, considering the short life spans of the previous News Directors. But who am I to judge? Soon I'm preoccupied with making my beat calls, trying to drum up a little business.

The morning is enlivened by a brief exchange between Calzone and Wallflower.

"Why can't you shoot the noon liveshot today?" she questions.

"My microphone cable needs tuning," he tries.

"Calling B.S. on that, there's no such thing," Calzone condescends. Then, challenging: "Do better than that, Norman." C'mon, c'mon. She must know what she's getting into. Challenging a four year old, that is.

He falls for it. "Listen, smart girl," he starts, a fake smile curling up under his own cheap moustache. "I didn't want to get technical with you. But you can't work on a Findlay microphone head without a Langstrom 7" gangly wrench. And the engineers don't have one handy. They have to order it. Got it?"

Many would succumb under that onslaught or technical jargon. Brilliantly, however, not Calzone.

"Wallflower you idiot. 'I-D-Ten-T.' I downloaded Steve Martin's "Let's

Get Small" recording when I was 12 years old. "Gangly wrench? That's his plumber's joke."

She smiles, I laugh out loud to punctuate her victory--that was classic. But our guest, The Candidate, seems perturbed.

In any case, eventually, we all drift toward the morning meeting, where Wilson evidently wishes to begin with a momentous announcement.

"Everyone and I mean everyone Billy Fotch put down the comic book you come over here too, and Tyler Hubbell please get off the phone, you always seem to be late for these meetings, and where in the world is Jen Nettles she's always here early did she go off on a story already?" Vaguely irritated that his underling is missing, Wilson looks around, addressing nobody in particular.

Aimee Flotsam lurches into the void, extremely happy to help. "My best friend's sister's boyfriend's brother's girlfriend told me it's a religious holiday today, Mr. Wilson. She's Jewish, so she took the day off."

Casually, Meredith Angle asks, "Which holiday is it?"

"Ramadan," Flotsam answers, definitively.

The Candidate actually flinches. But Wilson, not catching the mistake, simply continues with his monologue.

"The company manual says everyone is allowed to take one religious holiday a year and that includes Jewish ones too but everyone, please pay attention I want you to meet Martin Purefory, who impressed me so much with the deals he gets on suits that are just as good as Hart, Schafner and Marx over at the Men's Storagehouse and will become our next News Director."

All indications are that we are on the cusp of a brand new era at Newschannel 99, The Martin Purefory Era, if you will. But...Martin Purefory immediately places his stamp on the proceedings. Having lagged behind Wilson for a few moments, he finally steps forward. We wait, anxiously, for his first pronouncement.

"No thanks."

This perplexes Walter Wilson. He actually stops talking, rubs his forearm--accidentally wiping off a yellow sticky note--and turns to Purefory. "You mean, you don't wish to address the staff because I know you're new and haven't even gotten situated in your new office yet and I know there's no computer in there right now but I thought we had an agreement and I mean, um, what do you mean?"

"No, thank you," Purefory replies to the group, evenly. "I do not wish to take this position, thank you. I wish you well."

A black hole of silence ensues. Grinning to himself, Martin Purefory simply checks the tops of his shiny Valu-Mart shoes, turns, and marches away. Straight out the back double doors to the parking lot. I marvel at his sense of direction.

"He may be the smartest of the bunch," Phillips observes, considering the category of The Shortest Tenure Of A News Director In The History Of Television News. There is little more to say. Wilson retreats quietly to his office. Collingwood's blank expression is a cipher. Calzone appears incredulous. But speechless.

Newswise--that which will be reported to the public today, I mean--nothing much seems to be going on. I'm assigned a feature story up in Oak Ledge. It's an extremely modest industrial town. Textiles. A local author has published a book revisiting a mysterious series of factory accidents that killed several people back in the 1940's. Called the Marberry Murders, after the name of the textile mill and the persistent belief that the deaths were more than accidental.

A small publishing house in town handles printing the book. The people there direct me to the author, a retired newspaper editor. Sour faced. All sorts of lines in the skin radiate from his mouth, indicating years of grim copy-editing. He's torn between publicizing his book and speaking with an, ugh, television reporter. When my questions are finished, he has a few of his own. "Do you need me to spell 'Marberry' for you?"

"Already got it, sir, thank you."

"Did you understand what I said about how the police investigation was flawed?"

"Yes, what you said about what happened was pretty clear."

"What I said? What I *said*? Those are facts, man. Look them up!"

"I'll try to. In the next couple of hours it won't be easy to verify all the research that took you years to finish. So I'll end up attributing a lot of things to you."

"Well thank you so much," he answers, vaguely defeated. It seems he would prefer I took his word for it. Good thing this isn't a present day homicide investigation. This career journalist would have me unquestioningly repeat everything the police tell me.

"What angle will you take?" he tries.

"Angle? Actually, it might have something to do with diversification of the economy up here. The textile mills are closing and people have to find other work. Publishing and printing might become one positive alternative. Tourism, driven by the stories you tell in your book, is another."

"What? You aren't going to focus on my book?"

"Yes, it's the 'hook' for the story since it was just published. But I'm going to broaden the story to widen our viewers' interest in it. I want the biggest number of people to care about it."

"'Largest' number. Not 'biggest'." He dismisses me. "You do what you have to do. 'That's Entertainment,' right, Mr. Ramble?"

Billy Fotch is the videographer. He finishes up, slowly. I get up. Had enough of this. "I'm sorry if you are offended. The stories you tell are very interesting. Aside from some allegations that police investigative techniques were relatively primitive when the murders took place, you don't seem to shed much new light on something that happened a very long time ago." He grimaces again, silently. "Frankly, they just seem to rehash old ghost stories for the sake of selling a book that you couldn't get accepted by a mainstream publisher. But I'm going to try to find a way to make your book relevant, so I will bring back a story that can air on my station today." Okay, get down off the soapbox, boy.

"Possibly if you understood what I was getting at with my book, you wouldn't have to go somewhere else to make it 'relevant'," the older man scoffs.

I guess we aren't going to be friends. "In any case, watch tonight at 6 and you can see how things turn out," I say, exiting.

"I don't have a television," he says, with finality. Thank goodness.

While interviewing a local book store owner who has this book on display in his window, she tells us about an octogenarian up in the hills who was around Oak Ledge in the late 1940's. Knew some of the victims. Supposed to be quite a character. "Doghouse Herman Riley." If the name is any indication, we'll have an interesting time.

The bookstore owner's directions are precise, and they had better be. Winding around a county road for miles, we take a right hand turn at "a herd of cows" and head down a dirt road. Things get even trickier. We are supposed to find "a John Deere driveway reflector" that marks the origin of a dirt track that heads up a steep hill. "The only problem," the book store owner informs us, "is that I hope the reflector hasn't fallen over." It takes us three passes before we find it, nearly hidden by overgrown underbrush. Stopping, Fotch considers the size of the hill and quality of the trail. Then he hits the gas.

We race up the track to the top of a ridge. Pine trees provide thick cover. And...there it is, one ramshackle cabin, made to order, on my left. A long porch covered by a flat roof extends out from the house. Empty fruit jars litter the porch and ground immediately around it. A rock chimney rises above the tin roof. No smoke appears at the top of the chimney, but wood is burning somewhere. I can smell it.

Fotch parks at the end of the drive, directly in front of the cabin. He gets out and routinely moves to the back of the SUV to get his equipment. Peaceful place, here. Nobody stirring. Birds chirp. I'm still in the passenger seat, taking a moment to quietly check my notes.

But everything changes in an instant. There's a thunderous explosion, which jolts me up out of my seat. Fotch shouts something. Heart pounding, I fumble for the door handle. Guess I'm not hurt. The SUV seems intact. Get out, out, out. Door open, I crouch down behind it, wildly searching for a source of the huge noise.

A five-foot, two-inch tall man stands in the doorway of the cabin, tiny black eyes peering in my direction. Obscured by a cloud of gun smoke, he's holding a shotgun that seems the size of a bazooka in his small hands. The man struggles to heft it up again, evidently with the idea of firing the thing in our direction one more time.

"Billy! Are you okay?" I yell.

"I'm fine. But the back of the SUV may need some work," he responds. I'm guessing that some birdshot has made a mess of things.

"Mr. Riley!" I try. "Mr. Riley! Stop shooting!"

Indistinguishable cursing. "What's that you say? Who are you?" a very old, wavering voice shouts. The weight forces the barrel of the firearm to sag in his aging hands. I'm afraid he'll suddenly whip it back up and pull off another wild shot. But one hand is tied up adjusting something around his ear. A hearing aid?

"Newschannel 99! I'm a TV news reporter!"

That does not exactly create the desired effect. More swearing. The little man, whom I assume is Doghouse Herman Riley, hefts up the shotgun and fires again. This time, it's over the SUV. A small bird thuds down next to me.

"Stop shooting and we'll leave!" Fotch yells. He slams the tailgate closed but doesn't move forward. The driver's side is directly in the line of fire.

Riley appears to be reloading. I'm ready to dive back in the car but want to try one more time.

"Mr. Riley! I'm doing a story on the Marberry Murders!"

That stops him. "Marberry, eh? Oh." He sets down the stock of the firearm, leans on it. "Well. Come on in then." Propping the shotgun next to the front door, Riley chuckles. Then, he turns and ambles back in to the dark of the cabin. I lean back and look towards Fotch. We are both frightened but I sense we really are welcome. Crouching low, Fotch hurries around the SUV to my position. We confer.

"Should we go in there?" he asks.

"He invited us," I answer, without thinking.

"Yeah, and he just tried to kill us." Good point.

"I have a feeling it was just to warn off strangers. Revenuers. Anyways, he set down his shotgun. I'll go on the porch to talk with him."

"Brave man. He probably has a musket hanging on the wall inside." Fotch scratches his spiky hair. He regards the dead bird, bleeding on a bed of pine needles. "If I hear any more gunfire, I'm out of here, dude. But I promise to call the cops once I get to town. The town of Filterboro, I mean."

"Thanks for the support, man." I squint through the sunlight, mottled by all those trees. Can't see what's waiting for me in the cabin.

"Mr. Riley! I'm coming up on the porch!" I holler. My voice echoes, unanswered, over the hill and across the holler. Okay, no time like the present. Walking low, I take tender steps around the front of the SUV, into the open. I feel like Scout and Jem and Dill approaching the Radley home. Nothing moves. Now, I trek carefully across the dirt drive, up four wood steps to the porch. Nothing. To the open entrance. Nothing. Peer into the darkness. Nothing. Look back at Fotch. Nothing. Wait— where did he go? Ah, hiding on the other side of the SUV. At least he hasn't driven off to go eat lunch. Deep breath, here goes. Step inside.

What is this place? My eyes adjust to find a living room. Mid-century furniture, skinny legs and all, neat but everything covered in plastic. Walls painted yellow. Upright piano. Sunburst clock on the wall ticks, indicating 12:30 pm. It's probably right, say, twice a day. Moldy smell. Newspapers are lined up on the floor, indicating a path to follow. Looking to the right it is brighter, there are more windows. A kitchen is there, surrounding a metal and vinyl table set. The newspaper trail leads there. A noise develops from somewhere below; feet trudging up steps. Doghouse Riley bangs open a door into the kitchen and emerges from the basement. He grasps a fruit jar half filled with a clear liquid. Uh, water?

"Like a snort?" he asks, a little sloppily.

"Um, no thanks. Too early," I reply earnestly. So that's the wood-burning smell. And the reason for the shotgun. There's a still out back somewhere.

Riley leans forward, peering up at me suspiciously. Eyes are two very tiny but bright points of light. "You sure you ain't one of them Revenoors, air ye? 'Cause we shoot Revenoors aroun' here."

"No sir," I say a little too quickly, a little too loud. He does have a hearing aid, right?" Just look at our SUV," I offer, a little more quietly. "I'm with Newschannel 99. You know, 'Where We're Right 99 Times Out of 100? '"

Evidently that's good enough for Riley. Out of the cupboard he pulls two water glasses. Refugees from a 1950's cafeteria, it appears. They don't look all that clean. But the stuff he pours in it from the fruit jar should thoroughly sanitize them.

"I don't seem to 'member you from seein' Newschannel 99," he remarks, pouring himself a couple of fingers. "And I watch. Right over there on that Zenith."

I'm new. Unlike the Zenith.

"Well, I like the look of ye, so find a spot and set on down."

Sitting on a plastic slipcover isn't necessarily comfortable. But my priorities have adjusted remarkably after nearly having my head blown off. I ask for an interview. Perhaps relieved we're not trying to bust his still, he grants it.

After a lot of convincing, and a taste of the 'shine, Fotch joins us. It's all pretty pleasant, actually. Riley gives us his first-hand account. He also tells us how an old company house rented by one of the murder victims is said to be haunted. Lots of strange sightings by people whom you'd think would know better. Now nobody goes near it. Could be a focal point for our story, I think.

As we pack up to go, Riley's voice gets a little louder. He's been sipping from the fruit jar all along. He starts asking numerous questions about our story, the equipment, the television station, our religious sensibilities and political proclivities... . He actually sounds a little desperate, as if his questions will hold us here indefinitely and ward off the loneliness that is sure to follow our departure. He holds up a fruit jar.

"Boys, this my best stuff. I'll prove it, too. Ye know how to test this whiskey...fer poority?" He waits, expectantly, for my full attention.

I'm unsuccessfully trying to look overly busy putting away an ink pen in my pocket. "Uh, no, Mr. Riley."

"Well, I'll show ye." He scrambles around the kitchen and picks out a tablespoon and a lighter. "Here you go."

He's got my attention. Fotch stops also. Scooping a few drops of the 'shine out of the fruit jar with his spoon, Riley flicks the Bic and sets fire to the liquid. "See! Ha ha! See!" The little mountain man bounces with delight as the flame burns a few moments in the spoon. "It's yella, see!"

I guess I'm supposed to be impressed.

"Wow, it burns," I reply.

Disappointment. "Nah," he settles down. "A course, it should burn yella. If it 'twer ta burn blue, ar red--whew--this wouldn't be fit fer drinkin'." Riley seems to wind down, reluctantly releasing us from his clutches.

We head out. Fotch seems relieved to get as far away from Doghouse Herman Riley as possible. But we have to drive even further into the hills to find the factory. It's not the direction he prefers to be heading.

"We have to get some video of the Marberry mill, anyways," I argue. "So we might as well stop at the company house Riley talked about while we're out there."

"Well, you can go inside. I'll record you on the porch or something," Fotch replies. He's still jittery after nearly dying at Doghouse Herman Riley's. Or maybe he's contentious because we haven't stopped for lunch.

The textile mill isn't dead yet. Only "mostly" dead, which means "slightly alive." It's a rustic setting: a holler cut through the hills by a slow river, or a glorified creek. Not much stirring in the hamlet of Marberry. A loose cluster of run-down homes, a church, and post office. The paint wore off this place a long time ago.

Around the bend sits a shack, alone in the trees and shadows. Slowly bio-degrading. I calculate a half-life of 11,395 years. No glass in the windows. No door on the hinges. No hinges on the frame, for that matter. It sits by itself, like a reproach. Perhaps waiting for justice to be done for the murder victim who once lived inside? I start considering what kind of prose to employ.

The quiet is a bit unsettling, even in the daylight. Especially after getting shot at. But I want some video of this place.

Fotch sets up his tripod next to the SUV. Normally he takes a little time, considering the angle, the distance, any obstructions. Not today. Shoot 'n' go. He starts to pack up.

"Hey, Billy. I want to shoot a standup here, also."

He hesitates. "I kinda figured we'd go down to the mill and shoot it, dontcha think?"

"Nope. This is perfect. I'll start inside and walk out on the porch."

"Inside? I can just shoot it from here, then," he replies, reattaching his camera to the tripod. Relief. He doesn't have to go indoors.

I attach the wireless lav microphone to my necktie and walk across an expanse of rough but intermittent weeds to approach the stricken home. Something smells funny. Have to be careful on the steps, most of the boards are damaged, some broken. I feel a complete sense of emptiness and foreboding. Okay, so, what am I going to say? Think, buddy. More pressure now. Fotch is too-obviously waiting. Practically tapping his fingers on the camera. My nerves are jangled. And I'm wondering about the lost soul who is said to still flit about this place. Too many people claim to have seen some ghostly apparition at the window. What did Riley say about strange moaning sounds? The hair on my neck is starting to raise and I'm not even inside the house. Get it together, bud. I quickly develop a short script for my standup. "In the daytime this place of death may not feel 'haunted.' But it does have a sense of tragedy about it that is unsettling, and at night, people around here simply stay away." That's good enough in a pinch, I think.

"Okay, Billy, I'm ready." Although I'm 20 yards away, I don't have to shout. He is wearing an earpiece connected to the camera. I look out and he gives me the "thumbs up" while looking into the viewfinder. Wait, though. Something's wrong. He's shaking his head. Thumbs down.

"Dude, my battery's just about dead. Give me a minute to go get a fresh brick." He starts fiddling with the battery on the back of the camera. Great. Thanks, man. I decide to get in position anyways. Sooner we're out of here, the better.

I turn to approach the empty doorway. Dark in there. Didn't I just do this at Doghouse Herman Riley's? How much courage does a reporter have to muster on a single story, anyways? My heart beats faster. You can do this. Take a deep breath. Can't sound scared in your standup. Focus. Practice. "In the daytime..." I start to rehearse to myself. Wait. Was that a shuffling sound inside? No. C'mon, dude. Do this, go. What's the children's song?" Put one foot in front of the other... ."

My legs start to feel heavy as I make the few steps through the entryway. One big step, and I'm inside. Eyes adjust. Okay, focus. Get ready to start. What were my lines again?" In the daytime this place of death." Uh...I hear breathing. Human breathing. I turn, look further into the room. Oh...my...God. There, crouching in a shadowy corner.

Its Luther Post.

I know it instinctively, instantaneously. It adds up. A very large, 50-ish, bald man hiding in a place a lot of people won't dare visit. I stare and tense up, expecting to be attacked. Instead, he speaks. Low, quiet. Breathing hard. "Help me. Get me out of here. I'm stuck, I'm stuck, I'm stuck."

Much of my fear melts once the unknown becomes known. Even if its manifested in a man twice my size. I don't move...not yet, anyways. "What's the matter, Luther?" I ask, trying to sound more calm than I feel. He's still in the shadows.

More heavy breathing. Slow words form. "Foot...went through...the floor. Same luck as always. Leg's...stuck. Ankle is twisted, killing me."

I move forward, with caution. If the rotten flooring gave way under Post, it could do the same to me. But he's much heavier, so I feel somewhat confident while gingerly moving forward. The dark begins to fade as I advance. Post is in a sideways lump. One leg planted in the flooring. Where is his handgun?

"How long have you been here, Luther?"

"I don't know. A coupla days, a coupla days, a coupla days." Post seems to draw a slight comfort in repeating himself. "Figured nobody'd look around here...because I don't have nobody around here. Then I got stuck. God hate me. Left me here. And this place...is supposed to be haunted... ." He looks haunted, head bowed, eyes staring ahead. Heavily breathing the pain of his leg in and out. "So even if anyone heard me hollerin', they'd run away before comin' in to help me."

A too perfect hiding spot. Post might have died of starvation or dehydration or gone stark raving mad before anyone would ever dare venture into this house. And then I came in to record a stand-up.

"If I pull your leg out, what are you going to do next?" I ask.

More breathing. "I can't help a "wanted" man get away... ."

"What can I do, man?" he answers in a sudden burst. "I can't run! I can't...catch a break! Now...get me out of here!"

I hear the slide on a pistol pulled back. Time to help the wanted man get away.

"Okay, okay! I'm trying to step towards you carefully."

A lot of rotten wood in here. Feels soft underfoot, mushing under my feet. The shadows lighten and Post rapidly comes into focus as I draw near. There's...confusion in his eyes. And a gun in his hand. I kneel carefully to figure out how to help. Its dark. But it only seems to require sliding his damaged leg out of the bad angle its caught in the subflooring. All I have to do is pry out some of the bad wood. There's two complications. He's big. And his ankle's swollen, quite stuck in there. And Post is going to feel severe shooting pain when I help him out. Don't want that to lead to some severe shooting.

"Luther. It may hurt when I pull on the floorboard. Get ready for it." He starts breathing hard again. "But I'll work with you to, uh, maneuver your leg at the same time you pull back."

"Alright, man... let's do it, let's do it, let's do it. Things can't get worse."

Now it's my turn to breath hard. I'm worried. "Okay, you try to slide back and to your right. I'll try to guide your leg."

It only takes a minute. Post grinds his teeth in pain loud enough to be heard. But he doesn't cry out. I push on one rotten joist near his ankle to make space. The rusty nails quickly give way. But from his position, Post couldn't have reached it by himself. As stuck as he was, all he really needed with someone to guide the way.

Laying on his back, panting, Post looks around. He's free. But it's not freedom.

A nearby crate suggests itself. I drag it over for Post to prop up his leg. He lays back and enjoys a slight relief. Breathing easier, Post flicks a look my way. Assumes I know stuff. "Did that taxi driver...die?"

"Still in the hospital, I think. I kind of lost track, to be honest. I wasn't exactly looking for you," I confess.

Post looks relieved. "You the only one not lookin' for me." Then he stares off into one of the dark corners of his world.

"But what about you? What do you plan to do next?" I say, almost like a father patronizing his son. "If you only made it this far in a month, then you probably aren't going very much farther--even if your leg wasn't in pain. Most people figured you were three states away by now."

"Easy for them to say," he snorts. "I didn't just run away blind. Tried to be smart, be smart, be smart...you know, careful. Very careful. But no. I'm not going very far. Everything seems against me." Voice quiets, eyes are looking somewhere else. "No. I got nowhere to go. I'm ready to give up on everything." What? Post surveys the handgun. Time to get scared again. But he only regards the weapon, as if to speak to it.

"I shot that man. But it was a...accident." Confession time. "I can feel the kick of this thing as it went off...and can see the look on the man's face when he realized he was shot. Can't get it...out of my mind. Driving me crazy, along with all the ghosts aroun' here." He looks up and around. "Its 'cause God hate me, He hate me. I had the safety on this thing." He holds up the firearm as some sort of proof. "But sure enough it went off anyway, despite my precaution...I didn't want to really pull the trigger...it went off despite what I really wanted. God hate me."

"But how could it have gone off on accident..." I start.

Post gives me a tired look like I'm an imbecile. Okay, okay. We're not into specifics right now. Here in the dark. And something changes.

"Who are you, anyways?" he asks. Challenging me now. His leg is still propped up, but now he leans forward slightly, on his elbows. Trying to focus on me.

I tell him. He draws a momentous breath. Sigh. He hefts the handgun again. It seems heavier in his hand now.

"Get outta here. Now," he announces. "I don't want to be in no news story."

But that's exactly what I want. Even if I have to wait. "Okay, I'm leaving. But here's my personal phone," I show it to him. "You can use it to call your people, if you want. And once in a while I will call you on it." I set the phone to vibrate rather than ring. Hand it to him. "There. It's quiet." Post doesn't seem much interested but this is the best way for me to keep the line of communication open.

"Don't use that gun again," I advise, backing out the door.

No answer. Post sits, contemplating his rather bleak future. Black guy with a gun? Who admits to shooting someone? Bye bye.

Out the door. Daylight. Fresh air. There's Billy Fotch, standing with his camera, intent, pointed at me. I briskly walk out to him.

"I got it," he says.

"Got it?" I wonder. Got what? It occurs to me that I didn't do the standup.

"I got it. I heard you talking and after a while realized you weren't alone. So I rolled on it," he explains. Ah. My wireless microphone was hot. Turned on, that is. And Billy Fotch was recording. Billy Fotch: savvy? I hadn't expected it. Possibly for the first time in his life, no one had to paint him a picture.

"Let's go," I command, smiling. But he's already removing the camera from the tripod. We're outta here.

No thought of recording a standup, not now. Our story has changed. We've got to get to a working telephone, call Collingwood, and figure out our next step.

I start to consider what we have on our hands. Wow, what a windfall. But it's also dynamite. What to do with it? Do I turn in Luther Post right away? Or do I somehow work a deal with the authorities to postpone it, at least until our newscast? Imagine the awards: AP, Murrow, Emmy, maybe others. Is there some way to stretch this out, to make the most of it? How many stories can I get out of this?

"You sure you recorded what we said?" I ask. Can hardly believe it.

Behind the steering wheel, Fotch chews his gum, loudly. "Oh yeah. I put the new brick on the camera, and then turned everything on to make sure everything was cool." He pauses to make a left hand turn. "Uh, then I heard you talking and thought you were just, um, rehearsing or something. Then I realized you were talking to somebody inside. For a moment I thought it was the, um, ghost or something. I almost freaked out." I look over at Fotch. For a moment he looks like a little boy. He blows a bubble and his features quickly harden again. "Then I figured out it was somebody alive and it sounded, you know, a little intense. So I rolled tape and waited for you."

I'm not speechless. Just shocked. "Billy, um, I never thought I'd say this, but 'Good job, man.'

"Aw, shucks. But the bad news, dude, is that's our last brick. When it runs out, all our camera batteries will be dead."

"Okay, that's fine. But the battery on my personal phone died. Do you have a station phone?"

"Nope, I forgot it.

I'm feeling the definition of "nonplussed" for perhaps the first time in my life. But then, for the second time, Fotch delights me.

"I do have my own personal phone. And it might work, too." Will wonders never cease? We develop a cell signal a few miles away, up out of the holler, Fotch pulls over at a gas station.

Gretchen Calzone answers.

"Hey lady," I start. "I have something hot. Don't say anything in the newsroom just yet. I can't tell you much right now. Can you send me over to Carl?"

"Is it going to change what we have you scheduled to do at 6?" she asks.

"Probably. And it might change the entire rundown," I reply.

Calzone stops, perhaps thinks of Tracy Scott, the producer of the 5 and 6pm newscasts. She won't be happy to have to change her newscast rundown. "Yeah, okay, but we have to tell Tracy right away."

"Yes, ma'am," I respond. There's no way I can explain to her what kind of hot potato I'm juggling. "Let me talk to Carl to figure it out."

Phone transfers to Collingwood. Brisk as always. "Hi, Wil. What's up?"

"Sit down, Carl. I've got a big one. I know where Luther Post is. At least for the next five minutes."

"What's that? I hadn't heard anything about an arrest."

"He hasn't been arrested. I ran into him today." Like he was at the mall or fruit smoothie place or something.

"Where were you today? Uh, Oak Ledge? Is he there?"

"Out near Marberry. Not quite all the way to Blue Hill. He was hiding out in an abandoned house with an injured ankle." I survey the gas station and nearby smattering of homes. There's so little activity, it also looks abandoned.

"Did you get video?" Always the $64,000 Question.

"Not much. There was no way to do that without someone getting hurt. Post was armed. But we have sound. I was in a house with Post, Fotch had me on the wireless from outside."

There's no response for a moment. Then, Collingwood, gently offers: "Wil, is there any evidence other than your word to prove that's him on the tape? How did you know it was him? Did Fotch see him?"

"No one did. Just me. But it was him, alright. He told me about shooting the taxi cab driver. And it's possible somebody nearby has seen him and didn't recognize him. What do we do next?"

"Sit tight. First, I'll call Sheriff Dank. If I ask nice, he'll keep it quiet on the radios as much as possible so nobody at the other stations understand what's happening on the scanners. But deputies will want to talk with you right away, so make yourself available. What I want to do is send out a truck to meet you for a liveshot at the top of the 6. But it'll be tough to re-assign the live trucks this late in the day. Let me get the list from Gretchen." A few moments pass.

"Here it is. The satellite truck is in the shop." I had been thinking the sat truck may be our best bet, considering how far away we are from the station. They send a signal to a satellite, accessible from anywhere on earth. "Sports is using one live truck, we can't use that." Live trucks, on the other hand, can beam a direct signal to a nearby antenna tower, which is relayed to the station. "Arnold's doing his weather forecast at the car dealership; they are sponsoring it, so a truck has to go there. And the last one is shooting a civic service award that Mayor Parody is giving to Ivory Eriss. That's live also for tonight."

"We were having a hard time with our phones, so the sat truck may be the only one that works up there," I advise.

"You're probably right," Collingwood advises. "We can probably get it out of the shop and send it your way."

"What's being fixed on it?" I'm worried that it's something like the satellite mast or video link inside, not something related to the operation of the vehicle itself.

"Brakes." Whew. That's all, just the brakes.

"I'll send out Buddy Furlong and a nighttime reporter to follow up on this. It'll be the new kid we just hired, Juan Cortez."

'New kid'? Guess I'm not the rookie any more. Already. Turnover is high in my line of work, and you can become a veteran in almost any news shop before you know it.

"All right. But I gave Post my phone in an effort to stay in touch with him."

"Wait--what kind of phone do you have? If it has GPS, then Post can be tracked."

I hadn't thought of that. Primarily, because my low-tech phone is an older model without frills installed like Global Positioning System. I explain to Collingwood, and make sure everyone knows to call Billy Fotch's personal mobile phone to reach us.

At this point, many photogs would be hanging over my shoulder, anxious to know what's next. Other would be busy straightening out their gear, getting ready for anything. Breaking a big story gets even jaded videographers excited.

Fotch, however, is off having a smoke.

"Let's go," I call. He flicks away the cigarette and we load up and head back to Marberry. We've got to try to talk to some locals, figure out whether they saw Post and what they think about him hiding out here. I assume he's gone from the house by now but wonder how he'll elude the law on such a gimpy ankle. For a moment I wonder about the sat truck operator being sent out to us.

"Who is Buddy Furlong?" I ask Fotch.

"Sat truck operator. Old guy. Been around almost as long as the station." Billy pops another bubble. Then slowly smiles, appraising me out of the corner of his eye. "And he gets a little lost sometimes, not very good with direction."

Direction?" You mean, he's not very good with directions? 'S? 'Can someone guide him?" I ask.

"No, 'direction.' You'll see."

Great, another mystery. No time for that; I've got to re-focus on my story.

An hour later, we have interviewed a woman who lives in the Marberry holler who didn't see Luther Post but sure knows him from "the newspaper reports." That'll be re-phrased as "media reports" in my script. But the woman was a bit frightened, worried for her children. "I just want that man caught, and right now!" So she makes for a good interview for my story.

That's the moral trade-off we make in television news. To us, it isn't a human tragedy, it's a news story. The more hideous, pathetic, or sadly ironic, the better. The story isn't necessarily judged compelling on its merits, but the made-for-television elements in it. Is there exciting video, a tearful interview?

Parenthetically, some reporters play the "advocate," searching only for "victims" they believe to be out there. To them, there is no "other side" to a story, only the perspective of their victim. That's why reporters have earned the reputation of the jackal, easily preying on the misery of innocent people or the political correctness of their cause.

For the rest of us, there's more to it than that. Reporters are supposed to be objective. That's more than just not taking sides. That also means flipping to the "off" position an emotional "Humanity Switch" designed to help a reporter disassociate events from the human toll they take. That makes it somehow tolerable to file a report on an eight year old slowly dying of an incurable disease or a defenseless elderly man pistol-whipped in front of his helpless wife. In this cold emotional state we cope with a daily stream of sordid details.

The irony is, we are called on to *not* present "just the facts, ma'am." The facts may be cold, but the people involved experience unusually powerful emotions. That influences a news story, because emotion is a compelling and essential element to any report. Also, the reporter reading the story is supposed to infuse it with proper emotion. You can't sound happy while telling people about a row house that burned down with a family of seven inside. Reporters make value judgments without the viewer even knowing it, based on their choice of emotion: whether it be shock, sadness, cynicism, or even a touch of anger. All that without the reporter actually becoming emotionally engaged.

The final product is some amalgam of pathos and logos; the messenger embodies ethos. So after the 6 o'clock news is over, on our drive home from work or over a drink at the bar, sometimes that Humanity Switch can't wait to be flipped back on to "human" mode. Those true gut reactions that have been put on hold are now free to move about the cabin. That's when many order that drink that pushes them across 0.08. Others kick their dog. And some simply pull over to the side of the freeway, and cry.

Tears are forming in my eyes when Buddy Furlong hasn't arrived with the sat truck less than an hour before the newscast. We are waiting back at the haunted house in Marberry holler. Luther Post is gone, apparently, but how far away? Sheriff's deputies crawl through the woods and underbrush around the cabin. Pretending to be busy-- outside his jurisdiction, by the way--Sheriff Dank hangs around to give me the opportunity to ask him for an interview.

Before leaving the gas station, I had tried to call Furlong's cellphone; it rang endlessly. No way to tell whether he's out of the service area or has his phone turned off or whether he even knows how to answer it. I don't know if Juan Cortez has been assigned a phone yet.

Awaiting a sat truck to which he can hook up, Fotch and his camera are positioned in front of the haunted house. My story script is handwritten on a series of messy pages from my "reporter's notebook." It has the verbal seal of approval from Collingwood, the eternal copy-editor. But we can't edit the video until the editing equipment arrives. So, we sit and wait for the sat truck. I strain to hear its large engine, which powers a converted full-size van. All I hear is occasional muted noises from the textile mill.

Finally frustrated, I have enough. There's no cell reception here, so I take the SUV and head down the holler. Gotta try to call for help. Leaving Fotch to Please Stand By, I hit the accelerator, taking turns on the long and winding road just a little too fast. Concentrating on my driving and on the signal strength meter on my phone, I almost miss spotting the sat truck, sitting outside a diner.

I don't recall ever leaving skid marks on a road before. Too careful a driver. But having slammed down on the brake pedal, I skid the SUV on to the shoulder, kicking up gravel and dirt before stopping. Then starting again, racing into the dirt parking lot of the diner. I bound out of the SUV, look inside the sat truck. Nobody's there. Quick step to the diner. Weather-worn hand-painted sign over a faded clapboard box indicates this is The Golden Ocelot. Deep fried smoke wisps into the wind somewhere from the back of the building. Gotta see if Furlong is inside.

I pull open a gray metal 1960's suburban screen door. The piston-like door closer screeches like a running catfight. Evidently this doubles as a security bell, warning the proprietor every time someone enters or departs. In this case, it warns about a dozen people of my arrival, because all movement simply stops when I walk in, blinking in the new darkness. All that's missing is the sound effect of a needle being scraped off a record album. When my pupils finally dilate, I realize everyone else's eyes are on me. Just like an old western film when Bad Bart enters the tavern. I can't tell, though, whether the patrons of The Golden Ocelot are afraid or contemptuous or just curious. No matter what, I don't like it.

Then, down at the end of the counter I spy a creature that gives the impression of a human snowman, or perhaps, a cue ball. Round body, round head, round eyes, no hair--not even eyebrows, it seems at first. Turns out they are thin and a very light blonde. He's sitting next to a more polished- and younger-looking man. The cue ball is enjoying an iced tea but takes the time to slowly look around when I approach. The other people suddenly go back to what they were doing.

"Oh, there you are," he starts in a grandfatherly-condescending way. "Thought you'd never show."

He probably knows me simply from watching Newschannel 99 newscasts. Or thanks to a quick whisper from the young man in a suit next to him. I certainly don't know the cue ball. But his blue Newschannel 99 t-shirt proclaims this must be Buddy Furlong.

"Why are you here? Why aren't you at the house where we are supposed to shoot the liveshot?" I ask, exasperated. No time for formal self-introductions.

Furlong blinks. This does not register with him. "Why, this is the diner I always stop at when I come out this way. We are supposed to meet here. I've been doing this for 31 years and always do things the same way. You should have known that."

I want to stick this cue ball into a corner pocket somewhere but don't have the time to argue.

"Let's go. I've got to edit my package."

Furlong slowly stands. He has an air of amiability that makes it hard to want to punch him. But I do want to.

"Okay, you're the boss," he says. But he's the manipulator. Furlong takes time to fish out of his pocket an ancient billfold, deliberately removes a dollar from it, and lays the cash on the counter. He winks at an ancient man, unmoving behind the counter, who wears a white cooking apron. "See ya, 'Bobcat'," he calls jovially to the man as he rolls out. The man does not RSVP. What a day: first a "Doghouse" and then a "Bobcat."

Its 40 minutes to air. "Buddy," (I nearly spit out the word), "We got to hurry. I still have to edit my report. But its only about a five minute drive to where we need to be."

He's in no hurry.

"Lead the way, young man. I don't know which way I'm going," he advises. I suspect that this is literally true. Buddy hoists himself--slowly--into the driver's side of the sat truck while the young man in a suit--Juan Cortez, it turns out--hops into the passenger seat.

Although I badly want to peal out of the parking lot, I must keep in mind the lumbering vehicle behind me. Slowly, it backs out, and after a careful three-point turn, it follows my lead.

We find Fotch and the house and the deputies still combing the property. Emerging from the driver's seat, Buddy moves like a Marathon runner in a 40 yard dash. Inanimate objects decay faster than he moves; I suffer an awful, fleeting image of Furlong and Miss Mercy as a couple.

While Fotch unwinds a heavy roll of audio and video cables from the truck out to his camera, I hop in the back with Furlong. It's a miniature control room. A generator powers the tiny quarters, equipped with a wall full of switches, meters, and monitors so Furlong can maneuver the satellite dish and put our video up in space. There is also enough room on a small counter for video editing equipment. With the deadline rushing upon us, I get so engrossed in my work that I don't notice Furlong starting to sweat. Eventually, he makes so many bleating noises that it captures my attention.

"What's the matter, Buddy?" I throw a tired glance at him while making an edit. 15 minutes to air.

"Uh, we don't have a clear signal yet. Uh. I should try something else." He heads out of the truck.

"What are you going to do?" I ask behind him.

Furlong doesn't answer, so I follow him out to where Fotch has finished hooking up his camera. Fotch glances upward; dusk is descending so he'll have to make a series of adjustments to his camera as it gets dark. There's enough light, though, to show the house behind me.

Furlong huffs and puffs his way over to Fotch.

"Billy...uh, which way is north? I gotta have the truck pointed north in order to send a clear signal."

Fotch glances at me. Ah, "direction"—without the S. "I don't know, Buddy. Um. But you do have a compass mounted on your dashboard, dude."

"Oh yeah," Furlong responds.

"Waitaminute, what does this mean?" I ask, knowing what it means.

Fotch flashes an innocent Alfred E. Neuman "What Me Worry?" smile. "He's gotta turn the truck around." That means Fotch has to disconnect all the cables and reconnect them--(if and) when Furlong finds his compass and gets pointed north.

Ten minutes to air.

Helpless, I try to use the mobile phone to call the station to tell them I am going to miss slot. No signal. The sat truck is equipped with a satellite phone that should work, but I don't want to interrupt Furlong. Shutting down the generator and firing up the engine, he slowly turns the truck around on the shoulder of the road while focusing intently on an object on his dashboard. He must have found the compass, situated where it always is--right under his nose.

I notice Sheriff Dank watching our confusion with his hands on his hips. It's exactly 6pm when I'm able to scramble back into the truck and grab the sat phone. I already know what's going on at the station: chaos. Gretchen Calzone is vainly trying to make a connection with our dumb mobile phone, an engineer is vainly trying to tune in our satellite signal, one of the other reporters has to finish earlier than they had expected because their report replaced mine as the lead story...and Tracy Scott is changing her rundown while cursing my name.

Calzone answers on the first half-ring. Her words rush out at me. "GAMBLEWHATINTHEWORLDISGOINGONOUTTHERE?"

"The sat truck..." is all I'm able to hiss before Calzone lets out a suddenly-enlightened "Ohhhhhh. Buddy Furlong is with you?" That seems to be enough explanation. "Okay. How soon do you think you can you get your story to us?" She actually sounds reasonable. I consult with Furlong, who seems to be having more success getting things up and running in the back. "Five minutes," I advise her.

"All right. Your satellite window was booked until 6:15, so we'll be okay. Tracy says your story can lead the B-block. That's about 6:11. And Gamble?"

"Yes ma'am?"

"You better be perfect."

I hang up. Gotta finish a last edit or two in my story. Haven't thought much about what I'll say in my liveshot. Well, there's enough to worry about in the intervening eight minutes, so that will have to wait. On the sat phone with an engineer, Furlong finally succeeds in sending a signal off to Filterboro. He feeds my newly-minted package and I rush out to Fotch and his camera. "You got two minutes," he says, handing me my IFB connection box and handheld microphone. "And it's getting darker," he adds, turning on the toplight on his camera. Furlong turns on two exterior lights mounted on the top corners of the sat truck, helping brighten the scene.

"Billy, during the open I want you to pan off me and push in to a medium shot of the front porch. Leave it there until I pitch to the package. Then, re-set on me when we come back from the pack. Got it?"

"Yez, bozz," replies Fotch, breathily inhaling a cigarette while focusing his lens on something.

Clipping the IFB box to the back of my belt, I plug in my earpiece and can suddenly hear the sound of our newscast. So far, so good. Notepad? Oh no, where is it? Jacket pocket? There it is. Flipping past the pages on which I wrote my script, I jot down the most crucial bullet points, and think of something clever to open with, such as "A ghost house that came alive today... ." Then I motion over to Dank, who has been hovering nearby. Even though I hadn't asked him for a live interview, he's smart enough to see our confusion and stand by to assist with a live Q&A. Good instincts. Publicity doesn't hurt his re-election chances, either.

"Sheriff, can I ask you a question during this report?" I call over to him. "We're going on in a minute but I want to wait until after the package airs."

Savvy. Dank understands our terminology, how things work. "Sure thing. I'll stand next to you, just off camera." He positions himself. "This work for you?" he asks, trying to look down at me. We are the same height.

"Uh yeah, that'll do."

Over the steady rumble of the truck's generator in my IFB I can hear Lavinia Fern start to read the intro to my story. I tense up slightly, knowing the camera will be live in just a moment. Finally, it's ShowTime. There's just enough light to see the house, all the equipment is functioning, everybody's in place, and I know what I'm going to say. But just as Fern starts to announce, "Newschannel 99's Wilson Gamble is live in Marberry where..." , the lights go out. The IFB goes dead. Sudden silence. Huh?

I stand stunned for a moment before calling out to no one in particular, "What in the blazes has gone wrong now?"

As the light of this day finishes fading to black, I hear Furlong's plaintive voice, sounding very distant over at the truck. "No power. Generator's out of gas. Time to fill it up, I guess."

Some call it a "newsmare," an awful day (or night, whatever) in this business. But just like any nightmare, you wake up the next day. Hopefully you get a fresh start. So, I'm present and accounted for, only a little hung over, at the next day's morning meeting. At least there's no bouquet left on my desk today.

After all questions are answered about my failure, Walter Wilson says that he wants Tyler Hubbell to do a feature on a new hybrid automobile that just happens to be arriving in the showroom of one of our sponsors. I sense Hornswoggle in the background, without actually seeing him. His tail swishes happily. Hubbell only wants to do it if she can squeeze a liveshot out of it. Collingwood thinks not. Then, Jack Phillips pitches a story about how the Soyfield city council may fire its City Manager.

Brian Fantana's voice rises incoherently over the speakerphone. Um...from the *Soyfield* Bureau.

Briefly translated through the garbled transmission, he says, "We have to cover that here, Jack! That's our story!"

"Why didn't you pitch it, then?" Phillips asks calmly. He checks his fingernails.

"I didn't have a chance yet!" hollers the now-overmodulated as well as distorted voice. "I know everyone involved, and I have to stay on the big stories in this town, or I'll lose my credibility here!"

"But I've already got an interview lined up with the City Manager, my man. Maybe you didn't know that I play poker with Phil Fortuitous and he will only talk on camera with me." Phillips looks at Wilson, holds up his hands to project a headline: "Newschannel 99 Exclusive!"

Wilson shrugs. The speakerphone has been defeated. Phillips will do the story.

Meanwhile, I'm thinking about Luther Post, what to do with him. That's when the lights go dim for a moment.

On cue, Ivory Eriss materializes. Haughty, Incorporated. She moves almost mystically, like the Lady of the Lake.

"Look what just creeped in," whispers Follicle.

Eriss has yet another prodigal in tow. Hardly Excalibur caliber. We can barely see him behind her thin frame. Warden the Doorman looms behind the two of them. The guest is a younger man--who doesn't look young. Haggard. How does he get polyester to wrinkle like that? Hair disheveled, sloping back, pasty skin, nascent beer gut. Shifty eyes. Clearly spends a lot of time at the computer--uh oh. Has a hangdog, sulky, guilty look about him. We know what's coming: "Will you come in, Mystery Challenger, and sign in please?"

"Ladies and gentlemen," starts Eriss, quietly, formally. No cigarette holder is allowed to be displayed down here among the common folk. "Allow me to introduce your new News Director, Arlen Rapier. He comes to us from Tulsa, only 24 hours ago he was the Assignment Manager there. Oh, and there will be budget cuts concerning your department. Mr. Rapier will convey the details to you." She gives me a quick, meaningless glance, turns on a dime, and floats outta here. Warden marches behind her—The Bodyguard. Back here, Rapier is on his own. We are in shock.

"Where does she come up with them?" wonders Phillips. Aloud. In front of Rapier, who stares ahead, lost. Wavering. Rocking back and forth slightly on the balls of his feet. He was Pip in the presence of Miss Havisham, but now she has departed, just as fast as Purefory the day before. No one answers Phillips' question. Station management evidently prefers not to promote from within.

"Uh, Arlen, this is our Morning Meeting," starts Collingwood, I think quite graciously. Would Collingwood ever want to be Officially Responsible for a News Department in such a crummy place as this? Who knows. "We are just about done," he continues. "Everyone is ready to head out. Do you have anything you want to say before we get started?"

Rapier regains some composure. "Done? How can you be done if I haven't been here?" he asks, sullenly, nasally.

"Um, well, we didn't know you were coming and it's a bit strange and we never heard of you and didn't know anyone would be coming in so soon to be the News Director especially not all the way from Tulsa that's in Arkansas, right? and I'm not sure why Miss Eriss didn't tell us about this before now and what's all this about budget cuts, nobody has mentioned them to me and what will it mean..." Walter Wilson rambles on.

Slowly, Rapier ponders, then simply talks over Wilson's babble. "You can't have a Morning Meeting without the News Director. I'm the, you know, I'm the News Director." His voice comes from somewhere in his upper nasal cavity. "We should start a new Meeting now." He seems to gain courage from the realization that he's really in charge. Sort of. Then, "Budget cuts? Oh yes." He scratches his uncombed head metaphorically, without lifting a hand. Clears his throat. Speaking mechanically, he recites, "Ahem. There will be certain cost-cutting measures implemented in the near future. No full-time employees will lose their jobs. But the company is taking steps to maximize our bottom line. Those steps will be announced soon." With that, Rapier marches into his new office and closes the door. So much for the new Morning Meeting.

"What was that?" I wonder.

"U.F.O. Unidentified Frightening Object," tries Nettles.

"Well, at least we have someone from the News side in charge of the News Department," tries Tracy Scott.

"Yeah...Ivory Eriss," replies Sherman Follicle, ending the brief discussion.

Just as we push back from the table, a muffled version of the James Bond movie theme song starts to play. It is Phillips' ring tones. He grabs at the phone in his pocket, and has a brief conversation. Scott whispers something to Hubbell, obviously about the ring tones.

Closing up the phone, Phillips informs Collingwood, "I have a new story."

"What is it?"

"That was a guy I know out at the Tree Sloths' stadium construction site. Says they found some bones buried where they wanna build Gate Number 12. Human bones."

"What about the Soyfield city manager story?" asks Hubbell, trying to needle Phillips after watching him steal the story from Fantana.

"The Soyfield Bureau should do that," replies Phillips, dismissively. "It's

Fantana's beat."

Glad to escape office politics. Assignment in hand, I head out with Fakir Johnson. Instead of a follow-up on Luther Post, we head out to a wastewater treatment plant that is under investigation by the federal Environmental Protection Agency. Some residents say they're getting sick because of too much bacteria in their drinking water. The utility workers tell us the filtration process works just fine. But the residents are barfing up...stuff....and doctors tell us why: the water is has more bacteria than a science experiment gone bad.

It's a so-called "good story" and I'm satisfied. On tape, I have a couple of people looking pretty ill, two doctors who say it's because of the water, and a home testing kit that shows a dangerously high level of fecal coliform in the tap water. We don't have any fixes but we did shine a spotlight on what looks like a serious problem. Golden.

On the way back to the studio, Johnson's scanner suddenly goes crazy. A fireball out on the interstate. It's called an "MVA"--motor vehicle accident. Numerous emergency vehicles dispatched. We aren't far away, so we call Calzone and tell her we are available to head out to the crash. We don't know what to expect. Only that if it is big enough, it could replace all the work we have already performed today. "If it bleeds, it leads," remains a truism is news, no matter the medium.

Lacking any better options at the moment, Calzone directs us out to the crash scene. Even if it turns out to be a "mere" run-of-the-mill fatal crash, it would still warrant a 45 second "vosot" report. Which, by the way, would be a definite upgrade over the feature vosot we shot earlier. An auto dealership—cynically hoping for cheap publicity--is taking a collection of toys for children victimized by a wildfire in California. It seems altruistic enough. But the dealership is only setting out a cardboard box, and wants customers to come in and fill it with donations. The dealer--a client of Hornswoggle's, naturally--doesn't spend a dime and gets potential customers in the door. P.R. genius.

It's tricky actually getting to crash scenes out on the interstate. It's tough coming up from behind one because of the traffic jam--Johnson would have to try to speed along the shoulder, ignoring cursing drivers and the possibility of earning a traffic ticket. Much easier to go ahead of the crash and approach from the other direction, which is what we do. It doesn't take long to determine there may not be much of a story here. A small Toyonda "Cubicle" sits forlorn and burned out on the shoulder. A small gaggle of people stand nearby. One of them is wearing a uniform, so I approach him to find out what happened.

The trooper is distracted but willing to give me a brief summary, with a half a grin. "Driver--he's a stan'in' right over there--broke down and pulled over. He's gonna fix it hisself, so he opens up th' hood and gets ta work. Closes th' hood, gets in and turns th' key: poom! Forgot ta re-connect the fuel line!"

"Caught on fire?"

"Yeaup. Gas onna hot engine. He only hadda half a bottla water inna cup holder. Not enough ta put out th' flames. Itsa goner."

I chuckle, he goes back to work. Me, too. Johnson has been spraying the scene including the car, the backed-up traffic, and bystanders who stopped to help. Cold as it may seem to the casual observer, the immediate aftermath of a disaster is the best time to interview a victim. They aren't worried too much about consequences; the worst has already happened.

Approaching this unfortunate driver, however, he doesn't appear all that upset. In fact, he doesn't seem to mind my request to ask a couple of questions. And it quickly becomes apparent why.

"I just got off the phone with my insurance agent--and he says I'll probably get a new car out of this." He glances over at the burned out wreck. "I really hated that car! !"

Johnson and I return to an angry newsroom. Evidently, some internal company news has been distributed to the staff--but it's not going to make our Six O'clock Report. Everyone seems personally insulted and studiously avoiding eye contact, so I don't feel like I can ask 'what's going on? 'My best hope is to check out my own messages on ENPS.

One of the notices in the "New Messages" box that appears when I sign in is from the new boss.

I click on the message, noting Johnson watching over my shoulder. "In keeping with the new fiscal realities confronting Newschannel 99, some aggressive budgetary steps will be taken. The first is to phase out the fleet of station SUVs. Fueling and maintenance are extraordinary expenses. Therefore, a new mode of fleet transportation will be identified in the near future."

"They're selling the SUVs?" asks Wash. Then, instinctively to himself, "I wonder if I can buy one?" They had been well-maintained, despite piles of miles and fast food wrappers. Since there aren't that many reliable taxi cabs that operate in this town, I wonder what mode of transportation may be an alternative to the SUV fleet.

I look over at Phillips, typing a story on his computer. "What 'new mode of transportation' is he talking about?" I ask.

"No one knows for sure." He lowers his voice so far that I have to half-stand and lean on the cubicle wall to hear the rest. "But I have a friend in the sales department who says we're trading out commercial time to a place that sells scooters."

"Scooters?" What?" Like, one foot on the frame, the other pushes you along kind of scooter?"

"No," he replies dismissively. Gas engine scooters. They might save gas but believe me, you won't want to drive them out on Mercury Highway because they don't do more than 45 miles an hour. And they are loud."

"That's ridiculous. How can we carry cameras and other equipment on scooters?"

"Oh, they have sidecars, with hoods. They can serve as a small trunk."

I sit down, convinced Phillips is kidding me. Not sure why I should believe him, actually. Back to work, writing my golden story about people vomiting their drinking water. Wondering about the SUV's, I begin to feel a little ill myself.

12

Later, at Haversack House, a logistical problem arises when the battery in my work phone goes bad. Kaput, must be replaced. Since Luther Post has my personal phone, this means that if I want to make a call it will have to be on Miss Mercy's landline. Naturally, she has some definite ideas about letting boarders use her Ma Bell-era black rotary dial telephone. Upstairs, a 4x6 card is taped to the wall next to an extension phone. "Local calls: 50c. No long distance. Ask before dialing."

So, I ask before dialing. I need some help from the Newschannel 99 assignment desk, to call somebody to change the time I had set up for an interview. But I am met with all the animation of a woolly mammoth encased in 16 feet of arctic ice.

"Mr. Gamble, I use that telephone to conduct my business," she replies, in a chilly tone that implies that this is the stock answer she uses to end discussion on that question.

"I need to make a single, short phone call for work. You said the landline phone was available for boarders to use. When am I allowed to use your phone?" I ask, hinting at my frustration.

The thin red slit in her oversized face twists into the tiniest of smiles. "If my business takes me out of Haversack House, it is at your disposal." She turns away, knowing that I recognize already that she actually departs the premises only to, say, attend the funerals of her aging friends, of which I am sure she has few.

Next morning, there's no official word of the new "scooter fleet," but it seems everyone has bought in to the rumor, damaging staff morale. The anchors and producers aren't much affected but the reporters and photogs take a serious hit. The morning rush is marked by a steady murmur: We gotta ride these things out in public? We are sullen, anticipating the ridiculous announcement will come at any moment.

Phillips seems aloof during this time of uncertainty; he's growing apart from the rest of the reporting staff. I recognize the symptoms--he's ready to walk. His contract is ending. And his status makes him a newsroom guinea pig; everyone else watches to see whether the station bean counters will do anything to try to retain him, or will they simply let him go and find a cheaper replacement? We all want to believe the station management values productive employees, but so few are willing to pay to keep them. We may not be indispensable but we also wish to be considered more than just interchangeable parts. So Phillips and his contract are the latest test case, to see how urgent it will become to prepare new audition reels as our own contracts come to an end.

Even station management usually hates to lose people during the so-called "ratings periods." July is the least of the four "sweeps" months, since it's in the middle of summer when fewer people stay indoors to watch TV. The other months are February, May, and November. This is when The Neilsen Company exerts its Total Control over all our lives. Not just the reporters and anchors. But the producers, editors, photogs, production staff. During these four months, no one may take a vacation. If you are sick, have a note from the doctor ready to prove it. The front line staff must be in place to ensure the greatest recognition by our viewers. This is also the time when reporters are assigned to produce multiple-part series of ridiculous "news" stories on such hard-hitting topics as "Overweight Hamsters" and "The Three Things Your Kid's School Did Right This Year." They are called "sweeps pieces" or simply a "Series." Some stations resort to the blatant expediency of on-air contests or stunts to sucker in viewers. No matter how we get 'em, the number of viewers translates into the dollar amount the station can charge for advertising. Simple as that.

My series is actually a strong one, on the online predators. Although the video is 'in the can,' and the stories almost completely written, it must pass muster with the new boss to make air during July sweeps. Collingwood and I approach the News Director's office, now occupied by Arlen Rapier.

It's not dark inside any more. At all. The blinds are open. I notice Warden outside washing the windows with a long handled squeegee. The overhead lights are evidently set to "tan" mode. Macula probably would have simply melted in so much light. But its Rapier who now sits behind the big desk, shifting around nervously in the oversized chair like Lily Tomlin's "Edith Ann" perched on her rocking chair. He nervously slicks his stringy black hair across his forehead. But he's The News Director, by gosh, so you had better take some notes.

"You guys want to do *what* for a series?" Rapier asks. We explain, again. And show him the rough drafts of my scripts.

After taking a long two minutes to consider, Rapier finally hands down his Judgment. "No way you can do this without talking to the people who were arrested, or their attorneys. You are treating them as if they are guilty!"

"Actually, Arlen," Collingwood purrs, "we are simply narrating what the video portrays. 'The camera never blinks,' and all that stuff, you know." He's expecting easy approval.

But that's not coming from someone who appears to have a serious inferiority complex. He's gotta announce his presence with authority. "This is just sensationalism! No real people are out there online tracking down little girls ("and boys" inserts Collingwood, consequently) to meet up for sex! You and the sheriff's deputies found four or five drug addicts who were completely blown out on smack, or crack, or whatever it is, who show up not knowing what they were doing, and you think you have a series? These aren't real people!" His thin voice keeps rising as he lays out his poorly constructed argument. "No way I'm putting that on the air!"

"Okay," tries Collingwood, still soothing. "You are right. It isn't the deepest form of journalism. But this was a legitimate police sting, one that's conducted in a growing number of places. With 'real' people getting busted, including 'real' people we know here at the station. And they gave us exclusive rights to it, thanks to Wil's relationship (I almost smirk) with the Sheriff's Department."

"I want more from the point of view of these accused men. They are 'innocent until proven guilty,' right? This is America, right?"

Clearly, there's no answer for that. So much for friendly, professional discourse. Evidently Rapier is looking for a way to establish some position. Particularly relative to the senior journalist in the newsroom, Collingwood.

The senior journalist isn't finished. "What, exactly, do you want us to get from these guys? You know very well they are going to be lawyered-up and won't tell us a thing at this point. We've got sound from some of them when they were busted. What's wrong with that?"

"Heat of the moment!" Rapier cries. "They've just been jumped by police, and you stick a camera in their face! That doesn't allow them time to think, uh, of something."

Collingwood stops. He looks at me. Then leans in with an ugly smile towards Rapier. Maybe he isn't just establishing his authority for its own sake. "Upper management isn't telling you to kill this because of Vlad Macula, and the negative publicity from his arrest, are they?" he asks, evenly.

The conversation stops. Rapier looks dull. Eyes glaze over. "Uh, no, of course not," he answers, quietly. Guiltily. Then he musters steam. "I want to make sure we cover all the bases with these very serious accusations! If you go no further, we go no farther!"

"What do you want us to do?" I ask, but Rapier begins fiddling with his mobile phone, then some papers on his desk, then his stapler. This conversation is over. Collingwood and I retreat in the face of his distractions.

"What do I do now?" I ask.

"Try to make some calls to those attorneys. But they won't say anything. I suspect the only place that video will ever see the light of day is on the internet, if you are willing to be fired for posting it there."

"Good thing for us that Rapier played his hand early," I say. "I'm going to make sure those tapes remain in a safe place."

But when I finally get ahold of Don Wash, who has been moved to a weekday schedule and is out on a shoot, I get some bad news. "Yeah, Arlen asked me about the video," he tells me over the phone. "Said he wanted to review our tapes."

"So you gave him everything? Even the stuff about your girl's soccer coach--and Vlad Macula?"

He takes a breath. "Yeah, pretty much. He's the boss, right? I didn't have a choice, right?"

"Guess not," I reply, hanging up the phone. I have a new-found respect-- and loathing--for how Rapier played us in the office, acting as if he wasn't aware of our series. But all that work, and our budding "relationship" with law enforcement, will be erased.

With a new phone battery installed in my work phone, I decide to try calling Megan once more. Never know what to expect when she answers: will she be articulate but vapid, wildly incoherent, or sedated by drugs?

"Hello?" answers a woman's girlish voice, full of childish wonder at this novel thing known as a telephone.

"Hi Megan, its Wil. How are you?"

"I'm fine, Wil, how are you?" she asks, mechanically.

Over the next 20 minutes I attempt to engage her in conversation but it's as slippery as separating the white from the yolk; she has forgotten much of the specifics of our time together. So, I try to awaken her mind with the remembrance of things past. She seems sweetly intent on recalling things, knowing how important I must have been to her once upon a time. I remind her of college, of our shared love of coffee and biscotti, or a movie we once saw. Little of it registers with Megan, who lives in the now, man. Maybe my problem is living in the past. After a while I simply ask about her Mom, and Meathead, and the latest clothes she bought while out shopping. And then I have to go. Goodnight, sweet princess.

The end of our conversation leaves me about three hours left to kill before sleep ends my day. Time for a drink. And to think about the future. Is Megan a part of it somehow? What responsibility do I owe her? We were friends, that's all. And she's gone away, in more ways than one.

Professionally? How many towns do I want to bounce in and out of before figuring out what kind of work I am capable of performing that could be permanent? Indeed, how can I even consider any other future before finding stability?

Laying on the bed, drink in hand, I consider the Johnny Bench card stuck in the mirror frame.

The important thing to know about the card is that Bench isn't alone on it. It's a "1968 Reds Rookie Stars" card that features Bench and one other player. A pitcher named Ron Tompkins. He's paired on a baseball card with a Hall of Famer, tagged together as "future stars." Tompkins' major league baseball career didn't amount to much. Never did pitch for the Reds. A handful of games elsewhere: a couple of losses, a couple of saves. Nothing else. But this card tells me something. Promise, potential...it sounds good. Ah, but its empty until you prove it on the field. While in college, interning at my first TV station, another intern and I were equally well thought of. Had similar skills, potential. I think of him when I look at my baseball card. After getting exactly one important break, he is at one of the cable networks, covering the White House. Next step: Big Three nightly news network reporting. Who knows, maybe he wanted it more, worked harder. But as I refill my drink, I consider the concurrent paths of me and Ron Tompkins, bouncing around the minor leagues, perhaps forever.

There's a lot on my mind as I track down my stories the next couple of days. I find myself in a bit of a slump, turning in a series of B-block stories. That's the second part of the newscast after the first commercial break. Meaning, they are often more feature-oriented stories than the harder-hitting A-block reports--you know: the crime that has been just committed or the controversy that has everybody riled up. It's not a bad thing to have your lightweight story featured as the B-block lead. That draws some attention. Better than having your hard news story buried at the end of the A-block when viewers are thinking about all the previous reports. In any case, I prefer reporting "hard" news because its more exciting and adds to your credibility as a serious journalist. Compared to reporting features, that is.

I'm not burnishing any credentials this week. My day starts off well, getting a tip from one of the sources I've been grooming in Frippin County. Utility workers have reported a human body about 30 yards from a county road, but sheriff's deputies don't want us to cover it. They won't say why, and suggest--off the record--it would be better to stay away. This means one of two things. Something is really wrong, maybe a deputy is involved. Or there is nothing really to the story but deputies can't say anything because the investigation isn't finished. Not knowing these guys all that well, I find it difficult to get a read on the truth. Things are complicated when a passer-by calls us from their cellphone, which has poor reception and cuts in and cuts out, finally ending when he tells Calzone, "it looks...a body by...of the road but it's only a man... ."

After a quick conference with Collingwood and Calzone, I grab a photog and head out.

This is reporting "on spec," with no guarantee of success. It's an all-or-nothing, er, gamble, that we sometimes take. On the way, I devise two or three plans for how to go about developing this story. A lot of that depends on what the scene of the incident looks like. I begin imagining different scenarios, considering what steps we will take to record and report this story. Might even lead the newscast.

My phone rings about 25 minutes into the trip north.

"Come on back," Calzone commands.

Bummer, dude. "Why--what did we learn about the body? Is it not dead anymore?"

"Turns out, it's not a body at all. Collingwood kept pestering the sheriff until he told him."

"Alright, we'll head back. But what did it turn out to be?"

"A mannequin."

I'm a little stunned. "How could they confuse a mannequin with a human being?"

Calzone's smirk radiates through the phone. "There was a truck accident there about two years ago. Guess what it was carrying? You got it. I guess they left one behind, and all the utility workers saw this morning was an arm and part of its torso in the bushes."

That's why the deputies didn't want us to come out. And that's why the caller said it was "only a man." The rest of the word "mannequin" was cut off.

So, this becomes the latest "big one that got away." Happens quite often, actually. The promising report that wasn't. Like a fisherman, I'm always casting about for stories. So, when I feel a solid "tug" on my line, and it turns out I've only hooked a rubber boot, it leaves the same disappointment and sense of loss that every good angler experiences from time to time.

Having thrown this catch back in the lake, I get back to the newsroom having wasted a valuable hour at a crucial time in the day. That leaves me with a report on twins with perfect SAT scores. It'll lead the B-block--if I'm lucky.

It's not much better on Friday. I'm covering the opening of a new coffee shop chain that only sells "fair trade" beans. This one leaves a bitter taste in my mouth when Walter Wilson lets it slip the story was pitched to him by Marvin Finkbeiner, on behalf of the Chamber of Commerce. My knee-jerk antipathy to any news coverage suggested by an official may not be entirely fair. But it comes as part of the critical attitude journalists have to apply to anything related to government.

In the end, however, I can't really complain; I haven't brought in strong story ideas to the Morning Meeting the past few days. That guarantees a quick trip to B-block purgatory. This doesn't endear me to the News Director, Arlen Rapier. But he isn't endearing himself to me, either.

This afternoon I'm typing out my story, kind of focused, when my concentration suddenly breaks. The reason isn't immediately evident to me. After five or six seconds of staring at my computer screen, I realize someone exists directly behind me. Turn. Its Rapier, staring at me.

"Yes, Arlen, what is it?"

"I'm here to collect your station phone," he replies tonelessly. He's swaying on his feet again. Breathing through his mouth, heavily. Its Darth Rapier.

Am I fired? I muster, "What's wrong?"

"I sent out an email message. Everyone is to turn in their phone. Our contract is being terminated with the service provider and we are going to try something new. It's a cost effectiveness initiative that should also allow you to do your job more efficiently."

"You aren't serious," I try.

He doesn't know an alternative exists. Standing there, breathing, waiting for me to give him the phone.

"We will assign phones daily based on need, but we'll only have three of them. You can always choose to use your own," he says without any irony. Very funny. I can't imagine where my phone may be right now.

"But my work phone is an absolute necessity. My contacts need to know my number, how to reach me. And vice versa--their phone numbers are stored in it. I use it to research stuff on the web. I write scripts on it while I'm in the field, and email them to producers. I can do webcam liveshots when necessary and shoot video with it. And I shouldn't have to pay the bill for using my own phone! How can my contacts know how to reach me otherwise?"

"You have a company-provided desk phone with a fully-functional voicemail system," he replies, noisily. "Not to mention a company-provided computer with a fully-functional email program. You won't be out of touch."

I show great restraint in not pointing out the incontestable observation that someone in this room is, indeed, out of touch. Instead, I go back to Rapier's first assertion. "What do you mean when you say I'll be able to do my job more efficiently?"

"Without its weight and bulk in your pocket you will be lighter and more aerodynamic. You won't weigh so much."

I smile at Rapier until I realize that he's not joking. Managers love spewing platitudes to pretend to make cutbacks look like they will benefit us, but this one takes the cake. The pound cake.

"Can I take ten minutes and go through the contact information I have stored on this? It would help me be efficient." Okay, no restraint that time.

Without a word, Rapier slinks off to Hubbell's cubicle to repeat the phone disposal process. Hmm. I don't feel any lighter.

After the newscast, I stay late. Reporters are required to provide a written version of our stories for our station's website, even on a Friday night. No extra charge--to the station, despite the extra labor. We just do it. You can't just cut and paste your television script because writing a script "for the eye" is different than one written "for the ear." For some reason tonight I seem to be running in mud; everything I do takes longer than usual. Eventually it's all finished, but when I glance around, everybody has departed. It's the dinner lull. Okay, I'm hungry. And thirsty. I recall the bottle of water I left in the studio while "fronting" my report at 6:11 pm or so. Let's go get it. I wander out of the newsroom, down the hallway, through the heavy cast-iron double doors, into the darkened studio. Quiet. Not knowing where the light switches are located, I kind of grope along, using ambient lights from sources like the television monitors and weather equipment in the studio. No problem, I can stumble over to the news set to locate my water bottle. Where is it? That's when I hear noises.

Human noises. Made by two people entangled with one another. Enjoying what might be delicately described as a passionate moment. The muffled sighs and moans are coming from an auxiliary studio set designed for interviews, where there a couple of chairs and a, uh, loveseat. Two people are feverishly engaged in this darkened area behind the cameras, which point away from them, toward the primary news set. Involuntarily or perhaps voluntarily, I glance in that direction. The couple is oblivious to any other presence. But even in the dark, a mere glance identifies Jack Phillips and Tracy Scott, involved in an intense one-on-one, er, interview. Okay. I'm outta here. There are some headlines that never get read.

Forgetting the water bottle, I beat a hasty retreat, heading back to the newsroom. Time to return "home" to Haversack House.

At least that image is something to distract me from another night watching cable TV. Talk about a vast wasteland. 53 channels of empty and often self-serving drivel, interrupted by random flashes of brilliance. But my remote control doesn't move fast enough to catch most of those glimpses. I confess the image of Phillips and Scott stays with me; not in an obscene way, simply in seeing them as real people, outside the office. Even if I saw them, um, inside the office. It must be like the average viewer who sees me in a place outside his television set. For that moment, I become a real person, after all.

What will this mean for our office dynamics? Never pictured the smugly self-serving and consciously-talented Phillips hooking up with the serious, career-driven Scott. Especially since everyone wonders how long he plans to remain at Newschannel 99. No matter. I try to put it away; I'm not the gossiping type, and their secret is safe with me.

Yet the following Monday I'm interested to see their interaction at the morning meeting. Scott is among the first at the table, of course, and chats briefly with Hubbell about a report she is researching. Phillips is among the last at the table, of course, and doesn't make eye contact with his paramour. As the meeting breaks up, they head in separate directions. It strikes me then and there that this kind of discipline is probably the result of long-practiced behavior. Fawning, newly-attached lovers trade hopefully-hidden glances. But the practiced eye of this here reporter caught none of that.

Today's story assignment tests the practiced patience of this here reporter. On the surface it seems seamless enough: members of the textile union are voting to elect their Local President. Except, everybody is afraid of the Immediate Past President, Paul "Papa Pomade" Prednizone. He is powerful, although for the next three-to-five years he'll be indisposed, at the service of the state. Additionally, the owner of a Filterboro textile manufacturer has indicated that if Prednizone's protégé is elected, he may close up shop and move the operation to Mexico. No pressure, folks. So, no matter how long I wait outside the union hall, no member of the rank and file will talk to me on camera about the election. And it is television news gospel that I record the thoughts of at least one Real Person regarding my story. It is crucial to tell a human story--inside my report--because viewers can relate more quickly to a neighbor more quickly than an official-type person. It's obvious this day that the union members have been warned: "Don't talk to the media unless you want some people to visit your home tonight."

So I stand, with Wallflower and his camera, among hundreds of full-size pickup trucks in the parking lot of the local headquarters. Members trickle out in twos or threes. Sometimes ones; the mill is shut down for retooling. Most wear baseball hats, blue jeans, and flannel shirts. They all, without exception, treat me like The Plague. They demonstrate a mixture of resentment, fear, and arrogance--like the last single girl at a crowded bar late on a Saturday night. "I've got something you want and it's not really worth much but just because you want it I'll act as if it were above you." Off camera, they flip the bird and holler "Screw The Man!" but to a man they turn me down for an actual on-camera interview.

"This is a rough story," I conclude to Wallflower. He's not sympathetic.

"Yup," he replies.

Three hours of my life goes by. Sam from Channel 7 is there in parking lot with a photog as well, and has as little success as I.

The Noon newscast happens, with no update from me, except the remaining local leadership is optimistic that the results will be available sometime tonight. Suspicious of the media, the acting union President grants me an audience--and indeed, a five minute interview. wow, with a lower case w. But out in the parking lot, as each union member turns me down, I feel like a Fuller Brush salesman with leprosy. At least it's a sunny day.

Wallflower isn't much company. He leans sullenly against the SUV, rubbing his mustache, while I approach various union members and get rejected.

"Well, I'll say one thing for you," he eventually offers. "You're persistent. How long'll you waste my time like this? I'm getting hungry."

Good question. I call Calzone.

"Whatsamatter, bored?" she asks, almost turning away from the phone-sounding distracted already.

I almost want to whine. "This is getting old. Nobody's talking to me. I don't see how I can turn a package with just one interview with a talking head."

"Do you have a better story to do?" Ah, the ol' Logic Ploy. She's got me.

"Nope," I admit.

"You could go into town there and see what regular people think will happen if they shut down," she suggests.

"Yeah. But we should be doing that story tomorrow. I'll stick around here a little longer."

Back to my stakeout.

Sam has disappeared, apparently throwing in the towel. More union members wander in and out of the building. They look at me with curiosity on the way in to vote, and avoid all eye contact on the way out.

All except one group of five men who come out together. Safety in numbers, I guess, when confronted by me and Wallflower, the human stick figure. They aren't afraid to walk past our position and start jeering us. Or, me, rather. Wallflower thinks of an excuse to duck into the SUV.

"Hey boy! Get on home! This ain't none of your business!" shouts one of the men, whose "I Grill With Beer" t-shirt stretches tight over an enormous gut that has patently played host to many a beer.

Ignoring him, I write down some gibberish in my notepad.

I...can't...HEAR...yewww.

A guy with a green flannel shirt and orange pants craftily throws out, "We don't like your kind 'round here!" Then, more ominously, "You never know when something might happen, dude... ."

I check my watch. Miller Time yet?

"Yeah Buddy. That's right. Time for you to go!"

My new acquaintances don't seem intent on really starting anything. They pass by while I study a plane flying overhead. They keep moving towards their trucks. But one of them tries one more crack, this time hitting closer to home.

"Hey, TV Star. Go on back to your office and file your nails, pretty boy!" The others guffaw, thinking this is the parting shot. Their job is done here. "Thatsa good one, Scabrous Bob!" says Orange Pants.

That provides all the encouragement "Scabrous Bob" needs. He fires another salvo, more bitter this time. "When you gonna work for a living? You got no idea what it's like for the workingman! You was never laid off! !"

Jerk. I stop tying my shoelace. Yes I was. Laid off, that is. Well, actually, fired. My first boss informed me that (insert formal parental figure voice) "You haven't truly worked in broadcasting until you've been fired." So, he furthered my career right then and there.

Despite the bright blue of the sky, I see red.

Throwing down my notepad and pen, squaring my shoulders, flexing my neck muscles, I go after "Scabrous Bob." I'm no longer just a Newschannel 99 reporter--a minor Filterboro "personality." I've been stripped down to a man defending his street cred. The other union guys have already proceeded to their pickups. Wallflower remains seated in the SUV, deeply interested in the workings of the cruise control unit. So it's just me and Bob. But he's going down.

I stalk up to him. "Come here!" I demand, in a tone that implies he's running away. "You don't think I know about dealing with life's crap just because I wear a necktie?" Vile thoughts and words course through my blood. I pull at my tie, skewing it to one side. Okay, okay. Gotta draw back--just a little. This dude is tall but thin. I notice small, disconnected details. Green and black checked flannel. Veins popping out of skinny arms. Bloodshot eyes that show...weakness. A shoulder draws back...a slow-motion flinch. I'm emboldened even as I draw up to him. The other union guys are at their pickups, watching what happens. One half-yells a half-hearted, "Tell him, Scabrous Bob!" But he doesn't leave his truck.

Stunned that A) I would actually come after him, and B) he finds himself on his own; "Bob" is silenced.

I get up in his face. "I'm actually doing my job. What are you doing?

Voting for a union president instead of working your shift?" Bob really does flinch. "You look like you've been on a six month drunk." He involuntarily glances into his truck's side mirror, hand feeling his chin. "I hate it when people assume their suffering is worse than anybody else's. I went without work for six months, eating Ramen noodles and playing games with the electric company to keep the power on in my apartment. I sent out 60 applications and was rejected each and every time--without any word back from a single News Director. I was hungry, you stupid *knob*. So think twice the next time you open that gaping piehole known as your mouth."

Scabrous Bob almost looks like he's gonna cry. "Yeah, this guy is weak," I think to myself, as his shoulder draws back in another flinch. Except, it's not a flinch. It's a punch.

When I wake up, the world seems to be at funny angles. The bright, blue sky is straight ahead. The sun's over there. A series of rolling hills seem to have tilted sideways. It's really warm underneath me. Then, Wallflower's face slides over top of my field of vision.

"Let me help you up from the asphalt. It must be hot in the sun," he says, with a hint of a smile. "That guy sure clocked you with that sucker punch. You okay?"

My pride will need some Bactine but nothing hurts too much.

"This is a rough story," I repeat.

Although he had pretended not to notice what was going down, Wallflower eyes me with a little newfound respect. I might just be worthy for him to work with. When he's done inspecting the cruise control on the SUV, that is.

Eventually, our sacrifice pays off in unpredictable fashion. An older woman hobbles out of the Union Hall. I hadn't seen her go in. No way she's voting. She must be somebody's grandmother, long past retirement age. In fact, at least three times the retirement age. But on her way out, she approaches me and starts in.

"I heard what you said to that man earlier. And I saw what he did."

"Yes'm," is all I can reply. I'm not sure where she's going with this.

"Well, you can bring that camera over here and ask me anything you want."

What for?" Uh, I'm looking for voting union members for my story. I want to know how they feel about their future."

Asperity. "Whatsamatter? Don't you think I have much of a future?

What in the world could Papa Pomade do to me?" Grandma sure is feisty.

"Um, sure. Are you a member of the union? Did you just vote?"

"Sure enough, buddy. I've tied ribbons at the factory for 35 years, so I have just as much a right as anybody to tell you what I think, and this election is a travesty." She proceeds to tell me why, making for a terrific story, rewarding my perseverance.

13

Morning and Noon producer Meredith Angle is getting married. This means two things to people in television. First, she's developing an Exit Strategy, a financial path out of her career in broadcasting. Second, it's an excuse for a party. Hey, I'm ready to grill with beer. After the 6pm newscast I tag along with everyone else to a nearby tavern, where we get started with Jager-bombs and beer. Off to a great start, we're feeling good. Then things move really fast. Someone suggests we head out to a drive-in movie theatre. Is there really one still in existence? Sure 'nuff. Now it's suddenly like high school, watching *Porky's* and guzzling "Pabst Blue Ribbon" that we snuck on to the premises. Thank goodness we've graduated to the more mature *Deuce Bigalow* and "Schlitz Malt Liquor." Loud and obnoxious, we drive away other patrons. Eventually, a manager and security guard drive us away, threatening a phone call to the police. Uh, that wouldn't look good in the *Daily Repellent*.

So, it's on to another nightspot, this one with dancing. The party tempo increases. Other Newschannel 99 staffers join us, including Jefferson Adams, who really seems to like his Bolli-Stolis. Lavinia Fern sips a Perrier. Others, however, are getting toasted. Eventually, I find myself on the dance floor, hooking thumbs with Gretchen Calzone. She smiles at me, complimenting my "moves." I tell her how alluring her frizz looks and can tell by her smirk that she marks it down to the drink. That's okay, I may be making a complete fool of myself but I'm still having an excellent time.

Most of us from the TV station congregate at a long table that terminates with a booth in a corner. Angle, who normally appears dour and mousy, has nonetheless earned a reputation for a certain moral laxity. Tonight she shares drinks with a couple of cab drivers at a different table. "Journey" plays on a cheap speaker system operated by a local DJ, but it doesn't bother me too much, nor does her flirtatious attitude. Something else does. Bother me, I mean. She should be the center of *our* attention, not theirs. In my haze, for some reason, I assume that that it's up to me to correct things. Geez, I hardly even know her.

We're seated again. "She should be over here!" I exclaim half-heartedly to Calzone over the music, nearly sloshing my frosted mug of Heineken when I gesture towards Angle and the cabbies. Follicle sits on Calzone's far side, opposite me. She sips a wine spritzer, he a Boilermaker. Follicle likes to pour his whiskey into his mug of beer.

"Leave her alone," he counsels kindly, but with finality. "Let 'er have fun. She's getting married." Um, yeah, okay. Does that makes sense? But that's his point, I guess. Tonight, she's not...Married, With Children.

People spill onto the dance floor as the DJ plays an old Billy Idol dance tune. For the most part, they seem to blend together in a pulsating mob. But in the crowd I note Adams, um, dancing with himself. Okay, time to focus back on the Angle Controversy.

"She's our guest! She should hang with us!" I try.

"No way, buddy," agrees Calzone. Then, slightly more alluringly, "Don't I have your attention?"

Aw shucks. "You shore do, Little Lady" I affirm in my best John Wayne voice. Angle, who? Shall we dance some more? To Journey, even? I'm ready to escalate this confrontation.

But then, Calzone suddenly turns to focus very intently on Follicle, engaging him in small talk while I'm left to converse with my Heinie. Er, Heineken. That's when Channel 7 Action News weather-guy Phil Connors enters the bar. It's the first time I have seen him in person. Using a hand to prop himself against the door jamb, he stands unsteadily at the entrance, evaluating the scene. His left foot appears to bounce in time with the music. Arnold Paul, in the corner of our table-booth, squares his shoulders while sizing him up. It's a Meteorologist Standoff, and I become...afraid.

Ignoring Paul--and everyone else--Connors marches straight over to Angle, brushes aside her bangs with his right hand and plants a wet, sweet kiss straight on her lips. She sits, unresisting, a little responsive even, head upturned to Connors. One arm thrown out behind her, wrist bent back and palm open. The cabbies don't move. Connors flips a ten dollar tip to the waitress, and leaves. Paul stares, speechless.

Soon, the night starts to wear thin. The cabbies disappear. Eventually, other people trickle away also, in ones or--more often--twos. TV news hookups are as numerous and enduring as Saturday night summer replacement sitcoms. Fern and Adams left separately a long time ago-- they have a newscast to do, although I find it hard to believe Adams can function well enough to even tie his shoes. As we leave, I'm in the "two for show" category. I want to drive home, but am reminded by Calzone about another bad potential headline in the *Daily Repellent*--complete with mugshot: "Reporter Arrested For Drunk Driving." So, since she's been sipping while I've been gulping, I let her drive me home. But that's all. The drive to Haversack House is a very fast blur, like a DVD at double-time. Pulling up to the curb, I want to pause, to think out this situation. But Calzone won't let it even become a situation. With a smile, she quietly opens my car door and I waddle inside alone, making lots of unnecessary noise despite my best intentions. A 4x6 card from Miss

Mercy certainly will be my reward in the morning.

Some of us have different rewards at the next Morning Meeting. Calzone ignores me entirely, instead focusing on angrily texting someone on her phone. I can only hope its Artie on the receiving end of her digital tirade. Follicle looks badly hung over, has little to say. This Morning Meeting doesn't have much zest to it. One item does catch my attention, though.

Hubbell, pulling a brush through her blondish hair, relates how a convenience store was knocked over last night near Khalishes. "They think it was Luther Post who did it," she concludes. I shiver, wondering what the man is doing out there. Hope he didn't flash my cellphone in front of anyone.

"Who thinks it was Luther Post?" asks Collingwood.

"The clerk, I guess. I buy my Lotto tickets there and the clerk knows me. So she called me! Wasn't that cool of her?" Tyler is so...*connected*, dude. "Nobody was shot this time," she concludes.

"Is there any surveillance video of him from a security camera?"

"Well, yes," replies Hubbell, suddenly less sure of herself. "Except, they told me the camera wasn't exactly pointing in the right direction. All you could see were his feet."

Groan. A lead story turns into a lead story. Lead, as in ponderous, dull metal. Sounds like a story I did once... . We gotta have strong video, even if the threat of Luther Post is invoked in a story.

Now, however, our attention becomes claimed by Arlen Rapier. He stands at attention, and has an announcement.

"Meredith Angle is no longer employed by Newschannel 99. We wish her well in her future endeavors." That is all, thank you very much. He starts to leave.

She was an employee just last night, right?" What happened?" I hurriedly ask, voice almost a falsetto.

Rapier mechanically turns to me. "Miss Angle did not report to work in a suitable condition this morning. It is a personnel decision, so I am not permitted to say anything more." Typical corporate dodge. But Rapier does offer one codicil. "Miss Angle is not to be granted access to this building under any circumstances, except with a security escort." Who? Warden The Doorman?

It takes several hours for the entire story to come out. Phillips knows, of course.

"She called in sick last night from the bar, knowing she wouldn't be sober this morning. But the intern working the night assignment desk forgot to forward the message to anyone in the morning."

"Intern? Don't we have a real employee working the desk at night?" I ask.

"Not anymore. Another budget victim."

"So what happened when the AM crew came in?"

"They called Meredith, who was still stone drunk. So then they panicked, called everyone they could think of to figure out what to do. Including our boy Arlen Rapier. He called Meredith, insisted she report to work."

"Oh, no!"

"Oh, yes. Like a good soldier she stumbled in, tried to do a couple of things, but passed out in an edit bay. The morning crew wouldn't have said anything--they were doing their best to cover for her. But the boss, since he's quick as a scabbard (Phillips chuckles at his own pun), he came in to work early." Phillips shrugs his shoulders. "He stumbled across Meredith, and out the door she went."

"Hope she made it home okay," I say, with a tone of condolence. It's all I can offer. I feel bad for Meredith, but she has a safety net. I feel bad for me, because I'll have to work for a guy who has this little mercy.

As the Morning Meeting rolls on, Rapier is otherwise silent. Eventually, he walks away. Out of boredom, my eyes inadvertently follow him, which is a mistake. Suddenly, he turns back towards us, notices me, and bids me to enter his office.

"Close the door, please," he starts. Never a good sign. I feel just like I'm going to the Principal's Office, and fear I'll be sentenced to wear a dunce cap or stand in a corner.

Rapier slides on a pair of reading glasses. Checks a manila personnel folder. Its uncomfortably thick, considering how short a time I've been working here.

"Mister, uh," he glances at papers inside a manila folder, "Gamble." Statement of fact. Yup, that's me. "You have been here a few weeks and done some good work."

Affirmative. Uh huh, that's me.

"So I am moving you to the evening shift, beginning Monday. Come in at

2:30 in the afternoon."

Nope, that's not me. My first reaction is: no way. Another threat to move me. Change is bad. Not inherently bad, but the New Boss Thinks You Shouldn't Be Performing For The Flagship Newscast kind of bad.

"Why?" I wonder.

"We need to beef up our nightside reporting. You are doing a good job, so you will help us there. Just don't plan to work any overtime."

Huh?" Why should I ask for overtime hours?" I ask.

"Because you might feel the need to stay late, following a story overnight. Don't do it; we won't pay you. I won't be here that late to supervise you directly, so just finish your shift and go home."

"You want me to ignore major stories that might happen to develop overnight just so that I won't get paid overtime?" I immediately feel that I understand the word "incredulous" even more intimately than ever before.

"That is correct. We will have an overnight videographer get the story."

"Uh, I'd hate for us to get beat on a story, but if that's the way you want it, that's the way I'll do it," I reply. "You're the boss."

"Please don't forget it," is his rejoinder. What a tool. I'm sure to be loyal to that, buddy.

There are benefits, however, to moving to the evening shift. If the producers like you, they'll make you a featured reporter during the 6pm newscast. Do an easy live shot on either breaking news or some scheduled event going on around the area. Then have less competition from other reporters for a juicy story for the 11pm newscast. If the station leadership doesn't like you, well...you'll be covering quilting bees in Washerville for the b-block.

Okay, I'm resigned to the change. You can't fight City Hall, right? And it's not like I have an extensive social life. In some other line of work, I might expect a co-worker to stand up for me, to explain why my absence may hurt the company's product. Not in television, where the only value is that of professional jealousy. Each on air person is a personal "brand," working for a station "brand." Part of our survival instinct is to promote individuals over team. So I prepare myself for a shift change, as Jimmy Buffet might hum, Come Monday,

Come Saturday, Collingwood has me over to his house. We lounge on the patio, not swimming in the pool, surrounded by sentinel Majesty

Palms in clay pots. Flowing fronds abound. We pull on our longneck beers. Something's been bothering me. After enough liquid refreshment, I feel ready to plunge in.

"So, when did you give up?" Offhanded, 'been-there.' I watch him.

Silence. Does he understand?

Quietly, brushing an intruding palm frond away from his ear, Collingwood answers matter-of-fact: "I haven't, yet." Implying, 'What do you mean? 'But accepting the premise. "Why am I still in Filterboro, you mean?" he continues, out loud. Pause. He really expects confirmation. I nod, slightly.

"Or, if you mean my childhood--or maybe childish--dreams, they ended for the most part when I moved from Michigan to California in 1985."

Surprise. You kidding me?" In 1985?" I ask. "C'mon. It was still 'Morning in America.' And didn't your Tigers win a World Series around that time?"

Collingwood chuckles. "Look. It's as simple as settling down. There's nothing wrong with getting married, having a family. I really wanted to, like most people, I guess. Seemed like the adult thing to do, as if life didn't start until you had your own family. But having a wife and a kid simply changes the dynamics of life from 'the possibilities' to 'the limitations. 'There's just too many obligations. After that, its paycheck-to-paycheck."

I consider this, perhaps for the first time. What are my "possibilities" and what are my "limitations?" Megan inexorably comes to mind.

"The other day, I heard a song from an old movie," Collingwood recalls. Have you ever seen 'The Goodbye Girl? '"

I consider. "It's pretty old, right? Didn't see it. Who was in it?"

"Richard Benjamin... no, wait. Richard Dreyfuss. He was a huge star in a lot of movies over the years. You can't pin him down to any single moment in our culture. More to my point: Marsha Mason. She was the co-star of that move, she was the 'Goodbye Girl.' To most of us, she pretty much belongs just to that point in time."

"Like, um, that model in the movie 'Weird Science.' Kelly LeBrock."

"'Weird Science.' Didn't see it," Collingwood replies.

"Guys my age saw it," I explain. "For two or three years in the mid-80's, Kelly LeBrock was The Fantasy Woman. But that was it for her."

"So yes, like Kelly LeBrock, I guess," Collingwood admits. "She belongs to a specific time." Drink. Okay. "Sometime in the late '70's...it's the same thing for Marsha Mason and the theme song of 'The Goodbye Girl', which used to get played on the radio over and over when I was 13. David Gates. You know, the guy from the band called 'Bread'."

"Never heard of 'em."

Collingwood digresses for a moment. "13. Do they really think that a 13 year old is a teenager?" He shakes his head. "18 is a teenager. You can drink, vote, go to war...but still think and act like a stupid idiot. 13 is still an infant, practically."

"You have to be 21 to drink now." Ah, but it's his digression.

Back to the topic at hand. "For me, 13 is Marsha Mason," Collingwood reminisces. "David Gates. The opening piano and violin coda takes me to a place of beautiful horizons." Whoa there, Mr. Lyrical. But I understand. He's talking about that sense of possessing unlimited possibilities. None of the choices that limited that ballad and artist to what they eventually became--one hit wonders. None of the hard realities that so forcefully define a life.

Flashback: November, 1985. Friday night, babysitting a couple of kids across the street. Easy to imagine a commercial for "Weird Science" playing on the television. The kids are finally asleep, thank goodness, after a strenuous 'Cheez Whiz' fight and an hour of "Miami Vice" on TV. I'm picking the bits of "cheez" out of the carpet. Pastel wallpaper abounds. I sneak whiskey shots from the liquor cabinet. With that kind of courage, I grab the new cordless phone and chat up a girl from school. Moussed, big hair blonde. Tight Jordache jeans. She's a little cooler than me. By the name of Jennifer. Kelly LeBrock has nothin' on her. We talk of teachers we hate, homework.

Then Jennifer says, "I'm home on my own, home all alone."

What's that? Ulp. Her home? I did not get off the phone.

She elaborates. "My Mom and Dad went out tonight. They're at the movies. We can watch "Falcon Crest' together!"

Whoa Nellie, Kelly. I mean, Jennifer. My fantasy? Too unbelievable to even picture. Sweaty palms. Other brief physiological changes. But...I can't. Kids here. I'm a...responsible person, sort of. The parents I'm working for are probably at the same movie as Jennifer's folks. Deep breath.

"I'm babysitting. You want to come over here?"

Silence. She didn't mean it, I guess. Testing me? Teasing me? The moment passes.

"So...are you gonna buy that new album by Mr. Mister'?" Jennifer suddenly answers.

Goodbye, girl.

Back here in Filterboro, Collingwood brushes away that palm frond that has been tickling his neck. "Diana Ross, I guess."

I wait. Evidently, Collingwood was reflecting on his own impossible schoolboy crush. "Growing up in Detroit everyone was pretty much immersed in the 'Motown Sound.' And, wow, she was a goddess." He considers for a moment. "Going back to life choice. I used the word 'limitations'." Swig. "I'm thinking about it, though. It may not be exactly like I said, 'Shifting from the possibilities of life to the limitations': no, not exactly. Maybe it's more like 'shifting from the possibilities to the fulfillment,' really. That's better. 'Fulfillment.' Early in life, all roads seem open to you. You think you could take any of them, or all of them. Some people seem to stall out right there, people like those 'career students' who never finish college. For the rest of us, later, after we made our choice, we think of all those other options, and wonder if we somehow missed out. It's called 'regret.' Well, satisfaction in life certainly doesn't come from the anxiety over the different things you didn't do; it should come from the knowledge that you actually had a choice in the first place, and took that road as far as it could go."

"So, there should be no regret. We should feel lucky to follow at least one path as far as possible."

"That's the philosophical viewpoint, I suppose."

"But what if it's the wrong path? What if I was supposed to do something more...useful?" Pediatrician? Charity Fundraiser? ValuMart Greeter?

"'Supposed to'? That's like contemplating the end of the universe. At least you *can* speculate and imagine. A vast majority of people in the history of this world couldn't even fathom that. Circumstances dictated they follow one single path, one that was infested with problems and usually ended early and often in violence." Another sip.

"So, it's a luxury to contemplate the alternatives, like Jimmy Stewart in 'It's A Wonderful Life'."

"I'm not a philosopher. I'm just in the mood for another beer." Collingwood leaves for the fridge. I allow myself a luxurious moment of regret; to consider the big-hair blonde--Jennifer--and what might have, or could have, been.

14

It's almost a three day weekend, since I don't have to report to work again until 2:30pm on Monday. Upon arrival I note that the newsroom is still tense, but there's a different rhythm, different tempo in the afternoon. Less attention from the bosses. Fewer window cleanings from Warden the Doorman.

Despite the unsettling number of changes at the top of the News Department, we all pretty much believe that we are battling to win the 6 pm newscast ratings competition, long considered the crown jewel of any broadcast news operation. Some stations, bowing to the reality that another station is a powerhouse in their DMA, simply shoot to win the 11 pm or the morning newscasts. We might not finish at the top of the next ratings book at 6, but at least we feel like we are competing for the trophy. Which is why I hate to move to 11.

But if I am working the top story for 11, prized liveshots will fall my way at 6, if for no other reason than to promote what we are doing for the late newscast. So I can be a "featured reporter." So I tell myself.

I wander in to the Afternoon Meeting, sensing an atmosphere of anticipation and curiosity. We convene without Jefferson Adams. Arlen Rapier isn't there either, but that doesn't seem to concern anyone.

"Where is he?" wonders Collingwood. We all know he refers to Adams, not Rapier. No one answers. He peeks out of his office into the newsroom. No Adams. Calzone shrugs. "Call him," Collingwood tells her.

"Okay, many of you haven't heard, but Tracy Scott here," Collingwood gestures with pride to our primary producer, "turned in her resignation this morning. Tracy will be heading to the scenic Harrisburg/Lancaster/Lebanon/York market, which is a pretty decent jump from here."

"What's the new gig?" asks Fern.

"E.P.," explains Scott. Executive Producer. That's Walter Wilson's job-- here, anyway.

"So you got a job promotion also!" exclaims Fern. She sounds genuinely happy for Scott, who just smiles.

"Gronblatchulayshuns," offers Fantana on the forever-distorted speakerphone.

"Thanks, Brian!" Scott says brightly, like she knows him as something more than just a garbled voice on a speakerphone. It's always an occasion for celebration when someone gets a new job in television. The perception is that a "new" job must mean it's a "better than here" job. Especially if it's in a bigger market. The truth is, most of the same leadership, technical, and personnel problems exist everywhere. Because, well, people--human, fallible people--are involved. Although I haven't been around here all that long, I sense our newscasts may suffer without the steady hand of Tracy Scott to produce them.

The grass might be greener somewhere else for Scott, but tonight I still have to cover a Cheeseport town council meeting. A lot of residents are plenty upset about a new rock quarry operation proposed by Slate Excavation Company. My videographer is Frank Sturm, who has been around Newschannel 99 since they used film and had to send it out to be developed. Stubby, chubby, and a little grubby. He smells like a bar because he smells like an old ashtray. But he's full of entertaining stories about the people in Cheeseport and the older employees at Newschannel 99. As he nearly sideswipes another car and barely avoids a pedestrian, I just hope he gets us back in one piece so I can tell my story.

"Yes, I've had a long run here," he concludes a lengthy narrative. His voice is a mellow barrel of Irish whiskey, with a twinge. Like Burl Ives. We're about 15 minutes out from the station. Sturm scratches a short, white beard. "When Carl joined the station, we only had me, two reporters, a writer, and an anchor."

"Who was that?"

"Well, let's see." he stares off above the road. While driving. I hope his peripheral vision is better than his focused vision. "It must have been Ken Brickman. Wait, no. Bill Kentman. Or Kent Brockman, oh, I forget which. He stayed for a few years, then moved on to the Springfield market."

"What was Collingwood like back then?" I ask.

"His hair was all black back then," Sturm chuckles. "But always perfect. He always dressed well. He always seemed so focused, so serious. For a long time I tried to get him to lighten up." Sigh. Swerve. "But I learned he just had standards that not everybody measured up to." Sturm's voice turns querulous. It's not a pleasant memory. "One day we were out trying to shoot a water rescue on a river. A boat tipped over. Back then I had to carry a camera and a separate recording unit that was pretty heavy. The sun was going down, so we brought a light, so I also had to wear a battery belt." Another 25 pounds. "We shot on the shoreline. But with all that stuff hanging off me, I lost my balance and fell into the river. Well, that ended that, our video was destroyed and the camera took weeks to be fixed. Collingwood never let me hear the end of it."

Sounds like a Sturm sore spot. Time to change the subject. "What about Ivory Eriss?" I try. "What kind of standards does she maintain?"

Sturm's eyes cloud over. He's lost in space for a while. Finally: "I don't want to talk about that."

We park in a mostly-dark lot and lug in the equipment. Momentarily blinking in the artificial light, I quickly survey the quiet newsroom. About 8:30 pm or so. Young assistant Aimee Flotsam mans the Assignment Desk, chin on hand. She was an intern promoted to a minimum-wage job with a title. The scanner volume is turned low. The text message on her cellphone is far more interesting. Somebody is in an edit bay, quietly editing an audition reel to apply for a job at another station. Hurd looks at videos on f-baumsworld.com along Producers' Row.

A new and youthful reporter, Juan Cortez, is the only inmate to wear a newsroom expression. Mixture fear, frustration, indecision. Sees me, seizes upon me.

"Wil, do you have time to help me? My story's blowing up in my face."

I glance at Hurd. Cortez sees. "I asked him." He pauses. "Marshall." I detect actual disdain; Juan's a fast learner. "He could only suggest waiting to see if something clears the wires."

Hurd turns another magazine page. The wires are often the last to know anything that happens in a local TV market. Useless suggestion. I glance at the clock. There's a little time left for Cortez to act, if he's capable. He's straight from a university with a good telecommunications program filled with lectures on the Communications Act of 1934. All the natural talent in the world is absolutely no trade for experience.

"What do you have?" I ask.

Cortez speaks as if I already know his story. I don't. "The people who run Pestilence Ridge Mall kicked us off the property." He's hurt by this. I grin. "And they aren't telling us anything about how the construction worker got hurt." I stop grinning. "I thought maybe the other construction guys might tell me something but nobody would talk to me. And no customers saw anything, because the construction was out of the way, you know, on the back side of the Mall that's blocked off to traffic."

"Do you have any sound?" In other words: Any interviews on videotape?

"No! No one. The Mall spokesman shut me down. The police aren't treating it like a crime scene--it's an accident. The paramedics aren't allowed to say anything about who the victim is."

"Federal health laws," I say. "It's called 'HIPAA.' Emergency workers can't reveal anyone's identity."

"I learned about that, today, I guess. Now, I'm out of ideas."

"It's a tough one." Cortez may be able to gather most of his information, but it's only a newspaper story if he can't get anybody to talk on tape. "Did you call someone over at the union local?" I try.

"No. Why?"

"This may be a union construction job. Even if it's not, chances are they'll know all about the project, the kind of work being done there, the name of the victim, and they may be upset about what happened. They'll dish all the dirt."

"It's getting late...do you think there's any chance I can actually reach somebody?"

"Who knows, at this point. I don't know anybody over there but I'll try to help you track down someone. But then I have to log some video and get going on my own story."

Cortez is suddenly more chipper. "Thanks, boss man."

In the ENPS contact files I quickly find two union local office numbers, pass them over to Cortez. While he dials, I search the union local on the internet. Three minutes later, a webpage. A list of local officials. Email addresses, no phone numbers.

"No luck," Cortez appraises me.

"Try the OSHA website. That's the government agency that investigates workplace accidents." I think of the SUV. "They'll be coming here sooner or later."

"What can I find there?"

"Lists of any past accident investigations and inspection reports at the Mall. If there was anything wrong, they'll list citations."

"Cool." He turns to his computer.

I go back to the online phone directories. No match for names from the union website. Think. One name stands out: "Paul R. Opscit." Unusual. Weird, actually. The online telephone directory has the name, though. And a number.

"Here, Juan. Call 867-5309." Cortez writes. "Construction Union Treasurer. Name of...Paul Opscit."

Cortez stops writing. "Paul what?"

"Paul Opscit. In fact, he has a middle initial. Paul R. Opscit."

"You're joking." But he starts dialing.

"What's funny about that?" wonders Flotsam at the desk, almost defensively. There had better not be any political incorrectness going on here.

Looking up from his video, Hurd interjects, "That name can't be right."

"I agree," I agree. "But I'm finding the name mentioned on some other construction-related websites. And now I see it on another page." I click on it. One moment, please. Finally, it opens. So does my jaw.

"What is it?" asks Hurd.

What I see seems strange and out of place. Intrigued, Hurd walks over. Flotsam floats by. We stare.

It's the state's "Sex Offender" website. There is a listing for a "Paul R. Opscit." It couldn't possibly be anyone else.

"Uh, Juan..." I start. Too late. I hear, from across the room, "...yes sir, Mr. Opscit. Thank you. I'll be right over." Beaming, Cortez hangs up. "I got the interview! He knows the victim, what happened, everything!"

"Juan, you may want to be aware of what you are getting into here."

"Why? The guy sounds down-to-earth."

"Just come here, first. Look."

Scratching his head, Cortez comes. He looks. He drops his notepad.

"Uh, yeah." Thinking. "Guess I'll find a photog to go with me."

"Have fun." I have my own story to finish.

Next afternoon, I'm at my desk. Surfing the web for story ideas. Go to Goggle's "News" search engine, type in "Filterboro," "Reproach County," etc. Also, check out the county clerk's public records, see if there's anything new. Nothing. I'm ready to start calling my contacts, see if there's anything shaking with them, when my phone rings. Dully, I duly recite our prescribed greeting. "Newschannel 99, Where We're Right 99 Times Out of 100: Wil Gamble."

Heavy mouth breathing for a moment. "The battery is running out on this thing, man. Its running out, running out."

What? It's a thick, heavy, hunted voice I hear.

"I need to recharge it somehow. Or get a new battery."

Great googly moogly, its Luther Post.

"Ah, no problem, ah..." I almost say his name. "...my friend. How do I get it to you?"

"I'll see you back at that haunted house. Tonight at 7. No cameras, no cameras, no cameras." Click.

7 pm? It'll be getting dark then. Me, alone, a long ways from home, playing a scene from Poltergeist with a guy wanted for shooting a man. Aw, I hate this job. But, at least he said, "no cameras," not, no other people. I'll bring Frank Sturm.

"No camera?" wonders Sturm. Slowly. "I always have my camera with me. Always." I'm about to interject when he accelerates backwards. "Except for June of 1983, when the leg on the tripod slipped and the camera toppled over and broke the lens. I had to borrow a camera so I didn't have it with me sometimes."

"Frank," I break in. "Bring your camera. Keep it zipped up in a camera bag in the back of the SUV."

"Why don't you want me to bring a camera?" he finally wonders.

"Because it would be the last video you ever shot," I reply.

On the drive up I consult again with Collingwood, at home.

"Carl, I probably won't have time to turn a package tonight," and I explain why.

Always the good manager, Collingwood pays respect to the TV news maxim that "you have to feed the beast"--all that broadcast air time sucks up content like a sponge.

"Um, well," he thinks aloud, mentally searching for a quick story to turn. His guttural pauses are endemic in broadcasting: can't let there be any dead air, you know.

"Um, well, there is a town council meeting in Oak Hill tonight to make a decision about whether they can afford a major jump in insurance rates for their hot air balloon festival. You could go see your buddy then grab a vosot at the meeting and front it at 11." Vosot: 40 seconds of video with a soundbite from somebody. Front it: a live report from the newsroom, to add emphasis to the story, and incidentally fill a few extra moments of airtime.

"Alright," I reply. "But will you call Marshall Hurd and let him know what I'm coming back with? I'd rather someone in management explain to him why I won't be bringing back a package."

"Glad to. Just be careful with your, um, assignment tonight," Collingwood signs off.

The sky darkens as we drive north. Everyone has their headlights on, even before the sun sets. No moon tonight. Exit the freeway, leaving the highway for a byway. We pass through the small version of civilization named Oak Ledge, and head up through the oaks into the dark hills.

"So what exactly are we doing way out here?" Sturm wonders for the 234th time.

"I'm developing a major story. Meeting a quiet contact," I answer. "Just like 'Deep Throat'." Now I'm speaking Sturm's generational language.

"That movie inspired me to change my major in college," he confesses, heading for another deep reverie. Good. It distracts him from questions about our present day mission.

The house at Marberry is completely obscured when we pull up to it. Of course I'm spooked by the scene: a vague outline of the abandoned domicile, haunted with weeds and hanging tree limbs.

"This is a heckuva place to meet a guy," observes Sturm. We are parked on the shoulder of the road. "Do you want me to back up and shine the headlights over where you're going?"

It's tempting. But probably a deal breaker with Luther Post. And he has a firearm. "Nope," I reply. "Stay here, keep the engine running and the headlights pointed forward. Oh, and leave the interior light on, and you in plain sight."

One last look through my window at the darkness. I check my flashlight. Okay. Deep breath, pull door handle back, and I'm out into the night.

In the "front yard," I have to step carefully. The flashlight reveals cameos of tall weeds, wild bushes, and uneven terrain. It seems to take hours. Step, step, step. The going gets easier as my eyes adjust to the strange conditions. Its deathly quiet. No frogs, crickets, high wind, or gunfire to provide the usual nighttime theme music. The only noise comes from the weeds whisking along my pant legs. I feel a funny vibrating sensation and realize that it's my hand, shaking. Even as small as it is, the cellphone battery charger feels bulky in my pants pocket. Finally my foot kicks against the worn out wooden front steps. I'll go up to the porch, but no further. Having stepped up and around the broken boards I turn and face back to the road, finding some tiny comfort that Sturm has not driven away.

For the first five minutes I stand awkwardly on the porch, facing out to my lifeline: Sturm, in the idling SUV. He sits upright in the driver's seat and smokes a cigarette. Realizing the only way to at least appear relaxed is to sit, I drop down on the top of the steps. Ouch. Stand up, remove battery charger from pocket, sit back down. Another five minutes goes by.

I'm almost getting comfortable when Sturm leans over, rolls down the passenger window, and calls, "How long we gonna wait?"

"As long as it takes," I reply back.

Restless, I want to make something happen--the kind of wish one has when forced to wait. So, I prowl. Back and forth on the porch. Then, working up my nerve, I step around to one side of the house and look around. Nothing there that I can see. Through the weeds and around back. The weeds poorly disguise mounds of aging trash. The smell is strong; some of it must be fairly fresh. Where did it come from? Twitching my nose, I move away and turn the corner.

And am instantly engulfed by the hulking form of Luther Post.

For a moment, uncomprehending, I struggle. He's way too big. For another moment I consider shouting, but a great big hand muffles my face.

"Shut up. Just shut up," orders a rolling, guttural voice.

I nod my head. Swiftly, silently. Not like I have much of a choice. Please don't break me in half, sir.

Post releases me, and I realize that upon inhaling that he has squeezed me hard enough to take my breath away. I take half a step back.

"How's your leg?" I ask, looking way up at him. It's difficult to make out his features because the flashlight was squeezed out of my grip. It lies helplessly, shining a wayward beam straight into a thick clutch of weeds.

"It hurts, it hurts, it hurts. Shut up. Who's that with you?"

"Just my cameraman. I have to travel with him. He's not taking pictures. And no one else is here," I assure him.

"This cellphone ain't working. It died when I needed it the most. Its 'cause God hates me. All this is because God hates me." Suddenly he changes directions. "You got something for me?"

"I brought a battery charger. You have to plug it in somewhere to charge up the phone." I show him how it works.

"Thanks. Now get out of here," he directs me.

No way. "I didn't come here just to become an accessory to a crime, Luther. I'm a Reporter. If I don't have anything to report, then I become an Unemployed Reporter. Then I couldn't help you like this."

"What do you want?"

I think for a moment. "The only realistic thing I can ask for is an interview with your family. They haven't talked to anybody and I want to be the first."

Luther considers. "I'll get word to them to call you. I got to go." He's fading back into the night.

"Wait. Who is it that are you calling on my phone?"

He taps the phone with a finger, speaking almost to himself. "This phone, this phone. This phone I am using to make...my..." his voice lowers, "my arrangements."

Arrangements?

"You know the law has probably tapped your family's phone, so you can't call there," I advise.

"I figured that. So I call my boy at the gas station store in Otis Mills and he gets my messages home." Post turns away, then turns back and smirks (I think). "But that's 'off the record,' my man." He's gone.

Where's the flashlight? I retrieve it and hurry back to the SUV.

"Is this guy ever gonna show?" asks Sturm, tossing a cigarette butt out of the window.

"He's come and gone," I respond, vainly trying to brush my mussed up hair with my right hand. "Okay, let's go." We have a deeply important town council meeting to cover.

Later, back at the station, the newsroom resembles a locker-room. In a rare moment of levity, Hurd and Cortez toss around an old, empty videotape box to each other like a football. Neither seems like much of an athlete. So its humorous when the subject of athlete's foot remedies comes up. At that moment Walter Wilson breathlessly rushes in to join the conversation. Nobody, I think, even knew he was still in the office at this hour. Then again, nobody can imagine where he would go after the workday ends.

"Does anybody need some jock itch medicine?" he tries, to nobody and everybody. This is met by absolute and utter silence. Hurd twitches like he wants to throw the tape box at Wilson...who is not tuned in to the general newsroom reaction.

"I've got some almost-new 'Notrimin Extra' and its hardly even been opened so if you need some jock itch medicine I can sell mine to you."

"Huh? Jock itch medicine?" answers Cortez. "We were talking about athlete's foot."

"Oh. But some of you guys are real athletes and if you need any stuff for jock itch, I've got a bottle because I saw a feature on cable once about jock itch probably, oh, about January and I sure wouldn't want to catch it and I think you'd like to have something on hand just in case," Wilson attempts, as an explanation: "Did you know ringworm isn't really a worm? My dog has ringworm."

Silence. The newsroom becomes riveted to this crazy narrative. Bewildered looks everywhere. What in the world is he talking about? Undeterred, Wilson plows forward.

"Ringworm is a fungus, you know, like jock itch and my vet, who is a woman but I trust her anyways, says you can treat it with stuff like 'Notrimin' but I went out to the store and bought 'Notrimin Extra' by accident at the Koupon Klub the other night and I found out later you can't use *that* on Ringworm."

Ohhhhh. Silence. Despite this plausible explanation, still nobody volunteers to accept the jock itch medicine from Wilson's personal medicine chest.

But, then, there at the assignment desk, a small voice belonging to Aimee Flotsam arises. The intern has some breaking news for Wilson. "If you return it to Food King, they'll give you their money back."

Wilson's eyes light up like he'd been offered a lifetime supply of Little Jennie Nutty Bars ("They're only 100 calories, you know, that's a lot less than the breakfast burritos at El Indio," he would say).

"But I didn't buy it at Food King," he tries, doubtfully.

"They'll take it back," she replies, innocently, assuredly.

"I opened the package," he returns, growing bolder.

"They'll take it back," she answers, unaware.

"I don't have a receipt!" he adds, smiling, throwing down his ace card.

"They'll take it back. They have to. It's part of the Food King Pledge. I've seen them take back loaves of bread that were half eaten." Trump. With visions of $8.69 jingling in his pocket, Wilson nearly dances back to his office.

Quiet reigns for three minutes. Everyone returns to their work, to find some semblance of normalcy in their routines.

Then, Wilson re-emerges, approaching Flotsam once more. In a lowered voice, with all the attitude and body language of a deal-maker, he asks her, "Uh, hey, Aimee, would you mind taking it back for me? The Notrimin Extra, I mean, because I'm real busy this week--I have to go to PaperclipWorld to get sticky notes for the station and then take my dog back to the vet to have his teeth cleaned--and so I wasn't planning on getting over to Food King anytime soon." By the way, Food King is situated so close to Newschannel 99 that in her tower, Ivory Eriss can spot station vehicles in the parking lot. But Flotsam's attitude seems amenable to the proposition, so Wilson seals the deal with an offer she can't refuse: "If you do it, we can split the proceeds 50-50!"

Next afternoon on the way in to work, I notice for the first time that the grass really needs to be cut around the station building. Funny, thinking back, I probably noticed how unkempt the place appeared before, but perhaps I had not wanted to believe it. Poor landscaping reflects poorly on a business operation, and I wanted to believe the best in a place to which I had committed myself for the next two years ("Unless the station exercises the morals clause...").

Nevertheless, this is a vibrant, almost painfully-bright early summer day, the kind that makes you believe the upcoming weekend will be impossibly terrific.

On the other hand, this parking lot seems to be designed to create a daily drama of "musical chairs": which employee will be left without a place to park?

Somehow, I spy an open parking spot. It's close to the "turret" that juts out from the front of the station. But suddenly a strange ballet, perfect in poise and balance and pathos, plays out in front of me. As I approach the spot, another vehicle--an old Chevy Nova--races from the other direction to intercept and occupy the location before me. As it does, a Great Big Pickup Truck pulls out of the neighboring parking spot without looking. The Nova slams into the side of the truck, leaving no motion or sound but the hissing of radiators as they leak fluid on the lot. Since it remains open, I feel, um, obligated to take the open spot. It's the closest place to park to render aid, anyways. A quick glance at the drivers shows they may need a little help. Stumbling out of my pickup, I race towards the building to get to a phone. My vision jounces as I run, but I spot Warden the Doorman inside, sedately performing his window washing duties with absolutely no notice of the accident just outside his domain.

I burst inside the lobby before Warden can move to the door to open it.

"Call 911!" I breathlessly instruct everyone, and no one.

Motionless, half leaning into one of the big plate glass windows, Warden simply asks, "Why?" He's genuinely dumbfounded.

The windows are clean. But apparently there's nothing worth seeing outside his palace.

I can't fathom his inability to have seen what happened, so I walk wonderingly to where Warden is rooted. I turn and look. I can see the Great Big Pickup, the Nova, and a growing crowd of onlookers. Warden, evidently, cannot.

At the reception desk, Shelley Winters, aka "Rose," reproaches me tiredly.

"Don't we have enough to do without having to get mixed up in some fender bender?" she asks. She saw it. And then tiredly sets down her nail file to punch all three emergency digits on the telephone.

Well, I grew up quick and I grew up mean

My fists got hard and my wits got keen

I'd roam from town to town to hide my shame

As a boy named "Wilson" I wished that my fists got as hard and my wits got as keen as A Boy Named Sue. Right now I can relate to the "roaming" part of the lyrics.

Despite Shelley Winters' attitude and Warden The Doorman's obliviousness, I'm not feeling mean. For 48 seconds, anyways, until I hit the newsroom. A staff wide memo greets me when I sign in to my computer.

"Due to the economic downturn and an increasingly-frivolous attitude toward writing instruments by Newschannel 99 personnel, ink pens will be no longer provided free of charge to staff members desiring to use them," reads the electronic note. "You may purchase one from Rose at the front desk for 99 cents or you can provide your own writing instruments for future inter-office written communications. Local dollar stores sell inexpensive packages of ink pens. Sincerely, Arlen Rapier."

That evening someone quietly collects 30 or 40 loose or stray ink pens from various nooks and crannies around the station, dumps them in a plastic bag, and hangs them on Rapier's doorknob. Apparently, he ignores the rebuke. That is, until the next day when we see an engineer hooking up a new internal security camera in the newsroom...pointed unflinchingly at the entrance to the office of Arlen Rapier. Apparently I need to head to the dollar store. When I get back to the station, though, someone has beaten me to the punch. Sherman Follicle has purchased a pack of crayons and is using them to write all sorts of unnecessary notes to various co-workers on yellow sticky notes.

On my voicemail is something eminently more interesting than the latest hot color from Crayola. A shaky woman's voice leaves a phone number for me to call. It's obviously someone close to Luther Post. I dial and a hesitant but terse female voice tells me to leave a message on the answering machine.

"Hi," I try, breezily but uneasily, "This is me at the television station. I got a phone message to call this number. I can meet any time. Call me back at the numbers you already have for me." Hang up. Tap fingers on my desk, hoping there's no tap on that telephone line.

Okay. What stories can I cover tonight? There's a Reproach County Commission meeting, so I fetch the agenda online and check for anything of interest. There's always something. Tonight, though, not much. But, since we are in television news, we know how to squeeze blood from a stone. It doesn't matter which end of the political spectrum wants us to cover the story, it's just a matter of timing. If I need a story, I'm gonna make some lemonade out of whatever lemons are available.

In this case, older residents are starting to agitate for a county senior center. Gotta have a place to drink coffee and play Bingo. Tonight commissioners are considering whether to spend $200,000 on a consultant who will determine the necessity of a center. An expensive, but perhaps crucial, step in the process. Yawn. I wander over to the Assignment Desk and get the booking sheets that have been sent over from the county jail. People arrested in the last 24 hours. Let's see if there's anything interesting. Hmm. No murder warrants. Lots of "VOP"--"violation of probation." No one of interest. Any prominent surnames?

Alias Smith and Jones. No one I've heard of. A few drug possessions, soliciting, and petit theft charges. Nothing newsworthy.

Time to make some calls. Although I haven't been at Newschannel 99 very long, there are a few people I've met who are worth checking with to see if anything of interest is happening. One of them is County Health Director Juniper Wetlands. Evidently she doesn't hate me from my reporting on the stray needles. In fact, she seems a bit flirty.

"Actually, we having a little get together for a staff member who's retiring," Wetlands tells me, a little breathlessly. "A field inspector. She's got 30 years here, so it'd be nice if you guys could do a nice little story on her going away party." Yawn. But I humor Wetlands. Gotta try to develop her as a source.

"Ah, sure. Maybe we can come." I assume Wetlands wants me to be there. "But you know, with breaking news happening all the time, I can't say I'll be able to go."

Ignoring me, Wetlands tries, "Well I hope you'll send Billy out. He was really great when you guys came out a few weeks ago."

Billy? Fotch? Wetlands wants him to visit? Oh no.

After hanging up I deal with my pointless disappointment. I wasn't much interested in Wetlands. But then she mentioned Fotch instead of me and that hurt my pride. "She'll find out his IQ is about the same as pocket lint and then she'll kick herself," I rationalize. Then I try to get big about it. Fine. I'll set them up. I march over to Calzone, who only has only one telephone conversation going on at the moment. So she's free for me to pester.

"Gretch," I start, quietly. "Gretch." She doesn't look away from her computer screen. "Gretchen." This time, more intense voice level. She flicks a glance my way, says a couple of words to the phone. This means I now exist in her world.

"Gretchen, can you send Billy over to the Health Department?" She's still focused on the phone conversation. "Major staff change," I tease. She looks, nods. "He can get a vosot, easy." Now she shoots me a sharp look. Uh, yeah. Nothing comes easy for Billy Fotch. Retreating to my cubicle I feel I've done a nice day's work. Before my day's work, actually. But I am still smarting from my deflated ego...and resolve to call Megan ASAP.

The rest of the day, morphing into night, goes no better. Sturm is in a menopausal bad mood. My computer crashes, losing much of my script. The Reds lose.

At least, all's quiet in the newsroom, relatively. Just another Tranquil Thursday. I'm deeply involved in re-writing my story. It's complicated, about a state Supreme Court decision on religious freedom. The city government will have to pay six and a half million dollars to an employee they fired for handing out tracts that promoted biorhythms.

Nothing much shaking. Jefferson Adams wanders in from his usual three hour dinner. Lavinia Fern is reading the latest industry gossip on TVwebspy.com's "Shopchat."

I'm in full concentration mode and don't hear the scanner traffic about an "incident" at Handout Heights public housing apartments. It's a common address for police scanner traffic. No one else pays it much attention, either. Including Aimee Flotsam, now actually being paid minimum wage to sit at the Assignment Desk. She is consumed by a reality show on a television monitor.

But she can't ignore the phones when they start ringing a few minutes later. I don't really tune in to her initial conversations. But after the third call in the space of two minutes, I'm all ears. At that point, Flotsam doesn't know what to do.

"Mr. Hurd?" Flotsam tries plaintively. The 11pm producer is busy working on a crossword puzzle. But since Wilson doesn't seem to be around tonight, he is nominally in charge of the newsroom in the absence of more official, er, officials.

"Marshall?" She turns singsong: Mar-shall!"

"What. What?" He turns on her. Why in the world would she bust up his crossword concentration like this? What's a four letter word for running mindlessly with a pack of similar animals?

She starts. "Well, Mr. Hurd. I've had all these calls from people telling us about the police finding the body of a baby in an abandoned apartment. All the neighbors are wondering when we are coming out there to cover it."

"Where? I haven't heard anything about this. Have the police confirmed this? Was there anything on the scanner? And I'm very busy, uh, um," he casts about his cubicle, "trying to write this tease. Is this really important? Call up the 911 Dispatch Center, see what they got." That buys him some time to go back to the puzzle.

"Okay," Flotsam replies sweetly, pleased to have some direction. She starts dialing. Hurd goes back to D-14. "What's seven letters that describes 'floating debris? '" he asks no one. No one answers.

I start editing my package, the deadline looms. But soon Hurd is called out of his puzzle again by the annoying girl who won't stop calling his name.

"Mr. Hurd? Mr. Hurd! Marshall?"

Finally, Mr. Hurd hears. "Huh? Yeah? What is it?"

"Emergency dispatch won't tell me anything, which is, um, you know, unusual. And all the police will say is that they are investigating a 'suspicious incident'. It's at Handout Heights. I took another call from a neighbor saying a county forensics truck is there and that yellow crime scene tape is all over the place. Should we send someone out there?"

Seems like a no-brainer. Which is a perfect conundrum for Marshall Hurd. "Who would we send? Its 9:30 in the p-m, we don't know anything for certain, Gamble is tied up, Cortez has the day off. Wait. Call a photog. Where's Frank Sturm?"

Flotsam ponders. "Oh yes. He's on break."

"Well, call him anyways, send him!" Hurd nearly yells. Get this distraction of a news story out of my face, honey. I've got a crossword puzzle to do. Never mind the newscast in an hour.

Flotsam dials, reaches Sturm.

"Hi Frank! How you doin'? Nice night, huh? Yeah...we have something we need to go shoot. No...I don't need a burger combo with cheese fries, but you go ahead and order." Pause. "Actually, and we're not real sure about this, but I think you need to hurry on something that sounds real important. And it's not too far from you." She gives him the address of the public housing apartment complex.

15 minutes later, Sturm calls in. Flotsam holds the telephone handset straight out towards Hurd, like a mendicant. "It's Frank. He says its urgent."

Hurd rolls his eyes. "Okay. Extension 248."

"Whose extension is that?" asks Flotsam, before embarrassedly recognizing Hurd's stare. She presses the requisite digits to transfer the call from her phone, hangs up. Hurd picks up.

"Hey Frank, what's up. Uh huh. Really? Mm hm. Okay." He hangs up, looks up at Flotsam.

"Who's on call?"

"You mean, which reporter is on call?" She consults a list. "Tyler Hubbell."

Hurd sets himself in motion. "Call her. Tell her to get out to Handout

Heights, immediately. I'll call an engineer, get someone to drive a live truck out there. It looks like we've got the body of a baby found in a toilet in an empty apartment."

Everything stops.

"A dead baby?" asks Lavinia Fern, incredulous.

"That's what Sturm says he heard," replies Hurd, picking up his phone, dialing. And Sturm has some credibility. He's been around."

Two more calls come in from neighbors telling us about the baby. They say it's an abandoned apartment, useful for crack parties. One woman must have had a surprise party.

"Sounds like we've got a new lead story," suggests Jefferson Adams, turning back to "Medialine" on his computer.

Hurd gets to work on his computer. He's got to change the rundown for the newscast to include the story in our news software, then tell the director, who has to change the camera shots and other commands in his computer system.

Flotsam reaches Hubbell. "Hi Tyler! Its Aimee! Yeah! Oh, thanks! I loved the cute little top you wore on camera today! You're welcome. Oh. We need you to go cover a dead baby story. No, really! Out at that yucky public housing place." She looks at her notes. "Handout Heights, that's it. Frank Sturm is already there and we are sending a live truck to meet you." She listens. "Well, we already made, like a hundred calls on it already."

Hurd glances over to the Assignment Desk. "Tell her she's gotta get moving."

"Marshall says you'd better hurry, we need you to go live. Oh, and Filterboro police are there so I'm sure no one will bother you. Okay. Have fun! Bye!" Flotsam hangs up, smiles, addresses Hurd.

"She has to curl her hair. But she says she'll be out there in time for the liveshot."

"I wish she'd be out in there in time to find out what's really going on," injects Fern.

Off in my own world, I finish work on my story. It's a pretty good one, but now it won't be the lead story tonight. I'm powdered, gelled, and suited up. I will introduce my story from the newsroom, in front of the newsroom camera, lonely, since almost everybody else still here will be involved in the newscast. The shot is operated by remote control from the studio, so there's no camera operator to talk with. Just me and my thoughts. It's almost time. My IFB is plugged in, so I can hear some chatter between Hurd, the director, the anchors, and Hubbell in the field. She sounds far away.

"Marshall! We're still not 100% sure of what's going on here. I wonder why none of the other stations are out here." Hurd mumbles something unintelligible. Hubbell answers, "Just have the anchors throw it to me as a 'suspicious incident that's under investigation' and I'll try to take it from there. Just tell them to be generic." Hurd mumbles a few more words of direction, this time at the anchors. Fine, it sounds like everyone is on the same page. Pretty remarkable, considering we had only an hour and a half to mobilize for it.

Commercial break over, our news music starts: insistent, driving percussion. I hear Adams and Fern.

"First at 11: A neighborhood in agony!"

"Reports of a human tragedy!"

"Worries about a crack party gone bad!"

"You're watching Newschannel 99, Where We're Right 99 Times Out of 100!"

Dramatic news music up full, strings and keyboards. The two anchors appear together on the news set. The city skyline scene behind them is darkened for the night-time newscast, tiny lights twinkling to represent lighted windows and stars.

"Good evening, I'm Jefferson Adams."

"And I'm Lavinia Fern. Police are investigating troubling reports tonight from several residents in the Handout Heights Apartment Complex near downtown."

Fern turns to her own camera. She and Tyler Hubbell appear in graphic "boxes" that split the screen. "Newschannel 99 is first on the scene with our Tyler Hubbell. Tyler, have police confirmed what they are investigating?"

"Well, Lavinia, sources in the police department tell me they are investigating a report of the body of an infant found inside one of the apartments." The camera, operated by Sturm, carefully moves off Hubbell and on to a two story cinderblock building. Can't see much, due to the dark but we can see silhouettes of people flitting around like ghosts among the shadows. And there are numerous emergency vehicles, many with lights flashing--possibly at Hubbell's request. Halogen headlights cross one another like light sabres, completing the impression of an incident scene.

More Hubbell: "Police have been here for an hour, interviewing neighbors. A medical examiner is inside the building right now." Sturm pulls back to reveal Hubbell standing with a police officer. "We're joined now by Filterboro police sergeant Miles O'Meter. Is this a death investigation, Sergeant?"

Although he is a practiced public affairs officer, O'Meter seems uncomfortable. "Uh, not at this time."

"What can you tell us about the calls from the neighbors here?"

"Well, um, you see, they, uh, we get calls that are a little exaggerated or perhaps confused sometimes. So, uh, we have to take that into account until we can fully explore what's going on."

"What can you tell us about that apartment police are investigating right now?"

O'Meter starts to answer, but is interrupted by a man with too-thick eyeglasses and too much hair wax. He's not a doctor, just a functionary of the Medical Examiner's office. He won't ever be admitted to The Country Club. And he knows it. So, the man isn't exactly shy about grabbing his 15 seconds of fame.

He blurts out to O'Meter, on our live broadcast, "We confirmed it. It was poop."

Turning to the man, O'Meter instinctively drops his voice to a harsh whisper. "What?"

The lackey, happy for a little attention, smugly plays out what probably happened. "Someone must have said 'there's feces up there', and other people heard 'there's a fetus up there. 'Isn't that great? Feces. Fetus. Get it?" Smirking, he moves on, leaving Hubbell and O'Meter in possession of the field. But not their composure. O'Meter simply withdraws. Hubbell nearly forgets she's still "live" until Hurd yells something in her IFB. She visibly jumps, turns to the camera, and stammers out, "Well, Jeff and Lavinia, uh, that would seem to close the case on this...um, case. Reporting live from Handout Heights, Tyler Hubbell, Newschannel 99, Where We're Right...99...times, um, out of 100... ."

Adams appears, full anchor voice. Forceful. Commanding. Clearly not paying any attention. "Tyler, will there be an autopsy?"

Returning to Haversack House after the 11pm debacle, I find one of the infamous 4x6 cards taped to the door of my room. I briefly wonder who could have placed it there. Miss Mercy can barely move around the ground floor, much less lumber up a flight of stairs. It could be Slab, I suppose, if he has a couple of free hours and is able to figure out which is my door. Then I consider my, er, unusual next door neighbor, the Troll. Him, maybe? Whatev. I read the note. "Because of complaints about noise levels late at night, the television cable will be cut off nightly at midnight." What, no late night comedians? This is downright un-American. Shoving my frustration into a compartment deep inside my head, I change into some sweats and head back out. The only way to call Megan is outside of the cellphone dead spot that is this house. I walk back out into the cool night, turn around the corner on to Chainlink Street, and climb back into my pickup. Leaning back the bench seat, I punch in Megan's digits. My hand is a bit sweaty. I hope she answers.

Ring once, twice.

Three times; the lady answers.

"Hello?" she tries, wondrously. Yet somehow, worldly, aware. Tired. My Megan?

"Megan, hi, its me." I offer.

"Oh, hi, Wil." Where is the automatic, puppy dog joy of hearing my voice? She is supposed to pick up my spirits! What's wrong?

"Hi Megan...I just wanted to see how you are doing. How's Meathead?" I try, forcing it, a little too boisterous.

"He's sleeping," she answers, with some finality. Uh, yeah, its past midnight. She's probably been sleeping, too. So I had better come up with an excuse for calling so late. What was I thinking, other than trying to make myself feel wanted? But Megan, in her confused innocence, will not ask the question, even though it's out there.

"I, uh, just got home from work. And I am, um, working the evening shift these days, " I start. Silence. Has she fallen back asleep? Better think quick. What do you want, dude?

"Um, I was hoping to maybe see you soon. I thought I'd invite you to come down to visit me. I know its late, and you sound tired, but I hope you will think about it, talk to your Mom. Hey, 'SummerFest, By Jove' starts in a couple of weeks. I know we'd have fun."

"Mmmm, okay, Wil. Springfield, yeah. Sounds good," Megan tries.

"SummerFest," I automatically and regretfully correct her.

"Sure, Willie. Springfest." She's as conscious as a five year old at the end of a 15 hour drive home in the car. At 4:30 in the morning. She's not really weighing the difficulty of a trip all the way down here. I understand. My letdown, however, is complete--on the heels of the bad kind of day I've just had.

"Call me when you think of it," I demand, offhandedly, bitterly, unfairly. "I'll let you get back to sleep. Good night." I punch the red button on the cell phone. Then, I punch my forehead until its red. Looks like this will be one of those days that live in infamy. Largely thanks to me. Time for bed, to start over tomorrow. It feels like the trudge from my pickup truck to Haversack House is, like, 15 miles. I dare not glance at the Johnny Bench card--or should I say, the "Ron Tompkins card"--on my way to bed.

15

Friday just kind of passes by. I don't "mail in" my work; it's more like "Fedexed" in. I find myself simply hoping I can just finish the week without something pointless and stupid happening. No such luck, not this week.

Since there isn't much going on in my free time, I ask Cortez if he wants to go with me to see a Tree Sloths minor league baseball game. Since Newschannel 99 is a sponsor of the team, it makes sense that we might score a couple of comp tickets to Saturday night's game.

I ask Collingwood, who forwards me down to our Sales Department. "Well, Wil. We have some great comp tickets, and they come with vouchers for free food and parking. But if you want a freebie around here, you gotta sell your soul to Sales. How important is it to you?"

I don't have much to do, and hanging around Miss Mercy's place is driving me out of my mind. My pockets are empty. In addition, star outfielder Jose Tejada has been sent down from his big league club for a week or so to rehab an injury, so it'll be fun to see a major leaguer playing down here in Filterboro.

Collingwood understands. But he offers a philosophical codicil: "You know how the Catholic Church has patron saints for almost everything?" He waits until I nod. "They have a patron saint for journalists."

"I imagine we need one as much as anybody."

"Guess who it is." He waits until I shrug.

"I'm Catholic, but couldn't tell you."

Collingwood pauses again a moment. Then: "St. Francis de Sales."

Oh no. We just can't seem to keep Sales out of the newsroom.

When there's a small break in my day, I head back towards the lobby. Each step seems more physically difficult to take as I plod along. I branch off down the stone-lined path hallway past "Legal" and towards the darkness only illuminated by the flashing neon sign.

Take a breath. Okay, buddy, you are only here to ask for a baseball ticket. Don't sell your soul.

I enter the Sales Department hallway. Dim. Brown paint, brown doors, brown industrial carpet. All the doors are closed, and blinds drawn, but

I hear scratchy activity within many of the offices. The final door, however, is slightly ajar.

Lester Hornswoggle is on the phone. He acknowledges me with a flick of his eyes. I stand at his door and wait. There are no windows in his office. Just the orange fiery glow of a salt crystal lamp and a computer monitor. His voice is an unbroken dialogue of slippery promises of implied good fortune.

The perma-smile has been applied, for my benefit. "Helloooo, Wil. So, you want something of me? Heh, heh, heh," Hornswoggle asks, flipping through a handful of baseball tickets like a poker dealer holding all the cards. Ugh. His chuckle reminds me of someone I'd hoped to forget.

"Tree Sloths? Does The Station have any tickets?" I intentionally avoid the personal pronoun "you" with reference to possessing the tickets. They don't belong to Hornswoggle. They belong to all of us. At least, in theory.

"Let's see," he continues, ignoring the obvious implication. "I have some good seats available for tonight... ." Using the personal pronoun to parry my omission, Hornswoggle leaves this offer hanging like a Florida ballot chad. He licks his lips.

"Great! I'll take two," I try--brightly--yet worried that there will be a cost, and it's not monetary.

During the workweek, Fridays are the worst days in TV news. Just like almost every other industry, truancy is highest. Ferris Bueller has his day off. Even during ratings periods, fewer "sweeps pieces" air on Fridays because viewership is down. Viewers who are asked to fill out ratings diaries usually get tired of the process by Wednesday, so their journals become increasingly vague as the week goes on. I guess that $5 they get for filling out their diary doesn't exactly motivate them for very long. These ratings are especially unreliable for the 11pm show. Hey, it's the launchpad for the weekend, dude. So in consideration of this, our editorial meetings are filled with talk about good "Friday story" ideas. No, not "Good Friday" story ideas. You know, lighter subjects. Such as how the local Ice Cube Factory is going to give five needy kids a trip to Antarctica or how the latest fad in high schools is athletes who sew the letters on their letter jackets backwards. No mention of Luther Post or the latest ballot proposal coming out of the statehouse.

I end up assigned to cover a Sugar Glider convention. The little devils are popular among kids, and the owners are trying to also raise money for the Reproach County animal shelter. Not that, in trendy Filterboro, anyone would leave their precious Sugar Gliders in the care of the state.

This, however, is only a tiny concern, compared to what happens next. Rapier skulks in to the afternoon meeting arm in arm with, uh, who is that: Aimee Flotsam? Are they a...couple? Nah, can't be. Rapier's tiny eyes are shining as he attempts to assert his sloping posture to dominate the conference table. Flotsam is beaming: Ain't I cute?

Rapier is so caught up in his moment of power that he doesn't speak. Until Fern bores in. "Is there something you want to tell us, Arlen?" she asks, challenging Rapier but holding her eyes steadily on Flotsam. The younger woman silently lifts her head so as to look down on us.

Rapier collects his few wits, realizes he's supposed to reply quickly to his main anchor; he's in charge here. But he's so used to being bullied that he gets flustered when he is not prepared to answer a question, only make a statement.

"Uh, yes." He readies a statement. His thin voice, which emanates from inside the bridge of his nose, gives everyone the creeps. And a feeling of imminent doom. Rapier clears his nose, then his throat, and recites: "In order to provide a seamless transition in the leadership of our afternoon newscasts, to replace Tracy Scott I have selected Miss Aimee Flotsam to produce the five and six o'clock shows. I am certain you will all help her succeed in this new endeavor." Pause. "And, Wilson Gamble will return to dayside reporting duties."

A chorus of "What?" around the table drowns out my "Who, me?" -- thank goodness. Calzone emits a single, loud guffaw. All reaction is temporarily silenced and superseded by Walter Wilson.

"Great choice Arlen! I think this is just great!" He's actually slow clapping. "Aimee is a great choice, she's a young version of Tracy Scott who, uh, can never be replaced but we will have to replace her anyways because she's leaving so why not promote from within and who better to learn from me and you Arlen and of course Tracy before she leaves... ."

Wilson is cut off by Fern. "No offense, Aimee," she starts, offering a dismissive glance at Flotsam, still drunk on haughty. "But Arlen, you are taking a girl (Flotsam winces) who has not produced a single show here and are promoting her to produce our flagship newscast. Do I understand that correctly?"

Rapier blinks. Stoic, he blinks again as we all turn to him. Except Collingwood, who stares off into an edit bay while absently patting his pocket for a cigarette. The nominal boss can't think of a reply.

"And what about the morning show now that Meredith is gone? Who's going to produce that newscast? What kind of decision-making went into all this, anyway?" Calzone demands. She's not guffawing any more.

Staggered, Rapier answers, sort of. "We will find it easier to hire a morning producer than for our Big Show. Aimee will be our new 5-6 producer. She has my full support and, um..." he searches. "...my endorsement." His eyes harden into two dark points of fear. "I expect everyone to accept her as my deputy in this newsroom."

With that, he simply turn on his heel and flees for his office. There is a general explosion of disgust and the meeting breaks up. Very few people even refer to Flotsam, left standing small and alone by the corner of the table.

The final ripple effect noises come from Wilson. "Arlen? Arlen? Arlen? Arlen? Arlen? Didn't you mean to say that Aimee was my deputy, not yours, because I'm the Executive Producer for Newschannel 99 and have been for years and she's a producer and that should mean she would report to me? Arlen? Arlen? Arlen?" His voice trails off into Rapier's office.

This is Wilson's side of the news process: producing the shows. Not content. But for the first time I notice Collingwood's dress shirt appears the slightest bit wrinkled. He hasn't said a word, and doesn't seem surprised at what has transpired. His mind is clearly elsewhere.

Still docked at the conference table, Flotsam immediately flourishes her newfound authority with the sting of a queen bee. Turning to Juan Cortez--the new reporter--she makes an announcement. To those who will listen.

"If we can all be adults here..." oh, the irony. "I have two orders of business. Juan, your name sounds too ethnic for our audience. Arlen and I have decided your air name is now John Curtis. Sorry, but it's a part of the biz." He appears too stunned to respond. I glance at Scott, who can't make eye contact with anyone; this is her fault, she's leaving, and now: there goes the neighborhood.

"And, Wilson Gamble returns to dayside. We will get by with Cortezurtis as our primary nightside reporter." So, after one week I'm back to my former schedule.

Upon this, and her declaration formally Anglicizing Juan Cortez, the grizzled veteran of perhaps four months returns to her place on a tall stool behind Calzone at the Assignment Desk. For the time being, she still has the night shift to cover.

Much later, my B-block story on sugar gliders gets bumped up to the A-block because Curtis, er, Cortez has missed slot. "Slot," "deadline," whatever. His story is not ready to be aired on time. The reason is not immediately made clear.

But as usual, I get the whole story later, this time Direct From The Source. Cortez explained how he had to work with Norman Wallflower, who had no choice but to fill in for a sick nightside photog. So, Wallflower ends up working at half-speed, like a man stuck on "slo-mo instant reply." Cortez claims that Wallflower dragged his feet. Forgot to bring a microphone. Drove the long way back. Stopped for food. None of this is shocking. There are a million more important things for a photog the stature of Norman Wallflower to do than the story he's supposed to help produce. Like spend an hour on "Hot-or-not.com."

Cortez also has a late interview, and is still kind of slow writing his stories. In his defense, he's probably still coming to grips with his identity crisis. Once its slowly copy-edited by Adams--always a bad choice for the job--there is only 10 minutes left for Wallflower to edit the package. They squabble briefly over it, and I hear Wallflower announce he'll probably miss slot. Unfortunately, Cortez--er, Curtis--fails to notify Hurd. The 11pm producer sends Flotsam (for perhaps the last time) to check on their package about three minutes before airtime.

Flotsam approaches the edit bay with all the contrived haughtiness of Marie Antoinette. She's the new 6pm producer, you know.

"Where is your package?" she demands of Wallflower with a toss of her blondeness. She might have said, "Off with your head."

"Right where you can feel it but can't see it," answers Wallflower, not looking at her. He wipes sweat from his forehead. Wanting to get rid of this human distraction, he does the only thing that comes to his mind. He farts. A real, gaseous one, born of pent-up fast food burritos and frustration.

Flotsam propels herself from the edit bay, perhaps never to return.

Eventually, Cortez makes his revised deadline and there's little harm. He won't suffer much from missing slot, this time. But he's suffering, nonetheless. For some reason, Cortez chooses to approach me about it.

The newsroom can be a lonely place during the late newscast. Few others are there, on a Friday at 11:15 pm. Flotsam is gone, having checked out early, with great importance. Wallflower is off in The Cage, fiddling with something. Seems like he never leaves. Someone else is in a back edit bay, editing another audition reel. An overnight producer scans the jail arrest logs sent to the newsroom's email address.

At my cubicle, I go to work re-writing my story for our website. Appearing distracted, Cortez sidles up to my desk. The fluorescents slowly burn. So does he.

"Wil." He starts, unsure of the doubts rising in his mind, or of me. Finally, Cortez takes the plunge. "This talk of changing my name; what do you think of it? Will I have to keep this Anglo name my entire career? What does it say about the station?"

"It's nothing new," I assure him. And it isn't. I'm not a student of broadcast news history, but plenty of names have been changed, for plenty of reasons. I once worked with a guy who was forced to discard his given name, "John" in favor of his middle name, "Mike," because the boss also went by "John." Their last names were crazy different, but that didn't matter. To the viewers in that town, he will always be "Mike."

In an age of political correctness, however, it's becoming a different thing to replace an ethnic name with a homogenous one. Reporters are encouraged to "be who they are." I don't like the recklessness of the decision. So I wonder who signed off on such a change for Cortez.

"What will I tell my father?" he asks one of the chairs in the next cubicle.

"What did you tell him about using makeup on your face so you'd look good on camera?" I try.

"Makeup? I didn't mention it," he answers. "Listen. You've been around some." I wince. "Tell me...is this the way things are at every TV station? I'll have a hard time working in an industry that regularly makes such decisions--decided by such shallow people. I signed up to do journalism," he concludes, sounding naive. Yet a little heroic.

Um, yeah. "Well, I don't think you are stuck being 'John Curtis' forever. When you move on to your next station you can explain to the news director that you want to change it back. Or change it to Pole R. Opscit."

Cortez doesn't smile. But his features relax.

"Let's go for some dinner," I offer.

"Okay. But I definitely feel like having ethnic food tonight." Cortez finally smiles.

"Well, it's not Cuban or Mexican, but I hear Marcini's is pretty good, over on Pushrod Road. You can pay."

"Yeah, I'll write a check in the name of 'John Curtis' and see if it bounces," Cortez responds.

Marcini's turns out to be a place with an identity crisis of its own. Is it an Italian restaurant that happens to have a very large bar in the middle? Or a tavern that is thickly flanked by full-service restaurant booths? Guess it depends on the time of day.

Cortez goes ahead while Marshall Hurd tags along with me. Evidently the latest issue of "Mad" magazine hasn't hit the grocery aisles yet, so he has time to kill. But he slows us down, first stopping at his apartment to find his missing wallet, then to the bank for some cash.

At Marcini's, Cortez has already become more wobbly than I might have expected. For the time being, he seems more willing to be known as John Curtis.

"Mi amigo--hey...dude!" Cortez starts, breaking away from a couple of people at the bar as we wander in.

"What are you drinking?" I ask as we head over to one of the immense wooden booths. We are positioned close enough to the bar to still feel a part of the electric tug of the night scene. Young people clubbin', music thumpin', dancers bumpin'.

"Jagerbombs!" Cortez replies. "I started doing theesh a la universidad, uh, in collage, college. Whatever, man." A waitress brings up his new drink, which actually looks like two drinks. Hurd and I order beer.

"Check it out!" Cortez neatly drops a shot glass of Jagermeister straight down into a tall glass of Burgundy Bull energy drink. It fizzes as he slams it down the hatch.

"Woo-hooo!" he celebrates, fists thrust skyward. People nearby applaud, and Cortez bows.

The commotion draws the attention of Channel 7's Sam. He has a tan, wavy hair, striped dress shirt, and a challenging smile.

"Hey there, 99'ers," he says, friendlily, sliding into the booth next to me.

"Hey Sam I Am," returns Hurd. We shake hands and I introduce him to Juan.

"Only, it's not 'Juan' anymore. My name got changed today," says Cortez. He explains.

Sam laughs. "Don't sweat it, my man. It's like you've got a secret code name for real life. Chicks secretly dig it if you let on that you have a alter ego." Cortez shakes his head--hmm, this change might have benefits--and polishes off his beer. Sam goes back to his table.

"How many of those have you had?" Hurd asks, pointing at the empty Jagerbomb glass.

"One, three, quatro. Or four or three. I think. That makes seven, right?" he answers, thinking, while looking over my shoulder for a waitress. She comes back and without asking me, Cortez orders Jagerbombs for each of us.

"Hey, man, this'll ruin the taste of my Lite beer!" Hurd complains.

"I'm not here to get drunk," is the nature of my weak protest.

"This'll just keep you going. You can just keep going and keep going because of the Burgundy Bull!" exclaims Cortez.

"We may need to get you a little air pretty soon," I observe, airily. But, who am I to interfere?

Despite our complaints, we down the novelty drink. The levity ends and we settle in for a little shop talk.

Cortez leans in towards me across the table, and looks me straight in the eye. "You've been around a little bit, I know. So, is this how things are?"

"How things are? You mean in TV news?"

"Yeah!" Cortez suddenly sits upright, and looks off. "Am I going to be 'John Curtis' the rest of my life?" he wonders.

"There are worse things to be," Hurd observes, even though the question was directed at me.

"But it's like turning my back on...uh...who I am," Cortez flashes angrily. "I'm not Anglo, I'm Latino, man. It's like I'd be play-acting my role as a reporter." Hmm, maybe he's more lucid than I gave him credit for.

"What country is your family from?" tries Hurd, awkwardly.

Cortez looks at him over his glass for a moment. "Fort Lauderdale, man."

"Maybe look at it this way," I try, sipping my beer. "As a reporter, you aren't representing any one group of people. You don't want to be pigeonholed as 'The Hispanic Reporter.' A generic name actually may open doors to story assignments of all kinds instead of being sent out only on what management wrongly thinks are 'Hispanic' stories, like ones on immigration or migrant farm workers."

This plays on Cortez's mind nearly as much as the alcohol. "An open door of any kind is better than closing it on my people," Cortez concludes sullenly. "Camarera!" Momentary pause. "Er, waitress!" he calls once more, darkly, without the verve he had displayed before.

16

On A Monday I Was Arrested

On A Tuesday They Locked Me In The Jail

A common destination for reporters: jail. By way of our profession, that is. Trying to catch up with crooks, thieves, and murderers on their way inside. We love those perp walks.

Unless you are a reporter for Newschannel 99 and are counting on taking a station SUV out to the jail. I pull in to the parking lot to find that several hours earlier the revelation is, uh, revealed, that the SUVs are now all gone. An email sent late Sunday night explains that gas prices are rising too high to afford to maintain them. And no, we are not going to have to ride scooters (A "silly rumor" nevertheless with enough credence in this place to force management to address it). Our new mode of transportation will be...rental cars. From the Schurtz Rent-a-Car company. In disbelief, I take a moment to glance out at the place formerly known as the SUV Stable. Yup. I can almost hear crickets chirping: its empty.

Equipped with a story idea and a Fakir Johnson, I head out front to find our new ride. There, sitting in the spaces where I witnessed the car wreck last week, await a couple of tiny gas-saving Hyundaewoos, complete with magnetic "Newschannel 99" logo signs haphazardly adhered to the doors. One has slipped to a funny angle, thanks to Nasty Old Mr. Gravity. This is your new ride, Mr. Gamble. Credibility? It'll work with the environmentalists, but practically, it sure won't work trying to get up a hill through bad weather. I'm not even sure the vehicle is big enough to fit say, Luther Post, should he want to surrender to Newschannel 99 one day.

"Where am I going to put my stuff?" wonders Johnson, thinking not only of his camera and tripod, but his personal emergency scanner, spare lights, battery operated fan, portable water distiller, 2000 watt power generator, etc.

Eventually, we manage to head out and cover my story. On the way back, Johnson offers up some breaking news of his own. "I'm leaving Newschannel 99."

Happens all the time. Not a big deal. But Johnson is a good shooter, and I hate for us to lose him.

"Where are you going? What are you going to do?" I ask.

Johnson mumbles a few inaudible words to himself, before replying out loud, "I'm hoping to catch on with Linear Video--that's a video production house downtown."

"Hoping? I'd think you would want to have that in hand before quitting."

"Well, the truth is, Arlen wants the photogs to clean up the trash cans around the newsroom during our down time. He thinks we spend too much time on "Facespace." Johnson frowns, because this really may be true.

"He wants you to do what?" I try, incredulously. "We have janitors!"

"Not any more. I hear Arlen convinced Miss Eriss fired the janitorial service to save money. And they think we photogs don't do enough to earn our keep."

"Wallflower won't stand for that."

Johnson rolls his eyes. "Oh, yes he will. They won him over: He's exempt. He won't have to actually empty any trash cans. He just has to supervise the rest of us. And ol' Warden will continue to clean the windows, just like always. He'd do that for free if he had to. Anyway, I can't deal with it, so I turned in my resignation in a sealed envelope just before we left on this assignment."

"I'm sorry that happened to you. Losing you sucks for us, too."

"Yeah," Johnson pauses, fiddling with the GPS he temporarily mounted on the dashboard. "And it's gonna suck even more. Word is that Channel 11 is now only hiring 'one man bands.' And once it takes off there, they will definitely start doing that here, too."

"One man bands." In other words, make one man play two instruments: shoot video and report. Saves money, naturally, but most of the time, there's no harmony. Either the video or worse, the journalism, gets messed up.

So--if someone new is hired--Fakir Johnson, with all his gizmos and techno toys, will be replaced by someone actually willing to shoot video as well as report, and then take out the papers and the trash. Because this person will understand that's the only way he will earn his spending cash.

Next day at the editorial meeting, we filter in to the table with our coffee, story ideas, and personal resentments. At first, I don't notice the absence of Collingwood. Walter Wilson is trying to talk with Fantana over the speakerphone to resolve a technical problem that cropped up just before last night's 6. Evidently, one of the engineers visited the Soyfield Bureau while Fantana was away over the weekend and changed the parameters on the edit bay computer. Supposed to be a "computer update" that improved the process of transferring video from his camera memory card to the edit bay computer. Only, he didn't bother to tell Fantana, who found out the hard way that he suddenly did not know how to upload the video for his package video--about 45 minutes before air. His story died in the edit bay.

"Rkwrvbfleeble" squawks the speakerphone.

"Yes, yes, yes, Brian, we all know and the engineers have assured us that they went out there last night to the Bureau and had dinner at that great little barbeque joint and really enjoyed the ribs but should have ordered a full rack instead of the half rack, but then they actually went in to the Bureau and corrected the problem."

"Wesbgglnff s rltkm eslgn scrtjlgn!" Fantana answers. He is unintelligible but doesn't sound happy.

"You don't have to say that, Brian," Wilson replies, defensively. Apparently he is fluent in Speakerphone Garble. "The engineers say you will be able to upload and edit your video from now on so that's all, I'm sure you will be able to edit tonight so go on out there and get some news covered!" Yay, team.

Allen Rapier hands out a three-page packet to everyone. A headline in bold print reads: "Rock 'n' Roll News." Uh oh.

"The way we write isn't active enough, people," he announces. "We can be more impactful by writing tightly and in the present tense, and inserting certain catchphrases throughout and within our scripts."

Follicle, already an engaging and even sometimes lyrical writer, critically flips through the handout. "Uh, 'impactful? 'You really want me to have the anchors say things like, 'Now! The absolute latest that Newschannel 99 is learning on this morning's crash that leaves two children dead tonight?' Aren't we confusing when the crash took place?"

"You'll get the hang of it, Sherman," Rapier scowls momentarily. "I will personally copy-edit reporters' package scripts, to make sure we are all on the same page." If Rapier had a sense of humor, he might have allowed himself a small smile at the unintended pun. Nope. "And I have already begun a writing seminar with the producers, so they can write the other stuff in a good manner." Aimee Flotsam smiles, self-importantly, obliviously. Tyler and others, who aren't exactly English majors, fail to back up Follicle. Opposition is faltering fast, so I say something. Just to be an obstacle.

"With all due respect, this just isn't English." I hold up the handout and point to a paragraph. "And it's certainly not conversational." I quote: "'Your identity at risk! Thousands stolen tonight and police searching. A hacker in a hospital computer threatening patient security!'" Wow. I observe, "This is just like Joe Piscopo's Saturday Night Live caricature of a sports anchor: 'Live! The Big Story: NBA! MJ...baseline! Triple Double! Bulls now!"

Not everyone gets my reference. Nettles giggles, Rapier does not. Naturally, he must play the role of Above Being Amused.

"If some of you can't adapt to a more modern style of writing, we will find people who can. I want a high story count, so we will churn out a lot of stuff. Aimee Flotsam and Walter Wilson are on board and will help me monitor all scripts to make sure the writing is profligate."

"'Prolific," Nettles sighs.

"But this isn't writing!" Follicle cries. "You can't force us all to write in such an unnatural way!"

"Yes I can. I'm the News Director," Rapier sniffs, neatly revealing a tiny snarl. And having played the only trump card life has likely ever dealt him, Rapier walks away. Flotsam and Wilson follow, the new Three Amigos of Newschannel 99 saunter off into the sunset, forming plans to turn the place upside down.

I have my "Rock 'n' Roll News" story assignment. But it's one that would leave anyone singing the Blues. A long-haul truck driver comes home to tragically find his young wife dead of a heart attack these last two days, with a small child screaming in a crib. It's an awful but compelling human tragedy. For most reporters, this kind of story heats up their day. But when we return to the station, I feel a chill north wind is blowing.

"Where's Collingwood?" I quietly quiz Calzone as I pass by the Assignment Desk.

"He was here, first thing," she replies, uneasily. "But it sounded like he had it out with Arlen and Walter in Arlen's office about 8:30. After seeing what Arlen came up with at the morning meeting, I can guess what that was about." She turns to answer two phone lines at once, and I'm left to figure out whether I should concentrate on today's story, locate Collingwood to find out what in the world is happening, or simply start putting together my latest audition reel.

Sensing this, Calzone pushes the mouthpiece of both phones down on to her shoulders to manually mute them, and states levelly, "You better go cover your story."

I'm assigned to work with Don Wash. Once I've made a couple of phone calls to set up my interviews and prepare for the day, I check in The Cage for Wash. The only person there, naturally, is Wallflower.

"I'm looking for Don," I announce. "Is he around?"

Brushing a fringe of stringy hair out of his eyes, Wallflower doesn't bother looking up from his "American Cinematographer" magazine article.

"He's around. Might be out at the dumpster, emptying out a couple of garbage cans for his sector of the building."

His sector of the building? This development that sent Johnson packing still astonishes me. "How could you let this garbage thing happen to them, Norman?" I ask too quickly, at the same moment realizing I've asked an innocent question of a guilty man.

"'Let them? 'I didn't have a choice," he replies piously, actually addressing me instead of the magazine. He has made A Separate Peace. "I simply offered to help facilitate what was bound to happen anyways."

"What's bound to happen is that they are all going to be like Fakir, and take off! Where does that leave us then?" I demand, still unable to help myself. I should know better than to attempt to come to terms with something ridiculous, because there is likely a less ridiculous--and more sinister--explanation at the heart of things. Wallflower pauses just long enough, the tiniest glint sparkling in his beady eye. He stops himself from answering and the glint is snuffed out. But I take it as a clue that these are much deeper waters than I had thought.

Eventually, I find Wash, angry and embarrassed. "I'm not gonna put up with this for very long," he proclaims to me as we load the back of the SUV with the camera, lights, and audio equipment. "I'd be outta here by now but I have to think of my family."

I'm thinking of Wallflower. "They are trying to make you quit. And turn everyone who remains into One Man Bands."

"MMJ's, dude," he responds. "That's the new euphemism. 'Multi-media journalists' is management's take on making one person do the job of two."

"At least for now," I try to reason, "let's do the job of two people who are qualified to do their two distinct jobs."

Wash is silent as we get into the front seats of the SUV. He turns the ignition key in the rental car and we pull out of the lot. Letting Wash contemplate his future, I notice fully for the first time just how weedy the access road really is as we exit the Newschannel 99 property and head through the business complex toward the main road. The assemblage of wild artichoke, gripe weed, and buckhorn is gathering faster than an aging biker gang at a "Lynyrd Skynyrd Karaoke Night" at the local bar. The wild growth is fast becoming the border between civilization and our own little Gilligan's Island.

"Maybe I could hang in there," Wash eventually muses, more to himself than me. So I let him. "Why couldn't I be a one man band? Shooting is half the job."

"So is hauling out the trash, for now, anyways," I remind him. "You'll have to put up with that unless you make your own deal, like Wallflower." This silences Wash, it turns out, for most of the rest of the day.

The "rest of the day" concludes with me finishing up the internet version of my report. This time, I post both the video of my story as well as a written narrative to introduce it. In the process of doing this, my "humanity switch" inadvertently flips "on" in the relative quiet of the newsroom during the tail end of the newscast. Among the few objects still showing life in the newsroom is Calzone. I notice that her telephone conversation is not, well, at its usual volume, which is "11"-- on a scale of 1 to 5. For that reason, paradoxically, from across the room I can actually comprehend her end of the conversation. Not because I am trying, but because it fascinates me to hear her chat in a lower tone of voice. She's not whispering, but she's not projecting her voice so it can be heard in the 253rd row of Orchestra Hall. So enthralled with the form of her conversation, I don't even try to catch the meaning of it. But in a few moments I get the drift, quite without trying.

"Yes, Artie. No, Artie. I mean, yes. Jerk. Yes, you. Yes, you are a jerk. Why else would you take tips off of tables in restaurants? No. No. Yes, of course I know. This place has just about gone off a cliff. But we have gone through this before, Artie." Her voice, and apparently, her resolve, seem to falter. Some. "I don't want California. Yes I said I liked San Francisco. But only because it's a nice TV market, not because I liked Market Street." Pause. "Yes, I said I'd go. Yes, perhaps 'now' would be a good time...I guess." Her voice drifts...in my direction. Although my rabbit ears have been pointed towards the Assignment Desk, I haven't tuned in the picture. My eyes are focused on the computer. Her eyes are focused on me, heavily. I feel them gazing at me. And if I look up to lock peepers, my instincts tell me we will make a connection. Gretchen Calzone will not leave Newschannel 99. Artie fails in the end, becoming an, um, Artie-choke. She and I...well, she and I... .

I do not raise my eyes, it is not my business, I cannot interfere. It's a Man Code thing. I have no right to interfere. Momentarily, Calzone's heavy gaze releases me, returning to the mother ship. Her voice lower now, I think I hear the sounds of travel plans being made.

Since Collingwood has disappeared, I am still stuck with no mobile phone. Gotta have something to communicate with. So, I hit up a convenience store on the way back to my cell. Er, room. They have both beer and a prepaid "trakphone." On my salary, I don't need the extra expense, but I have no choice, since Miss Mercy is not quite as charitable as Ma Bell with the use of her landline. So, my choice of beer gets downgraded to something sporting a red sash painted across the white label. My first call, once back in Big Blue, goes to Collingwood.

His electronic voice answers; his voicemail records. I leave a message, cautiously imprecise in its content. "Hey Carl. Just wanted to catch up. Talk about what to do next with that story we are working on." I leave him my new phone number and hang up. I don't plan to drive out to his home, not at this point, anyways. Instead, I point my pickup towards Miss Mercy's Institution. I'll pop open a cold one for dinner and call Megan.

All the usual parking spots seem to be taken on Chainlink Street. I idly wonder if someone is having a party or if they are conspiring to keep me from parking in their neighborhood entirely. Anyhow, I have to park around yet another corner, over on Deciduous Street. That forces me to approach Mercy's house from the front and walk along the side to get to the "Boarder's Entrance." Squeezing between the house and a barrage of overflowing hedges that mark the property line, I turn the corner and nearly run into a man taking apart what looks like the cable box. He fills out his work uniform quite amply. I apologize for bumping into his girth and offer an innocent question, to be pleasant, since we find ourselves caught such in close quarters. "Oh, hey. Is it tough to keep cable in working order in an older house like this?"

The guy seems friendly enough, but keeps working, bumping his gut up against the wiring more than once. He surprises me with a high, wheezy voice. "Nah. All the wiring was replaced a few years ago. You a boarder here?" I nod yes. But the beer I carry is getting warm, fella. Gotta go.

"So each of you get a high speed connection in your rooms, hah? Is that covered by your rent along with cable TV?"

"Connection? No, not at all. Do you mean internet connection?"

"Yeah. There's seven...no, eight high speed lines working here. Hah. I figured each room in a boarding house must get a separate line. I woulda thought maybe a single WiFi connection would make more sense."

"Actually...I was told there was no internet hookup here."

The repairman stops for a moment to consider. "Then what do you suppose they have all these lines for, hah?" he wheezes. "And why not the WiFi?"

I breathe. He's got me wondering, not caring quite so much now about the rising temperature of my brew. Then I think of the phone I just purchased, and how my old phone didn't work inside the house. Juggling my six pack with one hand, I pull out the new trakphone and flip it open. No bars, no service. I wonder if this technician might have a guess about why that is. "By the way, do you have any cell service here?"

He looks at me for a moment. "Funny you should ask. I just tried to call the dispatch center, and couldn't get any bars on my phone."

"Did you know you can get perfect service about 15 feet off this property?"

The repairman absently scratches his best friend--his belly--and tells me, "Well, I'm no expert on cell service" (blast it all) "but there could be some building material in this old house, maybe if the roof is really old, that could block cell signals."

"What kind of building materials could do that?"

"I don't really know. Lead sheets, maybe. Hah. I'm just guessin'."

"Mm, okay. Thanks and good luck straightening out all that wiring," I offer as I move towards the door.

Inside, I pause in the kitchen. Mercy isn't there. Slab must be immobilized elsewhere as well. But as little as I wish to linger on the ground floor, where Mercy tends to lurk, the cable situation has aroused my curiosity. So, I simply stop, and listen for house sounds and movements for a few moments. Eventually, I do notice a low but steady stream of noise coming from the parlor. I can't see in from the paneled hallway, but it sounds like a television; no, at least two TV sets, playing indistinguishable, overlapping audio. But they sound of sporting events. Cheering crowds. Hard to say which kind. Baseball perhaps? Horse racing? I would not have guessed Mercy Haversack enjoyed sports so much.

Wishing to lower the odds that she emerges to find me here, I head upstairs. Where, naturally, another new Mercy Rule is taped to my door. This 4x6 card informs me, "Do not have personal mail sent to my home address. Please use a post office box instead." Dropped on the floor, half shoved under my door, is a bank statement and an ad for a magazine subscription, with my name on both.

Maybe I'll have that warmish beer now. Or three.

I hurt myself today

To see if I still feel

I focus on the pain

The only thing that's real

My drive in to work the next morning is a bit more tentative. Big Blue's accelerator lacks the bouncy excitement of the challenges of a new day at a new-ish job. The Newschannel 99 Honeymoon is, finally, officially over. My truck slowly slides past the buildings in the office complex. Along with the growing weeds I notice another sentinel guarding the driveway back to the TV station: a yellow, diamond-shaped sign that reads "Dead End." You know, I think the sign has been here a while. I just hadn't noticed it until now.

Despite taking it slow, I can't seem to help rushing headlong into more work-drama. Yes, Collingwood is missing again at the morning meeting. No one is sure what that means, since his nameplate is still affixed to the door of his office. But that door is closed and the lights inside are off. I almost feel a chill breeze originating in that direction. But the meeting soon heats up when Rapier appears. He's half pushing forward a Platinum blonde young woman who is strikingly pretty--in a cold, formal way. She's tall, thin, coated in Calvin Klein and Cover Girl.

"Can I have your attention please," he starts. No one around the table stops their conversation to give him attention. The man is rapidly losing our respect, so no one perks up to hear their master's voice. Even if it really does sound like it comes from a Victrola. So, he claps, twice, sharply. As if ordering a bowl of rice: chop chop.

"Can I have your attention, please," Rapier tries again. This time, the odd hand clap and sight of the latest blonde TV prodigy gains some of the attention he craves. The men at the table all sit up a little straighter.

"Everyone, I have two personnel announcements." My stomach churns, thinking of Collingwood. "Jack Phillips is no longer employed by Newschannel 99. We wish him well in his future endeavors." Murmur, murmur, around the table. I notice Scott simply stares unflinchingly at her daily Outlook packet. Rapier brightens as he turns to the newcomer. "Second, I want you to meet our newest reporter hire, Britnee Flaxen. She comes to us from Montana State University, which as you know has one of the most well-spoken-of broadcast communication programs in the country. And, she was 'Miss Bozeman! '"

With this flourish, almost everyone is slightly shocked at Rapier's summary of her qualifications. My mind, however, is working on something else. I've seen, or met, this young woman somewhere. TV news can be a small world. While Britnee is introduced all around, to smiles from the guys to scowls from the gals, I'm searching the databases of my mind. My turn comes around, and I shake her cold, tiny, and perfectly-manicured hand. I look into her flawless face, ringed with immaculate blonde curls, I note that she already seems self-satisfied in an impossible way for someone so new to this biz. She's not going to be a good soldier here. That's when I make the connection: soldier. "Little Napoleon"--from my last gig. And Miss Bozeman. The same girl my former boss wanted me to see--who all this time apparently hasn't been hired there, or anywhere else. How on earth could that be?

During my deliberations Rapier attempts to communicate with Fantana over the speakerphone. Two nights ago, we all remember how an engineer fooled around with the equipment so that it was impossible to upload the video for his news story to the computer editing program. His report was lost. Then, last night, Fantana discovered--the hard way, of course--that the same engineer also changed the software shortcut commands on the video editing system. Again, without informing Fantana. Slowed down to the Speed of Nightmare, he could not edit his report in time for the newscast. Today, Fantana's speakerphone gibberish rises to a new level of ferocity.

"Hsdfljk ob sfdccs ugfp!! Wfdv tok fasdc?!?!"

Even someone as dense as Rapier recognizes he has to soothe and smooth.

"Brian, yes. Mr. Fontana, Yes," he purrs towards the speakerphone. "Yes. I have every assurance, believe me, straight from the engineers, that they touched nothing else in the Bureau. At least, nothing they didn't tell me about."

"Gherjryjrjkrkryu!!! Thaghuj tahjyl hsuu waohdd voiay ur dhuhngh??" How do Rapier and Wilson comprehend this?

"No, Brian, I promise. They didn't tell us about any of the stuff they were going to do." Rapier glances at Wilson to peremptorily shut him up. They knew. "Uh, Brian, the engineers say there are no more surprises. Really. Cover your story and report with confidence today." Report With Confidence? This sounds like an deodorant commercial.

Rapier simply walks away from further unpleasantries and leaves the morning meeting in the hands of The New Brain Trust of Walter Wilson and Aimee Flotsam. Although she is the Assignment Manager, Gretchen Calzone seems on the fringe of today's decisions. She is quiet, mostly. Distracted? Her hair, usually so complicated, seems to have gone straight. This leaves Wilson to his own devices, which run decidedly towards the latest press releases previously placed in the "future file" for this calendar date. He deals these "news items" written by commercial advertising executives to us like a blackjack dealers at The Sands.

"Tyler the people who are organizing the annual children's' cancer charity are putting the final touches on their wine tasting event tonight at the River Park so you can front a story live down there. I went last year but don't recall too much after about ten o'clock but I did wake up the next day on a park bench hugging an 'MD 20/20' bottle for some reason and Juan I mean John here is your story; it's all in this press release from Reproach Industrial Power and you can see they have won an award from the American Public Power Association for having the cleanest restrooms in their public buildings and I stopped in there once recently and wow! they had an attendant and everything in there but I felt a little self-conscious while I was standing at the urinal... ."

Follicle blurts out, "Another feature on Reproach Industrial Power! Sorry, Juan, that's R.I.P. for your story, ha ha!" Groans all around.

Wilson turns to Follicle, having been only temporarily interrupted. "And oh, Sherman, I think you'll like this one, it's the grand re-opening of that homeless shelter that burned down last year you remember in the middle of the night but then they built it up again... ."

Wilson is cut off at the pass by Follicle, who suddenly thinks these story assignments are not so very funny. "Walter, another softball feature on this place? We reported precisely the same story last week." Follicle looks around for support.

Calzone temporarily awakens. "Yeah. We did a vosot on it."

Wilson has apparently prepared for this moment. "That was the ribbon-cutting," he starts, with decision. "This is the Grand Re-opening and you know there's a big huge difference which a longtime reporter like you, Sherman, should appreciate."

"But Walter," Follicle tries patiently. "How am I supposed to do this story any differently than last week?"

Unflinching, Wilson replies, "Do a whole package on it, Sherman, not just a vosot because that way you can get more emotion in there than you can from just one soundbite which would make for a very good story and I think our viewers like very good stories and here's proof: someone stopped me at Hamburger Heaven today, not the one on Archibald Road but instead the new one over on Highway 747 and he told me he really likes very good stories." Before Follicle can cut in, Wilson dances away. "And Jeanette, you need to get over to the Trans-Area Blood Bank where I almost donated blood one time but nearly fainted so instead I went to a diner and had a bacon deluxe cheeseburger and now you need to catch the start of the blood drive challenge between Filterboro and our sister city from Colorado. What's that place called again?"

"Leadville," almost everyone sighs. I'm amazed "almost everyone" knows this. Apparently Leadville, Colorado has long been on the radar screen of people here in Filterboro, several hundred miles away. The fact that almost everyone wants to demonstrate their knowledge of this is enough to neatly undermine any resistance Nettles might have offered to covering this "news item." I find myself impressed that Walter Wilson just may have counted on that. I'm less impressed when he turns to me.

"And Wilson Gamble," he starts, significantly using my last name. To offset me from him, I suppose. "Mr. Hornswoggle in Sales who really knows how to grill salmon very delicately using a spinach marinade says the Toyonda Motor Company is announcing special rebates to get customers back in their doors after a bunch of recalls. Not that I ever drove a Toyonda, because I haven't and my cousin Vinnie says they are junk, but that's really only because they are expensive and foreign and so I never did; but the local dealer seems like a good guy and he says he's hurting because of all these TV news reports about recalls and nobody thinks his cars are worth buying any more and he might have to start laying off some people and in fact he did lay off one or two. So we could talk about the rebates and see what customers on his lot are looking for and show our viewers how a major national story is hurting people here locally." Wilson drops off this press release with me as he circles the meeting table, like the kid who is "it" in a game of "duck, duck, goose." But then, he gooses me. "Oh, and Wilson Gamble, I want you to take Britnee with you to show her how we do things here."

Ugh. I'm not much for training rookies. But I do have a few questions for her about coming to work here at Newschannel 99 and, frankly, she is extensively easy on the eyes. So I put myself into Full Operational Mode, waving Flaxen along with me to my cubicle.

"Grab a chair. You can sit over there," I tell her. "We will get with our photog in a couple of minutes. But I want to make a phone call or two before we go."

Unexpectedly, Miss Bozeman speaks. Coherently. But in a challenging manner. "Why do you need to call someone? Didn't The Desk set this report up for you?"

What is she, the Story Nazi? Time to patiently esplain to Loocy. "I'm gonna try to find someone to balance out the story. The Better Business Bureau, or someone from another consumer watchdog agency, or a consumer product specialist at the college. They can provide an objective analysis of this company's cars.

I don't expect a response, much less opposition. Nevertheless, she provides it. "But that wasn't your story assignment. I heard that sloppy-looking guy tell you to just go to the dealership and find people there."

Sheesh, just shut up, Miss Bozeman. My instincts are to simply ignore her. Maybe she will go away, or dissolve, or something. If I have to explain everything about Journalism 101, I may just call in sick--from my cubicle. Instead I go for the "I wasn't born yesterday but you apparently were" response. "Yeah, it'd be a shame if our advertiser was selling dangerous cars and then we had to tell our viewers about it."

That flies straight over Flaxen's concrete blonde head. I let her play mental catch-up while I find someone to interview outside Walter Wilson's assignment parameters. After three phone calls, a stroke of good fortune puts me in contact with someone local who has created a "Toyonda Means 'Lemon' in Japanese" Facespace website. They boast hundreds of registered members and thousands of hits in the past few weeks.

Soon we find Wallflower. Motivated by the prospect of spending the day with "Miss Bozeman," he actually hurries out to one of the Newschannel 99 rental cars and straightens the magnetized logo on the door. Soon, we drive out to chase down the story. I rub my hands together, hoping to rob Wilson of his press release report. In my exuberance, I turn my attention to Britnee Flaxen, primly balancing herself on the center seat in the back of the small car. Feeling vicious, I call shotgun while Wallflower drives.

"So, Britnee. What was your last gig?" I ask carelessly, feigning innocence.

Innocent, she actually tells me. "Well, I was working at a restaurant in Denver, when this customer wouldn't let me alone." I yawn. She notices, turns querulous, speaks faster. "Anyways, this guy sits at my table and keeps talking to me and eventually tells me he's a News Director of one of the biggest local TV stations in the country." My attention perks up. "Well," Flaxen smiles, "Its Arlie, er, Mr. Rapier." Arlie? You mean 'Arlen,' right? She moves on. "I came to Filtertown and he auditioned me last weekend up at the station and, well, here I am, finally doing what I always wanted to do!"

"And, what's that?" I inquire, again, smiling, viciously, quickly, before Wallflower can correct her "Filtertown" gaffe.

"To be on TV, of course! To do, you know, this stuff. News."

"I see," I say. "Where were you a journalist before you came here?"

"Well, at Montana State I anchored a local cable access news program, KGCM Channel 1. That's for 'Gallatin County, Montana!" she recites, proudly. I note that Wallflower has managed to lock his eyes up in a semi-permanent roll even while driving. "It was all students at MSU who wanted to do TV but couldn't at school."

"Why not?" I ask involuntarily.

"There's no broadcast news program there," she responds promptly.

"Did you send out a lot of audition reels?" I inquire, recalling Little Napoleon.

Flaxen thinks hard. For her, I mean. "Yeahhhh... . I had an interview in one place, I forget where, and the guy only seemed to want to take me out to show me around the city. We went out to eat, then a show, then out for drinks... ." The recollection abruptly fades, intentionally or not. "But I decided to move to Denver instead," she abruptly concludes.

Wallflower adds his own snide question. "What did 'Arlie' tell you about Newschannel 99 during your, uh, interview?"

The blonde brow furrows in deep thought. "Well, he said we are a ratings leader and research tells him we should be all about 'more weather' and 'viewer benefit' but I didn't ask him what any of that meant. Anyway, he said he could take a direct interest in helping me get to the next level, and I am so excited!"

It's time for me to bore in on this apparent wanna-be co-host of "Access Entertainment." "So, what do you hope to accomplish here in

Filtertown; what is your goal in news?"

"Oh, that's easy. Now that I'm out of waitressing, I want to host 'Access Entertainment.' But I'll settle for starting as a reporter there." She glances at me for a moment, calculating, I think. It flashes across my mind that in a nanosecond, she has sized me up and determined whether it would benefit her career to sleep with me. The thought lasts as long as Ron Tompkins' major league pitching career. But I notice it and that cements my early conviction of the character or this, er, character.

Throughout the day I use my trakphone to stay in touch with Calzone and later, Scott, to let them know the progress of my story. The manager of the Toyonda lot is media-savvy and tries to maneuver us to putting the dealership sign behind his shoulder in the interview. I laugh; it's an old trick. Wallflower is on to it, also. So, claiming that the sun would be better if we face another direction, we turn the manager around to put behind him the sign for a bail bonds business located across the street.

The guy from the Toyonda Lemon website begs off at the last minute, putting my report in jeopardy of becoming a glorified press release on behalf of the auto manufacturer. But I pull another card out of my sleeve. We head over to an American Motors dealership. Quickly briefing the manager there of our intentions, we are permitted to try to talk to customers who are presumably inclined to favor American cars over imports. Even if the imports are actually built here in the U.S.

The first dozen or so people I approach treat me like Lorena Bobbitt at a sex offenders convention. Figuring the video camera is scaring some people away before I can warm them up, I send Wallflower off to stand by the used car lot. I keep Flaxen and her visual charms nearby for when any young guys wander nearby. Heck, any middle-age or older guys as well, for that matter.

"Are you doing this right?" Flaxen asks. "Because you haven't got anybody to talk to you yet."

No, but I bet I could get a lot of people to talk if I killed Flaxen by running her over with a brand new car from American Motors.

Eventually, though, I find an outgoing older woman with big hair and bigger opinions. She watches Newschannel 99 and recognizes me, sort of. "You wouldn't remember me, sweetheart" she starts, grasping the shoulder strap of an enormous purse that appears to weigh 75 pounds. "But I met you once before." Wink wink.

"Really? I haven't been here that long." I fear that she was at Collingwood's party and wonder if we "hit it off" in some way. The thought is terrifying but I really need this interview.

Without wanting to make her feel entirely forgettable, I try: "Were you part of the tour group that visited the station a few weeks ago?"

The woman actually cackles. "My Lord no, honey. It was seven-eight years ago at the Hilton. You know, sweetie, the charity thing for the policeman's Fallen Heroes fund. You know," she coaxes.

"I'm sorry, wasn't me. I only moved here earlier this year."

Silently staring at me for a moment, the woman weighs her bag and her thoughts. "Junior, you aren't Jack, uh, what is it. Let's see, Jack Mobil? er... ."

I put her out of her oil company memory-association misery. "Jack Phillips. No, 'fraid not. I'm Wilson Gamble. Can I still ask you some questions about shopping for a new car?"

Another pause. The woman calculates for a moment. I believe she is deciding that, why not? she has already invested three minutes in pointless conversation. But, I'm wrong. "Naw. I gotta get home."

The woman and her hair and her purse all stalk off together. Flaxen doesn't laugh or smirk. She just opens one button on her blouse and turns toward a couple of nearby male customers. Hi there, boys.

After, oh, about five minutes we have three interviews recorded and are back in the rental car. I'm silent; some job skills just can't be taught. Anyways, I make myself feel better by recording a standup in front of a junkyard, just to tick off the sales department. Sounding tired, Calzone gives me the green light to do it and we head back to the station.

The color red once was thought to launch bulls toward matadors. But in less civilized pursuits, such as the business world, red actually restrains. Such as: red flags, red lights, red herrings. The flashing red light on the handset of my desk phone demands that I stop and find out who activated it. The voice on the voicemail recording is smoothly familiar: Carl Collingwood.

"Wil, this is Carl," he starts, briskly, business-like. "I'll be back in the office in a few days, but we need to talk about a story I've been following up on. Call me at home after work tonight."

Ah, relief. Some good news inside this newsroom for a change. My mental observation is interrupted by a conversation that starts to sound a little tense. Its Aimee Flotsam at Tracy Scott's desk.

"... a big part of producing, Aimee," Scott says. "You have to be able to write coherent teases so that viewers will want to stay with us, not change the channel during commercial breaks. So the teases have to make sense!" Her voice sounds a little agitated, which is unusual for her.

"My stuff makes sense!" Flotsam responds, defensively. As if she's been told she's not all that smart, oh, only about four hundred billion times. "Just because you don't get it doesn't mean no one else will get it! Its conversational! Its 'Rock 'n' Roll News! '"

"But listen," Scott tries, a little more patiently, "Although you are trying to be 'conversational,' some of the phrases and words you are using are just wrong. You have to write teases crystal-clear so the anchors can read them cold."

"What's wrong with the 'B tease,' then?" Flotsam demands.

"First of all, you wrote 'The council died in fact raise concerns about the fissure.' You have to be careful about writing 'did' instead of 'died' and 'fissure' instead of 'future'."

"Those are just typos."

"Yes, but then you wrote, 'Their complaints fell on death ears.'

"What's wrong with that? Its conversational!"

"But it's not correct. Any person who ever read a book would recognize it's not right." Scott's patience is impressive. But it's clearly breaking.

"Read a book! Who needs to read a book? I don't read anything and I am just fine!"

Incredulous, thy name is Tracy Scott. She's a little confused. "You haven't read anything recently?"

Flotsam doubles down. "I don't read at all!"

"That's just ridiculous," Scott replies. "How can you know anything about our world if you don't read anything?"

"Ridiculous! That's not a professional critique, that's personal! I don't have to put up with this kind of trash from you." With such menacing words, Flotsam stalks off towards Rapier's office.

Scott silently continues her work producing the newscast, but I notice from time to time she stops to quietly fill a cardboard box with the personal belongings from her cubicle. At one point, I notice her taking a brief phone call. As she grimly replaces the handset, I notice across the office that Rapier is hanging up his phone as well.

In the cool of the evening, sitting in my truck--parked on Chainlink Street (evidently no birthday parties in the neighborhood tonight) where I can get a cell signal, I make my own phone call, to Collingwood. This time, he answers. "Hello, Wil. It's been a long couple of days, but I haven't been this happy in quite a while. It's nice to have a break."

"I'm just happy to hear your voice. Care to tell me what happened at the office the other morning?"

"Well, let's just say I threw a little weight around and then decided to take a vacation. I don't think Arlen understands that he is not going to last long here. And it's not just because of 'Rock 'n' Roll News.'"

"What do you know that we don't know?" I try.

Pause. "Enough. But it'll come out soon enough, at least in certain quarters," he replies, consequently. Subject change. "I've been working on a juicy story, and I think that's why I've been so happy. Actually covering news, digging up the story. Feels good to get my hands dirty again." Collingwood's voice does indeed seem to have an excited edge to it.

"Sounds good, Carl. Can I ask what you are working on?"

"Nope." Why am I having this conversation with someone who won't tell me anything?" But it's a story I'm going to give you, and it's about Luther Post."

I stop breathing for a moment. If Collingwood is working on a Luther Post story, it's probably gonna be good.

"What do you want me to do?"

"Just quietly gather up all our 'file' footage of Post; the shooting, the manhunt, when you caught up with him, everything. And, without telling him anything, have Fakir stand by. He's the most reliable shooter we have, even if it's only for the next couple of weeks."

"I'll take care of it. Is Post still over in the Marberry area?"

"No--he's been moving around. I can't give you any more information on the phone, but we have to hurry on this."

"Why, Carl?"

"Because Sam at Channel 7 has caught a break and is following it also. But we have a head start," Collingwood asserts.

I'm not sure what he means but I promise Carl I'll be ready, and promise myself I'll even stay sort of sober, in case the call comes at an odd hour. But, I tell myself, that won't be tonight, or Collingwood would have said so. So I smuggle a bottle into my manbag and head into Haversack House.

Miss Mercy and Slab sit heavily at the table like a couple of Easter Island statues, again blocking the kitchen. I've got nothing for them except a short, "Hi" as I pass by. There is no reply at all.

But as I pass the parlor, I try to listen carefully. Haversack can't see me, so I stop for a moment. Yes, once more I can make out the vague noises of sports being broadcast on television. There's so much cross-talk and crowd noise, I decide once again that there is more than one TV playing. And it seems that I hear live voices, too. It's just that every sound is so muffled.

Just as I make up my mind to move on towards the staircase, the parlor door starts to open. I nearly make a run for it back down the hall to the kitchen but there isn't enough time. The door opens all the way. Instead of Slab or The Troll, however, a young man emerges from the parlor. He does not look like he belongs in the 1890's. Golf shirt, dress slacks and shoes, slick black hair. Looks like a Player, a Sport. He's busy counting bills in his hand. Huh? Lots of bills. Dollars. Clams. Greenbacks. Do-re-mi. He's so intent that he nearly mashes me against the hallway wall.

"Hey, sorry kid," he says smoothly. Even though I may actually be older than him. There will be no further conversation, however, as The Player moves obliviously through the hall and out the front door, still counting his money.

"That's alright," I say to myself, wondering what on God's green earth this person is doing in Mercy Haversack's parlor. Some things start adding up, vaguely, and I begin to think about which steps I may eventually take. After I ascend the steps in front of me and have my drink, that is.

There is a lot on my mind at the morning meeting, hangover headache aside. Phillips is out, Flaxen is in. Collingwood's ambiguous story about Luther Post. The latest technical glitch out of Soyfield. The Mystery of Haversack House. The question of why I hate tomatoes but love salsa. In any case, the morning meeting is slow to start. Rapier is habitually absent, Flotsam can't really assert herself on her merits, Calzone seems to have been self-neutralized for now, and both Wilson and Scott are missing. Nobody minds Wilson's disappearance, it's a welcome relief. Scott's and Collingwood's absences, though, raise alarm bells...immediately answered by Calzone.

"You guys are about to get an ENPS message." Calzone does a mock Alan Rapier voice, flimsy and nasal: "'Tracy Scott is no longer an employee of Newschannel 99. We wish her well in her future endeavors.'"

"What does that mean?" asks Flaxen.

We all look at Flotsam, who reverts to checking her manicure.

"At least she has a job to go to," says Nettles.

"Yeah, Harrisburg/Lancaster/Lebanon/York. I guess the training period is over, huh Aimee?" asserts Follicle.

Flotsam silently answers by allowing Follicle to inspect the nail polish on her middle finger. End of discussion. But I wonder if there is any feeling left behind by the interlude I happened across a few weeks ago between Scott and Jack Phillips...and if they may try to work out some long distance relationship. Ultimately, I decide: it's not likely in this industry. You don't know which market you will end up in next.

But there's more drama. Hubbell apparently suspects Flaxen's presence is more a threat to her position than as a replacement for Phillips. So, Hubbell contrives to sit far from her, and tries to start conversation with the rest of the group to isolate the newbie.

"So, did Jack end up at Champaign-Springfield?" she wonders.

"I thought it was a little bigger. Something like Flint-Saginaw-Bay City," tries Calzone.

"Prfrde cjrr ud mz Mobile-Pensacola-Fort Walton," Fantana tries. His voice sounds resigned after his report died for a third straight night. Even though Fantana has figured out A) the new way to transfer video from his camera to the editing computer, and B) the new computer shortcut commands for editing the video, he was not prepared to meet the latest unexpected challenges of C) the new method of sending his finished product from Soyfield to Filterboro. His video successfully uploaded and successfully edited, he discovered the engineers' final unannounced alteration. The longtime Vyvx video cable link was disconnected over the weekend and replaced with a computer-based FTP file transfer site.

"Wfhkeovr fhs hhfs ghsp blszsp, man." This last somehow comes out clear. But no one here has an answer, so no one tries.

Three days, three strikes. The engineers have just struck out the Soyfield side. Fantana's voice sounds defeated. It occurs to me that it must be tough to be so isolated out there in little Soyfield—alone-- except for a receptionist, sales associate...and the occasional nocturnal visit from an engineer. That's his problem, however. There are other things on my mind.

"How is it that Jack just disappeared?" I ask, wishing I could ask about Phillips' interest in Luther Post. "Didn't he give 30 days' notice?"

Follicle snickers. He knows but doesn't answer.

Nettles knows and does answer. "He tried," she explains. "We had dinner last night, and Jack told me what happened. He went into Arlen's office, pointed out his contract is up in 30 days, and turned in his notice."

Knowing a little about the breed known as "News Directors," I can almost sense what must have happened next. But I am wrong.

"First, Arlen started crying," Nettles relates.

No, that isn't what I expected.

"What?" asks Hubbell incredulously. "Crying? You mean, tears?"

More Nettles. "Jack said he nearly laughed at that, but then just stopped what he was saying and waited for Arlen to blow his nose. Then, he says Arlen got angry with him, accusing Jack of not being a 'team player'"-- Nettles raises fingers to emphasize the quotation marks--"and abandoning the station at a really bad time."

"It's true. Jack's not a team player," Follicle observes, emphatically.

"But it's never a, quote unquote, 'good time' to leave," adds Hubbell.

Nettles ignores both statements of the obvious. "Anyways, Jack just shrugged his shoulders and said this is the nature of the business and he's willing to work hard the next two weeks, but Arlen didn't like it."

"Two weeks?" asks Cortez, sitting off of a corner of the table. "I thought you said he gave his '30 days.'"

"Well, he still has two weeks' vacation coming to him and was planning to go to the Caribbean. And when he pointed that out, Arlen just went crazy. Told him he could take his vacation and stuff it up his Bahamas, to get out and good luck getting paid for days he doesn't work."

Ah. That's more like the breed known as "News Directors."

Follicle whistles. "Wow. Sounds awful. What's Jack gonna do?"

Spotting Wilson finally exiting his office and heading our way, Nettles lowers her voice. "He's going over to Channel 11 to quietly tell them about our strategies and research. All the inside stuff. He knows the EP over there."

How, and how well? I wonder.

As Wilson reaches the table, I offer out of the corner of my mouth, "If he cares, he could get in a lot of trouble doing that."

But Nettles has the last word. "Ah, but he'll be in Flint-Champaign or wherever by then!"

No one else may have ever confused Flint with Champaign, or even more so, Flint with Champagne. But no one seems more confused than Jeff Adams this afternoon. As I put the finishing touches on my masterpiece report about budget troubles in the school system, I note that Adams and Lavinia Fern are huddled with Rapier and our Chief Engineer. The two anchors are asking a lot of questions. Adams looks befuddled and Fern appears upset.

"What's the matter over there?" I quietly ask Follicle over the cubicle wall. He's busy typing up his story for our website.

"Oh, to save some money we are printing scripts for the anchors any more. The scripts will appear on electronic notepads that they will hold at the anchor desk."

"Instead of 'crash copy?'" I ask impulsively.

"That will be their crash copy," replies Follicle, in a tone of voice that betrays his personal struggle between corporate loyalty and practical reality.

"They don't look happy," I observe, as Adams theatrically walks away from the discussion, pretending to need to consult with the normally-useless Marshall Hurd about something.

Follicle softens for a moment. "Doesn't matter, you know. When the push of saving money--not using all that paper, comes to shove--the anchors' objections, the anchors will lose in this environment nine times out of ten. Or, 99 times out of 100. They will simply have to get used to it, just like when they were given a foot pedal to run their own teleprompter."

I wonder how long it will take an entrenched old school TV Reader like Adams or a Professional Celebrity like Fern to learn how to use all the new technology. How long will it take before one of the electronic notepad display screens is fouled with ballpoint pen ink?

17

One of the unpaid duties we are occasionally called upon to perform is to make "public appearances" on behalf of the station. It's another way for me to meet people in my official capacity, which can help me develop contacts. And it demonstrates our involvement in the community--which is augmented when the station diverts a videographer from covering actual news to shoot video of me...for the purpose of showing me to our viewing audience. The sponsors of the event we attend theoretically benefit from the excitement and attention that a mini-"celebrity" may bring. So, everybody wins.

Most of the requests at Newschannel 99, naturally, come in for the best-known faces. Fern and Adams receive a steady stream of invitations, but Chief Meteorologist Arnold Paul probably gets the most. People are always interested in the weather, and they are at once fascinated and horrified by the prognostic capabilities of the local "weather guy."

Our Promotions Department, nevertheless, wants me to "get out there." The first opportunity is to give a brief career talk to 3rd graders at Thermopylae Pass Elementary School. Its first thing in the morning. For me, that means 9 am. For public school kids, that means 7:30.

It's an energetic bunch in Mrs. Applebaum's class. While I am seated in a white rocking chair, the children--well coached--plop down in front of me in a wiggly semi-circle on a braided rug. I have done this kind of thing before, but really should have given today's chat more attention than I gave mixing the perfect Long Island Ice Tea last night. So when I hesitate during that single, opening moment of attention, this pack of hyenas senses...fear. 25 hands punch the air, but none of their proprietors bother to wait to be called on. Their mingled and confused shouted questions and statements are overwhelming at this early hour, and I meekly turn to Mrs. Applebaum. Three commanding thunderclaps from her calloused and practiced hands instantly restores order. She raises a pair of calloused and practiced eyebrows at me: better take advantage of this second chance, buddy. "Children," she advises, sternly. "I want you to pay attention to Mr. Gamble. He's a TV news reporter for Newschannel 99... ."

"...Action News!" cries out one young prodigy.

"No," I try, "We say... ."

"Eyewitness News!" shouts a second wunderkind.

"Actually, it's not... ."

"Where The Entertainment Comes To A Screeching Halt!" announces a third, in mock monotone. A third grader listens to WDMZ Radio?

This time I regain control by clearing the air on our over-the-air slogan. Then, I downshift into talking to the kids about what they and their families watch on TV, and how children like themselves grow up to make those programs. Then I talk about what I do in particular. A good 10 minutes goes by, and I'm feeling better. But wrapping up, I realize there is another five minutes to fill...a challenge that any self-respecting broadcaster should meet. So, gamely I open up the floor to questions. There is no shortage, and it goes from relevant to inapplicable in about 20 seconds.

"How much money do you make?"

"Who cut your hair that way?"

"Did you get your tie at All-mart?"

"Are your eyes always that red?"

"Do you live with your girlfriend?"

"Why don't you work at something important for a living?"

"Why does my dad always get so mad watching your news?"

Okay. About the challenge of filling the rest of my allotted time? Never mind. My self-respect is out the door--with me in hot pursuit.

Back at the station, my self-respect and I are about to take another hit. I'm picked to cover a fatal shooting downtown. The choice is made by default, because everyone else is tied up. Despite the violent nature of the incident, it's a run-of-the-mill story. As a "joke," a young guy was left behind by his "friends" at a nightclub. He decided to walk home, and made it about 25 paces when someone tried to mug him. Joke over. The dude is pumped up with liquid courage and tried to shout down the barrel of a gun. Its bite was worse than his bark, so now he's in the morgue.

Nowadays we take advantage of social networking sites like Facespace. First, I find the victim's personal page and lift two or three photographs of him. Then, I put out a call to my "friends" and the network of people in our region, looking for a witness, or at least a friend of the victim. None steps forward right away, but one party girl eventually does reply, claiming she was at the nightclub last night. Her interview and comments I get from the police round out a decent news report. I waste two hours on false leads in an attempt to reach the nightclub owner, but I still have my story.

Since it is a Friday, and the clubs will be busy again tonight, this is an obvious choice to "front" with a liveshot at the scene of the shooting. Yes, it happened 16 hours earlier and there is nothing related to the crime left to see. Not even yellow police crime tape. But the liveshot adds a fresh coat of immediacy and the imprint of importance. At the same time, however, we are going to have to play "Beat The Clock" to get downtown in time to get the liveshot on the air.

The package is edited. I fetch Fotch and load up a live truck (these have not been replaced by rental vehicles, yet) and prepare to go back downtown. I have brief but deep misgivings about Fotch's ability to get the liveshot set up in time, and verbalize them as I pass the Assignment Desk.

"Five bucks says this doesn't make slot," I tell Calzone. She knows I'm probably right. But it was her decision to assign Fotch to the lead story, so her professional rep is on the line.

"Alright, buddy. I'll take that bet," she tries, bravely. I'm out the double iron doors, but am followed with a "Don't slow him down, though!"

No worries. On a Friday night, with the promise of 2-for-1 shooters at Marcini's afterward, Fotch is as motivated as a guy could be. He skids the live truck into a "No Parking" zone, raises the antenna mast, unloads the camera and attendant cables. He's moving faster than Clark Kent changing in a phone booth.

Ten minutes to air. While Fotch scurries about, I consider the best way to make the liveshot visually interesting. Don't want to simply stand in front of the nightclub building, with few people ready to go clubbin' at dinner time. Decide the best thing to do is provide my own reconstruction of the shooting. Fotch will have to start with the camera pointed at me. When Fern introduces me, she and I will be in separate graphic "boxes" at the same time. Soon after I start Fotch will turn the camera away to show where the attacker probably lay in wait. At that time, I plan to back up a few steps behind the corner of the building, so that I will be hidden when Fotch swings his camera back around to me. Then I can step around the corner just as the victim did, back into the camera shot--and what would become a crime scene.

Nine minutes left. I congratulate myself on the plan. It is, however, a lot of live-action motion for the photog. And the photog is racing to turn on all the switches and connect all the cables to send a signal back to the station. And the photog is Fotch.

Eight minutes. I use my trakphone to call Flotsam, who as the new 6pm producer, is now in the control room. I feel a shiver of confidence-deficiency at both ends of this deal.

"He's got to make it. Will he make it?" she asks, almost panicking. I smile, suddenly feeling better at her anxiety.

"Can't say," I say.

"Well, if we don't see a picture of you during the Open I'm not going to kill the liveshot. I'm not going to float our lead story to some point later in the newscast, not knowing if Fotch will ever get it together."

Ending the phone conversation, I'm disappointed. Once you are standing by, ready to do a liveshot, the adrenaline begins to build.

Seven minutes. All that adrenaline is sucked out of me at the sight of Billy Fotch, stopping to take a cigarette break at the live truck.

"Do we have a signal yet?" I shout at him. Meaning: does the Control Room see our signal?

"Almost!" is his reassuring reply.

"Get the shot up first, then take a break!" I warn him. "Get moving!"

Fotch takes a drag on the cigarette and shakes his head. But, mumbling to himself, he begins to move.

Five. While Fotch begins to speed up the process, I do what I can to slow down. The nightclub is behind me, I am in place. As he plugs in the IFB I attempt to share my plan for the liveshot with Fotch. His spiky head nods up and down in acknowledgement but I start to wonder what will really happen when--if--we actually make our deadline.

Four. Tension rises as Fotch swears hopelessly at something inside the truck.

"Everything alright?" I try, easily, too breezily. I'm feeling stress bunch up the muscles in my shoulders.

"Flippin' ghost-riding charlie seashell!!" is what I think I hear coming muffled from the truck in response. Never mind.

Three. Fotch sprints out to the camera, which is mounted on a tripod and linked to the live truck with the cables he has been laboring over.

"Everything ok?" I try again.

"Uh, yeah, of course," Fotch mumbles, defensively. Looking through the viewfinder, he twists the lens on the camera. I feel just a little less than assured.

Two. This might be a good time to review with Fotch what I had hoped to do with the liveshot. Not only do I have this plan ready in my mind to implement physically, I have mentally prepared a script to match the movements. It will be very difficult to change course.

One. I'm beginning to clench up like a mafia informant with a price on his head the day of the big trial. I have no idea where this liveshot is, uh, headed.

And....it is ShowTime!

I hear nothing on the IFB. And see nothing on the monitor. And I say nothing into the microphone. A trifecta of wise monkeys all rolled into one.

Fotch instantly backs off of the camera and starts to check connections. I calculate. It takes about a minute for the taped opening to roll. Flotsam is deciding right now to kill the liveshot. I'm ready to start cursing. Instead, I dropkick my notepad at Fotch. But in this attitude of frustration, a voice in my head speaks to me.

It takes a moment but I realize the voice belongs to Lavinia Fern. And she is saying my name.

"Newschannel 99's Wilson Gamble is live where the shooting took place. Wilson, are people planning to stay away tonight because of the violence?"

The camera stares at me. I stare back. And then blink. Um, this evidently means Fotch has fixed the problem.

Fern's voice once more. Sounding self-possessed as usual, but a touch more tense. "Wilson? How are people reacting?"

Oh. Yes, it's my cue! Ah, yes. Okay! I literally clear my throat while vainly attempting to compose myself. The little fink Flotsam lied to me.

"Thanks Lavinia," I start, trying to buy a moment to recall my script and what I had planned to do with the liveshot. Fotch sprints from the truck to the camera, offering further distractions. He is so out of control that he bumps the camera in his hurry. He then fumbles with the viewfinder as I attempt to remember what I was supposed to say. Some people who have gathered to watch the liveshot start snickering. On top of that, Fotch's little wind sprint leaves him, well, winded. He sounds like Darth Vader, sucking air behind the camera. Within the first five seconds I am convinced that a recording of this liveshot will be posted instantly on Wetube or somewhere else on the internet so that the entire world can have a laugh.

Fotch dispenses with the camera moves. I'd like to bust a move, right out of there.

Ultimately, I sputter out a few facts about the shooting but to end my own bloodletting, I simply stop talking. Play the package, please. I want to die. Or drink.

The director rolls the package and Flotsam climbs into my ear. "I don't think you'll want this one on your resume tape, Wilson."

Thankfully, the rest of the report goes without incident, and we are finally free to leave the scene of what now amounts to two crimes. Worst of all, despite this disaster, I still owe Calzone $5.

Minutes later, while helping Fotch break down and stow the equipment, I get a taste of Flotsam's sticky fingerprints on the newscast.

The monitor in the live truck is still operational, carrying our news broadcast. The volume is low, but audible, providing a bit of a soundtrack for our labor. I glance at the monitor as Adams reads the tease that leads into the commercial break." ...the Chef of Staff wants to 'hold the curse' on military funding, but we'll tell you why many Members of Congress are worried about the cost of fighting insurgeons, right after this."

Rock 'n' Roll News, baby. For half a moment I almost smile. I'm still discouraged by our disaster. Fotch, of course, seems unfazed as always. Thinking about those weekend plans, he briskly packs the truck.

We find ourselves back at the station before the newscast is over. In fact, back before either of the other crews running liveshots tonight. This timetable affords us the advantage of a visual that I'm guessing no one was meant to see: Britnee Flaxen entering the passenger side of Arlen Rapier's car, a self-consciously trendy Nippon "Square." He's sporting shades and an open collar. She's scrunching down in the seat as they exit the parking lot. Where to--and how far? I wonder. At that moment I happen to notice a slight movement in one of the windows upstairs in Ivory Eriss' quarters. But the person backs out of view before I can make an identification.

Back at my desk, my telephone is ringing. A raspy male voice, one I can't quite place, starts.

"Wilson Gamble. I need to talk to you."

"Okay," I reply cautiously, although it's not. Okay. At least until I figure out who this is. It's clearly not the deep, mellow, yet nasal voice of Luther Post.

"I can't tell you everything over the phone, or else it might all blow up before we can control it." He's using a low whisper that implies everything he says is an important secret. Oh. Wait. That description sounds familiar.

"We met one time here in Filterboro a few months ago, Wilson. At the time you were hired by Newschannel 99."

It comes to me. Alibi Wallace, the, um, "associate" of Allen Pratfall. I'm finally able to respond, guardedly. No names. "Right. Here's a better number to call me at." I pass along my Trakphone number.

"Good," Wallace whispers. "The other number I had for you was answered by a guy who swore at me, said God hated him before he hung up."

The cloak and dagger theme continues when I reach my car. The Trakphone rings.

"Wilson. You figure out who I am yet?"

"Yes, I know. I figured it out."

"Don't say my name. My friend and I want to meet with you. We have a very interesting proposition for an enterprising reporter."

"That's me," I respond sing-song, half-enthusiastically. I wonder if his "friend" is Pratfall. And if they are simply going to complain to me about the justice system making life hard on the guy. It's a common complaint made to reporters.

"Go to the Hamburger Heaven over on the east side, on O'Shaughnessy Street. Take a booth as near to the door as possible. Grab the sports section from the *Daily Repellent* if you don't think you are being followed, and pretend to read it. That'll be our sign that the coast is clear."

I'm not sure that he can hear me rolling my eyes. But Wallace can hear me pause.

"Well?" he breathes, impatiently.

"When do you want to meet?" I ask.

"In 30 minutes. Will you be there?"

Of course. It's not like I have an extensive social life happening here, especially on a Friday night.

If the definition of an "extensive social life" includes spending Friday evening at a "Hamburger Heaven," then there are more bored people in this town than I realize. The place is packed with heavy, slow-moving people. Ordering a cup of coffee, I manage to find a booth fairly close to the door. The restaurant is located on the corner of a failing commercial area, breathing its wheezy last few gasps of breath. Out of the floor-to-ceiling windows, hopefully lacquered with ads for meal combos, I watch older cars, buses, and a few poorly-dressed people pass by. A light rain starts to fall, completing the cloak-and-dagger scene.

While awaiting my clandestine rendezvous, I read the sports section. Slowly. The Reds lost the night before, so I try to avoid the box scores on page D-3. By the time I get to the racing form for Aqueduct, a skinny kid comes slouching up to me. He looks less like a teenager than a wise guy, one who hasn't seen the inside of a school building for a while.

"These two dudes gave me this to give to you," he says, sullenly. Each word seems a struggle for him to identify and pronounce. Meanwhile, I notice his hands are in the pockets of his massively-oversized jeans. He's holding them up, is my guess. One of the hands withdraws a small envelope. His pants shift slightly down that one side.

"Thanks," I offer, taking the envelope. Turning away, I open the envelope. Go away kid, ya bother me.

But Flunky hasn't moved an inch. "So, man, what do I get for my trouble?" he challenges. "The two dudes said you would have something for me."

Although I'd prefer to swat him in the forehead with the rolled-up newspaper for his trouble, I opt to buy a little peace and quiet for five dollars. The kid slouches away to the restaurant order line without another word. A five dollar bill is enough for him.

The note inside the envelope is not what I expected. Written in careful, block letters on a scrap of paper from a racing form, is a declarative: "HAVERSACK RUNS A BOOK OUT OF HER HOUSE. THE FEDS ARE PLANNING TO BUST IT."

That is all. There's no invitation to meet, no elaboration. Just a Deep Throat tip-off. Funny, I don't feel like Woodward or Bernstein. Just Wilson E. Gamble. But this could explain a few things, like high-speed cable lines, slick-looking Sports leaving the parlor, and televisions perennially tuned to sporting events. But this is a Friday night, when presumably, no one is watching.

But now, not only is there a professional consideration but a personal one. Do I get out of there to avoid guilt-by-association, or try to investigate from the inside? It's time to leave Hamburger Heaven and head home.

Back at the scene of the impending crime, I turn it over in my mind. For the moment, I have no answers. A few drinks later, however, it ceases to be an issue.

She walks these hills in a long black veil

She visits my grave when the night winds wail

Nobody knows, nobody sees

Nobody knows but me

On Saturday, without dialing ahead, I call upon the Collingwood home. Troubled over Luther Post, the dramatic changes at Newschannel 99, the Haversack situation, and Collingwood's future, I need to work out some answers.

Marie Collingwood answers the door. "Carl isn't here," she states breezily, as her greeting. Um, okay. For a moment, I'm not sure how to respond. Without hesitation, however, Marie steps back from the open door, beckoning me inside. "He only drove up to the store to get a fresh LP tank for the grill. So come in and visit until he gets back. If you're lucky, you'll get a steak out of it."

I'm grateful, following into the big open space of their living area. Cool jazz plays from a digital music streaming player off to one side.

"Can I get you a drink?" Marie, the consummate hostess, is ready for all intruders. "Bottled water? Pepsi? Heineken?" She's gauging the intensity of my visit.

"I'll take the Heineken," I return, trying to seem relaxed.

"Go ahead out to the pool deck and grab a chair," Marie instructs. "I'll get a frosted mug ready for you."

Sounds good to me. I amble through the sliding glass door and settle into a comfortably-padded wicker patio chair. But once there, I realize that I am not alone.

It's a big, airy space around the pool, where I spent the night one night. And draped like a slipcover over a wicker patio couch, about 10 feet away, is Ivory Eriss. Deja vu, all over again. Sporting a finger-wave hairstyle, frilly day dress--belt below the waist--long baubled necklace. Flapper, redux. She has certainly seen me before I notice her.

"So," she breathes breathily, quietly, motionlessly. "I suppose I should say that it is nice to run in to you again here on the Collingwood pool patio." Her voice is that of aged whiskey, with hints of aromatic Romeo Y Julieta.

Yaggghh.

"Miss Eriss," I return, slowly, cool-ly. "When are you going to show me that art collection of yours?"

Not bad for a startled response. Pretend the ball has been in her court to keep our, er, "relationship" going forward.

Eriss ignores this. With Marie entering the patio with my drink, she shifts into maternalistic employer-employee patter. "Marie, my dear. Have you been following the progress of Mr. Gamble here? I think we shall make something of him yet."

Marie hands me my Heinie, replying, "You know I never watch television, Ivory. But Carl speaks very highly of the work that Wil does."

Eriss looks at me directly. "Well, I do believe we shall make something of him," she repeats. Is she talking about my job, or something else?

"Ah, well, thank you, Miss Eriss. I have had a very, um, eventful, time so far at Newschannel 99."

"I'm sure you have," Eriss replies. She flicks the ash from her cigarette toward an ashtray stand. "Have you managed to settle in to a snug little domicile here in town?" So inquires the General Manager of Shoddy Properties, LLC.

I don't want to feed her habit of enjoying my discomfort. So I use a little artistic license. "Yes, actually," I try, a little too brightly. She blinks, slightly disappointed, I think. "It's a home in the historic district." Advantage, me.

Marie settles into a chair. "Isn't it some kind of quaint boardinghouse for professionals?"

Advantage, Eriss. The taut, flat line of her thin red lips curls up ever so slightly. "Ohhhh," she offers, multi-syllabically. "A room rental? Yes, that is so very quaint. And in the historic district. As a member of the Historic District Preservation Board, I seem to recall there are some very distinct guidelines for how these darling old buildings must be maintained."

"Well, this 'darling old building' is pretty plain... ." I try. Eriss' lip curl stretches upward into a downright wicked smile. "Oh Yes, I recall private rooms are not allowed to be upgraded to 'en suite' status and there is to be no central air conditioning. And Marie my darling, it can be such a beastly hot summer here."

Sipping an iced drink in a tall, clear glass, Marie "Mmm hmm's" her assent.

I feel it's necessary to defend Haversack's Purgatory House and Bookmaking Emporium, at least to smear away Eriss' petulant smirk. "Actually, we all have window a.c. units. And the rooms are very spacious--you should see how tall the ceilings are." Ur, let's not have Eriss over to see for herself how high the ceilings are. Try again. "It's pretty cool to sit on a rocking chair on the long, wide porch--They don't build porches on homes any more. I wonder why?" Hoping to change the nature of the conversation, I direct this last question to Marie.

She is a hostess, though, not ready to engage in questions of sociology. "I wish I knew. My childhood home in Turlock had one, and looking back, it seems we spent all summer out on it."

Unfortunately, Eriss ignores this, bringing the conversation back to where I don't want it. "Air conditioning units in the windows? Tsk, tsk," she adds musically, like the Cheshire cat. This is a cat *with* a grin, flourishing on the patio. "They aren't allowed, either. I must have a conversation with the city code enforcement bureau. What was that address again?"

"Oh, Ivory, let Wil have his air conditioning," offers Marie.

I add, "And, Miss Eriss, it's not just me, but the other, uh, professionals who board there. I don't want them to suffer in the beastly heat." Ooh. Shouldn't have used her antiquated adjective.

Her response mocks me like a hurricane. "Yes, Mr. Gamble. It is not just me, either, but the other homeowners in the Historic District, who are all required to live by the same regulations." Trumped. "Everyone who moves in is provided with a document that identifies the special codes that apply to that neighborhood, so no one goes in without counting the cost."

"No one, " I reply dryly, "except those who rent from the owners."

I almost feel sorry for Mercy Haversack, whose business will suffer. But if my confidential informant is right, it's about to suffer, big time, anyways. In any case, I'd rather not take up for Mercy in this conversation any longer.

The three of us sit on the patio, now silently sipping or smoking, waiting for Carl Collingwood to return with the LP gas tank. All quiet on the sequestered front. As I sip the last, now-warm mouthful of my carefully-nursed beer, he enters the front door, calling my name. Whew.

"Wil! I saw your truck parked outside." He greets me with an exuberant handshake, as if we were old fraternity brothers meeting at a tailgate party. Collingwood lugs a replacement LP tank for the grill, setting it down with a heavy 'thunk' on the patio. "You are just in time to enjoy an afternoon of steaks marinated "a la Collingwood," baseball on the tube, and," he glances significantly at the dry bottle in my left hand, "a few more of those. Not warm like that one, though."

The wimmin-folk take their cue and move away from the pool area, leaving the grilling to the men-folk. It's a temporary relief, though, because I eventually figure out that there will be multiple place-settings at the dinner table. So, it's easy to accept another beer--and turn down a cigar. Undisturbed, Collingwood lights up and manages to keep the ashes away while preparing his marinade at a massive outdoor brick kitchen and grill. There's plenty of time to talk; the marinade needs time to work its flavor magic. A portable television shows a satellite broadcast of the Tigers and Indians, but the volume is turned down to "two."

"Carl, I'm sure there must be a good reason...but why don't you want to become the News Director at Newschannel 99?" I ask, taking a cool swig. "I mean, it doesn't affect me that much--I'll catch on somewhere else sooner or later, no matter who's in charge. But you are obviously the best thing they have going there." He doesn't respond. "And that would help stem the flow of the best people leaving the newsroom."

For the moment, Collingwood is silent, adding a shot of bourbon to his marinade mixture in a re-sealable freezer baggie. Eventually, he replies, still bent over his work. "I guess I keep believing we will find a News Director from the "news" side of the industry, someone who 'gets' what journalism is at its core. Or, someone who at least appreciates that's what we are supposed to do in a newsroom. I don't want to handle a budget, or personnel issues. I'd rather be free to be more valuable--in my mind—you know, to spend most of my time concerned with the content of our newscasts, and using my credibility to back up the tough decisions someone else would have to make."

It's a classic journalist's dilemma. As a reporter, it's easy to advocate purity in journalism, without any hint of interference from moneyed interests. But someone has to pay the bills. And that's going to be advertisers. Remember St. Francis de Sales? So, news executives usually have to come to some level of compromise with The Money. The goal is to make The Money respect you. If you are perceived as honest and fair, advertisers will always come back. If you are perceived to be "for sale," advertisers will only remain in the bidding until a competitor comes up with a superior bid--then they simply back away, with the all-too credible excuse that the newsroom can be bought.

"In any case," Collingwood continues airily, "I am actually working out an alternative solution, and hopefully soon. I'll let you in on it as soon as possible." He seals the freezer baggie and lays it out on a plate on the counter. "But here's something we can finally talk about. Are you ready to get your phone back?"

"My phone. My personal phone?" Je ne comprends pas. "My trakphone? Or, do you mean, the company phone that Rapier took away?" Collingwood shakes his head, and it dawns on me. "My personal phone? You found Luther Post?"

Collingwood wipes his hands and sits on a patio chair. "Well, let's say I called that phone number a lot. Luther didn't answer at first, and then he hung up on me quite a bit, but I kept after him. He's a smart guy, actually. Knows my name. Eventually I convinced him his only chance of not getting shot by Dank's deputies was to turn himself in."

"That's all it took?" I asked, a little incredulously.

"Oh, that and the reward money. If we do this right, he turns himself in through his family, and they can claim the reward. He'll do time for the shooting, but at least his family will have this windfall to carry them through."

"But the man is angry and desperate. He seemed more inclined to kill himself before he'd get caught. After all this time and all he's suffered, why would he simply give up?"

"He has a network of friends, but it doesn't extend out of the county, so he can't really run far. He's had a lot of time to think. He's tired and hurting and, while he's succeeded in hiding for this long, he knows that each day the odds grow that deputies will catch him. And at heart, he seems to love his family, so in his calm moments he realizes that they need him alive in jail rather than dead and buried."

Well, okay then. "So, how is this going to go down?" I ask, swigging from the bottle.

"Luther has ways of communicating with his family. It'll take a day or so for him to take care of business and then get back to me. So, on Monday morning, you, Fakir and a camera will ride out to Marberry, where you ran into him before. I will show up to help broker things, make sure Luther Post doesn't become another Rodney King."

"What time will Post show up?"

"Well, he made me promise to not tell law enforcement where or when until the last moment. He wouldn't even tell me what time, but that he would call a short time before he gets there."

"So deputies won't have time to set up a perimeter around the house?"

"I'm sure that's it. Like I said, Luther's smart. He wants as few deputies there as possible, although I couldn't guarantee him anything."

"Have you talked with Dank yet?"

"Oh yes. And he's gonna be the hero. A win-win for everyone, in a way. Dank gets his fugitive, Post survives and his family gets the reward, and you get an ex-cloo-sive." For fun, Collingwood once again emphasizes the "cloo" in a sing-song voice. We can afford to stand back from the human element and enjoy the reporting victory.

"What other elements will we put in the story?" I ask, forever concerned with the reporting, not so much about the lives of the people involved in the actual events.

"I'm not sure we'll need much," Collingwood replies. "This will be pretty intense, simply showing Luther Post turning himself in. He might say something, might not. Dank will certainly have something to say. We'll have Nettles or Hubbell do a sidebar story with the family of the victim or on community reaction and get Follicle to talk with someone at the community college about law enforcement procedure. It's a good story."

"Yup," I agree, thrilled to be a part of it. "It's a very good story." Although I'm starting to get a little Heineken Hazy, I need to tell Collingwood about the clandestine allegations of a Book Operation running at Haversack House. As I recount Friday's events, Collingwood rises to flip over the food marinating in the freezer baggie.

"That could be some good stuff. I'll ask Dank for some insight, although as Sheriff it's not his jurisdiction. We'll try to find out when we need to be at your house with a camera. This is a really good day for us!" Collingwood smiles a little smile while puffing on his cigar.

Leaving it all in his hands, I start to forget all about Haversack House. But not about Megan.

Megan? Wait a minute, here she comes. But...how did my thoughts run in that direction? How did Megan insert herself into my mental conversation? I realize that I've been trying to forget her, make a clean break. I don't owe her anything. She was never more than vaguely interested in me, romantically. Now, in many ways, she would be a liability in my life, barely capable of taking care of Meathead, much less herself. So, why is she still on my mind? I feel the responsibility of a friend, to be sure. Its more than that, however. Her face, her person, stays with me. I smile at the thought of her goofiness, at the memory of the smell of her hair, the innocent wonderment in her eyes. Lifting another Heineken, I stop, having come to realize that Megan--whether she's physically with me or not--for better or for worse, for richer or for poorer, is my companion.

Come Monday, I'm sure it'll be alright when we are there to watch Post turn himself in. I call Fakir Johnson on Sunday afternoon to make plans, and we head up early Monday, with a bright clean sun throwing a brilliant key-light on Marberry. We stake out the haunted house.

"So, where do you want me to set up the sticks?" Johnson asks, pointing to his tripod. He will hold his camera for now, thank you.

"Can't say at the moment. But for now why don't you put 'em at the edge of the property on the shoulder of the road. We'll adjust when Carl gets here."

Johnson complies, then starts rummaging in the back of the SUV, ultimately producing a tablet computer. "Hey Wil. I've got a satellite hook-up on this thing--with a webcam. If Buddy Furlong can't get the sat truck pointed in the right direction for your Noon liveshot, you can always use this as a backup."

I hope it doesn't come to that but realize Furlong's track record pretty much always requires a "Plan B." Johnson sets up a black, hard plastic camera case as a stand for the tablet and spends the next 25 minutes fiddling with the software.

Meanwhile, I start to get nervous, thinking about this major story--and all that can go wrong. There's too much time to consider the possibilities.

I recall the time I had an athletic trainer with dubious credentials wrap my arm after a muscle strain. He used an ace bandage. At first it felt snug, solid. But he kept pulling it tighter around my arm. And tighter. Soon I felt my blood trying to squeeze through, becoming an arterial traffic jam. Then I almost felt like I couldn't breathe, even though it was my arm and not my chest that was wrapped up. The growing, unstoppable tightening seemed to squeeze my lungs. More like the growing tectonic pressure that crushes coal into a diamond rather than the steady velvet glove rubbing of an oyster creating a pearl. Momentarily I worried that I was merely passing a kidney stone. Then, I realized it was all just indigestion, and suddenly, my arm didn't really feel that bad any more.

That memory calms me down. So does a swig from my water bottle. Wish it was a stronger drink; at least a beer.

An hour passes. No sign of life. I don't have cell service, although I could communicate over Johnson's satellite computer connection if necessary. But I'd rather just pay attention, let things play out.

Another hour. One single, sketchy-looking pickup truck has passed on the lonely road. The driver gives us a long, slow look as he passes. It's not Luther Post, but it could be someone with whom he is in contact. The sun is still bright, but begins to lose the fresh glow of a new morning as it rises to the top of the sky. The temperature goes up also. I pass some time writing possible leads for my script, and teases for Aimee Flotsam. I can see it now; if she writes the teases, they will be undoubtedly pockmarked with "rock 'n' roll news" malapropisms: "First on Newschannel 99, a gunman unleased on society! We will fresh out details of his arresting situation!" I shiver, despite the building heat. Then I consider my own rock n roll news script, which could be hideous. "The Phantom of Filterboro--every mother's living nightmare run amok--manifests himself to our reporter! Deputies send in The Squat Team, disarming Luther Post, throwing the thug into the slammer! !" I shiver and feel sick.

Still no movement at the house. Johnson has kept himself busy with his gadgets, including his ostentatious smartphone. When that technology starts to get boring, he shifts to his tablet, still mounted on the camera case, pointed towards the empty house. He surfs the internet, playing around with his Facespace webpage. For him, that activity could potentially kill several hours.

But it won't have to.

A solitary Sheriff's Department squad car kicks up piles of dust as it carefully winds its way through the Marberry holler, growing larger as it approaches. Ultimately it pulls up to our position. Johnson turns away from his computer, me from my notepad. Carl Collingwood and Sheriff Dank deliberately emerge from the vehicle, as if every single step has been negotiated, choreographed. Astonishingly, Luther Post instantly appears from the tall grass around the side of the house. He's holding his handgun, pointing it at the sky.

Johnson and I silently man up, a tri-cornered Mexican standoff under the noonday sun. Hugo Montenegro's whistling theme music from "The Good, The Bad, and The Ugly" might as well play now. Collingwood is good, Post is bad, and uh, let's say Johnson is The Third Man.

"Fakir," I stage whisper. "Camera! ! !" He finally moves, slowly, careful to not disturb the dynamic playing out in front of us. Difficult to be a part of a news story, yet be apart from a news story. Gingerly, he hefts the camera to his shoulder, checks the viewfinder, sighs, presses "record." Moments later, shockingly, the fragile silence is broken by the sound of a half-dozen patrol cars, emitting deputies as they pull in and are disgorged. Guns drawn, they aren't smiling.

Johnson caaaaarefully pans around, capturing the amazing scene. It's as tense as a mob of supermarket shoppers impatiently waiting behind a customer with a full cart in the "ten items or less" express line.

Post is surrounded, or confronted, but carefully refers to his own firearm. Recognizing his weak negotiating position, he waves the gun and--amidst the sound of multiple firearms instantly brought into firing position--brings the barrel to his own head. Dank quietly curses; this guy is smarter than he had calculated.

For the moment, Post remains in control of himself and the playing field." Who all you? I said two-three police and it's a whole mob!"

"We're just making sure everything and everyone are gonna go home safe," Dank tries. "Standard operating procedure."

But Post clearly thinks a deal has been breached. "There's too many, Cop! Too many! Too many!" Now he tries to play the deputies. "I got nothin' to live for, man!" shouts Post. "If I gotta die, I die right now!! Who pull the first trigger, make it happen?" he challenges. I'm close enough to hear him mutter an aside, "God hate me anyway, it's too late."

"Luther, put down the gun, man," Dank half-commands, knowing it won't work.

Ever the Voice of Reason, Collingwood intervenes. "Nobody wants you dead, Luther. Think of your family. These gentlemen," he glances at Dank and two or three nearby deputies, "will honor their agreement for you to get a decent lawyer and a fair trial."

Post doesn't move, doesn't say anything. He keeps the gun barrel pointed like a judgment at his right temple.

Dank and the deputies are at a standstill. They don't like "suicide by cop" and worse yet, nobody wants to shoot this armed fugitive while a camera rolls. It's not like they could fail to hit him, a firing squad facing a single man. Yet, Post has what appears to be his own loaded gun--one that we believe has been in production for use at least once before.

Another dry silence.

Collingwood speaks up once more. "Luther. I have already contacted a skillful attorney who has agreed to help you." Pause to tease the name of the attorney. "It's Randy Sillocan."

Post doesn't change his position, but his demeanor alters noticeably. He straightens up and looks at Collingwood. "'Randy Sillocan, attorney to the working man!'--that guy?" Post asks, reciting from a well-known television commercial. If not impressed, he seems interested.

"Yes, that's him. He's willing to work pro bono on your behalf."

Post, handgun still menacing his temple, seems confused. "What's that mean?"

"For free. The hottest defense attorney in Filterboro is ready to represent you, Luther Post, right now."

The gun barrel starts to lower.

That is, until an SUV with unfamiliar but garish exterior markings captures Post's attention, racing through the hollow, completely oblivious to the dramatic incident unfolding before us. Dank and Collingwood fully turn toward the growing sound of the racing engine as the vehicle rapidly approaches. The deputies, guns drawn, do not allow themselves to be distracted from the armed shooting suspect,. But each of them inches back and triangulates, based on where they think the new vehicle will enter the scene.

And enter, it does, sliding to a stop at the edge of the haunted property. A standard-issue TV station white SUV with black, blue, and red logos all over it that read "WOMP Channel 11 News in High Definition." And a non-standard issue Jack Phillips hops out, followed by two others: Katie the reporter and a videographer, who quickly slings a camera up on his shoulder.

Post is not happy with these brazen party-crashers. "What is this?!" he yells, starting to back up. "We had a deal! First, I got a platoon of hairy cops showing up, now this stuff? I don't want no circus here!"

"Luther, you can't go anywhere. It's all over," Dank asserts, loudly. Several of the deputies take a step forward, slowly, eyes now locked on Post. They still have eyes on the newcomers, as well.

Post is increasingly agitated. "We were going to do this right!" It's evident that he believed it would look like he was voluntarily walking into the sheriff's office to clear his innocent name, not dragged in like, uh, a criminal. His agitation meter suddenly rockets upward. "What is this, man? I ain't having this! No, no, no!!"

Phillips and his crew show no compunction; they aren't leaving this news story. Post instantly makes it a bigger news story. Suddenly, astonishingly, he turns and runs, handgun wildly and loosely gripped in his right hand. The deputies instinctively move forward as a single entity, careful but quick, guns held out front like compasses directed towards their quarry. There is no order to shoot--parameters are unclear here. Meanwhile, Post sprints through the high weeds of the corner of the haunted house. Guess his leg is feeling better. But he makes a panicky mistake: wildly firing two shots behind him. Pop, pop. One pings off of the passenger side of the Channel 11 SUV. The other round is still traveling, for all I know, since I've dropped to the dirt. But this is the cue for a dozen honest replies from the gun barrels of a dozen well-trained lawmen. Their volley, however, is a fraction of a second too late. Post has disappeared once more into the tall weeds and trees around the back corner of the house.

Now the deputies accelerate into high pursuit, still careful to mark one another's positions as they head into the hillside brush. Dank gives Phillips a quick but sincere glare, before moving forward himself. "That might be worth an arrest, Jack, obstructing law officers in the line of duty."

"I'm just doing my duty, Sheriff."

Dank calls over his shoulder, "Me, too, Jack. We'll talk, real soon."

Briefly, Phillips looks over at me. "They should have tazed him, bro."

Lugging his camera, Johnson tries to start off in pursuit of Post and the deputies. I go with him; we have to ride to the sound of the guns, no matter how frightening. Or, no matter how quiet; there is no more gunfire, because there is no more Luther Post. One by one, the deputies return, bearing only sullen expressions. I hear one of them talking about spots of blood found along a trail in the woods. I can't get it confirmed but the general assumption is that Post was hit by one of the deputies' bullets.

Nevertheless, Post once again somehow disappears without a trace. After many hours of honest effort, the deputies' latest manhunt ends again in failure.

We try to interview Dank as he departs. He refuses, but while brushing past The Assembled Members of the Press, has a question of his own for Jack Phillips. "How'd you know this was goin' on? We had radio silence." This question might be for the benefit of Collingwood, to indicate that he hadn't given away our exclusive. He might not mind taking liberties with his agreement with Post, but not with the media.

Phillips' trademark Cheshire cat smile slowly appears. "I happened to notice Fakir's webcast."

This means nothing to the low-tech Sheriff, who mounts his horse, er, squad car, and rides off into the sunset without comment. But it means something to me.

"What do you mean, 'Fakir's webcast'?" My face speaks at Phillips but my shoulders turn to confront Johnson. He shrugs, looking sheepish-- but innocent, not a wolf in sheep's clothing.

"It looks like the webcam on my tablet might have been streaming to my weblog, where there would have been a live picture of this place. Sorry, Wil, I didn't think about that."

Phillips finishes. "When I saw it at first, I didn't realize that anything was going on. But then I recognized the place, and heard you guys talking--I decided it was worth taking the risk to run out there. Guess I was right."

Although we still have a pretty good story for the 6 o'clock newscast that night, I feel the disappointment that it wasn't an amazing exclusive. And I'm still ticked off at Johnson--because I still don't have my mobile phone back.

One pretty good story down--for now--one to go. Even though he's still mad the next day, Dank confirms--on background--that the FBI, in charge of investigating illegal bookmaking--is indeed ready to pounce on Haversack House. They won't say when. Apparently there is an inside man who knows who I am and what I do. But its somebody else's jurisdiction, so that's all Dank will tell us. "On Background" means we can report it if we get confirmation from someone else--and don't identify any of the sources. We won't. Report it, I mean. Collingwood and I would rather quietly devise our plans in case Someone Else turns out to be wearing a badge and leading a raid.

"Here is a decent mobile phone with a great video camera to keep for now," he advises, handing me a dark, rectangular gadget. "All you can do is stay close and if and when you hear noise, go to the proper screen on the phone and tap the "Video Record" button. Look out windows, down staircases, anything you can record before they stop you. The feds don't invite cameras to their busts. And, Will?" Yeah?" Don't forget to call us right away. We want to be first on the scene with a real camera." Better than Second On The Scene. Nobody but Linus Van Pelt remembers who finished second.

While putting the finishing touches on my report, my focus is interrupted by a lot of knees-bent running around in the newsroom. No surprise: it's a technical glitch that's igniting the panic.

The anchors have nothing to read. Newschannel 99 management jumped on the latest newsroom bandwagon, and has forsaken paper news scripts for e-scripts. It started last week. Fern and Adams are supposed to use computer tablets for the "crash copy" scripts they keep on the anchor desk. There haven't been too many problems so far, but today the tablets are malfunctioning, not receiving data. Nobody is sure if it's because of an electrical storm that happens to be burning the sky over the TV station. The anchors are worried that if the teleprompter doesn't work they will have nothing to read. They get, well, a little unreasonable about things like that.

Even worse, the storm has claimed other casualties. Our printers go on the fritz. There are three digital printers in the newsroom, all in a row. And a lightning strike seems to have suddenly incapacitated all three. We can print the occasional document off of an email or website. But with 15 minutes left before air, and the computer tablets apparently out of commission, Flotsam is having a terrible time finding a way to print a complete set of scripts from ENPS. As a result, Fern and Adams are moaning at increasingly-higher decibels over the fact that they don't have their scripts early enough to "mark up," that is, to make last-second changes.

Adams is particularly agitated. He follows Flotsam around like a little brother. "Aimee, I don't feel good about this. I knew we shouldn't have gone off on this cockamamie e-script thing. Now they aren't working and I don't have crash copy! I need my scripts!"

"Yes, I know that, Jeff," flusters Flotsam, her voice rising to match his. Evidently she hadn't calculated "stress" as one of the hazards of her new job. In fact, stress is the primary hazard of her new job.

"What are we going to do? What's the plan?" Adams persists.

Flotsam breaks instead of bends. Stopping her aimless rushing around the room, she turns on Adams. "Go sit down and leave me alone. I'm working on it. Let me do my job, Mr. Adams!"

Mr. Adams turns juvenile as well. "What, in fact, is your job, Aimee? You don't seem to be able to produce our scripts!" He sing-songs the second half of "produce" into about three mocking syllables.

"Producers...yes, we produce. I will produce!" she sputters. Then she has an idea. "Producers produce, in television, Mr. Adams."

He begins to look amused, which makes her mad. So she starts to recite. "Directors direct. Writers write. Reporters report." And with a sudden, wicked gleam in her eye: "And anchors...ank! I will produce and you, go 'ank,' Mr. Adams!"

Touche! Triumphant, Flotsam marches off with a ream of blank paper under her arm, in search of a printer with which to match wits next.

That doesn't end the crisis, of course. The clock ticks. An engineer moves on his own time in and out of the newsroom, encouraging the appearance of attempting to fix the problem. He has no deadline. But the general hubbub level rises as an actual deadline for everyone else approaches. Rapier, out of touch with everything but the station's budget, has no idea what is happening as he slinks by me.

"What's wrong here?" he asks, more out of annoyance than interest.

I take a breath. "The printers don't seem to be working," I inform him. "I tried printing my script on each of these printers and nothing's coming out. Oh, and the anchors' computer tablets aren't working, either."

"Is that all?" he looks at me accusatorially, as if I had broken the Society of Professional Journalists code of ethics. "They can use the teleprompter, can't they?"

"They say that isn't always reliable," I remind him, turning back to my own work. Not my problem, bro.

Flustered Flotsam flits forward. "I tried to put a new ream of paper every machine I could find, Arlen! But nothing is happening, yet."

Rapier thinks for a moment; it takes actual kinetic energy to begin. And then: "In Portland-Auburn I was told by our printer repairman that this kind of problem cropped up when the reams of paper we were using were too moist. The, uh, atmospherical conditions in the newsroom were too, um, moist. Humid, I guess. He recommended we microwave the paper to dry it out before putting it into the printer."

Microwave the paper? Rapier's position as The Boss doesn't save him from a derisive hoot from Sherman Follicle. "That's hilarious! Ha! Did he sell you any swampland in Florida, too? Whaddya pay that guy? Can we get him here?" he adds, turning his back on Rapier for good measure.

There's clearly no answer for that. Follicle's intellectual seniority fills the center of the room like Wilt Chamberlain in the paint, defying anyone to challenge it. No one can--except in the midst of the Desperation of Deadline.

Time ticks. The printers are still not working. The engineer is now trying to route printing duties to a tiny inkjet printer in the accounting office. At that rate, the anchors will have scripts, by say, Thanksgiving.

That doesn't solve the e-script problem. Flotsam senses disaster and complains loudly to nobody and everybody, "I won't be able to get scripts out to the anchors!" This propels Rapier back towards the printers. Nearby stands a stack of cardboard boxes filled with virginal reams of blank white paper, ready to be sacrificed to the almighty printer.

Hard at work finishing my own story, my attention is distracted momentarily by a burst of scanner traffic at the Assignment Desk. Involuntarily, I glance up. Amidst the chaos, Gretchen Calzone is having another private moment. Focusing, I realize she is pondering an object in her hand. It's a quarter. But the noise of the newsroom rushes around me again and I lose track of everything but my script.

Soon, however, I realize Rapier has been rushing back-and-forth between the printer station and the break room. On one return visit I stop him. "Where are you going with all those reams of paper under your arm? Is there something I can do to help?" I ask, innocently. Okay, semi-innocently.

A condescending return glance. "I'm microwaving the paper so it will work in the printer!" Rapier replies. Get out of my way, fool. A quick glance determines the paper appears slightly tanned, with curled-up corners. Yup, no humidity worries here.

The printer remains dysfunctional. Apparently, now its jammed because the curled-up edges of the microwaved paper are an impediment. Fortunately, however, the Teleprompter operator is on her best behavior. The anchors have no crash copy, but the computer tablets come online about five minutes into the newscast, and Fern and Adams manage to survive with little damage to reputation or ego.

Every question that I ask, I get a lie, lie, lie

For every lie you tell, you're gonna cry, cry, cry

Back at Haversack House, I find myself more intently checking out everything--and everyone. So...tell me more about this Book operation, hmmm? Slab draws my most intense level of suspicious scrutiny when his unbalanced bulk actually moves to repair the mounting on a television satellite receiver on the side of the house, up near the roof. And that slick Player I saw a week ago has come and gone a couple of times since then. Miss Mercy drifts aimlessly around the place at the tempo of an adagio.

It's not easy relaxing in a, uh, facility, that could be raided at any moment by the FBI. In a way, it already feels like a penitentiary. Trying to maintain my cell block routine, I heat up a frozen dinner while coping with the latest 4x6 Mercy Rule card. Taped to the microwave, it states, "Let's Go 'Green! 'All Settings Have Been Disabled Except 'Defrost,' To Save Energy." As a result, when the display panel asks "how many minutes" I want the microwave to run, I punch in the digits "4" and "8." That'll be sure to save electricity.

Eventually, avoiding all eyes, I sneak my warm-ish meal up the stairs, past the Troll-neighbor (vague talking noises emanate from behind the door tonight, but it's clearly not TV sound). The tray contains three bony samples of chicken thighs, a dollop of "whipped potato," a handful of greenish beans, and an indistinguishable, sugary mush called "compote." It would become "compost" if I wasn't so hungry for both spoonfuls. It only takes half a beer to wash it down, which wasn't bad, so I have one more for dessert.

Finally, with the beautiful new phone in hand, out in Big Blue, it's time to call Megan. "Wil? Hi! It's me, Megan!" she starts, bouncily. Long experience has taught me not to correct her about who called whom.

"Wow! How are you!" I start, joining in on the excitement. Then, hearing a lot of ambient noise behind her voice, I have to ask, "Where are you?"

"Oh, wow, Wil. It's this, uh, place to eat. A restaurant. Mamie's here too! Hi Mamie!" There's indistinguishable noise for a moment, then, she remembers I'm on the phone. "Wil! Its great! You tell them what you want to eat and it comes out fast, like, right away." Fast food?" And they have spicy wings!" This last with an excited flourish. At least she can remember something she has always enjoyed. Might I be another?

Querulously: "Wil?"

"Yes, Megan?"

"Where are you?"

"What do you mean? I'm at, uh, home."

"No, silly. Uh, geographically, where are you?"

Geographically? Oh, that. I tell her. A long ways away, in so many ways.

"Okay. Mamie says it's okay, I can make the trip, as long as you pick me up at the airport."

"Great!" Make the trip? Airport? Uh, hadn't expected this. "When are you coming?" I try, pretty much anticipating the response.

"Oh, pretty soon..." she trails off, noncommittally. "I have a ticket."

"Great! Okay. Maybe you should find it and let me know what date is printed on it. And, um, where do you plan to stay?" Oops. That just slips out. "I mean, can I help you find a place to stay?"

Silence for a moment. Then, quietly, shyly: "Well, I was gonna stay with you, I guess, Willie."

Miss Mercy would love that: Couch Girl in her parlor.

"Well, come on down!" I try, shakily, attempting a light-hearted TV Game Show Host approach. But, I'm suddenly nervous. And a little sick to my stomach. Is it nerves or--the thought occurs to me--the beer? One more doesn't sound bad now, but I have to cope. And think. Then, after hanging up, devise plans to make a reservation at the Placid Place Motel. For One.

18

A day later, there is a new paper-related issue to confront us at work. And I don't mean microwaving the printer paper or disposing of The *Daily Repellant*--which due to its own budget cuts has simply devolved into a massive reprint of Amalgamated Press wire reports.

Having finished my report out on the news set, a naked roll of toilet paper waits expectantly for me on my desk. Huh? Its fresh out of the package; the leading edge is still lightly adhered to the rest of the roll. My first thought is that it's not Halloween yet and therefore it is not time to t.p. my own house. The roll is accompanied by a plastic-wrapped miniature bar of soap, like those left on the sink at hotels. In fact, The wrapper reads, "Western 6 Motels." What's this all for? Road trip? The mystery isn't revealed until I look at my email.

Message for you, sir.

"Help us save the environment! There are 'Green' ways to pursue personal hygiene." There's that word again--abused to save some business a dollar in the name of ecology--actually at someone else's expense. "The bar of soap and roll of paper on your desk are the last such items that will be provided by The Company. Once they are gone, you must provide for your own bathroom toilet and sink needs. We will, of course, continue to provide city water for your use. Thank you." It's not signed, but Rapier isn't smart enough to realize that when he sends messages from his computer, his name is automatically attached to every one. Wow. I note that on every desk there is Charmin, and chagrin on Calzone's face at the Assignment Desk. The ridiculous scene conjures an image in my mind of a black market and barter system developing in a place like this. Follicle will certainly become the Godfather of Roll.

All this makes me even more appreciative of my newly-assigned station mobile phone. I try calling Luther Post on my old phone. No answer, so I leave a message. He has utterly disappeared once again, avoiding an intense search effort by law enforcement. It is difficult for them because it turns out Post has a rather extensive family that is spread out throughout the region. Investigators can't keep an eye on everybody, and they don't know to watch the "gas station store" in Otis Mills where Post told me he sends messages to his immediate family. But I do.

Nothing better to do, I drive up to Otis Mills after work. No specific plan in mind. The town is not incorporated, just a ragtag collection of worn out clapboard homes and old singlewide trailers. More satellite TV dishes than functioning automobiles. There is a bar and an "internet cafe" in which to sin, and two or three churches in which to atone. And, to dramatically narrow my search for Post, apparently only one gas station.

Big Blue really does need gas, so I pull up to a pump. It's a Noble station, familiar blue and green logo of a gushing oil rig smiling down on me as I exit the truck. Nothing else is smiling. A posse of five young men-- bulging with biceps and criminal careers, lounging near the door to the convenience store--turns on me with a single, burning stare. Conscious of my business attire, I loosen my necktie but otherwise pay no attention. Uh, let's fill 'er up.

I pump. They stare. I need to talk to someone who won't be spoiling for a confrontation, or to simply take a bribe and send me on a wild goose chase looking for Post. But, how to get inside the store? I'm stuck, the gas pump steadily ringing up a healthy bill on my debit card. Should I just come back at, um, a more opportune time? Just when the pump display hits $30, I get a break. A man in his 50's, blue short-sleeve company shirt, hair graying at the temples, exits the store--doorbell jingling--and walks straight at me. Aggressively.

"You!" Me? I tense up. Yup, he's talking to me. His short sleeves flap as he walks. "You, I recognize you. You work for that TV station that's after Luther," he challenges me as he reaches my pump.

"Yes, that's right." That stops the man. "I'm Wilson Gamble. I'm Luther's friend. I've helped him--given him a phone, in fact--but now we have to figure out what to do next."

The man pulls back the aggressive attitude. He knows something.

"I know something," he says. Join me in my office." He shambles back towards the convenience store. And towards the Staring Posse, staring at me. I don't like it. But I'm stuck between a rock and an Otis Mills, and I need this man to escort me into the store. So, I jam the hose nozzle back into the pump, pat the keys into my pocket, and catch up with him.

There is an-already familiar jingle of bells as the glass door--coated with iron bars--opens and closes on a wheezing contracting piston. No one is inside, and I follow the man past the checkout counter, through an aisle stocked with car air fresheners and a glass refrigerator sporting 40 ounce bottles of Olde Anglican Malt Liquor. He proceeds directly towards a small hallway lined with restrooms and video games. Through this he holds open an exit door at the end. Nothing said, I proceed out the door. Its dark green out here, all shadows, high trees and wild weeds. A closed-in, private place. Remaining inside, the clerk closes the door behind me. Leaving no one here but me--and Luther Post.

"I figured you'd figure it out," he starts, breathing heavily. He looks worn out. Torn shirt, bloodshot eyes, wild hair while leaning there--his back against the building.

"My back's against the wall, man. God hate me." I don't know how to respond to that, so I wait for him to continue. Still leaning, he bends forward a little, apparently in pain. I'm not sure that it's his bad leg that's hurting him. "There's no way I can keep doing this. I wanted to turn myself in, but that was a crazy set up back there at that house. I coulda got shot up with all those boys with guns. Woulda been big news for you, huh?" he flicks a tired but still-defiant glance at me.

"My offer still stands," I reply. "You want a safe way in, come with me now. To the TV station. They can't do anything to you there. Not with me and my camera."

"What's the catch this time?" Post asks, panting a little, now pivoting on his shoulder that's pinned against the wall to angle his body towards me. Still leaning. Something is wrong.

"We get to the station, I call the Sheriff. While we're waiting, I tape record a couple of questions with you. You tell me what really happened, what it's been like running from police."

"Huh! It hain't been no basket of chocolates," Post snorts. Then he slowly sinks as his knees give out, and he slides along the back of the building down into a sitting position. This does not compute--until I figure it out: Luther Post has been shot.

"Them deputies didn't get me, man, not really," Post breathes, explaining. "One nicked me on the arm when I run away. But this," his head tilts toward his hurt shoulder, "this from on my way here, last night." He starts a recital. "Here I am, going along one of my trails through the woods--I guess holding the phone in my hand--and this dude just pops up outta nowhere, got a gun. Mine's in my pocket. He wants the phone. I tell him screw you, I need this. Can't believe he actually pulled the trigger. He knows I woulda give it up eventually. Just gotta hold my own for a coupla minutes. Now I'm bleeding." He turns his other shoulder--the one farthest from me, on which he did not pivot. Its red.

"Holy smokes. That changes everything. First, I call EMS and then the Sheriff."

"Not here!" The old fire smolders in Luther Post's commanding presence. "When we get into the city, man." Tiring again, he calms down. "Just, let's get going."

"Slow down, Luther," I start. "There's a reward out for you. And you might have some friends around here, but there's a bunch of goombahs out front, and I'm guessing at least one wouldn't mind trying something if he thought he could cash in a reward check." Suddenly an image of my poor ol' helpless Big Blue at the gas pump pops into my head--with a bunch of convenience store loiterers staring at it all this time.

"Luther," I continue--ball is in my court. He looks up. "I'm going to drive a quarter mile south out of here, pull over on the shoulder, and wait for you. I'm driving a blue, full-size pickup truck. Can you make it back through the woods that far?"

"I can go that far," Post claims. "I'll be there in 15 minutes." A quarter of an hour feels like it will be forever, but I don't see any other way without attracting more attention than I'm already going to get.

"Uh, one more thing, Luther. Where is your gun now?"

"Had enough of it. Useless piece. Tossed it in the woods somewhere. I don't know where."

Without another word, I go back through the door and snatch up the first sale item I pass, a bag of pork rinds. I'm alright with that--you know, junk food doesn't deserve the bad rap that it gets. As I wait for my new friend the clerk to ring up the purchase, I note that the label boasts one serving contains 2% riboflavin.

"You find everything okay?" he asks me, double meaning loud and clear.

"It's all good," I assure him breezily. No worries here, my man. Except, I glance out the front windows to see two or three guys leaning up against my truck. I really don't want a confrontation of any kind right now. Thinking quick, I grab my phone to my ear as I exit the store. Everyone out here stops what they are doing, which isn't much. The fluorescents attached to the aluminum awning overhead hum awkwardly, lonely.

I pretend a phone conversation. "So, who is the reporter covering the free beer giveaway at the Otis Mills Food King? Wow--who ever thought up the idea of giving away beer? ! ? !" I offer in a stage whisper to the phone, head down, pretending not to notice anyone nearby. These loungers all heard the clerk call me the "TV Guy" earlier, so they already have a vague idea of who I am, or at least what I do. I step farther forward.

"Whaaaaaat you talkin about?" mutters a tall guy hiding inside a tight, black wife-beater t-shirt and knicker-length shorts that barely hang on to his groin. He glances at a squat, fireplug type of guy with medium dreads and no shirt at all. This guy looks back, implicitly believing The TV Guy, instantly recognizing an opportunity.

Then, the coup de maitre, as I saunter towards the truck. "Tyler Hubbell? Sounds great!" I ask the phone, incredulously. Hello: blonde goddess, anyone? "She's covering this?" I continue, out loud. "She'll be there, at the Otis Mills Food King, really?" Pause. "Didn't she just break up with that football player boyfriend, what was his name?"

A mad scramble ensues, heading rapidly away from the gas station. The loiterers quickly disperse, and Big Blue is suddenly free to go. I briskly climb aboard, fire up the engine, and head south. Bye bye, sweetie-pie.

Dusk dawns and the roadside grows dark as I drive along. Looking for Post a little too early, I start worrying that I've missed our rendezvous point. Where is he? The tires roll.

Eventually, he seems to magically emerge at a random spot in the woods at the end of a long roadside guardrail. Bingo. I pull over, and accept my new passenger: a character who has recently made the FBI's Most Wanted List.

Post leans into the truck kind of funny, because of the wound. But he does not get in all the way. All power draining away, he remains half-in and half-out. It's obvious: We're not making the drive into town.

"Luther, I'm calling 911 right now. I'm getting an ambulance."

He has a small burst of energy, but it isn't to object. Post finally hauls himself into the truck, resignedly. "Okay, man," he whispers.

I dial the numbers and tell the communications officer what happened, who is hurt, and where we will be waiting. Then I dial Sheriff Dank.

He answers, "Yeah?"

"Sheriff? Wilson Gamble, Newschannel 99." I try to sound calm so as to not alarm my companion. "I am right now with Luther Post."

He sounds business-like. "Stay where you are, and we will have two deputies there in five minutes."

I tell him that I have already called for emergency help, and the report of a gunshot wound will already draw a law enforcement officer. "But Sheriff--you can meet him at the hospital and make an announcement to the rest of the media."

He swears and hangs up.

I look at my phone, contemplating the dropped call, and wonder if I have handled this right. At that moment, nevertheless, I realize there is still a way for me to pull off an "exclusive" while doing all the right things—from a legal perspective. It's the same phone Collingwood had given me for the pending FBI raid on Miss Mercy's place. The same phone that has a quality video recorder on it. I don't even hesitate to think about ethical considerations; I just can't let this story slip away.

"Luther."

He's been quiet and still but has remained alert. He slowly looks at me. "Yeah?"

"You doing okay?"

"Yeah." He just sits there, tired but not in any more pain as long as he doesn't move.

"Luther. I'm going to use the video recorder on my phone and ask you a couple of questions while we're waiting." I don't pause to ask permission--I just hope he makes sense. I flip on the truck's interior lights and hold up the phone towards him. "Tell me why you tried to rob that cab driver."

Slowly, but not painfully, Luther gives me thoughtful, award-winning material. "I lost my job a couple of weeks before that. God hate me. I got family and I got to take care of my family. Those cabs collect a lot of cash by the end of the shift, so I went in and was just gonna take it. That driver was so scared he made me all crazy and my hand was shaking and the next thing I know the thing went off, so I just run outta there. Didn't even know where I was or where I was goin'. I just run. No way I really wanted to shoot him!"

Post stops his narrative to catch his breath. But I sense time breathing down our necks: the law will be here any second now. "Luther, what has it been like running all this time?"

Post pauses, which makes my heart flutter for a moment--as a reporter, I want more material. Then, he answers. "It ain't been no basket of chocolates out there." I've heard that one before. "I stayed up in the woods when the weather was good and in that haunted house when it was bad. But the hardest part was finding some food. I checked out behind restaurants, climbed up come apple trees, and got some help from some people I won't never say who they are." I hear the ambulance sirens coming now. "But it just seem like I couldn't catch no breaks, no breaks, no breaks...kept gettin' hurt, and then this," his head nods down to his wounded shoulder. "I'm just worried 'bout what will happen to my family."

Okay, that's a wrap. I hit "stop" on the recording. Two sheriff's patrol cars pull in behind us. Lights flashing. Leaving my dome light on inside the truck, I wait for The Law to tell us how to proceed. It only takes a moment for a deputy to command us from behind. "Get out of the vehicle and keep your hands in the air!"

Luther doesn't move at their command. I pause also, to make sure we move in concert. But this concert is over, and Elvis has left the building. "Can you make it, Luther?"

One more sigh. "I don't think so."

"I will make sure nothing bad happens." For the first time, Luther Post does not spit disbelieving venom at me. Tiredly: "Okay, man. Okay."

He sits, I stand. Opening the door I step out--and reach for the stars, with my feet on the ground. Facing two deputies with trained firearms, leaning forward in a firing position behind their car doors. Measuredly, I call to them. "He's hurt--been shot. He can't get out of the truck on his own."

I am commanded to walk back towards the deputies, and open the tailgate to give them a better view of the truck. One of the deputies then moves out, flanking the open driver's side door, to carefully check for danger. It doesn't take long for him to find that Post is helpless. The emergency medical technicians from the ambulance--waiting a quarter-mile away--are called in and they haul him away, sirens and lights going full speed.

The deputies have holstered their sidearms but before they ask me questions, I ask to make a call. It's not to my lawyer. It's to our Assignment Desk. An intern with a squeaky voice picks up my call.

"Newschannel 99, Where 'We're Right 99 Times Out Of 100, this is Lynette!"

"Hey, uh, this is Wilson Gamble... ." I feel I had better do more to identify myself to an unpaid part time college-age volunteer. "I'm a reporter at the station. You need to send someone to Malpractice Medical Center right away. Stake it out. Luther Post is being transported to the emergency room right now!"

"Someone? Who is this Luther Postal? And, um, what was your name again?" Squeaky Lynette tries.

Oh no. Walter Wilson has met his newsroom equal. Gotta think fast--what are my options? I'm disconsolate. But then, nirvana. "Never mind. Just get me Marshall Hurd."

"Right now? On the phone?"

Great Day In The Morning. "Yes. Right now. On the phone--but, don't transfer my call, you may lose it. Don't use the intercom system, either, to call him over, because you will probably electrocute yourself. Just shout the following words--out loud, I mean. Ready? Yell: 'Marshall, come to the telephone' and hand him the handset."

The intern sounds a little unsure, as if I had insulted her. But at least sensing the urgency in my voice, she does not argue and does what I tell her. In fact, I can hear her distant and querulous attempts to gain Hurd's attention. "Marshall Hurd! Marshall Hurd!" Naturally, Marshall Hurd takes his time, and the seconds pass painfully. Likely he feels the need to finish his game of "Angry Birds" before tending to his work duties. Eventually, he picks up the handset. "It's Marshall, who is this?" he tries, tiredly.

"It's Wilson. Gamble. Get somebody over to Malpractice Medical Center--Luther Post has been shot and is in an ambulance right now on his way in to the E.R.!"

Despite his native ambivalence, that ignites a fire under Hurd, who occasionally gets in touch with his inner Cronkite. "Got it. I think Curtis or Cortez or whatever name he goes by can be good to go. We'll be there."

"I recorded a quick interview with Post on my smartphone. Do you know if we can upload that into our editing system?" I ask, a bit breathlessly.

"Is it a work phone or your personal phone?" he asks.

It takes me a moment. "Work phone!" I almost shout.

"Then it should be compatible," Hurd pronounces. "Even if it's not, we'll upload it to MeTube video sharing website, and then download it into our editing computer. We're good either way."

Thank goodness. Who knows what Juan will get at the hospital--video of an ambulance or the family or law enforcement. But that end is covered for my Surefire Emmy-Winning Report at 11. Except...I have some pressing legal matters.

"Come with me, Mr. Gamble," instructs a deputy.

"What for?" I ask.

"We need to get your statement down at the Sheriff's Department before we can prosecute anyone. Including you, maybe, for aiding and abetting a wanted felon."

I play the "reporter" card with them. "Okay, here's my cards on the table: I'm a reporter with Newschannel 99. I'm simply covering a story, and I've been working directly with Sheriff Dank on bringing in Luther Post. In fact, I just did--and I think you ought to give me a medal and a very long vacation...and let me come in tomorrow to give a full statement. I have a deadline to meet."

The deputy pauses to ingest this logic. While he's off-balance, I simply start to dial another number on my phone. Naturally, it rings, like, 23 times before Collingwood's voicemail picks up.

"Carl!" I almost shout. "Luther Post is under arrest. And I am in the, uh, presence, of deputies who think I am somehow culpable. I need you nowwwww," I try, persuadingly.

The next couple of hours are a blur. The deputies hold me for a short time at the guardrail, and take a brief statement. Then, evidently instructed from above, they wordlessly let me go. And without a word on my part, I jump back in to Big Blue and shift gears straight in to town, to Newschannel 99.

It's close to 10 o'clock before I roll in through the cast iron double doors. I have no idea what video or sound I will have for the 11 o'clock news. "Marshall!" I call out. "What do we have?"

Catching my meaning from across the newsroom, he replies, "Whatever you have on your phone!"

Just as I suspected; it's all on me. I glance around to decide where I can work. "Okay, try to get me an engineer. I'm in Edit Bay 3!" I announce to the newsroom. And I head that way, alone. So now I have to figure out how to plug in my phone to our editing computer, and then transfer the video of the interview into our software editing program, edit it, and send it electronically to the Control Room to be played during the newscast. Oh, and then go and write a script.

I'm sweating out this routine in the edit bay when eventually I realize someone is watching over my shoulder. My Guardian Angel, of course, Carl Collingwood. Immaculate, even dressed down, in a blue track suit with a white stripe on the legs and arms.

"That bite, 'It ain't been no basket of chocolates out there,' could be a cold open," he suggests. Meaning, we start the newscast with that quote, and then the anchors read their introductions to the story. "I'll go tell Hurd to put it in. You do the rest, but come to me as quick as possible to check your script. Cortez is going live from the hospital after your report."

"Alright, bozz." Working as fast as I can, I edit my cellphone interview and marry it to some hospital video sent in from the live truck by Wash and Cortez. I pick two more "soundbites" from my quick interview with Post. This will not be a "package"--a pre-taped, all-inclusive report. It will be a report with me presenting the story live in the studio during the newscast. Cortez will provide "team coverage" by establishing his presence at the hospital. He's not the only one holding vigil. Sheriff Dank smells publicity in the air and is standing by.

Script approved by Collingwood, five minutes to spare. I race in to the studio and find my spot, which this time is a single-person news desk-- more like a podium, really--to the right of the anchor desk. Its close enough for one of the studio cameras to fit me and the anchors into an angled shot. And yet another camera can focus solely on me.

Everyone is smiling--even Adams--in the knowledge that we are about to kick some serious news-butt. The video is ready, scripts are printed, everyone is in place--nothing can go wrong now. The LED clock on the set displays 10:56:30. Three minutes to air. Ah, a rare moment of television peace and harmony. Then, over my IFB, Hurd asks, "Wilson, where's your tie?"

My...what? Oh no. I reach for my neck. Open collar. I took off the tie in the truck when I stopped at the gas station in Otis Mills. "I forgot it in my rush. I don't have time to get it."

"You know we have a dress policy," Hurd reminds me.

"I'm wearing a blazer..." I try. This just shouldn't be important.

"I don't want to have Arlen yelling at me for putting you on the air looking like this," Hurd carps. While the clock ticks.

Adams is Mr. Thoughtful, but without a dozen roses. The eternal Alpha Male, ready to remove competition if necessary--sees an opportunity. "Marshall," he speaks into his microphone to the Control Room, "you could just have the anchors read his copy, before we throw to John out in the field."

"No!" I insist. "I have been working this story for weeks, it is mine, I'm involved, I am breaking it!" I argue forcefully. I get some backup, sort of, from an unexpected source: Fern.

"He's right, Marshall. Why don't you ask Carl--he's there in the control room, right?"

Silence. I guess Hurd and Collingwood are chatting, and I already know what the answer will be.

"Okay Wil. You remain in the show. But this is on you and Carl if Arlen or Ivory Eriss gets bent out of shape." Amazing what becomes important in a television newsroom. I ought to be able to break this story in my birthday suit, much less my business suit. Knowing that Collingwood stands with me erases any uncertainty.

No time to think. The clock has expired.

"It ain't been no basket of chocolates out there," starts the somewhat distorted cellphone video of Luther Post. Followed by Fern and a reluctant Adams, while more video plays.

"The fugitive. He sees only darkness," starts Fern.

"But in that darkness, fate moves an uncompromising hand," follows Adams. "And an Attempted Killer comes to justice--only here on Newschannel 99! !"

I shift slightly behind my podium, unhappy with the sensationalism. Quickly touching my naked neck as one would check an unopened zipper. A studio camera silently faces me. For some reason I feel threatened, like it's a mute mugger. The central studio camera is focused on Fern and Adams. She starts.

"Luther Post, wanted for attempted murder in the shooting of a cab driver several weeks ago...is finally in the hands of Reproach County Sheriff's deputies tonight."

Adams' turn. "But first he's in the hands of doctors at Malpractice Medical Center."

The Technical Director in the control room calls up a "three box," a graphic screen that viewers see that includes the two anchors in one square, Cortez in another, and me in a third. Adams continues.

"We have team coverage tonight, including Newschannel 99's John Curtis at the hospital with Sheriff Don Dank, who has been closely involved in the manhunt."

Back to Fern. "First we turn to Newschannel 99's Wilson Gamble, who was there when Post was finally apprehended. How was he discovered, Wil?"

I'm faintly surprised by Fern's informal handling of my name, but that implies that I'm accepted now by senior staff as a part of the team. At least by Fern.

"Luther Post's long run from the law ended the way it began, with a bullet wound. He was shot in the shoulder by an unknown person in the woods near Otis Mills. Having been in contact with him previously, I met with him tonight and called for help. But it took four minutes for that help to arrive, and in that time, I turned on the video recorder on my smartphone."

Boom. Take package. The Director presses a button, my report rolls, and the rest, they say, is history. As long as this tape plays through to the end, I already know it will win me some awards. That's what many in TV news live for. To participate in, and win, annual broadcast news awards competitions. Associated Press, Edward R. Murrow, Emmy, sometimes Society of Professional Journalists. For me, it isn't even a conscious thought, but it is a certainty. With this material, I am a lock for an S.P.J. and an A.P. award...and at least a regional Murrow. Possibly a national Murrow and maybe even an Emmy. Considering in advance how I will accept these honors, I touch my open collar once more and hope I don't get fired tomorrow.

There are some anxious moments when a light goes out on Cortez during his liveshot at the hospital. Fortunately Fakir Johnson--called in to run the liveshot--has set up full three-point lighting that drenches Cortez in fluorescence, so no one has to rage against the dying of the light. He interviews Dank, who provides three clichés and a platitude for good measure. But that is oh-so-much-more than the competition has tonight.

It's an impressive "win" for Newschannel 99. After I leave the studio and return to the newsroom, the first thing to do is turn to the bank of television monitors. Collingwood is already there. Channel 11 Eyewitness News actually carries a report in their "B" block--the second segment after a commercial--that Luther Post has been "reportedly" caught and they are in the process of "checking to confirm the story." They are watching us--and quoting our report! I high-five Collingwood, who glows in the thrill of a News High.

"We will have to make some room on the Awards Wall after tonight. Too bad it's not a Ratings Month," Collingwood adds. February, May, July, November...really the only months that count in TV news. These are the windows of time in which the Nielsen ratings service determines our fate--by telling us how many people are watching, and what percentage of those watching television are locked on to our channel.

Ratings Month or no, we will honor the television tradition of celebrating a Win like this. It's almost an obligation to retire someplace for drinks. It was my report...so it's my call. And it's gonna be Marcini's. Everyone among the nightside crew shows up except Adams, who mutters something about "A party of one" and goes out gentle into that good night.

Call it "blowing off steam," or perhaps, "team building." Yeah, that's the ticket. Just don't call it "an excuse to go drink"...even if it is. We make for a merry crew at Marcini's. Even Jeanette Nettles and Sherman Follicle and a couple of other daysiders make an appearance. Calzone does not. Several smartphone photos are taken before the hour grows too late for such things. A disc jockey spins jubilant tunes on speakers set on "11" all over the joint. It almost feels like a Friday on this Wednesday.

Katie, the reporter from Channel 11, happens by our table. So does a bottle of Canadian whiskey accompanied by a couple of *Daily Repellent* reporters I don't really know--bearing fake smiles and $8 haircuts. They all want to know how I managed to haul in a story that really just fell in my lap. But I'm circumspect. There's much more to this story and I'm a gonna maintain my lead on it. So I'm careful to switch to cranberry juice before my jaw gets lubed and loose. Which gives me a strange and unexpected rush--I can get by tonight without the hard stuff!

Eventually, the juice gets noticed--it is really, after all, a Wednesday. The music turns as sullen as Billy Squier and everyone drifts away. It really is Wednesday, after all. I get a text from Calzone apologizing for not making it--she can't explain right now. Then, the music stops altogether. Marshall Hurd and I are last out the door. We part ways in the parking lot. Curiously, moments like these I find to be a time of reflection. And again, my thoughts turn away from the St. Pauli Girl to Megan.

Geez, here we go again. Megan, spontaneously materializing. She's appearing soon--in person, isn't she? Guess I'm a little hazy here. When, exactly, is that? I find myself hoping its sooner rather than later. To introduce a little stability in my life, right? Or, something else? Megan is hardly stable, I argue to myself. But she is downright and utterly loyal to me, someone a drifter can count on. Like a dock that this dinghy can tie up to. Ugh, that metaphor needs to change. I fire up Big Blue, flip on the CD player, and allow my mind to go blank. But even the music conspires against me:

I keep a close watch on this heart of mine

I keep my eyes wide open all the time

I keep the ends out for the ties that bind

Because you're mine, I walk the line

I drive home, still riding on that news high and now, on another burgeoning emotion that I will try to keep tucked away. For now.

In television, not all deadlines are driven by the start of a newscast. The newsroom is a brusque, intense place in the last few minutes before the morning meeting. Reporters feel the pressure of bringing that strong, "turnable" story idea to the table. The decisions made at the meeting determine a reporter's fate. Will they have the lead story, or be buried in the B-block? The search for lead stories is a nonstop struggle. Except for today. Waking up, I already know what I'm going to do. The only question is: what angle to take in following up on the Luther Post story? When I arrive in that brusque and intense newsroom, however, I'm hit hard by another compelling human story--one that the viewers won't see at home.

I pull up past the weedy dirt drive and enter the Newschannel 99 parking lot. That is becoming familiar enough. But something I come upon there is not. A grim gaggle of familiar faces has circled like a wagon train on the sidewalk out front of the building. Nettles, Johnson, Strum, Wash, and two or four others look downcast. Warden the Doorman watches like a sentinel from his glassy portal lookout post. Anyone approaching the scene would be curious, but possibly reticent to impose on what looks like a wake. I'm a reporter, though, so any native reluctance has been long obliterated having approached scores of similar settings.

Parking next to a news staff rental car, I walk up. "Somebody die?"

"Yeah," affirms Nettles, but does not elaborate. I'm left to linger in a brief silence. Johnson steps in.

"Gretchen walked into Arlen's office first thing this morning, and there's been a lot of yelling in there since then. We've been trying to figure it out."

"Do you think she's giving her notice?" I suggest.

"Yeah, that's what we were thinking." Johnson decides: "I'm going back inside." Everyone else does, too. We find the newsroom nearly silent, even though the entire staff is at their work stations. Well, it would be silent except for the slamming of drawers and cabinets at the Assignment Desk. Its Calzone, packing. Angry expression, hair at an all-time frizz. No one else approaches her, so I do.

"What can I do to help?" I ask.

"Answer the phones. Monitor the scanners," she replies, more to herself than me. But she seems a little relieved someone is acknowledging what's happening here.

"What's happening here?" I ask, trying to sound light-hearted. "I hope you aren't taking any station-bought ink pens with you." Calzone doesn't smile or slow down, filling a cardboard box with her personal stuff. Her speech is clipped in her hurry as well.

"Gave my notice. 30 days. Arlen flipped out. And you know, I don't exactly mince words. So he went off to get Warden a minute ago. Or, get permission to get Warden."

"To escort you out? Today?" I can hardly believe it.

"Yes indeedy. You remember how he treated Phillips when he quit." Calzone slams home the lid of the box, and hoists it. "But I don't need anyone to show me the door." Her work space is left just as untidy as ever, but there's just fewer objects strewn about. One of them is a "5 Years of Company Loyalty" plastic clock. The second hand, I note, is stopped.

"Let me walk you out, instead of Warden," I offer. She doesn't reply, but tilts her head at me before making her way through the newsroom. Brief parting exchanges with a number of people on her way out. Most recognize her departure as inevitable, acknowledging also this is apparently the way things are done here now. And they are considering what their exit will look like someday.

Her conversations are brief, so we hit the big double doors to the back parking lot fairly quickly. I help her load the box and two or three other loose items into the trunk of her car. There might have been more to say at this moment, but that chain of events is missing a link or two.

"Artie is heading to Carolina," Calzone starts. Ah, speaking of the Missing Link. "And I was planning to follow in a month. Now we'll just go together."

"When did you decide to go?"

"Last night. Artie has family there, I know a few people." She looks away, then goes for her car keys. "We flipped a quarter to decide where to go. It was tails."

"Flipped a quarter? I'm not exactly rooted anywhere myself, but isn't that kind of random?"

"You know, Wil, I've been flipping quarters my whole life on things. When it lands on tails, it's usually time for a change."

"Good luck. The newsroom will suffer. And we will miss you--I will miss you." We hug, and my instant impression is that her frazzled hair doesn't feel rough, but instead is delicate. But then she pulls away, gets into her car and once in it, pulls away. Not another word.

No need for me to dwell, either. Yes, apparently this is the way things are done here now. I turn and head back into the newsroom. As the natural light yields to the artificial, I see that Arlen Rapier has convened a staff meeting. Everyone is gathered near the Assignment Desk. Reporters, producers, photogs, anchors. Everyone. Rapier, looking a little wild-eyed, pushes a long strand of combover off his brow. As I approach, I catch up with him mid-sentence. "...go onward and upward. And I already have hand-selected a replacement."

"Hand-selected?" whispers Follicle. "Is that like 'hand-dipped' or 'hand-rolled'?"

No one responds. We want to know who was hand-selected. To move instantaneously like that, Rapier must have promoted from within. But who is it?

"There will be an adjustment period, but I think my choice will adapt quickly," continues Rapier. "Norman Wallflower, come up here please."

Why? I wonder--for a moment. Then it dawns on me, even as Wallflower, at this pre-determined moment, slouches forward to join Rapier.

"Norman has done a terrific job over the years leading our videography department. But now that it is being folded into the news department, this is a perfect opportunity to move him into management here in the newsroom. I have every confidence that you will give Norman the respect he has earned."

Absolute silence. Not even Follicle has words to respond to this crowning folly foisted upon us, even with the seemingly impossible-to-miss opportunity to hurl an insult using Rapier's ironic final words. The slowest, laziest, least-engaged employee of the television station has just been handed the fastest-paced, most complicated job in the news department. Everyone sullenly drifts back to their work stations, accompanied by a low but threatening murmur.

That's when I realize Collingwood is not in the newsroom. Walter Wilson happens to head in the same direction as me, muttering something about his breakfast burrito, Mayor Fulsome Parody, post-it notes, and "i-Trade" online investments. Concluding with: "And don't you think Norman will be really great handling everything at the Assignment Desk and he will probably put up some of his pictures from The Cage and I think he will be. Great, I mean."

There is no good reply, geo-politically, to his question, which isn't rhetorical but isn't really meant to be answered anyway. So I ask one of my own. "Walter, where'd Collingwood go?"

"Well, I think Norman will catch on just fine but Carl probably doesn't even know yet that he's getting the job because after we had our breakfast burritos together and heard all the shouting in Arlen's office Carl took one look at what was happening and went up front I think to go see Miss Eriss even though it's way too early in the day to hope to see her because she has her own private time until later in the morning."

I shake off Wilson and head back to my cubicle to try to make sense of the succession of beanballs thrown at us today. Worst part is, the clock is ticking on this news day. As a staff, we should be designing more award-winning coverage of the Luther Post story. But Rapier has disappeared, Collingwood hasn't appeared, and Wilson is still looking for a new pad of sticky notes. Into the abyss strides...Aimee Flotsam. She actually claps her hands for attention.

"Okay, so this has been a big day so far but we still have to, um, do the news." She flips her hair back with a jerk of her head. "So can I get everyone over here for the meeting?"

Big words from a pipsqueak voice. But this actually makes sense to the newsroom. Thank goodness for normalcy. But then, as we roll up chairs to the meeting table, I note who stands at the front. The trio looks, one to another, before convening: Flotsam to Wilson to Wallflower. Not quite as inspiring as Tinker to Evers to Chance--they strike this baseball fan as more like Miskus to Smalley to Addison Street.

Speaking of which, it's time for us to pitch our story ideas.

"So, what do we have today?" Flotsam asks.

In this surreal atmosphere, I'm glad to have the security of a lead story. "Well, I plan to follow the Luther Post story."

"That's old news," states Flotsam. "We aired that last night. What else do ya got." Declarative, not inquisitive, statement.

I'm now stunned beyond comprehension, so I actually try logic. "Yeah, we reported his arrest and everything. But there's so much more to this story to tell today... ."

"He's not getting out of the hospital, so he's not going to be booked into the jail or make a first appearance in court. So there's no 'hook' here," asserts Flotsam. The other members of The Brain Trust nod slightly in agreement. My head, and hands, start to shake in disagreement.

"Listen. It's a huge story. We don't just stop covering it because we ran a report last night at 11. We need to have multiple reporters on it today to continue to own this story!"

I look around for some support. Nettles throws in. "At the very least we have to revisit what we ran last night, to hammer home how we are leading everyone else on this."

This isn't the full endorsement I am expecting.

On the ersatz speakerphone, Fantana makes a lot of undistinguishable noise. I wishfully believe it to be supportive. Then Follicle chimes in. "Wil, this isn't all about you. While it's a good story you are personally tied up in it and that's clouding your judgment. And there could be other lead stories out there for tonight."

Flaxen "uh huh's" in assent.

I seriously cannot believe my ears. Briefly, I wonder if he feels threatened by another journalist in the newsroom, and is taking advantage of this opportunity to neutralize me. I reply, "Sherman, this isn't about me. It is about a major news story that everyone is talking about, one that everyone has been talking about ever since I got here."

Drawing on all her many days and weeks of journalism experience, Flotsam still seems unconvinced. "So, what's the follow up?" she asks, doubtfully.

I gush out, "The full story of how he managed to remain on the run. I can talk with his family. The family of the cabbie--what's his name, Chowdhury. Ask people around Otis Mills if they feel safer now that this 'dangerous' and armed fugitive is no longer wandering around their neighborhoods."

Wallflower starts to see the light. But some things are still dark. "Where would you go live? It would be repetitive to be at the hospital again."

"But the point is, this is an ongoing story! It didn't just end last night! Even if we did go live at the hospital, it would make sense because Post is still inside." My voice is starting to rise.

"Settle down, fella," Wallflower barks. Nice to see the job change hasn't altered his condescending manner. Nevertheless, that just about puts me over the edge. I catch myself, realizing that if I say anything at all the result will be nothing but bad. I simply don't know how to respond.

"Shut up Norman," commands Tyler Hubbell. "This is obviously our lead story." Nettles makes a noise in agreement. But, will wonders never cease? Tyler Hubbell backing someone or something other than herself? My ballooning anger immediately deflates. And then Collingwood enters the newsroom. He looks a little flustered--a hair or two is out of place--but he's still all business as he strides over to our gathering.

"So, how are we covering the Post story today?" he starts. "We really killed it last night, but we have to own it today, too." Nail, meet coffin. Flotsam's position is swamped.

At the end of the day, we do a credible job covering the Post follow-up story. But the story I want to hear is from Collingwood, who had not explained his disappearance during the early controversy. But I have learned that he can be elusive when the mood strikes. So, I head home. I can be satisfied with winning an early battle with The Brain Trust, and with our reporting today. But the fact that it took a battle in the first place is a major concern for the future.

It's about this time that I normally hit up a convenience store for a little liquid refreshment. Especially after a newsroom battle. Things are different tonight. I hold a strange sense of triumph after last night's voluntary trade from beer to cranberry juice at Marcini's. I enjoyed having a clear head. And I don't want to lose this power, however ephemeral, over a companion that has held the upper hand for so much of my adult life. It's not that I have come to some crisis with my steady drinking, I tell myself. This just seems to be an opportunity to show who's boss. So, to keep busy, I trade my wingtips for a pair of Air Jordans, and head out to Meatmarket Health & Fitness to work some machines and the treadmill. Then, a late dinner, a little baseball on the television, and bed at the Haversack House. Who's afraid of a big bad Wolfram cocktail? Tra la la, not I.

The end of the work-week comes with the end of our "Continuing Coverage" of the "Developing Story" of Luther Post's arrest. At least, the excitable full screen "stingers" with music proclaiming these exclamations will stop, because Alan Rapier and Walter Wilson don't bother watching the weekend newscasts. Oh, as a news department we will stay on top of the story, when Post actually faces a judge and eventually a jury. For now, though, it won't self-perpetuate just because it once was a "Big Story." Once he is released from the hospital, I promise myself to get attorney Randy Sillocan to take Post's case, and visit Luther in jail, to make sure all deals are observed.

The weekend poses other problems. For me, I mean. With few other distractions, I am lured to the liquor. Only, I've come to the conclusion that I don't want to go this route any more. If I can help it.

Friday isn't too hard. I remain late at work, and go out for some Chinese food with Hurd. His faintly racist vocal impressions of the wait staff make me regret this choice, so I exit as soon as possible. It occurs to me the minor league Tree Sloths may be playing at home tonight so I head to the franchise's aging stadium. Tonight, I'll buy my own ticket, instead of selling my soul to Hornswoggle.

Named after a one-time drifter who became amazingly wealthy after winning a military contract to manufacture napalm in the 1960's, the old Charles Veacey Stadium was actually a horse track in an earlier life, complete with cupolas over the grandstand. No wonder they're building a new stadium. But for whom? A "crowd" of about 90 or perhaps 100 people (counting the ushers) is on hand, which leaves me feeling as lonely as a cloud in the Charles. So, after nobody scores for three or four innings, I round third and head for home.

Back in my room, I remain in baseball mode. Flipping on a sports channel on the TV, I briefly notice the Johnny Bench baseball card in the mirror. But my reflection in that mirror starts to resemble Ron Tompkins right about now: struggling to get by while somebody else makes the most of their skills to succeed. Who from Newschannel 99 will make it big in our business? Tyler Hubbell will. She has the cool, beautiful look that News Directors and endless delusional TV news fans dream about. And she's savvy, in her way. Enough so to parlay those looks into some nice job promotions. Jack Phillips, although he's ex-Newschannel 99, now: he'll move up. We'd all rather be lucky than good. He's cornered the market on luck--and, he's a pretty good reporter, to be fair. And, thanks to his skill level and vague ethnicity, Cortez may make it as a "network affiliate" reporter. That's the "reporter" who provides the voice and on-camera appearance for national stories the network offers to local affiliates. It's not real reporting, usually. It's a simple regurgitation of information others have compiled. But in these Politically Correct days, anyone sporting a non-Anglo look and who can speak English fluently can quickly catch the eye of the network Masters. In another sign of the times, the same forces in this Trade that made him change his name, will eventually make him change it back.

Baseball, again. I wonder what kind of luck Tompkins had. He had been a prospect considered worthy to share a Topps card with Johnny Bench. From there, though, what changed for him? On my smartphone I type his name in the web browser, not finding much. Just his sparse Major League playing statistics: two years, a handful of games pitched. No wins, three saves. He had, at least, made it to the top. Even if it was for a cup of coffee in The Bigs. Back here in my room, I start considering a cup of something else.

My attention drifts again to the reflection in the mirror. And the image of Megan standing next to me. Whoa, wait. She disappears. Megan? Okay. I need to call her, right now. Of course, I have to head out of

Haversack House to make a telephone connection.

"Hello!" It's an exclamation rather than a question.

"Hi Megan, its me."

"Wil? Oh, hi! I'm going to the movies tonight!" she reveals proudly.

"Really. What are you going to see?" I ask, playing along, although I'm desperate to ask a different question: When are you visiting?

"Oh, hm. What is it? I can never remember stuff. But I know it..." as she dithers, I wither. I need to know. "Let me ask." Distorted sounds on her end of the line. "He says its 'The Other Side Of Darkness,' that movie about someone who comes out of a coma."

Wait. Suspicion torments my heart. "He" says? This can't be a date, can it?" Megan," I try, slowly, "who's 'he' you are talking to?"

She doesn't immediately answer. I immediately jump to all sorts of conclusions. Until she does, um, actually answer. "The guy at the ticket window, I guess," she finally replies. Considering who Megan is, I smile and relax.

"Megannnn," I admonish. "Is Mamie right there?"

"No...." she answers. "A guy named Fran. He's, um, French or something." She asks off the phone, "Right, Fran?" Back to me. "Tique. Fran Tique. That's his name. I met him at the library the other day. He's nice, but not like you!" she exclaims again.

Thank goodness for that. But, what does that mean? I don't want to take chances. "Megan?" No answer, indistinguishable noises on my phone. "Megan!" I try louder. "When are you coming to see me?"

No answer. I hear rustling but happy noises. Sounds like people walking into a movie theatre, I think. Video game noises, a popcorn machine, voices talking. Where's Megan's voice?

"Wil?" plaintively.

"Yes!" I exclaim.

"The movie is about to start." Pause. "OOH, look at that!" I hear as her voice turns away from the phone, towards the noise generated by someone or something else. Megan has lost contact. I press the red "disconnect" button, and quietly sigh.

The beast in me

Is caged by frail and fragile bars

Restless by day

And by night rants and rages at the stars

Saturday morning isn't too hard. Although I'm used to awakening to some level of a mid-grade hangover, I didn't expect a light headache this morning. But it's there, in the sinus system. An inner voice tells me this isn't fair--I didn't earn it this time! I feel just a wee bit sorry for myself. This is forgotten as my right calf explodes in a cramp. Yow! I leap out of bed with only one thought: to stretch that muscle and relieve the shooting pain. Once the episode is over, I ask myself, why did this happen? Dehydration is a common trigger of cramps. Let's see, what dehydrates the body? Running a marathon. Sweating heavily working in the hot sun. Ingesting diuretics--such as my favorites: coffee and alcohol.

Let's start with coffee, to which I have given myself a long time ago. Now my challenge is to keep myself busy. For a while it's not too difficult to distract myself. There are errands to run: banks and supermarkets and auto parts stores. But with no long-range plans, time slows as the sun moves into the third quarter of the sky.

Now, almost fran-tique to stay away from the juice, I whittle away a couple of hours driving out to Otis Mills, Marberry, anyplace that is connected with Luther Post. Places not connected with Luther Post, as well. I find a blood donation bus in a church parking lot in Khalishes. To kill some time I stop and give a pint.

But I want to go buy a pint. Or more. Resisting the notion that Weekends Are Made For Michelob grows tougher as the shadows grow longer. Driving back to Haversack House, I realize that I should have made plans tonight with someone, anyone. Even Walter Wilson. On the other hand, maybe that's going too far. Patting my pants pocket for my wallet on the drive home, I slowly pass by two liquor stores...but somehow manage to keep going. The clock ticks way too slow for my taste. And...oh, for a taste of something. I never gave this drinking thing much thought before. It was just there, a companion. But now it's my chaperone. With a long stretch of empty evening in front of me, I start to compromise. Just a couple of drinks, I tell myself, while watching a baseball game on television. Nothing hard, I reason, maybe just some, let's see--wine coolers. Ugh: wine coolers? No thanks for that support. But Big Blue slows, almost independently, in front of a convenience store. There's beer there, always handy in a pinch. As I park, the image of Megan briefly materializes in the passenger seat, entreating me to find some other treat. But her image dissolves again quickly, and all I'm left with are the demons assailing me.

Okay. The battle is a lost cause, for now. I made the effort, right? Saturday night's alright for fighting...something other than this beast in me.

19

Finally, I have the opportunity to get some questions answered. Collingwood calls at noon Sunday and invites me to meet him at a pizza joint up by Oak Ledge. My hangover is manageable and I am relieved at the prospect of doing something other than just killing time. I order up a slice of pizza and a slice of life at Newschannel 99. Collingwood doesn't waste any time delivering.

"Rapier is on his way out," he starts, fondling a table-top dessert display. Stunning news, but I know better than to be elated. In television, the rule of thumb is, "Better the devil you know than the devil you don't know." No matter how bad your current boss is, The Next Lucifer may very well be worse. Just look at the procession of winners we've had in my short tenure here. And, I have almost figured out how to cope with This Present Darkness.

"So, what happened?" I ask, curiosity tempered with the tone of experience.

"Honestly, I drew the line at his battle with Gretchen Calzone. He abused her, verbally, in his office. Even put a hand on her, which is the same as threatening her."

I snort. "You didn't go to Ivory Eriss with just that, did you?"

Collingwood regards the dessert offerings. Tiramisu, perhaps? before digesting my question. With a sudden resolve, he responds. "Nope. Did not. I went to her with certain other evidence to convict Rapier."

"Such as?" I ask.

"Well. Obviously he's been involved with Britnee Flaxen. I happen to have," he regards the dessert display once more, "some photographic evidence. A boss with an employee, exerting 'undue influence' upon her for career preference. Does not look good."

I cringe at the "boss with an employee" reference. But--photographic evidence? That sounds sufficient to me. "How did you get the pictures?"

Now Collingwood looks away. Regards a chalkboard sign covered with the day's specials. His answer isn't terribly surprising. "I know a P.I. who owes me. Asked him to tail Rapier. Wasn't that difficult. I gave him Rapier's home address and, well, Rapier is a sloppy housekeeper. Sometimes keeps his blinds turned open."

Ewww.

"So, with Ivory Eriss, what's the catch?" I ask.

Collingwood pauses again. Regards his manicure now. "I am retiring."

"What? Why in the world do you have to retire?"

"Let's just say that Ivory has had enough of me actually preserving standards in a television news operation. It's a pain in her neck and doesn't actually add anything to the bottom line."

My voice gets a little whiny. "But why would you have to give up your job when you have all the evidence you need on Rapier?"

"Because there's a secondary issue."

"I don't care how many issues there are. I really don't want to remain here if you are leaving."

"Oh, but I really hope you do," his eyes lock in on me. His next words take the wind out of the sails of my defiance. "The secondary issue is, she wants you to be the next News Director."

The pizza falls out of my hand. I almost faint. But manage to slowly gasp, "What did you say?"

"Ivory Eriss wants you to be the next News Director."

"News Director?" Does not compute." Me? Why me?"

"Seemed odd to me at first, I'll admit, but she apparently thinks she could, uh, work with you."

Gulp. "There is no way I want to be a news director--anywhere in the world--much less at this operation."

"But I hope you will take it," Collingwood urges. "In any case, my time is up here. Marie brings home a nice paycheck. I'm close enough to retirement, and can always teach over at Reproach County College." A tight little smile appears. "Maybe put my boat in the water finally. Or, do a little political consulting with our buddy Marvell Thyme." Just kidding. "In any case, if I have to leave, I'd really rather have someone like you in charge. You would be the first trained journalist actually running this newsroom in a long time."

"What happens to you if I say, 'no'? Is the deal off?"

"Nope. Either way, I'm retiring. For you to leave the station also would feel like we lost this battle entirely."

No pressure. My head is whirling. Honestly, I can't imagine Collingwood not working in a newsroom somewhere. It's like hand and glove. Then, I think of what I'm up against. "I can't do something like this without you,

Carl. Who would I turn to for some help? I've never been interested in management...I can't imagine how to even get started."

"First, pick up your pizza off the table. Second, you need to go out and hire a competent Managing Editor," he offers, his smile twisting ruefully. "They can be your conscience and guide. And," he adds, "I know exactly who that person is."

"Who is that?" I ask, somewhat hopefully.

"His name is Abel Toller. Former network, like me. But was N.D. in Burlington, Vermont when his news operation was shut down. I give him a high recommendation."

Name seems familiar. TV news is a small world. I think for a moment, then it comes to me. "I think I worked with an Abel Toller in Odessa-Midland."

"Is that right? It's possible. He's been around."

"So have I. Well, why don't we make him the News Director, then?"

"He was a disaster as the man in charge. Couldn't make personnel decisions."

I think of some of the blockheads I've worked for, and Abel Toller doesn't sound any worse.

Collingwood continues. "Couldn't fire anybody because he worries too much about peoples' feelings. At one point he had become close friends with one of the producers, who later became the Assignment Manager. Passable producer, awful Assignment Manager. After six weeks it was abundantly clear this guy couldn't do the job. But someone else had been hired to take his old job, so he couldn't go back. After six months the place was in shambles. He constantly missed stories, often assigned two reporters to one station car, demanded way too much from our news contacts--ticked them all off. He even failed to report a station gas card that went missing, and the next bill came in for, oh, a thousand stolen bucks or so. But Abel wasn't, you know, able to cut him loose. Finally the guy forgot to renew the station's auto insurance--for the entire fleet. Sure enough, somebody got in an accident, and it cost the station a small fortune. So they shut down the newsroom, and everybody lost their jobs."

This finishes off what was left of my appetite. "Remind me, then, why we want him here?"

"He won't have to make those kinds of calls. You will. And he is a big league journalist, with the same level of news sense that I have."

That almost puts me on the road to assurance. "But if Ivory Eriss wanted to get rid of you, why would she let me hire anyone I want?"

Collingwood's smile morphs into a grin. "That's the final part of our deal. You have hiring and firing discretion--but be careful of how you manage your budget. That's where she can--and will--put the clamps on."

"Meaning, I may have to move dollars from a line item for fuel or bonuses and into someone's salary category in order to get him."

"Something like that. See, you catch on quick--you're gonna be just fine. And, you can call me as often as you want."

"So, when is this all supposed to happen?"

"Rapier will be terminated immediately," Collingwood starts with an unhappy smile. "But the station has to advertise the job and go through the motions to be compliant with government hiring guidelines. So that will take at least a month. In the meantime I will act as the interim News Director. Then, I will announce my happy retirement and you will get the promotion."

"Carl," I hesitate. This is a lot to ask of me. He knows it. Yet, Collingwood is the type of guy I would hate to disappoint. "All this is a lot to process. I haven't said I'm willing to take this job. It may take the next month to figure it out."

"Good. You remain true to character. It wouldn't be like you to jump at this. But I think you will eventually see the value of taking over."

That'll be the day. Then I add, "One last thing, though. I am not giving up on you. I need you to remain in the newsroom, for a lot of reasons that I think you must already know."

Collingwood looks away, stoically. "Perhaps. The odds are really against you--and I'm okay if the Fortunes oppose us." Then he warmly smiles at me. "But, I confess that I'd love to re-energize a newsroom with someone at the top who cares about journalism. It doesn't have to be me."

My thoughts nevertheless turn to imagining what life at Newschannel 99 may become without Collingwood. There are images I don't want to picture, others I think I could learn to enjoy. The pay raise would be more than enough to leave behind Haversack House forever. Dealing with Ivory Eriss is a great big question mark. But I happily consider the prospect of putting an end to The Brain Trust.

The station's plan to consolidate the Videography and News departments is a telltale sign of how our jobs are all going to change. Reporters will be shooters and shooters will be reporters; dogs and cats living together...mass hysteria. But this will be a party of one, babe. Traditionally, we worked as pairs: grandly titled "videographers" and "reporters." What used to be known as "one man bands," used in a pinch, has been politically-corrected to "multi-media journalist." "MMJ." Almost as cynical and sterile as the "Going Green!" campaign. Meaning reporters like me will have to learn how to shoot our own video. And videographers like Wash will have to learn how to report. Two jobs in one. It's a malodious bouquet from the station Front Office to the Newsroom. The accompanying greeting card might as well read, "Content may suffer, don't worry. Just fill time. The Sales Department will handle the rest."

Journalists and Videographers are all there for the Morning Meeting. But there's no mass hysteria. The newsroom is strangely quiet, and it's not because there is one fewer employee. Rapier is indeed absent. His only parting gift is an instantly-outdated ENPS message directing staff to stop reading the online version of the *Daily Repellent* with the hopeful but forlorn object of suppressing their website readership numbers. His closing folly is followed by a management missive to staff that ends with the classic closing line: "We wish him well." Flaxen sits by herself, mum.

I can't quite put my finger on the subdued tone in here. The scanners seem pretty quiet, the TV monitors are muted, the coffee pot has fully perked. It is very quiet. In years gone by, the steady clacking of the cast iron newswire teletype machines provided a steady and comforting undertone. Yet, they have gone the way of the open reel video player. And, I surmise, the television journalist.

As we hasten to gather together, Flotsam struggles to get Fantana on the speakerphone. Finally, she gives up, asks Wallflower for help. He pretends to not hear her and wanders off to find a "Snackers" candy bar in the Break Room. The corner of my mouth curdles up in anticipation: Oh, I can't wait to fire him.

Then, I stop, and think. First, I have to be The Guy In Charge to fire him. Then, I have to consider the person and his family, not just the lazy caricature of an employee. Also, I wonder: what has his complete body of work been like at Newschannel 99? Another conflict here. Love to get rid of Wallflower, but I am a little troubled to possess that much authority.

A stray engineer wanders by, hoping to snatch a doughnut from the box that usually adorns the meeting table. Perfect. He won't get away scot-free this time. The price: fix the speakerphone. Caught, he bends to his new assignment.

There is a low murmuring of disbelief over the announced departure of Rapier. But no one addresses the group as a whole over the matter. It's not considered much of a surprise, the way News Directors implode around here with the frequency of a "Spinal Tap" drummer. Some quiet questions are asked about "who the next victim will be" and I instantly suffer more misgivings.

A few strips of duct tape later, Fantana is back online. The engineer is offered a second doughnut and speedily disappears.

"They move out of the newsroom so much faster than they enter it," observes Follicle to no one, to sage nods of agreement by everyone.

Collingwood is in charge but the Assignment Manager should run the meeting. Wallflower wanders in at the other end of the newsroom, chewing the last of his candy bar. Everyone turns his way. Enjoying the attention, naturally he takes his time. Meandering towards the meeting like a three year old who doesn't want to come to the dinner table. Collingwood is ready to make a meal out of him." Norman, why can't we hear the scanners?"

Oh. So, that's what was missing from the newsroom soundtrack. Wallflower simply shrugs as he approaches the table." I turned the volume down. The noise was bugging me."

"Noise?" Follicle asks. What do you mean, 'noise'?"

Wallflower sounds whiny and annoyed. "All this back-and-forth about a raid. And a chase. Maybe some shots fired, something like that."

Suddenly there is plenty of noise in the newsroom. Exclamations ranging from surprise to wonder to disgust. It's clear we have to do three things: find out which law enforcement agency is responding, whether the incident is real, and where it is located. The Assignment Manager should know all these things almost instantly. But Wallflower is eliminated from the Search Party quicker than a small college facing the Top Seed in the NCAA Tournament.

Collingwood, Follicle, and Nettles start working the phones. Wilson fires up the scanners and is ready to take down details on his sticky notes--all while swallowing the last of his breakfast burrito. I hit the internet--checking social media sites like Tweeter and Facespace, as well as our competition's sites. Some news outfits post stuff online as soon as possible, to claim being first with the story. Thank yewwww.

How useless is that? It's like giving away what you know...to the competition, and practically nobody else. This, despite the fact that the towering preponderance of news consumers won't know anything about any news story until they watch the evening news. All that online posting does is alert the competition--us this time--to news stories we otherwise might have missed.

Sure enough, even as our contacts start providing information, the internet comes through as well. Nettles strikes gold first, learning that there has been a bank robbery in Cheeseport that didn't go as planned, and as a result a pair of thieves are holed up in a neighboring bookstore. The police have surrounded the place.

Collingwood mobilizes his resources like a general officer moving units on a battlefield. Nettles gets the lead assignment, due to her connections in Cheeseport. Wash goes with her, to shoot and operate the live truck. Even in this new economy, reporters can't run their own liveshot. Not yet, anyway. Flaxen is sent out as well, to provide sidebar reporting--and maybe learn a little at the same time.

A problem arises, though, before they hit the road. Nobody placed the usual order for rental cars late last week, so there are no station cars in the stable. So everyone has to schlep on out to the scene in the live truck.

The scanners are now back at full volume, but Wallflower doesn't seem to be. He's snickering at a video on WeTube when Collingwood approaches. There's gonna be a showdown.

"Why don't we have any rental cars ready for us this morning, Norman?" he asks, viciously.

Wallflower is no shrinking violet. And he's had plenty of evasive maneuver practice. "I'm new at this job, Carl. Nobody ever told me that was my responsibility," he replies defiantly. With a tone that implies it shouldn't be, either, baby.

Whose responsibility did you think it is...Norman?" Collingwood returns. He includes "Norman" just to sound patronizing, and succeeds.

Norman doesn't rock that easy. "The News Director. It was Arlen's idea, wasn't it?"

Haughty, Collingwood knows better than to be dismissed this easily. "Apparently. But the keys are kept--and handed out to reporters and shooters--at The Desk. Someone has to return those keys to the rental agency at the end of each week." He grins, mercilessly. "Who did that on Friday?"

Pause. Then, brainstorm. "We are supposed to return the keys every week?" Wallflower answers. "Did we do that last week?"

It's a standoff. Collingwood gives Wallflower a meaningful look-- meaning, his time is about up. Wallflower looks away. Not just because he comprehends this, but because he does not face facts well.

With this opening salvo fired at Wallflower out of the way, I turn my attention to today's story. First, the problem of finding a shooter. Fakir Johnson's two week notice has expired. He is now gone, still hoping to land that gig at the production house, or possibly somewhere else. Don Wash and one other shooter are assigned to work that lead story. Sturm is on vacation. Wallflower isn't going anywhere, which leaves...Billy Fotch. Sheesh. I'm almost ready to begin those one man band videography lessons right now. I have learned that it's easier to find Fotch by calling his cellphone rather than searching the station.

"Hello?" he answers on, oh, about the 14th ring.

"Billy, its Wilson Gamble. We have to head out on a story. Where are you?"

Pause. "Umm, let's see. I'm in the drive-through at the bank. Or," I can picture him scratching his head, "the drive-through at McDaniel's. I'll let you know when I get up to the window."

"Uh, that's okay, Billy. Just get back here in ten minutes and we'll head on out."

Another pause. "Get back where?"

The abbreviation "OMG" was created for this guy. "Back at the TV station. Where you work. You remember where we're located, right?"

"Oh, ha ha, yeah," he rejoins. "See you in a few." He tries to close the conversation.

Not so fast, my friend." No really. Do you need directions?"

"Ah, no. I've got it," he tries to sound positive. I let it go for now, and hang up.

The story I'm developing starts out at the interstate. At the "Pump 'N' Run" gas station near the Placid Place Motel where I once stopped to fill up when I first came to Filterboro. The station with the creepy, jowly clerk with a camera. Turns out, the man has a hobby. Imagine those motorists who have waited perhaps one exit too many before stopping for a potty break. When they exit the freeway here, in a bladder-induced panic, he videotapes their hurried entrance to the store.

Apparently he enjoys their frenzied expressions, particularly when he intentionally points them in the wrong direction, and then sends them to a restroom that is locked. His undoing is posting these videos to the internet. They have become viral sensations on WeTube, which has many onlookers laughing but his victims screaming bloody murder. Eventually his computer's IP address was tracked down by a private investigator working for a wealthy lawyer in a neighboring state. This morning the lawyer exposes the clerk by telling everyone in Filterboro media his name and contact information. Hilarity ensues, as you might imagine, and I can't wait to be a part of it. The scramble is on to get the best story possible, and we reporters are like stock car drivers, all at the same starting line.

Only, my crew chief is AWOL. My arrangements are made, the manbag is packed, I'm fueled up with coffee. Still no Billy Fotch. I punch his digits, try not to imagine punching his head. No answer. Just a vaguely-female computerized voice telling me "This mailbox is full." I try texting. "Billy get #$%&@ to NC99 asap!!!" That goes off into the ether, emptily. Is anybody listening? There's no reply at all.

Time's a-wastin'. I don't want to start thinking about my options but I had better. There aren't many. Options, I mean. If Fotch is driving around looking for a McDaniel's drive-through in, say, Cheeseport, there aren't any other shooters. Guess I'm going to have to pick up a camera myself and develop my One Man Band skills a little earlier than I had expected. I grab a camera and a magnetic "Newschannel 99" sign to throw on to the side of Big Blue, and head out.

The long, harrowing, frustrating details of this day are better left unrecorded. Coping with focus, iris, filter, and other professional camera functions that are unfamiliar to me, I record two hours of video. Three minutes and 12 seconds of that excessive total is actually acceptable to use. The audio is another thing. A brief interview with a victim who happens to live in Oak Ledge--but who has to be convinced to talk--might as well be straight out of *Birth of A Nation*: No sound. It turns out the camera had been left with the engineers to repair a bad microphone connection and it was handed back without being fixed. No explanation.

The microphone does work on one other interview, so I have just enough material for a "mini-pack." That might as well be a television euphemism for "No story here folks, keep moving along."

Fotch may have eventually returned to the station but not while I am around. Good thing, or else my mugshot would have led the 11pm news on every channel...for committing Fotchicide.

Well, I woke up Sunday morning

With no way to hold my head that didn't hurt

The fog of sleep and dreams is slow to disperse the next morning. But I slowly realize it is a new day. Ah, but an old one, at that. My head throbs, from the temples around to the base of the skull. Rotating around, I note a glass bottle of something brown, about half empty. No. Maybe. Yes. I am disappointed, but tell myself that Billy Fotch has no doubt driven better men than me to drink.

Day? Um, Tuesday. Well, what time is it? Okay, I'm not yet late, but am on my way to being late. And getting there, to work I mean, won't be easy. Gotta start moving, no matter what.

Then I fumbled in my closet through my clothes

And found my cleanest dirty shirt.

Then I washed my face and combed my hair

And stumbled down the stairs to meet the day.

Although I am in no condition to harbor a grudge when I finally arrive at work, Fotch does perhaps the smartest thing in his entire life: he calls in to work sick.

This Tuesday isn't all frowns, however. The workday ends with one of those hilarious and totally-unexpected moments that can only happen in television. Cortez--aka Curtis--has developed a story about a telephone scam that targets senior citizens in the town of Khalishes. It's a light news day so even though Cortez is working nightside, Flotsam wants him to "front" a brief live report for the 6 pm news. Sending a live truck to Cortez means he won't have to spend a lot of extra time coming back to the station before going back out to complete the fieldwork for his full-length report at 11. That doesn't mean, however, that this will be easy for him. Cortez has to quickly shoot and edit together some video for the looming 6 o'clock report. And what he ends up showing makes Filterboro news history.

Per custom, we watch at the bank of television monitors. On the Newschannel 99 monitor, Adams and Cortez soon appear in "boxes" and Cortez begins his report. He's standing in front of an Eastern Union money transfer station. "At least seven people from this area have contacted the Reproach County Sheriff's Department about a man who calls them and says he's a bail bondsman in another state. Claiming the victim's 'grandson' has been arrested and is in jail, he asks for bail money. Without really checking into the story, the worried grandparent comes here, and actually sends money to a stranger."

Roll tape. So far, so good. Cortez continues his live description of the scam, and the investigators' reaction to it, under video. All fine and dandy until we notice that one of the shots, up for three seconds or so, is what passes as a random smartphone. But it is really not random. Its Cortez's smartphone. With his phone number prominently displayed for all of the viewers in Filterboro to see. Every one of us watching in the newsroom flinches. You do not want to display your digits for every crackpot in our television market to see. Because they will call, without compunction, at any hour and for every reason.

"It was on only for a coupla seconds," Nettles reassures herself-- and everyone around us. We shake our heads hopefully.

But that's just the beginning. Having evidently recorded very little b-roll for his report--so far--the same close-up of Cortez's phone appears in this report two more times. To us in the newsroom, knowing what is about to happen, this elongates his otherwise-short report to the equivalent of, oh, eternity. I scan the newsroom and spot about a dozen staffers wearing the same facial expression: "Uh oh."

And Cortez instantly pays for his mistake. Back on camera, finally, he tries to wind up his report. "Investigators have traced some of the calls to a phone number in Jamaica... ." Suddenly, Cortez freezes. All of us watching freeze as well. Live, on camera, Cortez reaches into the breast pocket of his blazer, pulls out his phone, and looks at it while it rings and vibrates. His ringtones: "Heavy Young Heathens."

"Yeah, he's about to get punk'd six ways to Sunday," declares Follicle. We are transfixed in horror, as if watching the Hindenburg going down. For a moment, Cortez stares at his phone, uncomprehending as to why a stranger should call him at this moment. Then, he actually presses the green "answer" button and puts the phone to his ear. It takes all of one millisecond for his eyebrows to shoot up at least six inches. Gamely, returning to the fact that he's still on live television, he snaps out of it and somehow regains his composure to finish his monologue. When he signs off, we all breathe a sigh of relief.

Follicle loves it--and he can be just as juvenile as the next unreformed frat boy. "I'm gonna send him an anonymous text message!"

A couple of us go over to his desk, where he retrieves his personal phone—an unknown number to Cortez. His chubby thumbs move slowly but resolutely over the tiny keypad. They spell out, "I wud luv to be a part of YOUR phonescam--ANY DAY—mr. yummy!!"

Next day, Cortez quietly approaches me. "I guess I won't make the mistake again of showing my digits to the whole world. But what do I do about all the weird phone messages I've been getting?" he asks.

"Don't answer them, just let it blow over," is my response--without looking in the direction of Sherman Follicle.

Cortez lowers his voice. "I got, like, seven phone calls and 11 text messages." I nod evenly, trying not to smile. "But I gotta admit I'm kind of interested in the person who called me 'Mister Yummy.'"

The week moves on. Collingwood points out that the News Director position has been publicly posted. Unnecessarily, I point out that he is much more qualified than me. Ignoring this, he announces that interested parties must submit an application form and resume, just to follow protocol. And, perhaps, a vial of Holy Water, to exorcise the apparent demons associated with the job. Am I really interested? I have avoided thinking about this too much. But events this week, from the laxity of Fotch, to Wallflower's silenced scanners, to the frustrations of One Man Banding, are three big problems that push me in this direction. Maybe I can make a difference. I'm no idealist. All our problems will never be fixed. But, two out of three ain't bad.

Then there is Rapier's legacy to deal with: "Rock 'n' roll writing." Flunking English--her Mother Tongue, and stuff--Flotsam persists with this idiotic form of communication. For good measure, she adds her nightly Malapropisms and typographical errors. "Naive" instead of "native," "panties" instead of "pantries." Fern corrects most of them before the newscast. Adams rarely thinks things through. As a result, in various newscasts, he calls out the "Squat Team" instead of the "Swat Team," chooses to "Stay the curse" rather than "Stay the course," and convicts someone of "man laughter," not "manslaughter." Then there are the non-error errors. Such as when Flotsam notes excitedly in a script that the first day of summer just happens to coincide with the summer solstice. And both coincidentally fell on the longest day of the year, too!

Numerous phone calls and emails of complaint make no dent in the assured demeanor of dimbulbs who possess just enough newsroom savvy to believe the laughter is directed elsewhere. This, too, might be corrected, I realize.

I know Collingwood's desire for our newsroom. Wish I knew what Gretchen Calzone would think about it. Or someone else I can trust, someone with perspective. Unreasonably, Megan comes to mind. Obviously, she's not right. Jack Phillips knows this place, but of course he's now with The Competition. Who could I just talk with on staff at Newschannel 99? Not Follicle. He's simply too aloof. Asking him for any kind of help would put me in his debt, a position of weakness I don't want should I become his--nominal--boss. Running out of options. Then, Jeanette Nettles comes to mind.

Its Thursday night. Not a weekend night with its potentially wild-ish overtones. Not an early weeknight, with a more business-like attitude. Just the right balance between the two. Nettles, with distinctive features and a boyfriend working in the Providence-New Bedford DMA, may be a little tough to approach. But she's got common sense and can tell the difference between a "come-on" and a "come on! let's go talk."

"So, what's on your mind?" Nettles asks while reaching for a nacho chip. Its "90's Night" and Marcini's jalapeno nachos are loaded, so here we are. Not getting loaded, but sipping a couple of high-end imported draughts. I tell myself that this drink is permissible, it's a part of the price of doing business.

Instinctively, I feel Nettles is trustworthy. Of course, any good reporter is that--at least, to sources. They have to lock up secrets, play poker-face with politicians, keep their word with sources. Loyal as a suspect to his alibi. Nettles has earned the trust of many reliable sources around our market, who regularly provide her with news tips. Guess I'm about to be one of them. But I need to ease in to it.

"It seems to me that we think a lot alike about how we approach our jobs," I smile. Nettles bobs her head slightly. Okay, good. "And I respect your work, as well as your common sense." Another bob for the guy. Get to the point. "We've had a run of pretty poor news directors, as well as decent people leaving... ."

"Only to be replaced by utter incompetents. Yeah, I feel that way, too." Nettles sips her beer, waiting on me again. On the same page, I turn one.

"Okay, yes. Every move has taken us further downhill, one step at a time. Rapier leaving might become an opportunity to reverse course. But I want to know, do you think there is something worth saving here? How vested are you in this?"

Nettles is younger than me, has only worked in two newsrooms. But she can assess the talent, the situation, just as well as I can. And she does. "Actually, I think we have a few decent people left. Start with Collingwood." I flinch, but disguise it by reaching for a nacho. "Lavinia is strong and smart. Adams may be high half the time"--Okay, so that's what happens to him--"but he pulls in the viewers. The reporting crew isn't bad. Follicle, you, me, even Cortez pulls his weight." Pause, pull on the beer, while she considers further.

"I don't know how the photogs are going to make it as One Man Bands, but Wash at least is smart enough to try. Our producers are pretty bad, but that's a common problem. At least Hurd knows the basics, I just wish he cared more. And I wish so many capable people hadn't been replaced by weak ones."

It's my turn to nod. Her assessment equals mine. I throw out, "Who is John Galt?" and this time, Nettles doesn't bob, she smiles, at the reference. But she wants to know where this conversation is headed.

"You are going to think this is crazy," I answer, "But it appears management wants to reach all the way down to...me...for the job."

Nettles' beer is suspended halfway between promise and fulfillment. "For which job?" she asks.

"News Director," I try out loud for the first time.

Beer meets mouth. Gulp. "News Director," she tries out, incredulously. "Of Newschannel 99? Do you really want it?"

"That's what I'm trying to figure out. My instinct is 'absolutely no way.' But I'm not getting any younger and this could be a passport to a new career. You know, something that pays better." Nettles bobs again. "More importantly, though," my voice sinks to Conspiratorial Level, "I would have hiring and firing privileges."

That's a game-changer. We both know that in our survey of capable employees, several names have not been mentioned, including "Walter Wilson," "Wallflower," "Flaxen," and "Flotsam." If I have my way all could become "jetsam" pretty soon.

Nettles looks away, then offers another assessment. "I can see you in charge. And it would be nice to have a journalist running a newsroom, not a bean counter or 'professional administrator'. Do you really want to deal with personnel issues? Or the budget? Making sure the cars are rented? Or constantly dealing with Ivory Eriss?"

My turn to gulp, so I turn to my beer. "Ah, uh huh. Right. I mean, I'm not sure. Which is why I'm talking to you. And Collingwood. And anyone I think can give me some serious perspective on this. It is not the career path I had imagined, to be honest."

"Well, what did Collingwood say? With all due respect, isn't he the most obvious choice for News Director?" Yup, Nettles hits the mark.

"Yes he is. But, he supports the idea. There is a complication." It's my turn to look away.

"What?"

"Collingwood is retiring. Or, is being forced to retire. I'm his compensation package, the knowledge that someone he mentored will actually take over the newsroom, with some real authority."

Now Nettles just looks at me. Her straight, practical hair, usually pulled back behind her ears, tumbles out on one side. She poofs it away with a quick burst or air.

"I'm sorry, Wil. This is just insane. Collingwood is easily our greatest asset, and you tell me he is willing to trade in his job so that you can be News Director?"

"Hey, look, Jen, he didn't ask for it to happen, and neither did I. The way he puts it, he's out, no matter what. I'm the consolation prize. And he has recommended someone strong who is ready to step in to take his place as Managing Editor.

"Who's that?"

I tell her about Abel Toller, the entire deal, finishing with another question. "How long are you gonna be at Newschannel 99?"

"Well, my contract has another year in a couple of weeks. When I came here, I signed a three year deal." There's a note of resignation in her voice. Actually, not just a "note," but an entire measure of music. "My outs begin in six months," she continues, more brightly. Outs. That means, contractually, she is able to leave early, if certain conditions are met. Such as, if a station in a specific market asks for her services. Or, if she is willing to pay a set sum to Newschannel 99 for her release. That's often thousands of dollars. Yup, indentured servitude is alive and well-- in television.

Nettles shifts on the wooden booth bench, as if she has suddenly realized the seat is uncomfortable. "So, Wil. Are you talking to me about this because you want my opinion about whether you should take the job? Or whether I would work for you? Or are you just trying to win me over?"

"I only want your advice. The dynamics will change if I become the boss, there will have to be a distance between me and everyone else." Which, it occurs to me, puts me in a lonely place. "I didn't have any designs on management, and a lot of me thinks it would be ridiculous to even think about sitting in that office. But then I look at the positive changes I might be able to make, and wonder if I shouldn't bite the bullet and take it. So, I need some perspective, and I couldn't think of anyone better than you for that."

A sip of beer follows a nacho chip. Nettles looks off to the side as a Smashing Pumpkins song plays on Marcini's speakers. She turns back to me. "I'm glad you think that highly of me, Wil. It's just," she is distracted by a chunk of pepper that drops off another chip, "It's just that, I guess I've grown used to coping with the dysfunctional leadership at this place. It's become tough to think of Newschannel 99 in terms of, say, 'professionalism,' or 'benevolence'. So, yeah, I'd love it if someone like you took over. Honestly, though, you are still pretty new here. I'm not sure how that would go over with a lot of older people, people like Tyler Hubbell or Sherman Follicle or Walter Wilson."

The irony doesn't escape me. Macula was new--to Newschannel 99. Rapier, also. Purefory would have been new, if he had decided to stick around for more than ten minutes. But she's got a point. It would be difficult to be *promoted* ahead of my more senior colleagues.

"I hadn't really considered that, yet. But if you are right, I guess that means I would stand a better chance if I have the support of people I respect, like you." Nettles looks at me, considers. Tough to read her, so I continue. "Look, I didn't ask for this. You won't support me, I may not take it. I can't take it. There are other reporting jobs somewhere else, so I will just leave."

"No, no," she answers quickly. "I'm behind you all the way. Considering the alternative, and how badly the place is managed, I think it's just that I'm more worried about your sanity than anything else." I smile: Another good point. "You can only bang your head against a wall so long before you have to be hospitalized."

After only two drinks I'm back at Haversack House. A lot on my mind, but nothing that can be resolved. Afraid I won't be able to sleep, I have a remedy handy. Already feeling a little loose, I run roughshod over any resolution to limit my drinking. The bottle opener goes to work, the baseball game appears on the TV, and a couple of innings later I am out at home.

> Well, if they freed me from this prison,
>
> If that railroad train was mine,
>
> I bet I'd move out over a little,
>
> Farther down the line

Just barely do I make a presentable appearance at the next Morning Meeting. Did I remember to knot my necktie? I'll find a mirror later. The Brain Trust temporarily relegated to Flunkey status, Collingwood calls the meeting to order. I'm assigned a high-profile visit by a member of the Royal House of a small European nation who happens to hold a major stake in one of the Filterboro tobacco operations. Its considered a pretty big deal but kind of fluffy, news-wise. She's a Duchess, a cousin to the son of a figurehead.

"Why me, Carl?" I ask, stepping in to his office.

"I want to raise your profile here a little. Have everyone see you in a featured role. So that everyone sees that you are considered important. The smart ones--the people we care to impress--will start putting two and two together. Then, you as News Director won't come as that much of a shock.

News Director? Who said? I'm still in a small state of shock. Gotta shake it off, though.

"Uh, who is this Princess, anyways?"

"She's not. And she isn't Annie Oakley, Dorothy Lamour, or Madame Chiang Kai-Shek, either. She's a Duchess. Just a member of a small country's Royal Family. But a big deal in Filterboro, any day of the week." He hands me two cardboard credentials contained within clear plastic sleeves. I throw the lanyard of one of them around my neck--it's a necessity for today's work, but a reporter's keepsake for tomorrow's cubicle display. The other credential has Wash's name on it.

A tightly-scripted series of events controls the Duchess's movements. As a result, I'll report live during the Noon newscast at one event, and front a package live at another event at 6. A lot of work. But its Friday, so both reports will lead. Hmmm, I like the idea of "featured reporter."

By 10:30 Wash and I find ourselves at a hotel conference room, where the Duchess will address the Chamber of Commerce. Wash has to stop by a department store to buy a necktie, which is required for all ladies and gentlemen of the press. A mixed security team of local and European officers first admits the media, allows us to set up our equipment, and then escorts us back out again. They want total access to our stuff so they can completely sweep the empty room. Only then are we allowed back in.

Five stations from neighboring markets join our four local TV stations, three radio stations, two newspapers, and one live-blogging internet reporter on a shaky set of risers in the back of the room. Most of us take notes as the event begins. Then the Duchess addresses the full house. But no matter what she has to say, as the clock strikes twelve she turns into a pumpkin to me and eight other television reporters. We form up in military order in front of our assembled cameras. Shoulder-to-shoulder, we prepare to perform our liveshots. Of course, to viewers of all nine stations, we are individually supposed to look like the only reporter on the scene. But that's difficult when the guy on my right has a shoulder as sharp as Gordie Howe's and the young woman on the other side has breath as livid as a plate of old seafood. Yeah, just a little distracting. And then, just as we are all about to go live--leading every newscast in the state--some self-important functionary from the Duchess's entourage decides to come back to monitor what the ladies and gentlemen of the press are saying about Her Somewhat Royal Highness. Remember, temporary risers are just that; they jiggle and bounce like a trampoline with each step taken. Magnified by the highly-sensitive video equipment we all use. Every step you take creates nothing less than a small earthquake on all our cameras. Although a couple of photogs momentarily try to stop her, the functionary wanders about self-importantly, and we all bounce. Disconcerting, but I tell myself that its part of the deal. And I must admit the sheer number of camera crews really energizes things.

The Noon newscast has started. In my IFB, which is working nicely today for a change, I actually hear my cue: I am live. Even as I start to address the camera, however, tremoring on the riser-trampoline, I can hear an exasperated shooter for another station stage-whisper-hissing, "Get the blazes out of here, lady!" Except, he didn't say "blazes." The Royal Functionary (sounds like a 1960's novelty band) finally disappears under a barrage of hooting antipathy from a firing squad of shooters. Unfortunately, most of this is picked up on my microphone as well as eight others during our simultaneous liveshots, shown throughout the region. Instead of reports covering a stately address about "what the world needs is a return to sweetness and decency in the souls of its young men and women," the average viewer sees what appears to be a natural disaster occurring live on a Seismic scale. Accompanied by shouted epithets.

As he wraps up the cables afterwards, Wash is philosophical about it. At my expense. "Guess this one won't go on your resume reel, huh?" Heard that one before.

After a day that is a royal pain in the neck, I drive slowly home to Haversack House, mulling over three invitations, of sorts. One, the job as News Director. Two, the still-obscure visit by Megan. Three, the sound of a light tropical breeze blowing over the open neck of a bottle, calling my name.

I put that aside after tiptoeing up the stairs. A new 4x6 card at the door advises guests to "Please Stop Tromping Heavily On The Antique Staircase, Which Is More Valuable Than Any One Boarder." All the words are capitalized. I trip lightly past The Troll, whose open door quickly slams shut as I touch the upper landing.

Survey of my room: someone else's four poster bed, nightstand, air conditioner, dresser, desk, chair, another dresser. My belongings are here, but compared to the history and stolidity of the place, they are quite temporary objects. My clothes, books, laptop, manbag all seem like children's' Colorforms vinyl cutouts, temporarily clinging to the permanent backdrop. They belong in a different dimension, and so do I. Some light enters the room through the pasted-on window skyline. This still creeps me out, so I keep the heavy ceiling-to-floor curtains drawn together most of the time. A 15 watt bulb feebly glows above, supplemented by every table and floor lamp I can drag in and fire up.

Unfortunately, they illuminate a bottle and glass on the double dresser. Hmmm. They are reflected neatly by the mirror behind them. That's the way I'd like it: neat. Just a salivating sip. Or two. Or seven. The thought of the bitter, tingling sting of that first sip makes me breathe more quickly, through my mouth. My silent Master calls me.

Whoa, whoa--its early. This is dinner-time, right? I glance at the Ron Tompkins card in the mirror. He was a pitcher. When pitchers are done for the day in baseball, it is said they take a shower. A good idea. Maybe a cold shower, put a damper on this desire that I'd like to gain a little control over. Time to formulate a plan. Its Friday night, so be careful. Take my time getting cleaned up, head out to a family restaurant, enjoy a slow dinner. Find a movie at the theater. Back home late--too late, too tired, to dive into a bottle. For one night, at least, it's a winning formula.

20

Dreamy mists clear from my mind as I regain consciousness. A night of sporadic if alcohol-free sleep does not produce an energetic awakening in the morning. My head remains foggy while I perk some illicit coffee. Food is banned in my room, but I'll risk another 4x6 card. Unnhh. Muscles tight, I stretch arms, neck, legs. Do a couple of knee bends. Nothing seems to clear up the haze. But I tell myself I'm supposed to feel virtuous to start this day--no booze in the system. So, why do I feel no different than every other morning after a couple of drinks? Not happy.

Desperately, I consider the big, gaping hole of a weekend in front of me. No plans, few errands. Nothing, really. Nothing, that is, except that bottle and glass on the dresser. Thankfully, I know I can hold off until at least the afternoon. Gulping my coffee, I consider what to do. Always with that bottle lurking over my shoulder, forever extending an invitation. I shake it off for a moment, decide to go grab a newspaper, see what's happening this weekend. Tree Sloths baseball? The infamous dog track? Some musical performance, movie, or arts festival? Anything to take my mind off of the monkey on my back.

Repeating last night's tactic, I start by taking my time in getting ready to meet the day. But only 45 minutes have passed by the time I rub my clean-shaven jaw while finding my keys, and close the Boarders' Door to Haversack House behind me. I'm still unsure where I will go to pick up a newspaper. Probably the Cluck Bucket over on Allergen Avenue. I can get a chicken breakfast sandwich and a newspaper out of a machine. These small plans now formulated, I step just a little more resolutely towards Big Blue. Feeling a little better, I start humming quietly. Not sure why. Then I realize I'm actually hearing music. I stop humming. It's something funky, streetwise, but with a basic melody. Takes me ten seconds to realize: it's my phone. So few calls come in that the ringtones are still unfamiliar. Fumbling to retrieve the device and determine how to activate it, I quickly grow worried I won't be able to answer before the call is redirected to voicemail. Not even worried about who might be calling.

"Hello, its Wil," I manage.

There's no immediate greeting on the other end but I hear ambient noises that are vaguely familiar. Background voices babble indistinctly, ignoring a louder but even more distorted voice--a public address speaker. Also: a steady machine noise, brute but not engine-like.

Occasional clunking or thumping. This noise-stew runs the course of five or six strange seconds, and I consider hanging up. Another couple of seconds, and I look at the phone to see where the "End Call" button is located.

That's when a clear voice speaks to me. "Wil? Hi Willie! Are you there, Wil? Hii-iii!!" This last greeting is two notes, in happy up-down notes.

What? I look at the phone and then push it so quickly back in place that I mash my ear kind of hard. "Megan?" I ask, while telling myself--of course, dummy, it's no one but Megan.

"Wil, I'm here!"

She sounds exuberant. So, I do, too. "Yes, I hear you, Megan! At first, you know, I didn't know who was calling."

"It's me! And I'm here!"

This suddenly takes on a different dimension. "Yes, I hear you," I repeat. But I'm thinking that her tone of voice means something different. "Where...are you?" I try, cautiously.

"At the airport," she answers, briefly. "Wait, there's my luggage!" She disappears from the conversation once more, apparently chasing down a suitcase or something from a baggage carousel.

Airport--oh my. Which airport? Megan returns, triumphant. "I'm here!"

"Where?" I ask. But the answer is already becoming apparent.

"Your airport! I just got Meathead from the, uh, guy who works for the airport. He looks a little nervous in this pet carrier thing but can you come get us now?"

'Get you now? 'I immediately realize there's no room to pause to calculate or think things through.

"Uhhhv course, Megan." That buys me about a two second pause just to catch up with this development--and its implications. But I can't leave her hanging. "I'm, uh, already on my way to my truck right now, in fact. Tell Meathead to hang in there. I'm on my way!" I try to end brightly.

Now I know how my weekend—and possibly more--will be occupied. That's good. After ending the call, however, there is a lot of stuff to figure out. The airport is maybe 15 minutes down the interstate so there's not much time to think. First, where to lodge her. Obviously she's not staying at Haversack House, although on the Harebrain Scale it would be a pretty good match.

Ouch, that's mean. I recant the thought. The Placid Place Motel was where I had previously considered renting a room for her. My concern is whether she would want to stay there. She countenances finicky and shifting standards. But I seem to have little choice. Before putting Big Blue in gear I check the mobile phone for a number, and press the digits.

At least half a dozen rings later a vaguely familiar voice answers.

"Placid Place, can I help you." A statement. The male voice doesn't sound bored, just...present. I quickly go through the files in my memory bank, and come up with the name. Too quickly, though.

"Is this Little Jerry?" Oops, didn't mean to add Miss Mercy's adjective. But I can almost hear a smile as the voice becomes more attentive.

"Only Mercy Haversack calls me that. You must know Miss Mercy."

Stupid, I kick myself, as I kick the truck into gear. "Yeah, this is Wil Gamble--you referred me to her boarding house a few weeks ago."

A pause on his end. Then, some recognition. "Yeah, you're the TV news guy. I got a commission for that. So, what do you want?"

Briefly, I wonder what other services Little Jerry might provide on the side. "I need a room at the hotel."

"Things that bad for you at Haversack House?"

"No, man. I have a friend unexpectedly coming in to town today and I need a room starting tonight. Do you have anything available?"

"Sure, sure," Little Jerry purrs through his missing tooth. "A friend of Miss Mercy is a friend of mine. Normally we don't take reservations but I'll make sure to hold a room for you." I hear him tapping away at his Front Desk computer.

"Jerry--Its a lady. Make sure it's clean, okay?"

Pause, chuckle. "Sure, my man. Will do."

This logistical problem solved, I'm now free to actually think about the more confusing elements of...emotion. That is, emotion and Megan. Megan and me, that is. My last image of her rears its ugly head. Wearing more paint than a Winslow Homer canvas. That crazy skin-tight spandex. Teased hair and heels. Now, I realize my right foot has fully removed itself from the accelerator. Big Blue slows to about 35 miles per hour. On the interstate. Suddenly conscious, I lower my foot again, slowly.

You know, in fact, I'm not really much of a romantic. I've grown accustomed to my own face. As I grow older, I have come to um, appreciate, my independence. My time is pretty much occupied by work and baseball and booze. Sometimes in a different order. It's true that I've been looking to end that last relationship. Maybe if I spent more time thinking about someone other than myself... .

This hits me pretty hard as I exit the freeway, heading straight into Airport-Land. But, now that we are both a bit older, where does our, er, "relationship" stand? We started out as friends which, I suppose, turned into a case of Puppy Love. When she left, it ended, then for a while turned strange. Fortunately, over the phone it matured into a distant but knowing Friendship. After her hiatus, I have felt a tad paternal while remaining deeply and fundamentally attached to her memory. Lately, however, I have found Megan popping into my thoughts at odd times: at work, at home, at drink. Almost like...a companion. Not the odd "character" Megan, nor the "college friend" Megan. The "current" Megan, at least the one I imagine. No one else has ever intruded herself into my thoughts on such a regular basis. So, as I struggle to weave my way through traffic to find a spot at the curb at the Arrivals Terminal, I determine that I'm going to think about Megan as a "special" friend...allowing myself the option to become more than that--if she feels the way I think she does.

In these last few moments before I expect her to materialize, I worry again about Megan's appearance. Embarrassing? But to be fair, then, what do I look like? Quick check in the rearview mirror. Faint lines under the eyes, crows feet. The eyes are purple--blue and red. Slight bags underneath. Ugh. Okay, squinting takes care of both, for now. Nose just a tad bright at the end. Signs of many long nights. Hair parted on side, suddenly strikes me as out of date. I reach to lift and muss up my 'do, just to add an edge to my "look." Realization: I have something to prove to Megan, also.

Finally I find a spot to stop near Arrivals for "Aerosplat," Megan's airline. Another nervous check of the mirror, and I exit Big Blue. Can't wander far, though, because of security rules. Typically, this isn't the busiest airport in the region--a spoke, not a hub--but apparently a couple of flights have arrived following Megan's. So there is a small scrum of cars and taxis and people and luggage and skycaps all hustling through the same limited space. Hanging back, I search the faces and outfits and hair. Nothing that matches Megan's description--at least the one I imagine. Slowly scan right, left, right again. And then, there she is. Seated on a concrete bench near the taxi line, legs crossed, one hand holding a leash for Meathead, the other pinching a cigarette between her fingers.

The burning tobacco isn't cool, but shockingly, Megan is smokin' hot. A fashion model posing on that bench. I literally shake my head in disbelief. Yow. Megan: knee-length, yellow, flower print summer dress; medium-height pumps; subdued but cool Vogue sunglasses; stylish crop hairstyle with long bangs swept all the way across the opposite eyebrow. The hair--a shimmering soft brunette. Straight, natural, not the teased bottle blonde that scared me away so long ago. On the other hand: All crazy bones, pop-eyes and tongue, Meathead looks utterly out of place next to her. Otherwise, she's a film star, surrounded by matching sunshine-yellow luggage pieces. And one odd, raggedy, oversized carpet bag. A childhood tunes leaps into my head: "One of these things (is not like the others)."

Then, there are also tiny, telltale physical signs that not everything is exactly 100% right. Although seated, Megan is in constant motion. Very slight, twitchy head motions. Almost imperceptible shoulder rolls, confessing muscle tightness. Nervous, tiny bounces of her crossed-over foot. All betraying someone just a little uncomfortable in her own skin. Which belies her epic lack of self-awareness. The kind which allows this striking young woman--who looks as if she'd stepped right off Rodeo Drive--to be paired with a scraggly, overweight, and hunchily-seated mongrel.

A smart and compassionate mongrel, however, confident in his master's love and loyalty. Meathead notices my approach first, of course. Leaning slightly against the slack in his leash, he turns, seeming to remember me. His mouth opens in a panting, crooked-tooth smile. "Arf!"

I make only another couple of steps before those expensive sunglasses turn my way. Flicking the cigarette away--I'm not sure she ever really drew on it--Megan turns her slender shoulders my way. A huge smile lights her face. But, ahem, she remains seated, a too-conscious attempt at composure.

"Megan!" I cry, suddenly, unreserved and yet in shock at her amazing metamorphosis from the image in my imagination. Happy shock. I find that I am overjoyed to have found a friend. My friend. This friend. She may resemble Holly Golightly, but I know the Lula Mae Barnes homegirl who exists under the cool exterior. Without breaking stride, using my momentum, I lift Megan off the bench and swing her around in my arms. I laugh. And forget to squint. She gives a little cry of surprise and happiness, adjusts her sunglasses, and gives me a small peck on my cheek. This reunion is the happiest moment I have had in a Very. Long. Time.

Feeling whimsical, I cradle-carry Megan like a groom back to Big Blue, and slide her into the passenger seat. Then I grab Meathead's leash and sprightly walk him in to the cab before bundling her luggage back into the bed. The raggedly carpet bag seems much more personal, more real to Lula Mae-gan. So I hand it to her to hold in her lap. She smiles again, and somehow, I feel like the sun is finally rising in my life. Wow.

We set sail. At first we are both wordless as I navigate out to the interstate. Because there's such a deep catalog of things to share, we can only remain silent--or completely burst open with questions, memories, and personal updates. Confessions must come much later. For several minutes Meathead's incessant panting and small frolicking provide a handy foil to our deep silence.

Taking a moment to reflect in these moments, I start by self-examining my euphoria. Is this about Megan's stunning appearance? Honesty washes over me like a waterfall: Partly, yes. Wait. Not really. Okay, maybe both. Beauty is in the eye of the beholder, right? And I'm beholdin', alright, every chance I can sneak a peek-a-loo over there on the other side of the tuck-n-roll bench seat. Wait. This is My Friend, and possibly much more. To me, anyways. Someone who has suffered deeply, maybe even a little at my hands. I kick myself: Fool. Yet, she is Someone who has chosen to forgive deeply, therefore binding herself to me in one way or another, for better or for worse. I know we're cool.

Yeeep. Did I just think that?" For better or for worse?" Whoa, horsie. Let's not run crazy here, okay? We have a long way to go, and not just to the Placid Place Motel, either.

"You must have started early today," I state with a smile.

"Mm hmm," Megan replies. That doesn't give me anything.

"Do you want to start by getting something to eat? You've been traveling and I'd love to sit down with you for a while. We can have a quick lunch at a great sandwich place called The Wooden Spoon, close to downtown off of St. Kilda Street," I try.

"Mm hmm," Megan repeats, a little absently, shifting her sunglasses. I'll take that as a "Yes," so, off we go.

It's the longest "quick lunch" that I can ever remember. While we are there, time doesn't mean a thing. It's still a little early for lunch, so we order breakfast sandwiches. I go for the ham and egg, Megan orders a tempeh and tomato. That's when the knowing quiet between us bursts open. Megan, of course, does not recollect many of the details of our time together in college. But there's lots to catch up on in her current life, not to mention Mamie and Meathead. And aside from my personal updates, I spend time trying to stoke those latent memories. This takes a while. Other customers ebb and flow through the restaurant. Once in a while Megan takes a break. She goes to powder her nose or heads out to visit Meathead in the truck to give him a snack and a drink of water out of a bottle. The sunlight slowly shifts through the long windows at the front of the building.

Long after our coffee is cold a waitress stops by--I hardly recognize the fact that she's the second one to work our table.

"We're gonna start charging the use of this table by the hour, kids," she expels through her nose. Her mouth is evidently reserved solely for the purpose of jack-hammering a stick of chewing gum. Or three sticks. Clickety-clack, clickety-clack. That's alright with me, though. Anything is alright with me, right now.

"Sorry 'bout that. We're just catching up after a long time apart," I look up and smile. Aw, shucks.

"More like, you're just catching on," Flo The Waitress replies. Clickety-clack. "We close in two hours." This announcement comes across as an ultimatum.

Megan to the rescue. She suggests to me, and Flo, "Why don't we order lunch?"

Smiles all around. I'm not really hungry, but on my budget in this scenario, I can do this and get away with just a snack for dinner. A club sandwich sounds good to me, and Megan is happy to find a stuffed Portobello mushroom on the lunch menu.

This gives us license to talk, laugh, eat, and check on Meathead until the sun shifts even further and then is covered in clouds. And then, I finally notice an employee is drawing the blinds on those big front windows. No other customers remain. Flo clickety-clacks a toe in time with her gum-chewing.

"Uh, Megan," I start, pseudo self-consciously. "I think it's time we got going," I tell her. Not sadly, of course. Her visit is just beginning. She instantly obeys, I notice, like a trained seal, promptly arising and gathering her things.

"Where to?" she asks.

Good question: Where to? I start to wonder if the Placid Place is fitting for My Megan. Whoops. "My" Megan? Uh, yeah, actually, maybe so.

"Well, the place I'm living is really a bachelor's quarters." Wow, sounds vaguely respectable. "Women aren't allowed, so I had to find something else for you." The Placid Place Motel? That's an acceptable "something else?" "Let me, um, go wash my hands before we leave, okay? I'll meet you out at my truck."

"Sure!" Megan answers, and heads out to Meathead.

Quick, formulate a plan, Dude. On a Newschannel 99 salary, my wallet can't stand a more expensive lodging than Placid Place. I try to slow myself down, run through some alternatives--and numbers. Then, all of a sudden, it dawns on me. The one person I know I can trust: Carl Collingwood. Even better: Marie Collingwood. Who better than to play chaperone? If only they are willing... . I dial their digits.

And get Carl's voicemail. I leave a message, strained and urgent. Leaving me with nothing but bluff once I get out to the truck. "Okay, ha ha, ready to go?"

Megan has already buckled her seatbelt. "I'm just waiting on you!" she rejoins, playfully. Her sunglasses are re-applied. Then, for a second time today: "So, where are we going?"

Quick calculations. Its 15-20 minutes up to Collingwood's home. That's not much warning time for them. Where else? I'm not taking her from one restaurant to another. Baseball? Don't be ridiculous. A movie? Great Day In The Morning. You never know what unnecessary and uncomfortable scenes they will shove inside even a PG film these days. The Community College? Not even Joe Cool has much to do on this campus on a Saturday. Waitaminute, here it comes. Newschannel 99? Of course, yes! A tour of my workplace could eat up a nice chunk of time.

"I thought I'd show you my TV station. It's still a little too early to check in where you are going to stay." Whether it's with the Collingwoods or at someplace to be determined later. Or sooner, I uncomfortably realize. Megan is her usual compliant self.

"Okay. Can we take Meathead for a walk while we're there?"

Thinking of the wild, weedy undergrowth around the place, I snort-laugh. "Oh, yes. There are plenty of wildlands around the building," I reply.

"Okay," she says again. Sunglasses removed, now at home in Big Blue, Megan starts to chirp away about everything she observes along the way. I consider that everything in Filterboro is all new and fresh to her. So, I reflect, her earlier reserve was probably a simple climate adjustment. Now she seems to feel at home with me, with Big Blue, even. Of course, Meathead is there to drool on her pretty dress. Now, however, she offers a steady commentary on everything from the number of clouds in the sky to the cameras we have on traffic lights to catch red-light runners here. Detail-oriented, this one.

As we drive through the back of the business park and head towards the Newschannel 99 property, however, she grows strangely quiet. The sunglasses make a return appearance over her eyes.

"There's something I don't like about this place," she offers, randomly, innocently, meekly. Yeah, like just about everything, I think. I say something different.

"What's that? What do you mean?" Her spirit, I realize, is as sensitive as a seismometer. I trust it.

"Oh, you know. Unusual stuff. I just have a feeling. It's not bad. I'm a little tired, maybe. You know." Megan trails off, her comments sounding much more choppy and distracted than before we arrived.

We drive past the "Dead End" sign and enter the parking lot. Not a problem finding a parking spot out front on this weekend day. I try to maintain a carefree demeanor, but as Megan follows Meathead out of the cab, she suddenly looks up, straight at the top of the Tower. My gaze follows, just in time to spot a figure pull back from a window. Instantly: Ivory Eriss. Must have been. Who else? Norman the Doorman wouldn't work on a Saturday, would he?

Megan is silent for a short time after, while we walk Meathead around the weedy grounds next to the parking lot. Meathead seems to be in a hurry and once his business is finished I decide he can stay with us as we go inside.

Everyone follows me through the front lobby to get the full feel of the place, front to back. I haven't taken this trip for some time now, and vivid memories of my first day here suddenly surface. The funny early impressions of everything from the walls to Walter. Wilson, I mean. In the quiet, relatively deadline-deficient Saturday, even that initial-impression smell of the cheap carpet comes back to me for a moment. Then, the sense of oppression that comes with this territory exerts itself.

Walking through these halls, I realize the oxygen becomes almost too thin to breathe. The slate-lined walls seem to rapidly close in. Meathead strains at his leash, easily dragging the wafer-thin Megan along. She seems to breathe in a strange, heavy pant.

"Do you...like this place?" she asks, doubtfully.

"Um, sure, yeah. It isn't always like this," I reply. Like this? What is this?

I'm feeling dizzy but at least I know my way forward. As we finally burst into the newsroom, the weight suddenly seems to lift and we stop to take a deep breath.

That's a relief. Except in that first breath I discern a strange yet familiar odor wafting our way. In fact, I can actually see it wafting our way, in the shape of smoke. It is, uh...perhaps...a cigar? What happened to all those "No Smoking" signs around the building?

A happy incandescent light burns in Collingwood's office, augmented by something else burning: tobacco. That's okay, he's here and I need him. I'll just follow my nose.

"Carl?" I try, tentatively. A skeleton crew is on hand, quietly preparing for the first weekend newscast, but the newsroom is so still that a normal call across the room could startle someone into an unplanned bowel movement.

There is movement, in Collingwood's office, and he appears, hand just pulling a cigar away from his mouth. He glances at the smoke. "Batteries died on the air filter gizmo." Yet, he's quick to notice company. "Well, hello, Wil. Giving a tour?"

I introduce Megan to Carl, hoping hard the two most important people in my life right now will hit it off. Shaking off her initial difficulties with the place, Megan smiles, flips her hair once or twice, and keeps her twitching to a minimum. She seems to intuitively know that Collingwood is an important figure to me. That means he's important to her. And naturally, any lovely young woman apparently on my arm is sure to make an impression on my mentor. So we start off on the right note.

Rudie, the weekend newscast line producer, comes by to offer a polite hello. Others kind of nod at us; they hardly know me yet, much less my guest.

Five minutes later Megan excuses herself to wander towards the ladies room. She leaves me with Meathead on a short leash, and a short lease on time to hit up Collingwood with my unreasonable request.

"Carl, let me tell you something. I wasn't expecting her visit," I start, confidingly. "She just showed up at the airport this morning. Like a lost puppy..." I happen to look down at Meathead, who looks backs up at me, knowingly. He shakes his big head slowly. "Okay, not like a lost puppy. It's a very long story I'll tell you later. She can't stay with me at the boarding house and I can't afford to put her up any place better than The Placid Place Motel."

"She sure doesn't look like a lost puppy," Collingwood observes. "Didn't she come here with some sort of budget?" Collingwood turns his head to blow tobacco smoke away.

I stop to indulge a small smile. That would require planning and saving:

long term endeavors. Politely: not Megan's strong suit. The airplane ticket probably gobbled a recent paycheck she may have just received. Another paycheck likely furnished her wardrobe.

"If I know my Megan (there's that stray "my" again) she didn't plan any further ahead than making sure she had my phone number stored in her phone. And then she tried real hard to remember to actually bring the phone. Honestly, as amazing and sweet as Megan is, the synapses just don't all fire in order." Coaxingly, now, "Carl, I'm really stuck and since I don't have time to be delicate or polite, can she stay at your house for a short time? Honestly, there isn't a better place for Megan than to be, than with you and Marie," I try.

Clearly, he has sensed this coming. Which is good, because it has given him time to start to get used to the idea. But Collingwood still tries some alternatives on for size. "Why don't you see if Jeannette or Tyler can put her up for a few days. Young women seem to naturally relate to one another."

These might be legitimate options. But I really don't know either of these young women as well as I do Collingwood. Generally: how they live away from work. Specifically: certainly not enough to ask such a heavy and sudden favor of them. In a few words I say as much to Collingwood.

He glances at Meathead. "Does the dog come, too?"

"Yeah, animals aren't allowed at the Haversack House. Its Rule Number 1,284 or something."

Collingwood sighs, removes the cigar from his mouth and scratches his head. "That could be an issue. Marie isn't much of an animal person. Let me call her and get a sense of where she's at. We do have a pretty big house for just the two of us--really, it is meant for hosting unexpected guests." I smile and wince at the same time. "So I don't see why we can't put her up in a guest bedroom. Maybe we can pen up the pooch somewhere in the back." I smile without wincing this time. But then he finishes. "We will just have to bleach everything that Marvell Thyme touched in the Guest Room." Now I wince without smiling.

Collingwood repairs to his office to call his spouse. While waiting on Megan I slouch over to my cubicle. Even with a few weekend drones hard at work elsewhere in the newsroom, I feel like the overhead fluorescents are glowing only on me. I fire up the computer, and sit back while it complains against the unplanned weekend workload.

Okay, the startup page is functioning (wallpaper set to a photo of Johnny Cash at San Quentin Prison), programs ready. Which one first?

ENPS and web browser feel a little work-impersonal on a Saturday afternoon. Ok. Let's see if there are any email messages of interest.

Spam. Spam. Spam. Spam. A lot. Much of it highly-inappropriate. More spam. I start thinking of canned meat product. Then, dramatically, there is a message from Mamie. Megan's Mamie, her mother. Its dated today at about Noon.

"Wil, I've lost Megan. This is much stranger than when she wandered off in the haunted house over at the Bison Club and ended up talking with the creepy clown character who carried a fake chainsaw. She's not answering her phone and your phone doesn't seem to work and all I could do is find this email address on the TV station website. Call me asap. Meathead's gone too so I guess at least they are together."

Desk phone, quick. I almost knock over a computer speaker scrambling to punch up Mamie's digits.

"It's Mamie," an older, syrupy, but roughened voice announces. She sounds a little tired and worried.

"This is Wil. She's here," rushes out into my phone.

Mamie pauses, sighs a veteran sigh, and chuckles lightly. "Well, I didn't have any proof she went down there but I had a sneaking suspicion she was headed your way."

"She forgot to tell you," I try.

"She forgot to tell me."

"She forgot to tell me, too, until she was here at our airport."

"Is she alright?"

"Mm hm. In fact, she's never seemed better."

A small pause of satisfaction on Mamie's end. Then, "Is she with you right now?"

"She's not far away." I look around. The only person I see at the moment is an intern checking her text messages. "We're at my office. Megan is probably giving herself a tour around the studio or something."

"Or something." Another sigh. "Where is she gonna stay tonight, Wil?"

Boy, do I feel seriously proud of myself right now.

"Don't worry, Mamie. I'm fixing her up with a great family I know--a couple. They are a little older, and some of the most highly-respectedest people in town." Eep. Did I just say "respectedest?" Selling this a little too hard, I think.

"Sounds like you've done some fancy footwork. Thank you."

"No problem, Mamie, I've got it covered."

"Wil?"

"Yes ma'am?"

"Megan is an adult, Wil. She's absent-minded in so many ways, but I never try to tell her what to do. She knows her own mind, she just kind of changes it from one moment to the next, and then back again. I just try to be there to give her, um, guidelines. Parameters or boundaries, you know what I mean."

"We're on the same team, Mamie. I don't know how long she plans to stay, but I'll do my best to be a, uh, guider. Guide, I mean." I'm simply butchering the English language here.

I give Mamie my new cell phone number as well as my office number, and promise to make Megan call home as we end the conversation.

Okay, so where is Megan? I feel like a parent looking for a lost child in a department store. Obviously she's not in the newsroom or the sporting goods department. I look in on Collingwood: nope. Surely she can't be still powdering her nose after all this time. Maybe Meathead had an emergency. I head out the double steel doors, the only obvious nearby exit. Nope: the former-SUV Corral is empty. Back inside. After the creepy reception we felt coming in the front, I doubt Megan would want to head back that way. And there aren't that many people around to ask if they've seen her. I try the Control Room: uh, uh. But a chance glance at the bank of camera monitors holds the answer. There's Megan, on the news set, primly seated in Lavinia Fern's chair at the anchor desk. She looks straight at me. That means--I quickly comprehend--she's actually looking straight at a camera. That's when I realize something is strange here. The cameras are always "on," always sending a signal. That's not the issue. But I can see every detail of Megan's face in the monitor, without heavy shadows. Ahh, the production lights are up. They shouldn't be. Normally they are dimmed after each newscast. Must save these expensive fluorescents for the next newscast.

This occurs to me in about two seconds. In the next one second, I can tell that Megan--although looking straight at the camera--is listening to someone. Her head tilts slightly to one side, like Meathead. The microphones are not "up," that is, they aren't activated. So I can't hear anything from the studio. But I can see enough in there to motivate me to hasten forward quickly now.

"Megan!" I call, busting through the heavy doors, striding past the plywood backside of the faux news set. I find: The lady is a vamp. Complete in her summery attire, Megan is a vision who has caught the attention of the Newschannel 99 weekend director--uh, you know, whatshisname. His attentions are unwanted by The Lady, correct? Except, they don't seem to be. I enter the studio in time to hear her giggle, and to hear him command.

"Okay, in a moment I'll go back into the control room, and switch you from '2' to '3,' so be sure to turn from this camera to that!" The guy leers at Megan, who is oblivious to him but not the novelty of seeing herself on the studio monitors.

Again I call, more questioningly, "Megan?" as I approach the set. Um, I had better paste a smile on my face. To marginalize Mr. Weekend Director, I have to join in the "fun," then send him off to cool his heels in the control room. He can become a functionary there while we stay out here and play. "Hey, Phil," I start. I don't really know his name.

"Rob." The guy says to Megan, not me. She smiles, vaguely.

"Hey, Roy. Go ahead and load up this morning's newscast script in the prompter, and switch some cameras for us. And, why not record it, too--okay?" I look to Megan.

"Oh, would you do that? Thank you!" Turning from him to me, Megan doesn't wait for an answer.

Rob, Roy, whatever, is neatly boxed out. He mutters something about "not spending too much time doing this because there's a newscast coming up." But ultimately he gives us a few minutes of his suddenly-valuable time to let Megan model. Instantly bored, I check my text messages, look around for Meathead, think about how to introduce the idea of her putting up at the home of complete strangers.

Soon, though, I realize I am hearing...gold. Megan looks straight into the camera, and reads the teleprompter flawlessly as it flows by. At first she sounds halting, getting used to the device. And some of the place names trip her up (Ersatz County is pronounced "err-sits"). Nevertheless, seated prim and straight, slightly leaning in on one shoulder--just like a seasoned pro--I could see that Megan would have really connected with the phantom viewing audience. Her appearance is electric, charismatic. And when she reads, the scripts sound conversational, like a trusted friend telling you secrets straight from her heart. Music plays. Quietly but suddenly, the horn of the theme to "The Natural" seems to play in my ears. There are only a few people in television who are "naturals," complete with charm, charisma, absolute confidence. I am not one of them. To my complete shock, Megan is. I scratch my head in a classic pose of wonder.

Having lost interest, Rob announces over a studio intercom that he's done. The prompter halts, and so does Megan. She simply sits...simply. Before I can start to express my amazement, Collingwood walks in from the control room.

"Miss Megan, have you ever done this before?" he asks, briskly.

"What do you mean...read stuff out loud?" She is sincerely stumped.

Collingwood is gentle. "Not entirely. I mean, worked in a newsroom, sat on a news set, read news copy on a teleprompter."

Megan blurts out a hearty laugh. "I've never even visited a television station never once in my life!" She chokes a little on her laughter. "Did I do something?" She leaves it vague, like that.

Collingwood and I exchange a glance. "Megan," I start, "You seem to be good at that. Really good. Reading the news script on the teleprompter, I mean. Showing up on camera. You were pretty amazing, in fact."

"What's a teleprompter?" Megan asks, sweetly.

Collingwood and I exchange a second glance. He clears his throat. "Uh, so my wife and I are hoping you and Wil will come over for dinner tonight."

As we drive across town toward Haversack House, its quiet inside Big Blue. Megan seems tired; she leans a shoulder back against the door, and gazes out the window to watch the town pass by. I add no comments about her on-camera performance. This is just the latest bit of craziness to cope with today. I don't have to ask what Collingwood thinks, and I don't want to. With some polish, Megan could be a major ratings-grabber. But she is no journalist. In fact, she could care less about journalism: you know, that stuff about shedding light on corruption or holding politicians accountable. Or for that matter, TV news exposés on overweight pets or most popular ice cream flavors. Megan is certainly not the archetypical bubble-headed bleach blonde who comes on at Five. But she doesn't come across as savvy, wary, or discerning. Not a Jessica Savitch bone in her body. Viewers will not really fathom Megan--not like me. She understands things, relates to things. Life, for instance. As much as she is unaware, as much as she has forgotten, she retains her passion, her love and compassion, her native common sense. She may not know the name of the President of North Korea, maybe not even the United States. But she sure does care about the plight of their people.

I'm heading "home" because, for now, I've run out of other places to go. Clearly, it has been a long day for Megan, who needs a break. I need a liquid break--and need to kill some time before driving up to see the Collingwoods for dinner. If nothing else, Megan and I can relax on the swing on that expansive front porch of Haversack House. Even if Mercy kicks us out, we can stroll around the neighborhood and find a park or look at the historic houses. But our gracious landlord wouldn't object to a gentleman boarder meeting his lady friend on the porch...would she?

There seems to be an unusually-large number of vehicles parked on Chainlink Street. Must be a party brewing. So, we find a spot down the way. Megan grabs Meathead's leash and goes around to the bed of the truck to retrieve her things. I stop her.

"Better leave them here, for now," I tell her. "We'll get them later." And I'll explain later where she's going to stay.

I figure if we just wander around to the front porch, quietly take the steps, and edge ourselves on to the swing, we can spend at least 20 minutes taking it easy without being noticed. Even if Miss Mercy is disposed to dispose of us immediately, I calculate she couldn't physically move any faster than that. Megan trudges a little heavily and Meathead plods along. Eventually, though, we fall into the swing and slowly push it backward with our toes.

"Willie?" Megan tries after a few moments. "Could we get some ice water or something? I'm parched and so is Meathead."

I look down at the panting dog. There is no other answer but "yes." By drawing attention to ourselves, of course, this may hasten our departure. It's an all-too-reasonable request, but I make an effort to buy at least a minute or two.

"So, what did you think of the TV station?" I try.

"Fine," she responds in a classically-vague mode.

"What did you think about seeing yourself on TV?" A standard question I'd ask a group of Cub Scouts touring the TV station.

"Um, it was pretty neat. I enjoyed reading that stuff and it was exciting to see myself." No more exciting than when the 18-49 male demographic gets a peek at her. But then she stops, politely not referring back to her request to wet her whistle.

"I'll get you that drink," I offer, moving off the swing.

"While you are doing that, can I borrow your keys?" she replies. "Silly me. I forgot my purse in your nice truck."

I fish out my keychain and hold out the correct key for her to take. Megan smiles, tells Meathead to remain on the porch, and heads out.

After briefly considering the logistics, I decide on pluck. Just stroll in through the front door, baby, boldly go where no boarder has gone before. Boldly, perhaps, but with circumspection. Crossing the threshold, I spot no living being. I pass the staircase (a new 4x6 card on the railing advises "Do not 'flick' the light switches harshly. Gently 'move' them up and down") and move noiselessly past the parlor. The usual sportsy broadcast noises emanate, and I hear the muffled chatter of many people inside. All male voices, natch. I pass through the dining room, which opens up into the kitchen. Even my cautious stride, however, gives me too much momentum to stop after realizing someone is inside. It is Slab. Seated at the table, at the one spot not covered by magazines. He's not reading any of them. In fact, he's just seated, apparently doing nothing.

"Thought you'd come in." Thus spake Zarathustra. Deep, primal, guttural. I'm thoroughly amazed.

"So you do talk!" I blurt.

In a move slow enough to rival construction projects on the Ohio Turnpike, Slab's mouth loiters into a smirk. "You have a lady out front," he admonishes, languorously.

I'm sure my face instantly blossoms into a deep shade of salsa. "I have a friend here who would appreciate some refreshment," I try, in my best Southern condescending manner. "Just a glass of ice water, if you can spare the ice," I add, um, icily. That doesn't break it. The ice, I mean.

"And the animal?" Slab accuses instantly. Instantly for him, I mean. Oh, that. Slab may be more shrewd than I give him credit for.

"Just her...service dog. They will both stay outside." Whew, the taming of the shrewd. I close the conversation and move to the kitchen sink. In the grate I find two tall glasses and a tumbler. I take all three out to the Boarders' wheezy refrigerator and find exactly three ice cubes in a vintage metal tray. Sheesh. I distribute them and head back to the sink for some nice, fresh tap water.

"They need to leave. And...dishes stay in the house," Slab challenges. Joyful menace gleams in his narrowed eyes. A nice touch, letting me go through the motions first. I start calculating. Slab's massiveness could fill a doorway. A swipe of his arm could flick me aside. And he's grown comfortably used to boarders' instant acquiescence.

But Slab moves slower than a decomposing milk jug. So, I decide he can't really oppose me at this moment if I cross this Rubicon. The eventual consequence, of course: I will have to really find someplace else to live. "Freedom!" I shout in my best William Wallace. And stride forward, wondering what a meaty backhand from Slab will feel like.

It never comes. Slab, flabbergasted. Up he rises. "Hey!" his voice climbs in sorry disbelief. "Mother said you can't do that!" is all he eventually conjures, crying in my wake. Over my shoulder I note that he actually lurches forward. But by the time I make the front door, it's clear Slab isn't following me. Instead, he veers into the parlor, laboriously closing the door behind him with a decisive "plunk." Why didn't he follow me?

Cradling the three drinks I push through the screen door...and bump full into a young man wearing a golf shirt and slick black hair. The Player, The Sport. Yes, I recognize him. No need to chat--I'll let him go by. Except he wears a determined expression. Much different from the breezy gambler attitude I recall briefly getting from him earlier. In the clinch he whispers, "Get your phone out, start recording some video."

Does not compute. Then, I realize, he isn't alone. And I can see that Megan no longer appears to be out front. There are several uniformed and presumably plain-clothed law enforcement officers poised on the porch and in Mulberry Street. They don't wait for my train of thought to leave the station.

"This is a raid!" commands The Player, barging inside the parlor like Elliot Ness. I hear similar noises in the back of Haversack House as well. Geez, here's this incredible lead story I've been waiting for, happening on a scanty Saturday, when absolutely nobody watches the news. Friday is bad, also, viewership declines while apathy rises. In fact, Friday at 5pm is often the juiciest time for press releases: powerful people know the news cycle will grind to a halt for two full days. By Monday, they can try to argue, "That's old news!" Breaking news is best on a Monday: we can milk it for most of the following week.

Back to today, Saturday. A quick glance outside shows Megan and Meathead are safely away out front. We make eye contact as she is escorted off the premises by an officer. She looks composed, but I know her and allow myself about one second to worry. To think that she saw this on Mulberry Street.

Nevertheless, I'm now on the clock. Apparently having been recognized as The Newschannel 99 Guy, for the time being I have been left to operate independently. Quickly I fire up the smartphone, fumble for a moment in finding the video camera function, but ultimately point and record. Steady, remember to remain steady. Moving a small camera like this makes a video recording look like everything is happening in an earthquake.

There is an uproar of noise throughout the building. It has the feel of the sound of air being let out of a balloon all at once: the game is up. Most of the officers, directed by The Player and another insider, quickly fill the parlor. Others investigate in the back of the house and climb up to the second floor. Unfortunately, some touch the walls along the staircase, which would have driven Miss Mercy out of her mind. There must be...57 cops up there. On the first floor, I head into the parlor, where the action seems to be. Sure enough, resistance is futile for those inside. A number of people are handcuffed, others are mimicking the old underarm deodorant commercial: their hands are up. So much movement and noise. One of the other Sports inside, wearing a porkpie hat and a golf shirt about two sizes too small, shouts something about a lawyer. The Troll is here--my neighbor. So, he does come out of his room, ha ha! He notices my freedom and my video-recording. Not knowing what to make of it, he half hides his face in the crook of his manacled arm in classic "perp walk" fashion. Thank yewwww, neighbor. How guilty can a guy look? This is really fulfilling. A third guy hollers a string of profane protests as he passes by me, so I follow for a few steps. As he is led away, he changes tune. Attempting to plead his case to my camera, he bleats, "But I'm just a hard-working American...at Sears!!" Wow--that could lead the newscast, even on a Monday.

During a lull in the action, I use the all-purpose phone to try to send a text to Collingwood. Odds are low that it will get a signal out right away. But the phone will keep trying until the moment it does.

The other inmates of the bookie joint are led away. Agents swiftly comb through the parlor and adjacent rooms. At this point, a heavy hand grabs my shoulder and my attention.

"You are done here, too," says a bored voice. I turn to face a tall, stocky man wearing a jaw and a chocolate-colored three piece suit. How does The Heat stand the heat like this?" Someone pulled a lot of strings to make sure you could stay in here. But now, everything here is evidence, so you can't see any more. Come with me." Although I'd like to stay longer, I'm grateful to have collected what I have on my phone. I realize, however, I don't have some images that I would treasure. I turn to The Human Jaw as we head out to the front porch.

"What's your name...Agent...?"

"Tanner. Simon Tanner. State headquarters. And you must be..." his voice trails while he checks his notes. "Uh, Wilson Gamble, Newsradio 95?"

Not quite. "Wilson Gamble, Newschannel 99. Television."

"Okay. I have been directed to give you some very limited information about this raid. Active investigations mean we normally don't say anything."

"Alright, Agent Tanner. Where is Mercy Haversack? Where is Slab? I ab-soh-lutely need to get them being led away in handcuffs."

"Oh, we'll find Mercy for you," Tanner grins. "Only, outside. Right now she is being interrogated in the kitchen." A smile involuntarily pulls at my face, imagining how crowded that room must be right now. "But, you won't see Slab."

"Why not?"

"This is off the record. We're not 'on background,' right now but 'off the record.' Right?" Tanner insists, fiercely. Jaw bulges in expectation.

"Fully agreed, I won't report it. Just help me understand it...since I live here."

Tanner and Jaw appraise me briefly, then decide this falls under 'some very limited information.' "Slab has been working for us the past six months."

Wow. Big Wow. So, along with The Sport, he's the Inside Guy. Maybe that's why he tried to move Megan off the property just now. He knew the raid was happening. But if this is true, I guess there will be no greeting card the next time Mother's Day rolls around.

"How did you get him to snitch on his own mother?" I ask, a little unconvinced.

Tanner rubs his thumb on that ample chin. "Well, they aren't actually related. Mercy took him in off the street a long time ago. And you may have noticed that she doesn't exactly treat people with much respect. All the work he did around here?" I shake my head--it didn't seem like much. "He was never paid. Just room and board. Finally, he'd had enough. And eventually, he figured out what was happening in the parlor, and we made friends." Tanner smiles. "That's all you are getting from me, except for what the law requires."

"Will you talk to me on camera?"

"Not a chance. Now, it's time for you to get off the property. We'll set you up out on that street that runs behind the home. We will take Mercy to a car parked out back. If you call your station right away," Turner looks at my phone with mock disdain, "maybe you can get a real camera out here in time."

At least my phone is state-of-the-art. And at some point it has indeed managed to send my text to Collingwood. Now, I dial his number. He doesn't pick up, voicemail does. So I recite a quick summary. Collingwood needs to get to the station to direct our coverage. The "B" team that works the weekends is actually not bad, but needs a strong hand from the A-Team to make sure a plan comes together.

A quick glance around fails to spot Megan and Meathead. A small worry tumor forms in my mind; I find it hard to shake its presence. But in the meantime, I have to call someone with the B-Team to request the on-call photog. Er, nowadays titled the "on-call multi-media journalist." After about a dozen rings, someone finally picks up the so-called newsroom "hotline."

"Newschannel 99, Where We're Right 99 Times Out Of 100." How can a voice sound juvenile, ambivalent, and treasonous at the same time? I instantly become cautious.

"Uh, hi. Hello. This is Wilson Gamble--who is this?"

"Who is this? This is Newschannel 99 Where We're Right 99 Times Out of 100. What do you want?" Now this comes indignantly, a demand.

Perhaps unfairly considering the fact that since this is the B-Team, this person has little right to cop an attitude, I become a little indignant myself.

"Hey--whoever you are, this is Wilson Gamble! One of your reporters! I've got a huge scoop on my hands and need some help--send a photog right away to Chainlink and Second!"

"Whoa, whoa, whoa, fella. Slow down," replies my condescending colleague at Newschannel 99. "You aren't one of the reporters on our schedule today. Who exactly are you?"

Blowing my lid won't make any impression. So I do indeed slow down and start, "Obviously, you need me to spell this out for you." So I do. I spell my name. Then I spell my job title, loudly overriding the lackey's impatient noises.

"Okay, okay," he finally interjects. Apparently he has consulted a staff directory and found my name. "But I have to call someone to get permission to call in a photog. That may take a while." The way he's going, it might take until the next lunar eclipse.

Suddenly, however, his tone changes. First, a muffled exchange on the other end. Then, I am gratified to hear a distinct change in attitude.

"Mr. Collingwood is here and says Don Wash is on the way."

"Thank yew," I reply, perhaps a little snidely.

Once again, I turn to the matter at hand. Surveying the scene along Chainlink, I can see the back of Haversack House. A stream of agents carries large, brown cardboard boxes of evidence out of the house and into waiting SUV's. Uniformed officers are keeping people off of the property. But neighbors are still gathered, to rubberneck and ruminate.

After snapping off a few decent clips of video on my phone, I use it to dial her number. Megan's, I mean, not Mercy's. No answer, naturally. So, I start asking bystanders about her. Eventually, a tall, thick guy wearing a "Beer Is For Lovers" t-shirt stretched tight over his gut responds affirmatively.

"She was pretty hot, right? The runway model walking a crazy-looking dog?" I nod, wishing he'd get beyond whatever fantasy he is experiencing at the moment. "Uh, she left in a pickup truck with a sketch-looking dude a few minutes ago."

Oh no. She took my truck. With a sketch-looking dude.

"What did the sketch guy look like?" I ask, a little breathily.

"Skinhead, you know, uh, dragon tattoo on his neck. Earrings everywhere."

Oh man, that sounds like "Little Jerry" from the Placid Place Motel. He was a friend of Mercy's, I recall. Referred me to her, in fact. There's not much I can do at the moment. Wash shows up and it's time to get to work.

While waiting for Mercy's perp walk, we interview three neighbors to gauge the general opinion of the reputation of Haversack House and its inhabitants. I'm not terribly surprised to learn that Mercy isn't exactly beloved. One neighbor tells me how Mercy had someone tape 4x6 cards to his front door every time his dog barked at night. Another related how Mercy called the police every time his teenage son cut across her property on his way to school.

I'll prepare something for the 6 and 11 newscasts, including a liveshot at 6 out front of my own home. Wash drove over in a live truck, so we will simply stay out here and work. No need to go back in to the studio. I'll edit my story in the truck and report live at 6. No such thing at 11, though; I'd be in heavy overtime. And no one watches the late Saturday newscast.

The clock is ticking a little too loudly towards 6pm for my comfort while we wait. I look around to see whether the other TV stations have been tipped off. Often someone working inside law enforcement will quietly call their news contact when stuff comes down. Little Napoleon, my former ND, had a standing offer of a bottle of wine to anyone in government who called in a legitimate tip. Other times, curious residents will call their favorite station to ask about an incident in progress, assuming the newsroom knows what is happening.

Eventually a reporter with the *Daily Repellant* does appear. I'm not worried about that at all. He might post something on the newspaper's website first, but by the time anybody reads it in the newspaper, it'll be old news. Then, however, a weekend crew with Channel 7 Action News races up as well. But their live truck does not come with them, I note.

Finally, the cherry on my Saturday sundae arrives. We hear her before we see her. In an unusual burst of energy, Miss Mercy Haversack is hollering her lungs out in an endless torrent of invective. Apparently its directed at The Law. Since we are kept back a distance, there's no way for me to even try to break in to her spitting, screaming rant. From my vantage point, all I can catch is something like, "...I know every bigshot in this town and I'll have you kicked off the beat!" Utterly ignoring her, agents expertly hustle her bulk handily toward a waiting car. Then, stopping to consider her size, they change direction and move her on to a nearby SUV. Another ten seconds, and they are gone.

Wow, life is good. Just like anyone else, reporters either enjoy or suffer through streaks. Runs of terrific stories or b-block boredom. And here I have yet another award-worthy report ready to go.

Except...I'm about to streak the other way. Welcome to this episode of "Please Stand By. The Technical Difficulties Are Not The Fault Of Your Receiver."

Wash approaches, breathing heavily, like someone who has just run a great distance but in fact is only trying to convey the great effort he has put forth in vain.

"I can't seem to transfer the memory card video from your phone over to our editing software." Wash has struggled for 15 minutes in the live truck edit bay. "It's not compatible. Looks like we will have to stick with just the video I shot." Consternation. Channel 7 will have pretty much everything what we have--which I rate as a disaster consider all the inside video I should have.

Thinking quickly, I prepare a package using the video and sound that Wash shot of the aftermath. But I always have a Plan B handy--this time, for my liveshot. And it will beat Action News senseless. During my live opening, I will hold up my phone to the camera while it plays my video. Wash will close in with a tight shot of the video playback from the phone, which no one else will have.

Genius. I am so happy with myself that I actually dance. But I sober up, recalling the self-deprecating parody-song of a videographer I worked with two markets ago: "I am so smart! S-m-r-t! I am so smart! S-m-r-t!!" Can't get too cocky here.

Just at that moment, naturally, I hear an apocalyptic electronic "beep" from my phone. Low power. The battery icon looks quite empty. I switch to panic mode. No need to ask where the battery charger is--its either safely cordoned off in my room in Haversack House or in one of the multitudinous brown evidence boxes, to disappear forever. Shutting off the phone, I will simply have to nurse along the battery for the next few minutes.

Despite all the obstacles, everything seems like it is in place for this liveshot. Wash assures me the generator has plenty of gas. We send a signal that the Newschannel 99 control room can see--and hear. My IFB returns the station's audio signal.

It's ShowTime. Gripping the microphone, facing the camera, I back myself up to yellow police tape that now defines the Haversack property. Deep breath, exhale. Shoulders come down in "relaxed" mode. Twist right shoulder forward, lean a little on one leg to affect a relaxed demeanor. Withdrawing the phone from my pocket, I switch the power back on. It fires up without complaining.

The weekend anchor--a former Miss Teen USA South Carolina-- introduces me. Her name is Mallory, I think. It doesn't matter much what she says, it'll sound like gibberish in my IFB earpiece anyways. But I'm treating my story like it's a ratings month Monday. A-game.

"It's the last place you'd expect illegal activity," I start, the irony melting off my tongue. "A quiet boardinghouse run by the Matriarch of an old Filterboro family--who is now under arrest." I look down and switch on the recorded video on my phone. It plays and I am gratified. "Here is exclusive video of the raid that we have obtained from inside the home." As planned, I hold up the phone video playback while Wash pushes in with his camera and attempts to fix his focus. So far so good.

But the video is abruptly interrupted by my phone's ringtones.

1980's musician Rick Astley belts out a tinny version of "Never Gonna Give You Up," and a graphic box appears in the center of the screen. Ten numbers and a name are plainly displayed for the Filterboro Designated Market Area to see: Megan. Oh. My.

The aircheck that I consult later portrays me literally jumping back from the camera closeup. I look stupidly at my phone. Rob--the newscast director who I dissed when Megan was in the studio--gets his revenge. He allows me to twist in the wind.

Live on camera, I panic. Hoping to clear the screen, I actually press the green button on the phone. Not good. It's on the "hands free" speakerphone setting. I'm pretty sure our viewers can hear Megan bleating, "Hello? Wil? Hiiiiii! Are you there Willie?"

That's when someone in the control room must have finally forced Rob The Disgruntled Director to cut to the pre-recorded package. Stabbing the red disconnect button with my finger, I want to run as fast as I can into my room in Haversack House to hide. But Willie won't go home. He still has to wrap up the report when the package finishes.

Recovering from a coughing fit behind the camera, Wash asks, "Uh, do you want to try that again? We can come back to you on a closeup on the camera phone."

What a trooper. I'm truly impressed. Even in my humiliation I recognize a gleam of professional respect for a photog who sees a colleague who has just tasted the agony of defeat...but is willing to quickly bounce back and give it the ol' college try one more time.

"Are you out of your mind?" I shoot back. Professional respect is for the birds. "Just give me a static medium shot, put the house over my right shoulder." That way, if I feel like it, I can turn and shoot one last derisive glare at Nightmare Manor.

Straighten up, Wil. Finish with a flourish. Over my IFB I hear the recorded package conclude and Rudie the producer tell me, "Go."

"One reason this raid is so unusual," I start, "is that very few such private bookmaking operations seem to exist on this scale." I jut my thumb over my shoulder like a hitchhiker towards Haversack House. "Agents tell me this falls someplace in between organized crime and those penny ante office pools run in many places of business." Alright, let's finish strong, buddy boy. "Coming up tonight at 11, we'll show you more of that exclusive inside video of the raid. Reporting from downtown Filterboro, Wilson Gamble, Newschannel 99, Where We're Right 99 Times Out Of 100."

"Clear," says Rudie the producer in my IFB.

"You nailed it!" calls Wash immediately, trying to encourage me.

"See you back here later...Willie," laughs Rudie in my ear, disconnecting.

Like I need to be taunted by some 20 year old. But there's nothing to do but yank out the IFB and skulk away.

Then I realize--once again--there's no destination to which I can skulk away. Can't visit my room--it's a crime scene. And Big Blue has bid adieu. No choice but to go straight back to the TV station. As Wash rolls up cables, I meander down the sidewalk and pull out the phone. I punch Megan's digits just a little too hard, and it takes three tries to get them right.

"Hello?" Megan tries timidly.

Deep breath. I exhale: "Hi Megan, it's me. Where are you?"

"Just checking in."

"Checking in? Where?"

"Oh, a homey little place by the interstate. Let me ask." Lips away from the mouthpiece, I hear a brief, muffled discussion.

"Flacid Place Motel," she states. More muffle-noise. "Oh. PLACID Place Motel. Whatever. Meathead likes it so we're gonna stay here."

"How did you get there?" I ask, actually already knowing.

"Oh, a nice young man with tattoos saw me looking tired and said he knew you and had already booked me in to the hotel and wanted to check me in to my room." More like wanted to check her "out" rather than "in." "So he gave me directions that were real easy to follow and so here we are!" Voila ici! "I hope you don't mind I took your truck, but I did have your keys...remember? You were so busy with work and we were so tired. I figured you could get a ride with your TV friend." Don Wash, she means.

Megan has a point there. But I can't help but to ask, "So the nice young man with the tattoos drove with you all the way to the motel?"

"Oh no! He got out on the way there."

Huh?" Where did he get out?"

"Oh, somewhere, I don't know. Wait! It was at the bus station."

He got out at the bus station? The wheels in my brain go round and round--but the resulting conjecture isn't difficult to develop. Little Jerry was a part of Mercy's book shop. Must have been in the betting parlor at the time of the raid. Noticed me with Megan on the porch before the raid and did some quick thinking. He slipped out somehow to the street and swiftly blended in with the crowd of onlookers before approaching Megan. Used her and Big Blue to escape to parts unknown.

Then I set aside the speculation. At this moment, other concerns override this issue.

"Megan, honey...do you have enough cash to stay there?" I ask, as sweetly and delicately as I can muster. "I can help... ." I leave this open-ended, with the hint that I'm not exactly flush.

"Enough cash? To pay for our room?" I quickly decide to assume that "our" means Megan and Meathead, not Megan and Willie. "Why, uh, no," she finishes, with finality.

"Worst fears," meet "realized." I truly want to help--and start a series of mental dollar calculations that circulate around my next paycheck as well as my current bills. Megan continues to stammer self-consciously, in my mind apparently just now realizing her vulnerable position.

Not.

"Uh, Wil...I meant, that, only, I'm sorry. Do you think they only take cash here? Because I was gonna use my debit card. I'm planning to stay a week."

Oh Happy Day. The sun starts to shine a little brighter in my solar system. Not only because I'm off the hook, but because Megan is executing a plan. She is not just here on a whim, she has saved money to pay for her excursion. New respect suddenly flows and I find myself even more attracted to this surprising bundle of contradictions in a summer dress.

> Hey, get rhythm when you get the blues
>
> Yes a jumpy rhythm makes you feel so fine
>
> It'll shake all the trouble from your worried mind

The rest of the weekend moves by rapidly. Collingwood seems a little relieved when I tell him how Megan's lodging predicament played out. But he still takes on a new temporary tenant: me. No longer able to live at Haversack House, I bunk up in the Collingwood guest bedroom--after making sure everything Marvell Thyme may have touched was disinfected, whether Collingwood was joking or not.

Moving into Sunday, I spend the rest of my time with Megan and none of it with Miller. Or Daniels. Or Adams, or Beam, you get the idea. So, if I'm a little groggy when the alarm goes off Monday morning, its only due to a lack of sleep for a change.

My routine has been dramatically altered in less than 48 hours. In this case, when I arrive at the Collingwood home, it means I start by leaving the Ron Tompkins-Johnny Bench rookie card in my luggage. Its baggage I resolve to no longer to dwell on.

On Monday, I arrive at Newschannel 99 some 45 minutes earlier than usual. Plenty of easy parking, ladies and gentlemen. Wallflower hasn't arrived, naturally, so I enter the newsroom to find an overnight photog manning the Assignment Desk. He alternates between dialing up contacts on the morning beat call list and turning the pages of an X-Men comic book. A young Morning Show lackey unconsciously sits in the wrong place: at Adams' desk, scanning the wires for any breaking news around the state that we may have missed. Adams will most likely complain long and loud later, wondering who took 75 cents in change out of his desk drawer. I'll never tell.

The scanners are pretty quiet. Most of the television monitors are muted, but the volume is just audible on one that plays a rival show. Its background noise. The coffee has perked just long enough ago to infuse the newsroom with its pungency. The fluorescent lights glow their usual sterile, early-morning blue. Only later will they somehow turn a more jaundiced shade of yellow. It takes me about 25 seconds to start feeling sickly, when I find a hand-written note, encased in an unsealed pink envelope, on my desk. My nose detects a soft Oriental perfume note. The fluorescents flicker as I withdraw the note and, er, note the signature.

"Call upon me, and I don't mean maybe," it reads. "My apartment. As soon as you arrive." It is signed, "Ivory Eriss." Not the familiar, "Ivory." Not the formal, "I. Eriss." Not even the informal and ironic, "I.E." It is the cold, complete and distant given- and sur-names. Very deliberate, I calculate.

Well, I'm here, so up I shall go. Up through the atmosphere, up where the air is queer--at the top of the Ivory Tower.

Heading out of the newsroom, I pick my way through the orange-carpeted hallways to the place where the flagstone hallway branches off. The strange, musty chill pervades the place, particularly when I pass the Sales Office. Now the sound of my footsteps echoes on the stone, effectively announcing my approach. That's okay. Whether or not things become unpleasant, I have my rock-solid answer prepared for Ivory Eriss.

Norman The Doorman waits at the elevator. Impeccably-uniformed, as always. Starched. But his expression, normally a practiced ambivalence, this morning betrays a slight antagonism.

"Madam is ready for you," he states. But his mechanical tone is tinged by a hint of sarcasm. And I note he bit off his customary "Sir" from the end of the statement.

"Even at this early hour?" I smirk. Shut up, Wil.

"Yes, Mr. Gamble. Do not keep her waiting." He sweeps an arm toward the circular stone staircase, and waits expectantly.

Uh uh. No way. "I'm not falling for that one again, Norman. I'm taking the elevator."

"There are strict limits as to who may use the elevator. Your name is not on the list."

"Then I suggest checking it twice. You're gonna find out who's not going upstairs at all without taking the elevator."

Evidently Warden has been pre-programmed to mess with me, but in a standoff like this, his default move is to simply give in.

"Yes, sir. Right this way." He opens the door, follows me into the carriage, and presses a button. No muzak plays on some kind of tinny speaker. So, for 30 long seconds we stand silently, listening to the equipment jerk to attention and pull us upward. At the top Warden opens the elevator door and simply waits. I proceed, alone, through the short hall to the heavy entry door of Eriss' apartment.

I decide to try to throw her off a little bit, and tap at the Gothic door with the old "shave and a haircut" riff--leaving her to answer with "two bits."

Unsurprisingly, she doesn't. Instead, the door swings wide, seemingly all by itself. I find Eriss in her eternal starting position, posing on the daybed in the center of the Great Room.

"You came. I'm so glad," Eriss purrs menacingly. She touches her slim cigarette holder to her lips, and stares into space.

"Didn't have much of a choice, according to your note." Then, a brainstorm. Or perhaps, a brain fart: I decide to play with her. "By the way, what was the scent on the stationery?" I ask cloyingly.

This, I immediately regret. Eriss' languid repose whips instantly into motion. Up she rises, and strides directly towards me. "Listen, smart guy. I have a valid contract with your name on it for the next 18 months. That's a lot of twisting in the wind. I can make your life extremely uncomfortable." She emphasizes the hard "e" in "extremely." "Or," she purrs again, "extremely comfortable." Nice kitty.

It's tough to hold my position as she gets into my personal space. She's just four inches less than my height. So Eriss can get in my face, literally. For one moment I experience the vague and unpleasant memory of being thisclose to her once before. Eriss sets her eyes about two inches from mine.

"It's Yves Saint Laurent, you fool."

Yet, despite her aggression, despite the contractual cards she holds, I have a couple of aces of my own. And they don't have to be hidden up my sleeve. Clearly, she is attracted to me despite her better judgment. That's "One." And "B," I'm not attracted to her impending job offer.

I twist to a right angle from her closeness, and take slow, deliberate steps forward, before turning around to face her at a distance of my choosing.

"What is it you want, Ivory?" A warning to her, using her first name. I'm not under the thumb of this Siamese cat of a girl. Her cigarette holder twitches like a whisker.

"Ah, so we are addressing one another in a familiar way." She slinks to a bar and pours a drink. I gulp. Boldness may have been a miscalculation on my part, or perhaps, simply misunderstood. She stirs her drink while questioning me over her shoulder, "Allow me to ask, my dear Wilson, what it is that *you* want."

No hesitation. "My inclination right now is to get the heck out of here. I do not like the direction we're headed."

Eriss turns to fully face me. She affects a slightly hurt look. "Do you mean your newsroom...or something else?" Heavy, deep "else."

Have to nip this confusion in the bud. "The newsroom, Ivory--uh, Miss Eriss. It's clear there is a rapid descent in management's concern for covering the news properly, much less practicing journalism. If the company wants to trade on whatever success we have in the newsroom, we have to have the tools to do the job right, without being compromised."

"Journalism?" Her voice pitches to a disbelieving falsetto. Then drops an octave to mocking soprano. "But my dear Wil, when we met, you claimed you weren't a journalist, that you were merely a reporter." No question, just a challenge.

"That doesn't mean I don't believe in journalism as a standard of practice."

"Oh, and you are the arbiter of journalism, one who is certain his standard is to which others should adhere? Incidentally, it is easy, Mr. Gamble, for you to espouse these ideals, while others have to get their hands dirty to make it possible. To underwrite the endeavor, in other words."

I ignore the Sales pitch; one thing at a time. "Well, someone has to be that so-called 'arbiter,' Miss Eriss, or else there's chaos. You have someone play that role in the newsroom, and here, it isn't me."

"Mr. Collingwood," Eriss breathes.

"Yes, Mr. Collingwood." I lay it on the line. "If he goes, I go."

"You won't work in television for quite a long time, Mr. Gamble. You know that," she warns. I know that. "Additionally, Mr. Collingwood and I have already made arrangements for his replacement. If he comes as advertised, Mr. Toller should be quite capable."

"You'll excuse me if I don't express much confidence in the recent hiring decisions that have been made for the News Department." Instantly I regret this comment, having just launched a big slow pitch right down the center of the plate.

Eriss swings from her heels and knocks it out of the park. "I'm certain you don't mean to include your own hiring in that category."

The only rejoinder I'm capable of conjuring is exaggerated exasperation. "The recent *administrative* hiring decisions for the News Department."

Eriss smiles to herself, sips her drink in celebration of scoring a point. A little happier, she floats around the room, airily admiring artwork and touching various decorative accessories. "In any case, Mr. Collingwood and I have already reached a firm agreement, on paper. The matter is settled. We wish him well." She faces me once again, this time from a less aggressive distance. "It's time to move on," she finishes, suggestively.

"Spell it out, Ivory. I am not giving up on Collingwood. But what is it that you want from me?"

"You don't know?" she replies, coaxingly. "Clearly, Mr. Collingwood has spoken to you about our proposed arrangements."

"I want to hear it from you," I insist.

Eriss does not like to be pinned down on anything. First move: "Surely you know what I want, Mr. Gamble."

Congratulate me: I do not answer. She continues her tour of the Great Room, pausing only to pet a brass cat that adorns a mantle. Another long pull on her cigarette. Then a stop at an aquarium to briefly feed the fish. I wait it out, motionless, in silence. I propose to fight it out on this line if it takes all summer.

Soon, however, Eriss is done blowing smoke and gives in to the inevitable. But she does not condescend to physically face me. "Mr. Gamble, I would like to extend to you an offer to become the next News Director of Newschannel 99," she recites to the drink in her hand. "With, of course, certain conditions and codicils that must be observed."

Ball's in my court. Pretty straightforward, which is unlike Eriss. My reply is straightforward as well.

"Nope. No thanks, no way. Under the current conditions I have no desire to remain in any capacity, much less one that forces me to be obligated to you."

Eriss probably expected me to demure. She may have even held out hope that I would accept the job. A flat-out, contentious "no" was not any part of her equation. I can see this hit home when her roaming stops. She contemplates her cigarette, stubs it out. Looking for an opening in my response, she tries a softer approach.

"'Current conditions,' Mr. Gamble? They can change, quicker than one of Arnold Paul's forecasts." She starts, humorously, alluringly. Then, she notes my smugness. I see it in her face. And her purr instantly shifts forward into cat scratch fever. "You had better start thinking straight, Buddy Boy. My offers don't last long, and the clock is ticking on this one. You owe me a year and a half of work, according to your current contract. And oh, it's going to be a torturous 18 months, my friend, if you don't work with me. And if you try to leave, you will owe me compensation. And my lawyers do indeed know how to squeeze blood from a stone. Meaning," her eyes glow like a feline at the moment of Pounce, "You."

Now it's my turn to pause to reflect. Unconditional surrender was not on my original list of options. But I want to buy time while still buzzing from her verbal assault.

"What are your terms?"

Withdrawing a manila folder from a writing desk, Eriss offers me a Cheshire Cat grin. "The details are contained within. Suffice to say, a generous pay adjustment is included in the offer. *Generous*." She pushes the folder towards me across a table.

"How long is the deal?" I move to the corner of the table but do not reach for the folder.

"No more than your current contract, Mr. Gamble. 18 months. You are an unproven commodity in a formal leadership role. We will consider this a probationary period. At the end of it, I will determine if I am finished with you."

Um, I seriously do not take well to that kind of phrasing. "Look, Miss Eriss. You are putting me into an impossible position. You want me--untested--to assume the role of News Director. A job that I did not ask for. And do it without the security of an extended contract, and without the help of the one person I can thoroughly rely upon in the newsroom. That's a recipe for failure. And I do not like to fail."

Eriss flicks a glance my way. "Well, the basis for any contractual negotiation is to start by finding common ground. We have it: I do not enjoy failure, either."

"Okay. You want me." Oops. "Uh, I mean, you want to hire me as News Director. I don't want the job. What other common ground can we find?"

Roaming recommences. "I suppose that depends on what I might...entice you with."

Steady, old boy. Again, I do not blink. I mean, literally. I'm afraid that if I blink, I might miss something between the lines. I hold my hands apart in near-apology. "You can only offer to raise my salary so much. I'm a, yes, 'journalist' by trade, not a pencil-pusher. And, other things are just as important to me."

An eyebrow rises, a smirk flashes by. "Just what I had counted on, my boy," she tries, coyly.

No flinching, now. Keep going. "First and foremost is Collingwood. If I am to take the job that he should have, I must have my own hand-picked person with me. Carl gives me immediate cachet with the current staff, and is a reliable sounding board for questions of journalism and administration." I wait a moment. "So much better than having a Britnee Flaxen as a Number Two."

Without flinching, Eriss clicks into Full Negotiation Mode. "I fully understand that you need a person such as this. But Mr. Collingwood and I already have an agreement, a Separate Peace, if you will. Mr. Toller is coming. It is done."

I'm really over this presumption. Moving around the table, I take two or three steps towards Eriss' position, which naturally, is fluid. It's my turn to go on the offensive.

"Then it can be un-done, if you want me to take charge of that newsroom," I firmly reply. "Anything on paper can change. And I must have complete hiring and firing privileges in my own department." Go, me. Unfortunately, I do not immediately grasp the fact that I am being drawn in to a position of not "yes" or "no" with this job, but rather, "what conditions will be arranged when I agree to take this job." Suckerrrrr.

"Well, then. If Mr. Collingwood is so important to you, I suppose I could attempt to talk with him about changing his plans--which I understood to be quite settled--if that makes you happy." "His" plans?" Whose" plans? No, no, no, this isn't enough.

"I don't want to mislead you, Miss Eriss. There is absolutely no chance of me taking this job without Carl Collingwood. So, if he is not on-board, I'm not going to captain this ship." Ha ha, I'm proud of my little quip.

Then, Collingwood actually appears.

"You called, Miss Eriss?" he asks, briskly striding into the apartment through the entry door I had left open.

"No, I did not," she replies, immediately, emphatically, incorrectly. Suddenly, she seems out of sorts.

"Hey, Carl," I try, loosely.

"Hello, Wil," he returns. Miraculously, we are a team, suddenly. Two-against-one here.

"Mr. Collingwood..." Eriss falters. She tries to draw on her cigarette once more but notices it has gone out. She doesn't move forward to confront him. "Ahem, ah yes, Mr. Collingwood. We had an arrangement." Slight pause. "Didn't we?"

"We did."

"So, what can I do for you?" she asks, disarmed, worried.

"The one thing you didn't imagine was that Mr. Gamble here would invite me to stay. You expected that he would want to hire his own leadership team, which would include people he could influence, rather than vice versa."

"That kind of leadership weakness is a concept that I wouldn't understand," Eriss replies, condescendingly. She regains her composure instantly, powerfully. I'm impressed.

"Then perhaps Wil here isn't the guy you want running your newsroom," tries Collingwood.

But the wheels turn quickly in Eriss' mind. It only takes a millisecond for her to consider. Then, she reacts as if there was no need to consider. "Oh no, no...you have it all wrong, Mr. Collingwood," she replies, feather-lightly. "My employment offer is ironclad. And I have concluded that if Mr. Gamble"--she does not turn to face me--"wishes to employ you in turn, that will be his prerogative. Only, that contract will have to be renegotiated from scratch. And I must express some misgivings about the fate of Mr. Toller, who at this moment believes he has a job waiting for him here."

That's his problem. She doesn't care. Eriss is beating a tactical retreat, only to prepare for a bigger and more important fight down the road. She will look for ways to dump Collingwood and control me. But it may ultimately surprise her that I relish the thought of fighting to practice actual journalism. Such a rare opportunity.

"I will take the job, Miss Eriss," I announce. She does turn to face me now. "And Mr. Collingwood will indeed be my first hire."

Eriss sets down her drink and strolls in close to me. Even with Collingwood there, she is unashamed.

"Yes, you will make Mr. Collingwood your first hire. But understand something, Mr. Gamble: I will be working very closely with you in this endeavor. Verrrry closely. In fact, we will establish some working parameters immediately. Such as: you will report to me here at the beginning of each work day."

"Here? Why not in your office downstairs?" But I already know.

"Because, my dear," she replies haughtily, laughingly, "my office hours don't begin until one o'clock."

Collingwood gives me a significant look as she turns to stub out her cigarette. What have I just got myself in to? Eriss continues as she flits into a chamber to conventionalize her wardrobe for the masses downstairs.

"I shall have Rose prepare the contract to send to you later today," she calls out to me. "Now allow me a moment to prepare to escort you to your new dominion, and introduce you to your minions."

"They are my colleagues, Miss Eriss," I reply loudly behind her. "Colleagues, not minions." Then I consider some who will not be my colleagues much longer, if this is all real.

"However you wish to refer to them, my dear, to me, they are all subordinates," Eriss continues from the other room. "As a Manager, you had better consider how to impart your will on them. Let us proceed," she declares, striding back into the Great Room with a fresh business jacket that somehow matches the flowing robes--and fresher breath, having just spritzed with a handheld spray nebulizer.

Collingwood and I step in line behind the Pied Piper, out of the apartment, and into the elevator. Norman drives us down to the ground floor. After the roiling seas of Eriss' apartment, I resist an urge to drop down and kiss the solid rock once we land. Collingwood assumes a somewhat amused expression as we step in formation through the hallways like the Armagnac vanguard advancing on the Burgundian line.

As we march forward, I notice an interesting phenomenon. The overhead lights in the hallways dim slightly as we approach. Turning back, I notice they resume their normal luminosity after we pass. It gives the impression of a rolling brown-out as we parade along. Of course Collingwood notices me noticing. Does this guy ever miss anything? And he briefly mutters an explanation.

"She hates bright light. Has a GPS-connected remote dimmer that automatically lowers them wherever she goes in the building. They also dim if someone mentions her name, as a backup should the GPS fail."

Wow, so it wasn't my imagination. But what an expensive way to act upon her proclivity.

There isn't any more conversation. In the strangeness of my new life, my thoughts drift back to Megan, and the Found Weekend we just shared. No matter what instability lays ahead, I find a firmness in my feelings for her and her support of me.

We enter the newsroom. The morning meeting appears to be loosely underway, with Wallflower nominally running things. But the center does not hold. Chatter echoes around the room in a variety of disconnected conversations. All of it dies off, however, as a swift realization sweeps over most everyone. Meet the new boss. Not same as the old bosses. The only noise that persists in the sudden silence are the scanners and Fantana's oblivious speakerphone gibberish.

I quickly survey the faces to find any support. At first I sense a complete power vacuum. Wallflower is going to be de-flowered. Flotsam is off to the side, cowering like a wounded animal. Then I realize how wrong I may be. Nobody in the newsroom really likes Wallflower, but then, he did not come from the newsroom. He and the other remaining shooters are now a part of the newsroom, and their shared history might have created a bond, if he wasn't so selfish. For pragmatic purposes he had allied himself with Walter Wilson, who I do not spot at the moment. Apart they are helpless. Follicle is a center of gravity, even though he is not personally close to anyone. Wilson once blathered something to me how back in the day Follicle led a newsroom uprising that ousted a lazy and mean Assistant News Director. His experience, intelligence, and force of character command a certain respect among the younger and less experienced staff. But, I wonder, in this place--how far does that go? Most of the other reporters are friendly with one another. Each, however, is climbing a career ladder--necessarily alone. Fern and Adams aren't here. Together they could be a powerful bloc within the newsroom. But as much as they are similar creatures--the stars of the show--they are wildly different personalities. There is no unity there. Only a few of the line producers overlap, so they have no common cause. This room is ripe to be plucked.

"Ladies and Gentlemen," Eriss begins with classic blandness. She already has their close attention, but pauses anyway. A reminder, I surmise, of Who is In Charge. Eriss takes a breath to speak, but just then one of the network speaker boxes blares out an announcement by a chewing gum-popping intern in New York.

"Attention all affiliates. Ah, the President's arrival on Air Force One has, um, been delayed by a haircut... ." Wallflower actually lifts a finger and kills the volume.

Eriss takes another breath. By her command, no other worldwide developments will interrupt this brief announcement. "Ahem. Ladies and Gentlemen. I would like to introduce your new News Director. Someone you all know and trust." Then I notice: all eyes turn to Collingwood. They think its him! And for good reason, he's the obvious choice. Oblivious, Eriss continues. "It is unusual for us to promote to this position of leadership from within, but this man's qualities and skills cannot be ignored. He has earned my confidence and I hope, your trust. Wil Gamble."

Eriss withdraws faster than a bad comedian on amateur night. The house lights come up, too, as she departs. Collingwood and I are left in command of the field. I hear two or three choking noises, and one person involuntarily exclaims a drawn-out, "Wait--who?"

I had better take over. "Obviously this is a, uh, bold move by the management." Other adjectives, such as "unusual," "risky," and "nutty" first come to mind. "Bold" was all I could summon that wouldn't instantly undermine my credibility.

"But in any case I look forward to working with everyone. Obviously I face a learning curve and I ask you all to give me a grace period." Silent response, the shock has not worn off. "You all know me to some degree, so you already know that I care very much about journalism, attention to detail, being aggressive." Now some heads nod. "Carl and I will be working very closely together to overhaul everything we think needs to be changed." Wallflower and Flotsam turn their sour expressions away at a sudden premonition of their respective fates. Nettles grins, Hubbell and Wash seem into the idea of letting me take a whack at it. Then Fantana manages to articulate something that sounds positive over the speakerphone.

Wilson finally wanders in, writing something on a sticky note. Then he notices the attitude of the room and he lets loose. "What did I miss, it looks like something has happened but I was told by a confidential source that the new Taco Del Gato is offering mini breakfast burritos two-for-a-dollar so I went to investigate but it turns out that was a hoax. I had to pay full price for both breakfast burritos and that restaurant was a good 15 minute drive and now I wonder why I even went all that way in the first place."

"We have a new News Director, Walter," declares Follicle. Then lets him stew in that for a moment or two. "Ivory Eriss has just introduced Wilson Gamble to replace Arlen." Do I detect sarcasm? I wonder if this is trouble brewing already. "And we are just about to start the morning meeting...right, Mr. News Director?"

Relief. It's not sarcasm, yet. With his tone of voice, Follicle has made it clear that he will cut me some slack. Perhaps not much, but I hope that a little is all I will need.

-30-

www.ingramcontent.com/pod-product-compliance
Lightning Source LLC
LaVergne TN
LVHW051619080426
835511LV00016B/2077